UFOS

Over New Mexico

A True History of Extraterrestrial Encounters in the Land of Enchantment

PRESTON DENNETT

4880 Lower Valley Road, Atglen, Pennsylvania 19310

Text and images by author unless otherwise noted

Schiffer Books are available at special discounts for bulk purchases for sales promotions or premiums. Special editions, including personalized covers, corporate imprints, and excerpts can be created in large quantities for special needs. For more information contact the publisher:

Published by Schiffer Publishing Ltd.
4880 Lower Valley Road
Atglen, PA 19310
Phone: (610) 593-1777; Fax: (610) 593-2002
E-mail: Info@schifferbooks.com

For the largest selection of fine reference books on this and related subjects, please visit our
website at **www.schifferbooks.com**
We are always looking for people to write books on new and related subjects. If you have an idea
for a book, please contact us at
proposals@schifferbooks.com

This book may be purchased from the publisher.
Include $5.00 for shipping.
Please try your bookstore first.
You may write for a free catalog.

In Europe, Schiffer books are distributed by
Bushwood Books
6 Marksbury Ave.
Kew Gardens
Surrey TW9 4JF England
Phone: 44 (0) 20 8392 8585; Fax: 44 (0) 20 8392 9876
E-mail: info@bushwoodbooks.co.uk
Website: www.bushwoodbooks.co.uk

Copyright © 2011 by Preston Dennett

Library of Congress Control Number: 2011941351

Designed by RoS
Type set in Hallmarke Black/Humanst521 BT

ISBN: 978-0-7643-3906-6
Printed in the United States

Dedication

**To all UFO witnesses -
You are not alone!**

Contents

WHEREAS, NEW MEXICO HAS A UNIQUE AND DYNAMIC MOSAIC OF CULTURAL ANOMALIES; AND

WHEREAS, EXTRATERRESTRIALS HAVE CONTRIBUTED TO THE WORLDWIDE RECOGNITION OF NEW MEXICO THROUGH THEIR MANY AND ONGOING VISITATIONS, SIGHTINGS, UNEXPLAINED MYSTERIES, ATTRIBUTED TECHNOLOGICAL ADVANCES, EXPERIMENTATIONS, EXPEDITIONS, EXPLORATIONS, INTRIGUES, PROVISION OF STORY LINES FOR HOLLYWOOD EPICS AND ACCOMPLISHMENTS OF ALIEN BEINGS THROUGHOUT THE UNIVERSE;

NOW, THEREFORE, BE IT RESOLVED BY THE HOUSE OF REPRESENTATIVES OF THE HOUSE OF NEW MEXICO THAT THE SECOND TUESDAY OF FEBRUARY BE DESIGNATED "EXTRATERRESTRIAL CULTURE DAY" IN NEW MEXICO TO CELEBRATE AND HONOR ALL PAST, PRESENT AND FUTURE EXTRATERRESTRIAL VISITORS IN WAYS TO ENHANCE RELATIONSHIPS AMONG ALL CITIZENS OF THE COSMOS KNOWN AND UNKNOWN; AND

BE IT FURTHER RESOLVED THAT A COPY OF THIS MEMORIAL BE TRANSMITTED INTO SPACE WITH THE INTENT THAT IT BE RECEIVED AS A TOKEN OF PEACE AND FRIENDSHIP.

"EXTRATERRESTRIAL CULTURE DAY" EST. 2003
NEW MEXICO HOUSE OF REPRESENTATIVES

THE SHEER NUMBER OF [UFO] REPORTS FROM CREDIBLE CIVILIAN, LAW ENFORCEMENT AND MILITARY WITNESSES FROM NEW MEXICO CRY FOR A SERIOUS INVESTIGATION AND A RELEASE OF ALL EVIDENCE AND MATERIAL COLLECTED THEREIN.

DR. STEVEN GREER MD
UFO RESEARCHER, AUTHOR[1]

NEW MEXICO HAS ALWAYS BEEN A "HOT SPOT" FOR UFO SIGHTINGS... IT WOULD BE HARD TO FIND A CITY, TOWN OR VILLAGE ANYWHERE IN NEW MEXICO WITHOUT A REPORTED UFO SIGHTING.

LINDA KERTH
UFO RESEARCHER, JOURNALIST[2]

Introduction

Human remains from the Stone Age (more than 10,000 years ago) found near Folsom in the northeast part of the state make New Mexico the location of the oldest known human civilization in the United States. The earliest identified culture in the area was the Anasazi Indians, who flourished in the San Juan River Basin in the first millennium. From the 12th to the 14th century, the Pueblo Indians (descendants of the Anasazi) lived peacefully in numerous towns along New Mexico's largest river, the Rio Grande. In the 15th century, nomadic Navajo and Apache tribes arrived, bringing four centuries of conflict between the groups. In 1539, Spanish Franciscan priest, Marcos de Niza led an early expedition to the area, followed one year later by Spanish explorer, Francisco Coronado. In the 1560s, the area was named Nuevo Mexico by a Spanish explorer. By 1598, Spanish colonization of the area had begun, and one century later, by 1696, the Spanish had conquered the entire state.

In the 1800s, the state had a population of about 30,000, consisting mainly of Pueblos, Navajos, Comanches, and Spaniards. In 1821, Spain gave up claim of the area to the new nation of Mexico. Under Mexican rule, the borders became opened for the first time to Americans, attracting merchants, trappers, pioneers, and others. In 1841, the new Texas Republic tried unsuccessfully to lay claim to the area. Then, in 1846, war broke out between the United States and Mexico. On August 18, 1846, New Mexico officially became a part of the United States. It was denied statehood, but instead, in 1850, became the Territory of New Mexico (which also included the area of Arizona.) In 1863, the two territories were divided.

For the next 62 years, New Mexico remained a territory, in part because Congress feared that democracy would not work in a Spanish-speaking community and because residents feared higher taxes. However, in 1898, public schools began teaching English, and fourteen years later on January 6, 1912, New Mexico officially became the 47th state. By this time, the population hovered just above 200,000.

The fifth largest state, New Mexico has an area of 121,593 square miles, approximately one-third of which remains owned by the federal government. Its lowest elevation is 2,817 feet at Red Bluff Lake, and its highest elevation is 13,161 feet at the summit of Wheeler Peak. The eastern third of the state is part of the Great Plains. The state is also very mountainous. The north central part of the state includes an extension of the Rocky Mountains. In the east are the Sangre de Cristo Mountains and to the west are the Nacimiento Mountains. There are numerous mountain ranges and desert basins in the central and southwestern part of the state, while the northwest quadrant is part of the Colorado Plateau. The climate is mild and arid, with low humidity and a wide temperature range.

New Mexico contains more than 6,000 species of plants, and 23 percent of the state is forested. The state is rich in natural resources, containing large reserves of coal, petroleum, and natural gas. It is also extremely rich in minerals including resources of gold, silver, copper, iron ore, lead, manganese, molybdenum, zinc, potash, and perhaps most importantly, uranium. The state ranks second in uranium production and contains half of the country's known reserves of uranium.

In part because of its rich uranium reserves and its isolated location, New Mexico was chosen as a location for highly classified United States Government research into nuclear energy. In 1943, the secret city of Los Alamos became the birthplace of the Atomic bomb. Later came White Sands Missile Range, Kirtland Air Force Base, and nuclear research installations in Albuquerque. These new developments and a fast-growing tourist industry soon caused the state's economy to boom. By 1970, more than one million people lived in the state. And so New Mexico's prominent position in the United States became assured.

Of all the states in the United States, New Mexico has one of the most complex histories of UFO and extraterrestrial encounters. Sightings began as early as 1880. However, it wasn't until the arrival of the Atomic Age in 1945 that UFO activity exploded. Perhaps because of its research into atomics, the state of New Mexico – in some ways perhaps more than any other state – became the focused target of the UFO phenomenon.

New Mexico's UFO history is rich with high-profile cases that have had a profound effect on how the phenomenon is perceived and understood.

The first sightings to gather widespread attention occurred in 1947, when a gigantic UFO super-wave swept across the United States. In New Mexico, much of the activity was concentrated over military and atomic installations. This was also the year of the now-famous Roswell UFO crash, forever putting New Mexico on the front lines of UFO research.

In 1949 and 1950, New Mexico was uniquely targeted by a wave of mysterious green fireballs – causing great concern at high levels of the Air Force.

The 1950s and 1960s brought dozens of "classic cases" including the Farmington UFO display, the Socorro Landing, continuing visitations over

White Sands, Holloman AFB, Kirtland AFB and other sensitive installations, dozens of car-stalling cases, UFO-car chases, the abduction of Sergeant Charles Moody, the contacts of Dr. Daniel Fry, several new UFO crash/retrieval cases, and a growing number of civilian cases. From 1948 to 1965, Project Blue book investigated scores of New Mexico cases, more than two-dozen of which remain unidentified.

The 1970s brought a new twist with the arrival of cattle mutilations, a phenomenon which was initially focused largely on New Mexico and surrounding areas, but was later discovered to be a worldwide phenomena. Focus also began to shift to accounts of UFO abductions.

The 1980s brought more sightings, landings and abductions, and rumors of underground alien bases, the unique "Taos Hum," and the deepening mystery of animal mutilations.

The next two decades produced virtually the entire range of the UFO phenomenon. New Mexico, although one of the less populated states, ranks well above average in the number of UFO sightings as compared to other states. Clearly, this area is of great interest to the UFOs.

This book contains a comprehensive history of UFO activity over New Mexico, including the most famous and influential UFO events and many other lesser-known cases. Accounts are organized chronologically and topically, beginning with sightings and then moving on to more complex and extensive encounters including UFO landings, UFO abductions, crash/retrievals, and more.

So, come along as we explore the exciting and true history of UFOs in the Land of Enchantment.

CHAPTER

TheARRIVAL

Back in the 1800s, the idea of space travel and extraterrestrials from other planets had not fully entered the public consciousness. Strange sights in the sky were usually explained, not as aliens or UFOs, but as astronomical phenomena, or religious manifestations. So when a wave of strange airships swept across the United States starting in the 1880s and culminating at the turn of the century, most people speculated that the objects originated not from outer-space and other planets, but from some foreign country on Earth. One of the earliest sightings from the massive "airship wave" occurred in New Mexico.

AIRSHIPS

On March 26, 1880, four men were walking outside near Galisteo Junction in Lamy when they saw a "strange balloon" shaped like a fish flying overhead. The craft, described as "monstrous in size," seemed to be guided by a large fan-like device attached to the back. Strange written characters decorated the sides. Even more startling, the four men saw about eight to ten normal-looking humans aboard. They spoke in a strange language that none of the witnesses were able to understand. The witnesses also heard sounds of shouting, laughter, and music. A few objects were tossed out of the craft and fell to the ground.

The craft then flew at a low altitude over the junction, and then gained in altitude and moved away towards the east. The objects tossed from the craft were quickly recovered and included a flower, a sheet of fine silk-like paper covered with strange Asian-looking writing, and what appeared to be a tea-cup. According to the *Santa Fe Daily New Mexican*, "It [the cup] is of very peculiar workmanship, entirely different to anything used in this country."

The objects were put on display, but were immediately purchased by an older gentleman who identified himself as a "collector of curiosities." The objects were never seen again.

This was one of the first airship sightings in the United States. Just over fifteen years later, the huge airship wave would strike the United States and usher in the idea of extraterrestrials from other planets.

Another early case occurred twenty years later. On March 7, 1901, Dr. S. H. Milliken not only observed an airship, he managed to photograph it with his Kodak camera. The photo allegedly depicts three cigar-shaped objects that appear to be tied together.[3]

THE FIRST UFOS

The dawn of the modern age of UFOs is usually said to have begun in 1947. However, in New Mexico, the first significant wave of sightings came as early as 1944. One of the first known sightings to attract military attention occurred one evening in March 1944 when a B-17 Air Force pilot flying over Carlsbad encountered a fast-moving greenish, glowing object which swept past his cockpit, illuminating the exterior in green light. The object then moved swiftly out of sight over the horizon. The brief encounter marked only the beginning of what would soon become a storm of activity.

At 11:00 a.m., on April 2, 1944, an aircraft engineering officer at a military base near Clovis was shocked to see a silvery, glowing object hovering over the base. It appeared to be reflecting the sun or actually emitting its own light. Most strange, the object was stationary in the sky. Before long, the object became the talk of the base, and dozens of officers went outside to observe it. Says one officer,

> THREE OF US, ALL B-29 ENGINEERING OFFICERS IN THE AIR CORPS OBSERVED THE OBJECT. THE DAY WAS WARM AND TOTALLY CLEAR. THE OBJECT WAS AT 11 O'CLOCK HIGH. IT NEVER WAVERED, JUST SAT THERE. REMEMBER, IN 1944, UFO WAS A TERM UNKNOWN TO US... I AM SURE THAT MANY HUNDREDS OF PEOPLE ON THE BASE SAW IT. WE SPECULATED THAT IT MIGHT BE A JAPANESE BALLOON AS WE KNEW SOME HAD COME OVER THE PACIFIC NORTHWEST. THAT EVENING AT MESS IN THE OFFICER'S CLUB, WE TALKED ABOUT IT.

Various other theories were raised, including everything from assorted aircraft to the planet Jupiter. The object remained in view for a period of one and one-half hours. In 2005, the witness finally reported his sighting to both the Mutual UFO Network (MUFON) and the National UFO Reporting Service (NUFORC), writing,

> THIS SIGHTING HAS TROUBLED ME FOR 61 YEARS NOW... I AM A HIGHLY EXPERIENCED ENGINEER AND LOOK HARD AND LONG AT SOMETHING BEFORE EXPRESSING AN OPINION. WHERE DO WE GO FROM HERE?[4]

PLANE PURSUES DISK

Like many intense UFO encounters, this one was told by a very old person who kept the experience secret even from family. About a year before he died, he finally told his nephew what he experienced during his period of employment at Los Alamos in 1944, where he worked on the super-secret Manhattan Project.

Writes the nephew,

> ONE DAY A BRIGHT SILVER DISK WAS OBSERVED IN THE SKY HOVERING OVER THE FACILITY, AND A PLANE WAS IMMEDIATELY DISPATCHED FROM KIRTLAND FIELD TO INTERCEPT AND IDENTIFY THE OBJECT. AS THE PLANE APPROACHED, THE DISK

ASCENDED UPWARD OUT OF ITS RANGE. A SECOND LARGER PLANE WITH A HIGHER
OPERATIONAL CEILING WAS THEN SENT UP TO CONTINUE THE PURSUIT, AND AGAIN
THE DISK ASCENDED UPWARD UNTIL IT DISAPPEARED.

The uncle told his nephew that the incident was witnessed by many
of the staff at the facility. Sensing the event was important to UFO history,
the nephew reported the sighting to NUFORC in 2009.[5]

"IT WAS NOT A METEOR"

It was 2 a.m. on a December evening in 1945, and ten-year-old Joseph
(pseudonym) lay on his bed looking out the window. To his delight he saw a
shooting star. Strangely, however, the shooting star appeared to be moving
very slowly. Realizing there was something unusual about it, he continued
watching it. Says Joseph,

BEFORE I KNEW IT, I REALIZED IT WAS NOT A METEOR BUT A SPHERE AND IT WAS
DESCENDING ABOVE THE HOUSE ACROSS THE STREET.

The object was very bright, but oddly it did not illuminate the area
around it. It moved very slowly, and then stopped, hovering above the
porch of their neighbor's home.

Amazed, Joseph ran to wake up his sister. When he arrived in his sister's
room, she was already kneeling and looking out the window.

"Do you see that?" Joseph asked.

"Yes," his sister replied, "and it took off real fast."

Looking outside, Joseph saw the object was gone.

Says Joseph,

WE NEVER TOLD ANYONE OR DISCUSSED IT. I DON'T THINK WE EVEN REMEMBERED
IT THE NEXT DAY, [NOT] UNTIL WE WERE ADULTS.

Joseph reported his sighting to NUFORC more than fifty-five years
later, writing,

I THOUGHT I WOULD TELL OUR STORY BEFORE WE ARE BOTH GONE AND NEITHER
ONE OF US IS HERE TO TELL IT AND BACK EACH OTHER UP.[6]

THE INVASION OF WHITE SANDS

On July 16, 1945, the first nuclear bomb was exploded on a test site near Alamogordo in the southern section of the state. Within two years, the world would be overwhelmed by an unprecedented super-wave of UFO activity on a level never seen before. Several researchers have pointed out the remarkable coincidence that the Atomic age coincides nearly exactly with the dawning of the modern age of UFOs of 1947. The fact that UFOs still exhibit a strong interest in nuclear power plants shows that this is likely no coincidence, but rather reveals at least part of the reason for the high levels of UFO activity from this point onward.

In New Mexico, it was early rocket testing that first attracted the attention of UFOs. The events that occurred in 1947 made it quite clear to military officials that they were dealing with an apparent extraterrestrial phenomenon. Researchers Charles Berlitz and William Moore write,

> IN THOSE SUMMER MONTHS OF 1947, NEW MEXICO EXPERIENCED MORE SIGHTINGS BOTH PER CAPITA AND PER SQUARE MILE THAN ANY OTHER STATE IN THE UNION.

The flood had begun.

In 1947, White Sands Proving Grounds was the location where the United States Air Force conducted much of its advanced experiments in atomics, rocketry, and aeronautics. It should therefore come as no surprise that the location became a powerful magnet for UFO activity.

On May 15, 1947, a team of scientists launched a V-2 (A-4) rocket at White Sands Proving Grounds. At first the test was routine. The missile climbed to an altitude of forty miles. Then something strange happened. Radar technicians tracking the rocket were amazed to see another target appear next to the missile. At this point, the V-2 veered forty degrees off its normal flight path and crashed two minutes later.

Lieutenant Colonel Harold R. Turner was the commanding officer and told intelligence investigators that he could not explain why the missile went off course other than the "peculiar phenomena" that were observed by the radar technicians. He later told reporters about this incident and others.

As one journalist wrote,

> Lt. Col. Harold R. Turner, commanding officer at White Sands said he had received reports that a track walker said he had seen a falling object near Engle, New Mexico and an Army captain flying his own plane reported seeing an object falling from the skies near Tularosa.

C. Jon Kissner, a former Republican State Representative from Las Cruces investigated the incident in detail and says that it:

> ...began an episode that would evolve over the next half-century into the most highly classified military and scientific research and development project in world history.

According to Kissner,

> Whatever had mysteriously appeared and vanished after observing a V-2 in flight and affecting its trajectory at a highly classified missile range became an immediate priority within a small closed circle. It involved highly ranked general staff officers and civilian scientists assigned to the Office of Scientific Research and Development and the Joint Research and Development Board of the Joint Chiefs of Staff, under whose authority White Sands Proving Ground was established and operated. Both of these national weapons research and development organizations were headed by one key man – Dr. Vannevar Bush.

Incidentally, Dr. Vannevar Bush has been implicated as one of the members of the controversial and secret UFO study group, MJ-12, said to be in charge of UFO crash/retrievals and the reverse engineering of UFO technology.

On June 27, 1947 Captain E. B. Detchmendy was at White Sands Proving Grounds at 9:50 a.m., when he observed "flame-like objects" moving over the base. W. C. Dobbs was in the town of Pope when he saw what appeared to be the same object. At the same time, just north of the base in the city of Capitan, Mrs. Cummins and her neighbor, Erv Dill, observed apparently the same object, which they described as "shiny." The object moved overhead and then it "seemed to land on nearby hills."

Meanwhile, yet another witness – Mrs. David Appelzoller – was driving about fifteen miles west of WSPG when she saw a "falling silver object... just as bright as shining as it could be. If it had been any closer it would have blinded us."

Other reports of sightings came in on that day. In Silver City, in the southwestern section of the state, Dr. R. F. Sensenbaugher and several members of his family observed a disk "half the size of a full moon" float slowly across the sky.

Later Lieutenant Colonel Harold R. Turner released an official statement in which he said that the sightings of the UFOs were actually caused by jet planes. He explained that the jets have circular exhaust pipes, and that these pipes, when heated, might give an illusion of disks. The Air Forces' policy of debunking UFOs as hoaxes, hallucinations, and misperceptions had begun.

White Sands continued to attract UFO activity. Two days later, on June 29, 1947, three naval research scientists had an incredible sighting while waiting at White Sands proving grounds for a test involving a captured German V-2 rocket.

At 1:30 p.m., the three scientists, Dr. C. J. Zohn, Curtis C. Rockwood, and John R. Kauke were out on the grounds when they observed a bright flash of light from above. Says Zohn,

> WE NOTICED A GLARE IN THE SKY. WE LOOKED UP AND SAW A SILVERY DISC WHIRLING ALONG. WE WATCHED THE THING FOR NEARLY SIXTY SECONDS AND THEN IT SIMPLY DISAPPEARED. IT DIDN'T GO BEHIND THE MOUNTAIN RANGE. AT ONE TIME IT WAS CLEARLY VISIBLE, AND THEN IT JUST WASN'T THERE.

Being trained observers, the scientists quickly made several assessments. They estimated that the disk was flying at an altitude of about 10,000 feet. They were very impressed by its silver mirror-like surface and its flat, elliptical shape. Dr. Zohn was a rocket expert and made a report of the incident to Army Intelligence in which he said that the object was unlike any rocket he had ever seen, and that it could not have been a balloon.

The very next day, there was another rash of sightings. The first reports came from the Albuquerque area. A railroad worker named Price observed thirteen silver-colored disks headed south low overhead. He alerted his neighbors, and within seconds the entire neighborhood rushed out to view the objects. People lay out on their lawns and watched the objects begin to maneuver, turning sharply to the east and then reversing direction again, before finally disappearing.

Meanwhile, while the wave of sightings swept across the entire country, New Mexico continued to be a main target of activity. On July 1, Albuquerque Chamber of Commerce executive Max Hood reported his sighting of "a disk-like bluish object following a zigzag path in the northwestern sky."

On the same day, Native Americans from the Navajo Reservations in the northwestern section of the state also reported sightings.

On July 2, 1947, Mr. and Mrs. Dan Wilmot observed a large "glowing object" pass very quickly and at a low altitude over their house, disappearing to the northwest.

Within a few hours of this sighting, the most famous incident in UFO history would occur outside the small town of Roswell. Known as the Roswell UFO Crash, or the Roswell Incident, this event is so extensive that it will be covered in a later chapter.

The 1947 sightings, however, continued at an ever-increasing rate. A few days after the Roswell crash, on July 6 or 7, Mark Sloan – the operator of the Carriozo flying field – was with a group of pilots (including Gray Warren, Nolan Lovelace and Ray Shafer) when the men observed a flying saucer move overhead at around 5,000 feet of altitude. As Sloan told reporters at the Roswell *Daily Record*,

> WHEN WE FIRST NOTICED IT ABOUT 10:00 A.M., WE THOUGHT IT RESEMBLED A FEATHER BECAUSE IT WAS OSCILLATING. THEN WE NOTICED ITS GREAT SPEED AND DECIDED IT WAS A FLYING SAUCER. OUR GUESSES ARE THAT IT WAS MOVING AT BETWEEN 200 AND 600 MILES PER HOUR. IT PASSED OVER THE FIELD AND ALMOST DIRECTLY UP FROM SOUTHWEST TO NORTHWEST AND WAS IN SIGHT IN ALL ONLY ABOUT TEN SECONDS.

Sloan's account appeared in the same newspaper issue in which the Roswell UFO crash was publicly revealed for the first time.

July 1947 was a very busy month. As reported to MUFON by one of the witnesses, on July 7, 1947, a family of five were on their way to California and had spent the night sleeping in their car off Route 66. The witness was 12 years old at the time. She writes,

> WE AWOKE AND MY DAD SAID, "LOOK UP." THERE WERE THREE DISCS HOVERING ABOVE US, VERY SHINY METALLIC. [THEY] MADE A SLIGHT WHIRRING NOISE. WE WATCHED AND THE THREE DARTED FIRST IN ONE DIRECTION AND THEN ANOTHER AT TERRIFIC SPEED. THEY WERE COMPLETELY OUT OF SIGHT IN SECONDS. MY DAD THOUGHT THEY WERE SOME NEW PLANE WE HAD DEVELOPED. WE HAD NEVER HEARD OF UFOS AT THAT TIME. IN LATER YEARS, MY DAD REFUSED TO TALK ABOUT THE SIGHTING ANYMORE AS EVERYONE HE TOLD SAID HE WAS CRAZY.

On July 10, 1947, a leading astronomer (whose identity was withheld by the editors of *Life Magazine*) reported that he, his wife, and two teenage daughters were driving from Clines to Clovis when they saw an elliptical-shaped object high in the clouds. The astronomer carefully observed the object and estimated that it was 160 feet long, 65 feet thick, moving up to 180 miles per hour horizontally and up to 900 miles per hour vertically, with what he called "a remarkably sudden ascent." He was puzzled by the way the object moved in a strange "wobbly motion." Most impressive was that the object was silent and "self-luminous" against the dark clouds. There was no exhaust trail. They watched the object for nearly three minutes until it moved behind the clouds.

Also on July 10, Mrs. Charles J. Carroll, the wife of the local jeweler in Belen, reports that at 1:30 p.m., she stepped outside of her home and observed a large glowing "white ball" moving across the sky. Says Carroll,

IT MUST HAVE BEEN WHAT THEY CALL A FLYING SAUCER, BUT IT DIDN'T RESEMBLE A SAUCER. IT WAS TRAVELING NORTHWEST AT A HIGH RATE OF SPEED. WHEN I FIRST SAW IT, THE OBJECT APPEARED VERY LARGE. IT LOOKED LIKE IT WAS THEN ABOUT OVER MUNICIPAL AIRPORT.

Thinking she was seeing things, Carroll ran back inside to call her neighbor. When she returned outside, the object was gone.

In August 1947 (as reported to MUFON by the witness), a dramatic sighting took place near Berrela Mesa. "I have never told anyone about seeing a UFO before," wrote the witness, "because it would be a story no person would ever believe... I was in the kitchen of my grandparents' house when I noticed a shadow suddenly flash across the house. In a couple of seconds I was at the window staring at a flying saucer moving directly away from me."

The witness watched as the "strange machine" dove downward into the nearby canyon and then turned upward, darted to the right and accelerated out of view. The witness was able to view the object from all angles and gives an excellent description:

THE DIAMETER OF THE UFO WAS ABOUT 60 FEET AND THE HEIGHT OF THE BELL-SHAPED BUBBLE AREA WAS ABOUT SIX FEET ABOVE THE BASE. THE UFO LOOKED METALLIC WITH NO WINDOWS.

Several other cases occurred in 1947. Pioneering researcher Coral Lorenzen interviewed a gentleman who reported sightings while working at Holloman base in 1947. Holloman is located in the Tularosa Basin, nine miles west of Alamogordo and a mere thirty miles north of White Sands Proving Grounds. Writes Lorenzen,

> A GOVERNMENT-EMPLOYED CIVILIAN WORKING AT HOLLOMAN AIR FORCE BASE IN NEW MEXICO RELATED TO ME TWO DIFFERENT INCIDENTS HE OBSERVED IN 1947. ONE, INVOLVING A GLOWING GLOBE-SHAPED OBJECT, TOOK PLACE ABOVE THE SAN ANDREAS MOUNTAINS TO THE WEST OF ALAMOGORDO AND HOLLOMAN. THE THING RESEMBLED A "BOUNCING MUSICAL BALL" USED IN MOVIE "COMMUNITY SINGS." THE OBJECT FOLLOWED THE PEAKS AS IT FLEW AT HIGH SPEED FROM NORTH TO SOUTH. THE SECOND INCIDENT TOOK PLACE IN THE VICINITY OF THE SACRAMENTO MOUNTAINS, EAST OF ALAMOGORDO AND HOLLOMAN. THE OBJECT IN THIS INSTANCE WAS A RED, GLOWING BALL-SHAPED OBJECT WHICH FLEW ALONG THE MOUNTAIN PEAKS FROM NORTH TO SOUTH.

A unique sighting involved a low-flying mother-ship occurred in 1947 to a couple who were driving late at night about fifteen miles west of Clovis heading west towards Santa Fe.

Without warning, a "huge craft" appeared 150 feet ahead of them on the road, moving from left to right. The husband screeched to a stop and together the couple watched as the gigantic craft moved across the road. It was at an elevation of just a few feet above the road. It was so tall that the witnesses were not able to see the top until it moved away. The object was also extremely long and took several minutes to cross the highway. It reminded them of a train, except it was much too large and it was floating above the highway. Otherwise, the surface appeared metallic, and they observed occasional portholes, both light and dark.

The couple estimated that it was moving at about 130 miles per hour. When it finally finished crossing the road and moved away, they were able to better guess its size, which they compared to the University of Texas Memorial Stadium.

After the object had passed, the asphalt underneath where it had passed was "hot, almost steaming, but there were no marks or anything."

The couple kept their encounter a secret, sharing it only with family members. In August 2005, more than fifty years later, their son "Dave" reported the incident to MUFON. He felt that the sighting was significant as it occurred only a few weeks after the Roswell UFO crash, and in the same general area.[7]

AN EARLY UFO CAR CHASE

From early on, UFOs began to exhibit a behavior known as a "UFO-car chase." On July 20, 1947, a family was driving near Raton when a glowing blue object zoomed down out of the sky and began to follow their car. The family continued to drive, and the object followed them for the next forty miles. Forty-five minutes later, the object zoomed upward "at a very high speed and then disappeared."

This case may be one of the earliest New Mexico UFO-car chases on record. Later, New Mexico would become a leading producer of this peculiar type of UFO encounter.[8]

BLUE BOOK CASE NUMBER 139: UNIDENTIFIED

Despite the earlier visitations over White Sands and the Roswell UFO crash of 1947, the first New Mexico case to be declared officially unidentified by the Air Force Project Blue Book staff occurred on April 5, 1948.

On that day, three trained balloon observers (also identified as navy missile trackers and a scientist) from the Geophysics Lab Section at Holloman Air Force Base were conducting tests when they observed a white object with a golden aura fly at "tremendous speed" over the base. The object performed incredible maneuvers including steep climbs and vertical loops. One of the witnesses described the object as an irregularly rounded craft with a slightly concave top. All agreed that it was roughly disk-shaped and about one-fifth the apparent size of a full moon, or an estimated thirty-five feet in diameter.

During the sighting, the scientists were able to train theodolites (telescopes equipped with cameras) to track their speed and trajectory. After being in view for several minutes, the craft accelerated to the west at a speed the theodolites measured in excess of 18,000 miles per hour.

Air Force investigators were, of course, impressed that the men had seen something that flew "faster than any known object" and labeled the case unexplained. (See Blue Book Case #139.)[9]

OFFICIAL GOVERNMENT DOCUMENT REVEALS SIGHTING

One of the most impressive sightings from 1948 was later revealed in an official Top Secret government document called "Analysis of Flying Object Incidents in the U.S." This document (Air Intelligence Report #100-203-79) dated December 10, 1948, was signed by both the USAF Directorate of Intelligence and the Office of Naval Intelligence, and contained more than twenty reports across the United States. The report was declassified in 1985 and was obtained by researcher Robert Todd using the Freedom of Information Act.

What follows is an excerpt from the document describing a dramatic sighting over San Acacia:

> ON 17 JULY 1948, A REPORT FROM KIRTLAND AIR FORCE BASE DESCRIBES A SIGHTING IN THE VICINITY OF SAN ACACIA, NEW MEXICO, OF SEVEN UNIDENTIFIED OBJECTS FLYING IN A "J" FORMATION AT AN ESTIMATED HEIGHT OF 20,000 FEET ABOVE THE TERRAIN. THE FORMATION VARIED FROM "J" TO "L" TO CIRCLE AFTER PASSING THE ZENITH. FLASHES FROM THE OBJECTS WERE OBSERVED AFTER PASSING 30 DEGREES BEYOND THE ZENITH, BUT THERE WAS NO SMOKE OR VAPOR TRAIL. IF THE REPORTED ALTITUDE IS CORRECT THE SPEED WAS ESTIMATED AT 1,500 MILES PER HOUR (2,400 KM/H), ACCORDING TO THE REPORT.[10]

SCIENTIST OBSERVES FLYING DISK

According to researcher Jacques Vallee, a scientist from New Mexico University (who insisted upon anonymity) was driving through the streets of Albuquerque at 8:35 a.m. on July 27, 1948 when he saw a "flat and circular object that seemed to be a metallic disk motionless in the sky." The object remained in place for ten minutes before departing the area. The witness was a former Navy pilot with more than 2,000 hours of flight-time. He is certain that what he saw was not a conventional craft. His case has never been formally reported.[11]

A CRAFT WITH WINDOWS

One evening in 1948 (exact date not given), an anonymous field-grade officer assigned to White Sands Proving Grounds, was driving through open country on his way to the base when he noticed strange-looking lights ahead of him above the road. Moments later, the lights zoomed towards him at an elevation of 400 feet. Says the officer, "I thought the Department of Army had a new type of pyrotechnics."

However, it quickly became clear that the object was some sort of craft. The officer then wondered if it might be a C-119 or C-123 transport plane. At this point, the object made a right turn above the road and the officer saw that it was unlike any aircraft he had ever seen. Says the officer,

> THERE WERE TWO ROWS OF WHAT APPEARED TO BE WINDOWS, BRILLIANTLY LIGHTED... I WOULD ESTIMATE THAT THEY WERE FIVE TO SIX FEET IN HEIGHT, AND SIX TO EIGHT WINDOWS IN EACH OF THE TWO ROWS.

Before he was able to approach any closer, the object turned at a 90 degree angle and moved off into the darkness. The officer reported his sighting to the Air Force, who recorded the event in Air Force Project Report 9, devoted to studying the UFO phenomenon. The event was kept confidential by the Air Force until being revealed by pioneering UFO researcher Major Donald Keyhoe (USMC, Ret.)[12]

PROJECT TWINKLE

In the last few months of 1948, a strange phenomenon made its first of what would become numerous appearances over the skies of New Mexico. A wave of enormous green fireballs – like meteorites – showered down on the landscape. In a few cases, the fireballs appeared to strike the earth, however, in every case no physical evidence of their existence could be found. The fireballs were first assumed to be a natural meteorological phenomenon. However, as their numbers increased, it became clear that these were not normal fireballs. Not only were they bright green. Not only were they too numerous. Not only were they totally silent. Not only did they leave no evidence of their passing. Most mysterious was that the fireballs – unlike meteors – often traveled in a nearly horizontal path at an altitude of 40,000 to 60,000 feet. There were also the questions as to why they had not appeared before 1948 and seemed to be centered almost exclusively over New Mexico.

From December 1948 through April 1949, at least thirty-nine reports of the green fireballs came to the attention of officials at the Air Material Command. One of the first occurred at 9:27 p.m., December 5, when an Air Force Pilot flying a C-47 at 18,000 feet over Albuquerque saw a huge green fireball fly upward, then level off to a horizontal trajectory.

A mere seven minutes later, another pilot saw a large orange fireball approach in a horizontal trajectory, turn green in color, then dart to the side and fall to the ground.

Before long the New Mexican skies were littered by the fireballs. Edward Ruppelt wrote that:

> ...EVERYONE, INCLUDING THE INTELLIGENCE OFFICERS AT KIRTLAND AFB, AIR DEFENSE COMMAND PEOPLE, DR. LA PAZ, AND SOME OF THE MOST DISTINGUISHED SCIENTISTS AT LOS ALAMOS HAD SEEN AT LEAST ONE.

Sightings of green fireballs were reported in the Los Alamos vicinity on the 5th, 8th, 11th, 12th, 13th, 14th, 20th and 25th of December 1949. Witnesses included Special Agents of the USAF Office of Special Investigations, airline pilots, Los Alamos security inspectors, scientists, and military personnel of varying ranks – all witnesses the Pentagon called "observers whose reliabilities are not questioned."

Lincoln La Paz's sighting occurred on December 12, 1948. He and others watched with alarm as a green fireball with a brightness magnitude of –6 (four times brighter than Venus) flew on a flat path at an extremely low altitude for at least eight miles directly over Los Alamos. The sighting convinced La Paz that they were not natural phenomenon. He later had an additional sighting.

J. Allen Hynek (the astronomical consultant for Project Blue Book) was also consulted about the fireball problem. He interviewed several leading astronomers and found that most were unaware of the fireball's anomalous features. He pointed to La Paz as the best source of information on the subject. According to Hynek,

> IT APPEARS THAT THE GREEN FIREBALLS CAN BE CHARACTERIZED BY BEING EXTREMELY BRIGHT, MOST OF THEM LIGHTING UP THE SKY IN THE DAYTIME, ESTIMATED MAGNITUDE –12, WHICH IS EXTREMELY BRIGHT. THEY APPEAR TO COME IN BUNCHES...

NO NOISE IS ASSOCIATED WITH THEM DESPITE THEIR BRIGHTNESS...THEY LEAVE NO TRAILS OR TRAINS... IF THESE DATA ARE CORRECT, THAT IS, IF THIS MANY OBJECTS ARE ACTUALLY SEEN, ALL EXTREMELY BRIGHT, ALL HAVING THIS PARTICULAR GREEN COLOR, ALL EXHIBITING NO NOISE, ALL SHOWING A PREFERENTIAL DIRECTION, ALL BEING HOMOGENOUS IN LIGHT INTENSITY, ALL SNAPPING OUT VERY QUICKLY, AND ALL LEAVING NO TRAILS, THEN WE CAN SAY WITH ASSURANCE THAT THESE WERE NOT ASTRONOMICAL OBJECTS. IN THE FIRST PLACE, ANY OBJECT AS BRIGHT AS THIS SHOULD HAVE BEEN REPORTED FROM ALL OVER THE WORLD...IF THE EARTH IN ITS ORBIT ENCOUNTERED, FOR SOME STRANGE REASON, A GROUP OF VERY LARGE METEORS, THERE IS NO REASON THAT THEY SHOULD ALL SHOW UP IN NEW MEXICO... IF THE DATA AS REPORTED BY LA PAZ ARE CORRECT, THEN WE DO HAVE A STRANGE PHENOMENA HERE INDEED.

On January 30, 1949, hundreds of residents across New Mexico observed one of the dramatic green fireballs sweep across the night sky. This time the response from Kirtland officials was swift. They contacted officials in Washington and began to organize an investigation. La Paz triangulated the path of the object and was able to estimate its speed as between 25,000 and 50,000 miles per hour. The lack of any reports of a sonic boom mystified him and he again wrote to the AFOSI that the objects were "surely artificial."

Not all of the fireballs were green. Sometime in 1949 over a period of several nights, (exact date not given) a series of bright red fireballs descended near the airport at Albuquerque. On the first occasion, a fireball reportedly approached to within 500 feet of the airport, dropped to an elevation of 200 feet, and then exploded with a shower of reddish spray. Writes Keyhoe,

AT FIRST IT WAS FEARED THIS MIGHT BE SOME KIND OF GAS, BUT IT CAUSED NO ILL EFFECTS. THIS WAS REPEATED ON THREE MORE NIGHTS, AT THE SAME TIME AND LOCATIONS, PROVING THE "RED SPRAY" OF THE UFOS WERE UNDER PRECISE CONTROL. THE INCIDENTS WERE CONFIRMED IN THE AF PROJECT GRUDGE REPORT, WITH NO OPINIONS AS TO THE PURPOSE.

Air Force officials now became increasingly concerned. The fireballs were appearing in increasing numbers over the sensitive atomic installations of Los Alamos and Sandia, and Kirtland Air Force Base. On February 16, 1949, a secret meeting involving Dr. Edward Teller (the primary inventor of the atomic bomb) and Dr. Lincoln LaPaz (director of the Institute of Meteoritics at the University of New Mexico) was held at Los Alamos Scientific Laboratory to study the phenomenon. After studying the reports, and having observed one of the fireballs himself, Dr. LaPaz concluded that the fireballs were artificial constructions, and might even be radio-controlled missiles. He strongly opposed the meteor theory.

Astronomer Clyde Tombaugh (discoverer of planet Pluto) agreed with La Paz that the fireballs were not meteors. As he wrote in a letter to researcher Leonard Stringfield, "I have seen three green fireballs which were unusual in behavior from scores of normal green fireballs." Later, in 1949, Tombaugh would have a dramatic sighting with a solid object with portholes, after which he became increasingly vocal about the UFO phenomenon (see below.)

On April 19, 1949, the Air Force Office of Special Investigations at Kirtland AFB issued a list of fireball reports to Air Force Headquarters, saying in part,

> THE COMMON CHARACTERISTICS OF MOST OF THE INCIDENTS ARE:
> (A) GREEN COLOR, SOMETIMES DESCRIBED AS GREENISH WHITE, BRIGHT GREEN, YELLOW GREEN, OR BLUE GREEN;
> (B) HORIZONTAL PATH, SOMETIMES WITH MINOR VARIATIONS;
> (C) SPEED LESS THAN THAT OF A METEOR BUT MORE THAN ANY OTHER TYPE OF NO KNOWN AIRCRAFT;
> (D) NO SOUND ASSOCIATED WITH OBSERVATION:
> (E) NO PERSISTENT TRAIL OR DUST CLOUD;
> (F) PERIOD OF VISIBILITY FROM ONE TO FIVE SECONDS.

In August 1949, the action Kirtland had been asking for was finally taken when the USAF created a special study called Project Twinkle. They brought in a cinetheodolite camera, which would allow them to track the objects and triangulate their size, speed, and altitude.

On September 20, 1950, more than 100 witnesses across Idaho and New Mexico observed "great fireballs" streaking across the sky. Project Twinkle failed to capture them on any type of instrumentation.

Then, from November 9 to November 20, the green fireballs were reported on seven of eleven consecutive evenings. The objects were witnessed by many military personnel and astronomers. Again, however, Project Twinkle was unable to capture any of the objects on their instruments. By this time, there had been more than 150 sightings reported.

Unfortunately, the Project Twinkle was, as Edward Ruppelt said, "a bust." It was dissolved on December 27, 1950, badly organized, pitifully funded, and without ever having tracked a single fireball.

In 1955, researcher Leonard Stringfield spoke with Captain Robert C. White of the Air Force's Office of Public Information. When he inquired about the green fireballs over New Mexico, Captain White replied, "They do exist. That's why thousands of dollars were spent investigating them."

White then said, "The projects' files have never been declassified," and told Stringfield, "The Air Force thinks the green fireballs are astronomical phenomena."

Stringfield disagreed and quoted Dr. Lincoln La Paz who had said, "They are not any kind of meteor I have ever heard of."

White then capitulated and replied simply, "We cannot explain them."

The fireballs continued to appear throughout the 1950s, though by the end of the decade, they slowed down and eventually stopped. They have never been explained. Scientists did find unusually high levels of copper in the atmosphere where the phenomenon had manifested. Some scientists speculated that perhaps the Earth was passing through a previously unknown asteroid cluster. However, this failed to explain why New Mexico, the atomic capitol of the world, seemed to be singled out as a target. Later, at least one UFO contactee was told that fireballs were intentionally generated by ETs and sent to the area in order to reverse the atmospheric damage that atomic testing had caused.

Every now and then, the green fireballs continued to make dramatic appearances. In January of 1952, three fireballs were seen over Taos. The first appeared at twilight; it was bright yellow and reportedly hung motionless over Santa Fe Highway for a period of ten minutes before suddenly vanishing. Shortly later, a second green-colored fireball appeared, swaying to and fro over the mountains adjacent to Taos. At 10 p.m., a third green fireball shot across the Taos sky and vanished. Several months later, on November 2, 1952, a green fireball, described as larger than the full moon, was seen over New Mexico, exploding in a "tremendous paroxysm of light."

For the most part, the wave of green fireballs was over. Only a few more sightings gained attention. On September 18, 1954, a wave of green fireballs was seen across Colorado, New Mexico, and Texas.

One of the last major events occurred on April 6, 1955. On that day, at least five different green fireballs were seen in varying locations across New Mexico including Albuquerque, Hobbs, Lordsburg, Roswell, and Weed. In each case, the fireballs hit the ground and exploded.[13]

PROFESSOR REPORTS UFO

In 1952, astronomer J. Allen Hynek interviewed several people who had seen UFOs in Albuquerque. One sighting comes from Dr. Everton Conger, Instructor in Journalism at the University of New Mexico. On July 24, 1948, at around 8:45 a.m., he saw a round, flat plate-like object. Writes Hynek,

IT APPEARED TO BE MADE OF DURALUMINUM AND GAVE OFF REFLECTED LIGHT VERY SIMILAR TO THE LIGHT REFLECTED FROM A HIGHLY POLISHED AIRPLANE WING.

Hynek spoke with other gentlemen in Albuquerque who had witnessed a UFO on the same evening (exact date not given.) Writes Hynek,

I QUESTIONED THEM SEPARATELY AND FOUND THAT THEIR STORIES WERE REMARKABLY CONSISTENT. INDEED, SINCE THEY VIEWED THE OBJECT FROM WIDELY DIFFERENT PARTS OF THE CITY, THERE IS SOME POSSIBILITY THAT THE PARALLAX OF THE OBJECT CAN BE OBTAINED BY MAKING THEODOLITE SIGHTINGS NOW ON WHERE THE OBJECT APPEARED TO THEM. THE POSITION OF THE OBJECT CAN BE IDENTIFIED NOW BECAUSE IT WAS VIEWED CLOSE TO A CANYON IN THE MOUNTAINS.[14]

UFOS TRACKED BY THEODOLITES

Although Project Twinkle failed to record any fireballs, there were, as we have seen, several incidents during which members of this team and others did, in fact, observe several classic "flying saucers" using a theodolite.

Beginning on April 6, 1949, there were several sightings of unknown objects flying over White Sands. The first incident to be captured on a theodolite occurred at 10:30 a.m. on April 24, 1949, over Arrey at White Sands proving grounds. Commander Robert B. McLaughlin (chief of the Navy's guided missile program at the base) was supervising an experiment involving the launching of General Mills skyhook research balloons. One of the members of the crew, Charles B. Moore was watching the small 350-gram weather balloon as it ascended. Suddenly, he noticed that another member of the group had the telescope trained on the wrong location in the sky.

Moore confronted the man, berating him for having lost the balloon, which Moore could still see. The man protested and said, "But I've got it right here!"

Moore looked and with his naked eye he suddenly noticed another "whitish spherical object" flying directly over the balloon, only at a higher altitude and in a different direction. He quickly took over and trained the ML-47 theodolite built around a 25-power telescope onto the object. The instrument revealed that the unknown object was actually a flat oval-shaped disk with a whitish-silver color. Moore kept the theodolite trained on the object for at least sixty seconds. During this time, he was able to determine that the object was 56 miles in altitude and was moving at an astonishing speed of seven miles per second or 2,200 miles per hour. They estimated that the craft was 40 feet wide and 100 feet long. As they watched, the unknown object suddenly dropped in altitude until it was below the horizon line of the nearby mountain range. Then it stopped, swung upwards and zoomed out of sight. The group of scientists were stunned and easily concluded that they had seen an actual craft and not a meteorite. Says Moore, "As I remember the object that I saw through the theodolite, my memory is that its edges were sharp and not diffuse."

Air Force Intelligence officers were brought in to investigate, and unable to find an explanation, reluctantly labeled the case unidentified, the second such case in New Mexico (see Blue Book Case #358).

J. Allen Hynek was assigned to research the case, and admits that he and the other officers did not give it the time and attention it deserved. As he later wrote,

> MOORE WAS DISGUSTED WITH THE AIR FORCE'S AND MY LACK OF ATTENTION TO THIS SIGHTING. WHO CAN BLAME HIM? IT WAS TYPICAL OF THE AIR FORCE'S PRACTICE OF SPENDING A GREAT DEAL OF OVERKILL EFFORT PINNING DOWN CASES FOR WHICH THERE SEEMED TO ME AN IMMEDIATE LOGICAL EXPLANATION IN SIGHT AND DEVOTING ONLY MODEST FOLLOW-UP TO A CASE THAT WAS TRULY BAFFLING.

Despite receiving almost no investigation, the sighting had far-reaching implications. Researcher Michael David Hall writes that the sighting impressed the base officials and that "it stands as one of the most credible [sightings] from the early years." Researchers Brad Sparks and Jerome Clark wrote,

WITH GOOD REASON THIS SIGHTING CONVINCED MANY INFLUENTIAL PERSONS THAT UFOS WERE REAL AND EXTRATERRESTRIAL.

Within three days of the incident, investigators from the Air Force Scientific Advisory Board arrived to investigate. The purpose of the visit, as revealed in a declassified memo, was to investigate reports of "unidentified aerial phenomena that have been observed in this area during the last five months."

Shortly afterwards, this incident and others were leaked to the press. Documents from the now-declassified Project Grudge (the pre-cursor to Blue Book) show that the Air Force officials were apparently more concerned that the news articles were revealing too much information about the saucers and the Air Force interest in them, than about the incident itself. According to Brad Sparks and Jerome Clark, the AFOSI "went into a frenzy to try to hunt down the source of the leak." They learned that Commander McLaughlin himself was the main source, but not the only one.

In a public press conference, Commander Robert McLaughlin told reporters:

FLYING DISKS HAVE NOTHING TO DO WITH ANY EXPERIMENTS CARRIED ON BY AMERICAN SCIENTISTS OR FOR THAT MATTER BY ANYONE ON EARTH. IF THESE THINGS ARE REAL, THEY COME FROM ANOTHER PLANET, WHERE CREATURES ARE FAR AHEAD OF US IN SCIENCE. I HAVE HEARD IT SAID THAT THEY ARE SPACE SHIPS FROM MARS, WHICH HAVE BEEN ATTRACTED TO THE EARTH BY OUR ATOMIC BOMB EXPLOSIONS AND, FASCINATED BY WHAT THEY SAW, HAVE CONTINUED TO KEEP AN EYE ON US.

Later, McLaughlin told *True Magazine,*

I AM CONVINCED IT WAS A FLYING SAUCER AND FURTHER, THAT THESE DISKS ARE SPACE ALIENS FROM ANOTHER PLANET, OPERATED BY ANIMATE, INTELLIGENT BEINGS.

Whatever the case, the information proved to be a thorn in the Air Force's side. One article, written by journalist Austin Conover, revealed several new sightings over White Sands. Writes Conover,

DURING A VISIT THERE LAST WEEK, I WAS TOLD BY A TOP NAVY OFFICER WHO HAD LONG EXPERIENCES IN OBSERVING HIGH-ALTITUDE MISSILES: "WHILE SUNBATHING RECENTLY ONE DAY, I SAW A MYSTERIOUS OBJECT CAVORTING HIGH IN THE AIR ABOVE US. JUST BEFORE THAT, I TURNED IN A REPORT TO WASHINGTON THAT TWO SUCH OBJECTS WERE OBSERVED BY A PARTY OF ROCKET EXPERTS VISITING HERE. AT THAT TIME I WAS SKEPTICAL. THEY INSISTED THAT I MAKE THE REPORT."

Another whistle-blower was Homer E. Newell Jr., a top civilian scientist with the Naval Research Laboratory at White Sands. Newell told reporters,

> I HAVE NEVER SEEN A FLYING SAUCER. I DISCOUNT ALL OF THE REPORTS EXCEPT A FEW. SOME JUST CAN'T BE DISPELLED AS PURE MYTH, HALLUCINATION, WEATHER BALLOONS, OR SHADOWS OF ROCKETS ON CLOUDS.

Meanwhile, the sightings at White Sands continued. On April 27, 1949, four U.S. Army personnel were stationed near Los Alamos when they observed a tiny object described as a four-inch diameter light with a metallic cone attached to the rear, fly directory towards them. The soldiers estimated that the object moved at a speed of seventy miles per hour and a height of only seven feet. It was only in view for a matter of seconds before disappearing to the southwest.

About one month later, in May of 1949, Commander Robert McLaughlin had his own sighting at White Sands. He and two other officers were observing the launch of a rocket when they saw another white glowing object pass slowly overhead, then suddenly accelerate at high speed and move behind some hills.

One month after that, on June 10, there was another similar sighting at the base. Two small white disk-shaped objects were observed from five separate observation posts. The two disks appeared alongside an Army rocket, maneuvered around it as it launched and then accelerated vertically into the distance at speeds estimated around 1,300 miles per hour.

Commander McLaughlin later revealed that he had been witness to this and other similar UFO events. Says McLaughlin,

> MANY TIMES I HAVE SEEN FLYING DISCS FOLLOWING AND OVERTAKING MISSILES IN FLIGHT AT THE EXPERIMENTAL BASE AS WHITE SANDS, WHERE, AS IS KNOWN, THE FIRST AMERICAN ATOM BOMB WAS TRIED OUT.

On August 31, 1949, the *Los Angeles Times* printed an article by Marvin Miles titled, "U.S. Officers Report Seeing Flying Disks." The article said that on August 29, "flying saucers or at least some mysterious objects" were seen by service personnel at White Sands Proving Grounds. Writes Miles,

ONE OFFICER BELIEVES THE OBJECTS WERE SPACE SHIPS... OBSERVATION MADE
THROUGH A PHOTO THEODOLITE, SHOWED SHIP TO BE EGG-SHAPED, FANTASTIC IN
SIZE, TRAVELING AT POSSIBLE THREE TO FOUR MILES A SECOND.

More sightings continued. In Fall of 1949, *Life* magazine reported a sighting over a "key atomic base" (presumably White Sands), during which a high-ranking Air Force officer and others visually observed and tracked on radar five metallic disks which flew over the base at "tremendous speed and great height." They were reportedly at 100,000 feet of altitude moving at 4,500 miles per hour. The case is missing from Blue Book and the only apparent documentation comes from the *Life* magazine article. Despite any official corroboration, UFO researcher Hynek says that there is "no doubt about its authenticity."

Clearly, by this time, despite public denials, Air Force officials on many levels were aware that the UFO phenomenon was real.[15]

ASTRONOMER CLYDE TOMBAUGH SEES UFO

In 1930, astronomer Clyde W. Tombaugh stunned the world with his discovery of the planet, Pluto. Although some astronomers downgraded it to a mere planetoid in 2007, the discovery of Pluto electrified the world and earned Tombaugh a permanent place in the field of astronomy. Nineteen years later, on August 20, 1949, Tombaugh's announcement of his own UFO sighting failed to generate the same publicity.

It was 10:45 p.m. and Tombaugh, his wife and mother-in-law sat in the backyard of their home in Las Cruces. It was a particularly clear night, and Tombaugh noted that even the faintest stars with a brightness of six magnitudes were easily visible. Suddenly, the three observers saw something they couldn't identify. Flying overhead in a geometric formation were six to eight blue-green rectangular-shaped lights. The lights were at a low altitude and moved quickly and silently from the northwest to the southeast. It soon became clear that the lights were attached to a single object which appeared to have a half-dozen windows or portholes along the front and side that emitted a bright light. Tombaugh concluded instantly that they were neither meteors nor conventional aircraft, but it was clearly a "solid" object. He wrote an official report to the Air Force stating in part,

THE REMARKABLY SUDDEN ASCENT CONVINCED ME IT WAS AN ABSOLUTELY NOVEL AIRBORNE DEVICE… I HAVE DONE THOUSANDS OF HOURS OF NIGHT SKY WATCHING, BUT NEVER SAW A SIGHT SO STRANGE AS THIS.

He also wrote a letter to NICAP stating,

AS I HAVE SAID BEFORE, I WAS SO UNPREPARED FOR SUCH A STRANGE SIGHT THAT I WAS REALLY PETRIFIED WITH ASTONISHMENT. CONSEQUENTLY SOME OF THE DETAILS I MIGHT HAVE NOTED WERE MISSED.

Years later, Tombaugh continued to be vocal about the phenomenon. For example, on February 13, 1954, he gave a talk to the Astronomy Society at Las Cruces, surprising the audience by predicting that there would be an increase in UFO sightings.

Three years later, he wrote a letter to researcher Leonard Stringfield in which he revealed that he had seen "three objects within the past seven years, which defied any explanation of known phenomena such as Venus, atmospheric optics, meteors, or planes."

Tombaugh wrote that on three other occasions he had seen the unexplained green fireballs over New Mexico. He closed his letter, saying,

I THINK THAT SEVERAL REPUTABLE SCIENTISTS ARE BEING UNSCIENTIFIC IN REFUSING TO ENTERTAIN THE POSSIBILITY OF EXTRATERRESTRIAL ORIGIN AND NATURE.[16]

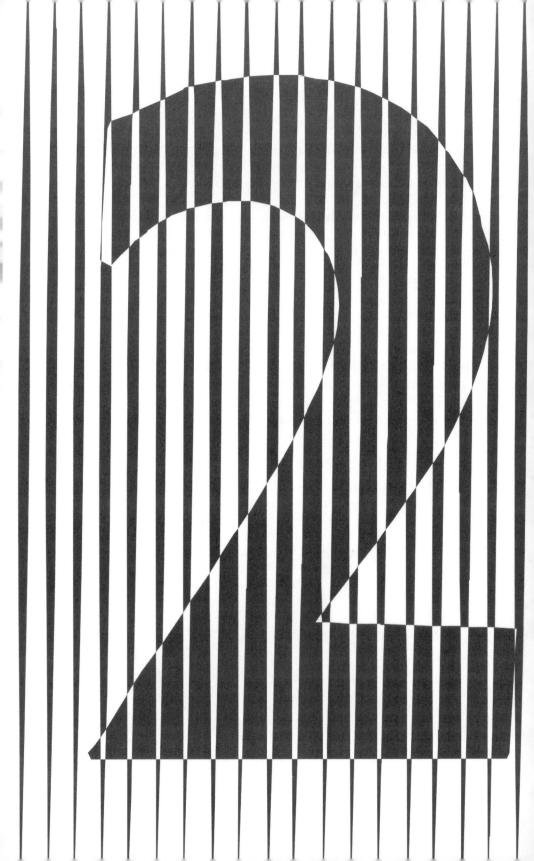

CHAPTER 2

THE Roaring 1950s

The dawning of the modern age of UFOs was, for New Mexico, the beginning of a long and ongoing series of escalating UFO encounters, and a mad scramble to deal with a phenomenon that was a largely unknown quantity. By the time 1950 had arrived, there had already been as many as seven separate UFO crash/retrieval events in New Mexico alone, not to mention the hundreds of sightings over sensitive military bases. Clearly by this time, the USAF was in no way ignorant of what was going on, at least not at the highest levels.

Again, much of the activity was concentrated over military and atomic installations. However, as the decade progressed, increasing numbers of civilians began to report their own dramatic encounters across the state.

UFOS OVER HOBBS

On March 15, 1950, Frank Bond – a painter and resident of Hobbs – heard a sound like a "jet plane" and looking up, observed four silvery metallic craft travel overhead at an estimated 2,000 feet, maneuvering in a follow-the-leader fashion. Bond described the objects as having a square-shaped fuselage with a rounded nose, and portholes along the sides. Bond was so impressed by his sighting, he not only reported it to authorities, but he constructed models of the objects he had seen.

Unknown to the painter, there may have been other witnesses to his sighting. On the same day in the neighboring town of Eunice, C.E. Hedpath and Ruth Hedpath observed a "flying saucer" fly overhead.[17]

THE FARMINGTON UFO DISPLAY

One of the most unusual UFO incidents in recorded history occurred on March 17, 1950, over the small town of Farmington (then a population of 3,600 to 6,100). At around 10 a.m. that St. Patrick Day morning, more than a thousand witnesses in Farmington observed an enormous group of *hundreds* of saucer-shaped objects maneuvering above the town, performing fantastic loops, dives, turns, accelerations and decelerations, and other fantastic gyrations. Panic ensued as half the population of the town poured into the streets to watch the display, which continued for at least two hours.

There had been scattered reports of sightings over Farmington for the past few days, but this level of activity appeared to be an absolute invasion. The craft were observed not only by the citizens of Farmington, but by several city officials including the mayor, members of the highway patrol, the local newspaper staff, and several pilots.

The next day, newspapers across the country carried the dramatic story. The *Farmington Daily Times* headline read, "Huge 'Saucer' Armada Jolts Farmington." The story was quickly picked up by other newspapers.

The *Los Angeles Times* printed an article titled, "Scores Report Seeing Saucers' Flight in Formation Over New Mexico." The article goes on to say that:

...50 PERSONS REPORTED A MASS FLIGHT OF FLYING SAUCERS OVER FARMINGTON, NEW MEXICO. GROUPS COMMENCING AT 10:30 A.M., AND LASTED FOR ONE HOUR. AMONG THE SAUCERS WAS ONE LOW-FLYING, RED-HUED SAUCER-SHAPED OBJECT. ALL THE SAUCERS EXCEPT THIS ONE WERE SILVERY COLOR, AND ALL APPEARED TO BE VERY HIGH EXCEPT FOR THE RED-HUED ONE.

The *Los Angeles Mirror* printed an article called, "Now What Was It, You Saucer?" The article says that:

ALL OF THE 250 PERSONS INTERVIEWED BY WALT ROGAL, EDITOR OF THE *FARMINGTON TIMES*, ADMITTED SEEING WHAT WAS GENERALLY DESCRIBED AS A MASS FLIGHT OF FLYING OBJECTS... ROGAL ESTIMATED 85% OF THIS TOWN'S POPULATION OF 6100 SAW THE OBJECTS.

The *Denver Post* headlined, "New Mexico Town Sure Saucer Mass Flight Seen," and reported that:

MORE THAN 50 WITNESSES – INCLUDING BUSINESSMEN AND PRIVATE PILOTS – SAID THAT THEY SAW A MASS FLIGHT OF DISK-SHAPED OBJECTS YESTERDAY WHICH CAME ACROSS THE TOWN IN GROUP WAVES AND NUMBER "INTO THE HUNDREDS."

New Mexico newspaper staff writer, Walt Rogal, also wrote for the *Las Vegas Daily Optic*, which carried the headline, "'Space ships' Cause Sensation." Rogal had become one of the major press sources regarding the incident. According to Rogal,

FOR THE THIRD CONSECUTIVE DAY FLYING SAUCERS HAVE BEEN REPORTED OVER FARMINGTON. AND ON EACH OF THE THREE DAYS THEIR ARRIVAL WAS REPORTED BETWEEN 11:00 A.M. AND NOON. FULLY HALF OF THIS TOWN'S POPULATION IS CERTAIN TODAY THAT IT SAW SPACE SHIPS OR SOME STRANGE AIRCRAFT – HUNDREDS OF THEM – ZOOMING THROUGH THE SKIES YESTERDAY. WHATEVER THEY WERE, THEY CAUSED A SENSATION IN THIS COMMUNITY, WHICH LIES ONLY 110 AIR MILES NORTHWEST OF THE HUGE LOS ALAMOS ATOMIC INSTALLATION. ONE WITNESS WHO TOOK A TRIANGULATION SIGHTING ON ONE OF THE OBJECTS ESTIMATED ITS SPEED AT ABOUT 1,000 MILES AN HOUR, AND ESTIMATED ITS SIZE AS APPROXIMATELY TWICE THAT OF A B-29.

The Air Force was contacted, but at first refused to release any statement other than denying any knowledge of the situation. An editorial in the same newspaper as above, on the same day, lambasted the Air Force's mishandling of the UFO situation. The editorial titled "Give us the Facts" said:

YESTERDAY HUNDREDS OF RELIABLE, SOBER PEOPLE IN FARMINGTON SAW "SOMETHING" IN THE SKIES. AT LEAST HALF BELIEVE WHAT THEY SAW WAS AN ARMADA OF SPACE SHIPS...THE AMERICAN POPULATION IS NOT COMPOSED CHIEFLY OF CHILDREN OR IDIOTS. MOST OF US ARE ADULTS WHO ARE WILLING TO EMBRACE NEW CONCEPTS OF TIME AND SPACE WITHOUT PANIC. ATTEMPTS TO KEEP THE PUBLIC IN THE DARK INVARIABLY HAVE HURT THE GENERAL WELFARE, NOT HELPED IT. WE CAN SAY, HOWEVER, THAT IT IS HIGH TIME THE GOVERNMENT OF THE U.S. CAST ASIDE THE CLOAK OF EVASION AND SECRECY SURROUNDING THESE MANIFESTATIONS, AND PRESENT THE PUBLIC THE FINDINGS IT HAS REACHED ON SUCH MATTERS.

Not all people were believers. At least two Farmington residents told reporters that the objects seen were not flying saucers, but rather pieces of "cotton" or which merely gave the appearance of flying saucers. Both witnesses claimed to have actually watched the bits of cotton land on the ground and rooftops.

Most witnesses felt differently. Orville Ricketts, editor of the *Farmington Daily News* says that the wind that day was very still, and could not have carried up cotton or other material in that volume or at that speed. Ricketts collected the names of at least fifty men and woman who observed the objects. One witness tried to explain the sightings away as "a star or planet," though this absurd explanation was ignored.

The vast majority of the town's inhabitants, however, believed that the objects were some kind of craft. Said Farmington resident John Bloomfield,

THEY APPEARED TO BE COMING AT EACH OTHER HEAD-ON. AT THE LAST SECOND, ONE WOULD VEER AT RIGHT ANGLES UPWARD, THE OTHER AT RIGHT ANGLES DOWNWARD. ONE VEHICLE WOULD PASS ANOTHER, AND IMMEDIATELY THE ONE TO THE REAR WOULD TAKE THE LEAD... ALL I KNOW IS THAT I SAW SOMETHING UP THERE IN THE SKY THAT I NEVER SAW BEFORE.

Farmington resident Marlow Webb also watched the objects, and is convinced they were craft. He watched as one of the craft "flew sideways, on edge, and at every conceivable angle. This is what made it easy to determine that they were disc-shaped."

Captain Clayton J. Boddy (ret.) the advertising manager of the *Farmington Daily Times* said he was with a group of five businessmen when the objects arrived, and all agreed that they viewed more than 100 of the objects which were silver-colored, disk-shaped, and fluttered through the sky without descending. Says Boddy, "We contacted the Air Force and they denied everything. They said it didn't happen."

Glen Pace was 10 years old when it happened. As he says, "I came out on the playground for recess and someone said, 'Look, up there!'"

Looking up, Pace saw no less than 30 silver, disk-shaped objects maneuvering and hovering overhead. Says Pace, "They were in a triangular formation, and they made sudden moves all together."

He watched them for ten minutes until they suddenly departed. Says Pace,

> WHEN THEY LEFT, THEY TURNED ON THEIR SIDE. THEY WERE GONE IN A SECOND. BOOM, THEY WERE OUT OF SIGHT.

Farmington resident Johnny Eaton (a real estate agent and insurance salesman) was 29 years old at the time of the incident, and recalls it vividly. Said Eaton in a 2002 interview,

> I'VE NEVER SEEN ANYTHING LIKE IT IN MY LIFE. THERE WERE FIVE RED OBJECTS. THEY WOULD HOVER, THEN IMMEDIATELY CHANGE DIRECTIONS, BUT STAY IN A GROUP. THAT WAS THE AMAZING THING.

Eaton said that a few minutes later, a much larger "cigar-shaped machine" appeared, moving rapidly across the sky. The red objects immediately flew towards it and disappeared inside it. Says Eaton, "It looked like they went right into the front part."

The next day, says Eaton, military officials showed up in the small town to interview the many witnesses. After interviewing him, the military officials told Eaton it was a weather balloon, and that he should forget about the incident. Eaton, however, was not persuaded. As he says,

> I'M NOT STUPID. I KNOW DANG WELL THEY WERE NOT BALLOONS. THEY TOLD ME TO FORGET IT. FORGET IT? YOU CAN'T FORGET SOMETHING THAT HAPPENS ONCE IN A LIFETIME.

There were apparently two waves of sightings, one at 10:30 a.m., and a second wave one hour later, at 11:30 a.m. The objects sometimes appeared to fly randomly, and at other times, flew in formations. Most witnesses agreed that the objects were very high in elevation. The reason for the wave of UFOs was unknown, but some of the witnesses had the impression that the objects were looking for something.

News of the sightings spread quickly and the Air Force was contacted and asked for an explanation. The next day, the Air Force released a statement refusing to explain the incident and concluding simply, "There's nothing to it."

The explanation – or lack of it – enraged the public, and as a result, more newspaper articles were published about the incident, criticizing the Air Force's apparent disinterest in the subject. Later, Major Edward Ruppelt tried to debunk the sightings, suggesting that they may have been caused by a Skyhook balloon which could have shattered into thousands of tiny bits of pieces, each of which would reflect brightly in the sun and appear to move at sharp angles as they were carried in the wind. Whatever the explanation, the intensity of the Farmington UFO display remains unparalleled in UFO history. According to a few sources, the Farmington UFO display actually took place on the anniversary of the alleged UFO crash at Aztec (the date of which is disputed among researchers.) Some researchers feel that the ETs were acknowledging the date of the Aztec crash and the lives of the ETs lost in the accident two years earlier (see chapter on UFO crashes.)[18]

MORE MILITARY ENCOUNTERS

By 1950, the Atomic Energy Commission (AEC) was apparently so concerned about the rash of UFO sightings over atomic installations that they solicited the public for information. The AEC prepared a questionnaire and asked anyone who had seen UFOs over atomic installations to fill them out. The form contained twenty-six questions, requesting a description of the object in detail, including the luminosity of the object, apparent means of propulsion, and even the odor. Writes reporter Robert S. Allen, "This is the first time the AEC has publicly evinced interest in flying saucers."

Apparently the reason the AEC was so concerned was because of the increasing audacity of the flying saucers, particularly over New Mexico. For example, on February 25, 1950, twelve AEC inspectors were visiting the Los Alamos Proving Grounds when they personally observed a "flying cylinder" cruise leisurely over the base. Only one day earlier, Blue Book officials had investigated another dramatic sighting over Albuquerque which they were unable to explain. They eventually declared that both sightings were officially unidentified (see Blue Book Cases #642 & #645).

As the UFOs descended over various New Mexican military bases, they seemed to exhibit no fears of being seen and would even put on displays. One such case occurred at Los Alamos on April 17, 1950, when more than fifteen people observed three UFOs for a period of twenty minutes. The objects maneuvered back and forth along the eastern horizon "faster than any known conventional aircraft" at an estimated altitude of 2,000 feet, as if putting on a show for the onlookers. One of the witnesses, a scientist from the University of California, observed one of the objects through a telescope and described it as flat, metallic, circular and about nine feet in diameter.

On April 27, 1950, a Twinkle team was on duty at Holloman Air Force Base. They had just observed a test missile launch and then fall back to earth when they also saw four unknown objects swoop down as if to examine the event. They trained the theodolite on the objects and were able to determine that the objects – whatever their origin – were around thirty feet in diameter, and hovered at an altitude of 150,000 feet. After several moments, the objects darted away at high speed. On that same day, at apparently around the same time, an officer at White Sands visually sighted the object streaking across the sky. He grabbed his camera and was able to capture a photograph of the object. Unfortunately, the photograph was labeled inconclusive.

One month, later, however, the UFOs were back. On May 29, 1950, officers at White Sands tracked an unknown object at two separate theodolite stations, and also captured theodolite camera footage of the object. Strangely, the case was never reported to Blue Book.

An even more impressive case took place at Holloman two months later, in July 1950, and is one of many UFO incidents which the Air Force attempted unsuccessfully to censor from the public. In this case, the witness was an electronics engineer who worked on the base. Over the past several months, he had seen "high groups of shiny objects" over the base, and had already accepted the idea that there was "some kind of phenomena" which hadn't yet been identified.

One warm summer July day, he was eating lunch in his office when the telephone rang. One of the nearby range stations phoned to say that an unknown aerial object had been sighted over the base and asked the witness to proceed to another range station that was equipped with a manually-operated Askania theodolite.

The witness and his co-employee rushed to the station and, obtaining the azimuth and elevation readings, quickly located the object with the theodolite. According to Coral Lorenzen, who interviewed the witness, the object was described as "cigar-shaped and metallic, with a straw-colored iridescent radiance or luster."

Fins extended from the body of the object, which also displayed at least three "smoky gray" oblong portholes. The object hovered in a horizontal position at an elevation of about 25 degrees.

Shortly after the object was located on the theodolite, it maneuvered, turned its front towards the camera, then dropped abruptly and stopped short. It then moved forward, dropped in elevation and turned on its side.

Alarmed by the extreme maneuvers, the witness left his post at the theodolite and made a call to alert other nearby range stations so they could also track the object. However, when he returned back to his own theodolite, he was unable to locate the mysterious object.

Afterwards, the witness and his co-employee turned over the developed film they had taken with the theodolite camera. Ten days later, he and his co-employee were called in and interrogated by an unidentified first lieutenant. They were surprised that they didn't recognize the officer as he wore a Base identification badge. Says Lorenzen,

THEY WERE ASKED OVER AND OVER AGAIN IF THEY HAD TAKEN PICTURES, AND TO DESCRIBE OVER AND OVER THE OBJECT THEY HAD OBSERVED. THEN THE TWO MEN WERE ASKED IF THEY COULD IDENTIFY THE FILM OF THE OBJECT THEY HAD PHOTOGRAPHED. ONE OF THE MEN BECAME QUITE ANGRY ABOUT THE QUESTIONING, TELLING THE OFFICER HE HAD SEEN WHAT HE HAD REPORTED, HAD PHOTOGRAPHED THE OBJECT AND WAS CONVINCED THE OBJECT WAS SOME SORT OF VEHICLE FROM OUTER-SPACE. HE WAS SHOWN A FILM OF FOURTEEN FRAMES ON A RECORDAK PROJECTOR. THE BLACK-AND-WHITE PRESENTATION SHOWED A BLURRED ELLIPSOID WITH A DARK CENTER, BUT NO DETAILS...THE MEN WERE THEN TOLD BY THEIR SUPERIORS TO FORGET THE WHOLE INCIDENT.[19]

THE WAVE OF 1951

By this time, the increasing levels of UFO activity over sensitive nuclear installation and military bases had reached a new high. The year of 1951 brought at least six high-profile cases over various locations in New Mexico.

On February 14, 1951 two Air Force pilots (Captain J. E. Cocker and Captain E. W. Spradley) were tracking a balloon over Alamogordo when they saw a flat, round, white-colored object move overhead flashing a white light.

Exactly five months later, on July 14, 1951, a fast-moving object was seen over White Sands. The object was first seen hovering near a B-29. It was caught on radar, observed visually through binoculars and also photographed on 200 feet of 35 mm movie film which reportedly showed the object as a bright round spot.

In mid-August 1951, Alford Roos, a mining engineer, was working on his ranch located about ten miles east of Silver City. About 10:30 a.m., his attention was drawn upwards by a strange "swishing" noise.
Says Roos,

> I SAW AN OBJECT SWOOPING DOWN AT AN ANGLE OF ABOUT 45 DEGREES FROM THE SOUTHERLY DIRECTION, TRAVELING AT IMMENSE SPEED, COMING QUITE CLOSE TO THE EARTH OVER FORT BARNYARD, TWO MILES TO THE NORTHWEST. REACHING THE BOTTOM OF THE SWOOP IT HOVERED FOR MOMENTS THEN DARTED UP AT AN ANGLE OF ABOUT 70 DEGREES FROM THE VERTICAL, IN A NORTHWESTERLY DIRECTION, DIRECTLY OVER FORT BARNYARD.

At this point, Roos and a couple of other ranch workers saw a second object which was now hovering next to the first object. Both objects quickly entered inside a mile-long cloud. The witnesses were shocked at what happened next. Says Roos,

> THE ASTONISHING THING WAS THAT THE CLOUD IMMEDIATELY SPLIT INTO THREE SEGMENTS, EVER-WIDENING, WHERE THE OBJECTS ENTERED. EACH OBJECT LEFT A PENCIL-THIN VAPOR TRAIL.

In a report to NICAP, Roos wrote a vivid description of the objects,

> AT FIRST THE OBJECTS APPEARED TO BE SPHERICAL, BUT AFTER THE HOVERING AND THE TURN UP, THEY MUST HAVE TIPPED, CANTED SO THEN I SAW THE EDGE-ON OF THE LENS-LIKE OBJECT. GOING TOWARD THE CLOUD THEY WERE DISC-SHAPED... AFTER THE OBJECTS TURNED ON THEIR SIDES AT THE HOVER, THERE APPEARED TO BE A BUTTON, OR SOME SMALL PROTRUSION ON THE UPPER SIDE AS VIEWED EDGE-ON. THE OBJECTS WERE QUITE CLOSE AND WE COULD ALL DETECT SOME SORT OF OUTER ORNAMENTATION OR PROCESS OR POSSIBLY ORIFICES OR PORTHOLES, ON THE LOWER SIDE JUST BELOW THE RIM OF THE LENS, AND THESE SEEMED TO UNDERGO CHANGE OF IRIDESCENT COLOR, ALMOST LIKE A BLINKING.

What most impressed Roos, however, was the way the objects maneuvered. Says Roos,

THERE WAS NO GATHERING OF MOMENTUM FROM THE LOW HOVER, TO THE LIGHTNING-LIKE SHOT. FROM ALMOST STATIONARY TO INSTANT 500 MPH, THE SHOCK OF INERTIA WOULD HAVE MADE HUMAN (TERRESTRIAL) SURVIVAL IMPOSSIBLE.

The object appeared to be "lens-like or disc-shaped" and had a "button or some small protrusion on the upper side as viewed edge-on." It hovered in place while several other ranch employees gathered to observe the spectacle.

Moments later, a second identical-looking object appeared and joined the first object. At this point, both objects turned on their side and "shot up at a steep angle, from almost stationary to an instant 500 mph."

Around the same time as the above sighting, Sandia AFB reported several air-space violations by an unknown object over the base. None of the above cases made it onto Blue Book's unidentified list. However, one case was about to occur which could not be ignored.[20]

BLUE BOOK CASE NUMBER 995: UNIDENTIFIED

Only twenty-eight cases in New Mexico were declared officially unidentified by the Air Force's Project Blue Book. Most researchers believe that this particular Air Force study was more of a public relations project than an objective scientific study, and was used to extricate the Air Force from the sticky UFO problem. Whatever the case, there were some cases that were so strange, even the skeptical Blue Book staff couldn't explain them away. One such incident occurred on August 25, 1951.

It was 9:58 p.m., and Hugh Young (a security guard at the Sandia Atomic Energy Commission) and his wife were outside their home in the outskirts of Albuquerque when they saw an enormous V-shaped "flying wing" move over their home from north to south at a low altitude of about 1,000 feet. It was so low that as it flew over Central Avenue, the body of the craft reflected the city lights below. They said that it was larger than a Boeing B-36 bomber, made no noise, and moved about 400 miles per hour. It was silver in color with dark bands running across it from front to back, and had about six or eight lights situated on the back edge. It was like a flying wing "sharply swept back, almost like a V."

Young reported the incident to officials. An investigation showed that no known aircraft were in the area, and Blue Book officials, impressed by Young's high-level employment, declared the case officially unidentified (Blue Book Case #995.)

Incidentally, on the same night, the nearby town of Lubbock, Texas, also experienced a dramatic and intense wave of UFO activity that later became known as "the Lubbock Lights."[21]

UFO DESTROYS WATER TANK - KILLS FOUR PEOPLE

On December 13, 1951, Lorenzo Gutierrez of Tucumcari, looked up in the sky and saw a bright ball of light – what he thought was a "fireball" – streak across the sky and land close to the Tucumcari water tank. It then moved towards the tank and collided into it. The tank (which had metal hulls 3/8 inch thick) held three million gallons of water (another report says 750,000.) When the fireball collided into the tank, it immediately collapsed. Four people were killed and twenty structures destroyed. Property damage was estimated in the millions.

Later, accident investigators inspected the tank and were puzzled that the breach in the hull of the tank was so clean that it appeared as if it had cut by a knife. There was no other evidence to show what exactly had crashed into the tank.

News of the event spread and later Dr. Lincoln De Paz was asked about the case. After reviewing the details, he said that the object was not a meteor or natural fireball. If it were, he said, it would have left a crater or some evidence of meteoritic residue.[22]

BLUE BOOK CASE NUMBER 1037 UNIDENTIFIED

The year of 1952 was one of the busiest on record, producing dozens of high-quality reports. The first occurred on the afternoon of January 16,

1952 when two members of a balloon project from the General Mills Navy Aeronautical Research Laboratory and four other civilians were watching a balloon at an altitude of 112,000 feet over Artesia. The balloon was 110 feet in diameter with an apparent size of about one and a half inches.

At this point, the observers noticed another larger round object that "appeared to remain motionless in the vicinity, but apparently higher than the balloon." The larger object was a "dull white" color. Its apparent size was two and a half inches in diameter, nearly twice the apparent size of the balloon, which would make it nearly 200 feet in diameter. The object then moved away.

A short time after the above sighting, the first two witnesses were joined by four civilian pilots who continued to watch the balloon from Artesia airport when the UFOs suddenly returned. According to the Blue Book report on the case,

> TWO OBJECTS APPARENTLY AT EXTREMELY HIGH ALTITUDE WERE NOTED COMING TOWARD THE BALLOON FROM THE NORTHWEST. THEY CIRCLED THE BALLOON, OR APPARENTLY SO, AND FLEW OFF TO THE NORTHEAST. THE TIME OF OBSERVATION WAS ABOUT 40 SECONDS. THE TWO OBJECTS WERE THE SAME COLOR AND SIZE AS THE FIRST OBJECT. THEY WERE FLYING SIDE BY SIDE. WHEN THE OBJECTS APPEARED TO CIRCLE THE BALLOON, THEY DISAPPEARED, AND THE OBSERVERS ASSUMED THEY WERE DISC-SHAPED AND HAD TURNED ON EDGE TO BANK.

Meanwhile, several other objects described as "round and flat disks" appeared. According to researcher Jacques Vallee, at one point "the objects scattered and then regrouped close to the balloon. When they departed, they did so in single file."

Although Blue Book officers listed the case as unidentified, their written conclusion as to the nature of the object was: "None."

Hynek was disappointed with the Blue Book investigation of the two sightings. As he wrote,

> NOTHING IS SAID ABOUT THE ASSUMPTION THAT THE TWO OBJECTS OBSERVED FROM THE BALLOON'S LAUNCHING SITE AND LATER FROM THE AIRPORT WERE THE SAME PAIR. DETAILS OF THIS SORT MATTERED LITTLE TO THE BLUE BOOK INVESTIGATORS.

Also, Blue Book investigators were alerted of the case on April 16, three months after it occurred. The report on the case reads, "Due to this time lapse no further investigation is contemplated."

Hynek again disagreed and wrote,

> DETERMINATION OF THE QUALIFICATIONS OF THE REPORTERS COULD CERTAINLY HAVE BEEN CARRIED OUT, EVEN AT A MUCH LATER DATE.[23]

MORE JANUARY UFOS

There are many cases on record in which UFOs have mimicked the appearance of stars to avoid detection. The following case provides a daytime solution. One morning in early January 1952, citizens in Gallup reported seeing groups of objects that moved swiftly and would, at times, stop and hover in front of the disk of the sun, where they were effectively hidden from sight.

Also in January, airport controllers at Santa Fe Airport observed a strange glowing object swoop down over the airport. One of the controllers switched on the airport runway lights. The object responded by immediately climbing at a steep angle. It then stopped at a very high altitude and hovered in place for the next twenty-five minutes, before darting away.

Later that month, three different witnesses reported seeing a green fireball-like object. One witness observed the object hanging motion over the road in Santa Fe. Another saw it "swaying to and fro" over the Santa Fe Mountains near Taos. The third witness saw it streak overhead.[24]

APRO'S FIRST CASES

The Aerial Phenomenon Research Organization (APRO) was founded by Jim and Coral Lorenzen in January 1952, and was the first civilian special interest group in the United States to begin collecting and studying UFO reports. The Lorenzens had already been researching the subject since 1947, when the Modern Age of UFOs began. Shortly after forming APRO, however, they were literally flooded with cases, the first group coming in April 1952 from the Albuquerque area. One particularly impressive case was that of Carl Hawk, a Sandia Corporation engineer.

Hawk was with his friend Marvin Harvey on the base when they looked up to see a jet fighter zoom overhead. Moments later, they saw a very strange object described as long, rectangular and black, with a clear, bright yellow-colored V-design on it. The object came streaking out of the Tijeras Canyon area from the east, raced silently overhead at about 300 miles per hour and 2,000 feet in altitude, and disappeared into a cloud over downtown Albuquerque. Hawk and Harvey viewed the object for about ten seconds.

Afterwards, Hawk (an amateur artist) drew an illustration of the craft and wrote a short description, then gave them to Air Force officials with a formal report of the incident. He later received a written response in which Air Force officials commended him for his objective and unbiased report, calling him a "well-qualified observer." Hawk was left with the impression that the Air Force considered his sighting "unexplainable."

Another case investigated by the newly-formed APRO occurred at 3:05 p.m. on April 11, 1952, when construction foreman Jesus Dimas and his crew observed "a strange object, possibly a flying saucer" flying across the Pintada Canyon sky. Says Dimas,

> THIS THING WAS WHITE AND LONG —ABOUT 60 FEET, AND IT WAS TURNING OVER AND OVER... IT WASN'T ROUND, IT WAS ABOUT 30 FEET WIDE.

One hour later, Dimas and his crew saw another object. This one was higher than the first and had the shape of a bow-tie. It appeared to somersault across the sky at an estimated speed of 700 miles per hour.

Also in April 1952, a physician was driving in the area of Newman when he saw a bright yellow disk flying near the Franklin and Organ Mountains. The witness said that the object traveled at high speeds, darted at a 90-degree turn, and accelerated straight up into the sky and out of sight. The entire encounter lasted only a few seconds, but was enough to convince the doctor that he had seen something unusual. The case was investigated by Jim and Coral Lorenzen, who called it one of the two "most interesting in our files" for that year.[25]

TWO DISKS OVER KIRTLAND

At 1:20 p.m. on June 28, 1952, two personnel at the Cargo Air Service hangar adjoining the southeast corner of Kirtland AFB in Albuquerque observed a strange object over the base. The case was investigated by Blue Book Officers, whose report says,

> THERE APPEARED HIGH IN THE SKY DIRECTLY OVER KIRTLAND AIR FORCE BASE AN OBJECT WHICH FIRST APPEARED TO BE A WEATHER BALLOON, BUT AFTER CLOSER EXAMINATION IT WAS DETERMINED BY THE OBSERVERS TO BE OF A DESIGN FAMILIAR TO THEM. IT WAS THEN NOTED THAT A SIMILAR OBJECT OF THE SAME DESIGN WAS NEARBY. THE TWO OBJECTS MOVED SLOWLY TO THE SOUTH...MAKING NO SOUND

WHICH COULD BE HEARD BY THE OBSERVERS. THE OBJECTS WERE OF A ROUND, DISC-LIKE DESIGN AND SILVER IN COLOR. BOTH OBJECTS SEEMED TO PICK UP INSTANT SPEED AND CLIMBED ALMOST VERTICALLY. ONE OBJECT CONTINUED ON A SOUTH-SOUTHEAST COURSE WHILE THE OTHER OBJECT VEERED TO AN ALMOST DUE EAST COURSE. THE ENTIRE OBSERVATION TOOK PLACE WITHIN 30 SECONDS.

Despite the obvious high-strangeness of the observation, Blue Book officials declined to label the case unidentified. After reviewing the case, Hynek disagreed, saying that the case could not be explained away as a balloon or conventional object. Writes Hynek,

AS IN SO MANY OTHER BLUE BOOK CASES, NO FOLLOW-UP WAS, TO MY KNOWLEDGE, UNDERTAKEN. THE CREDIBILITY OF THE OBSERVERS (OTHER THAN THE FACT THAT THEY WERE AIRPORT PERSONNEL) OR THEIR MOTIVATION IN MAKING THE REPORT OR THE MANNER AND ATTITUDE IN WHICH THEY MADE IT WAS NEVER ESTABLISHED.[26]

THE WAVE OF JULY 1952

During the month of July 1952, a huge wave of sightings swept across the entire nation, producing such high-profile cases as the Washington National Sightings and others, including dozens of Blue Book unidentified cases. New Mexico, not surprisingly, was again targeted by the UFOs.

On July 29, 1952, Major General John Samford, Director of Air Force Intelligence, held a press conference about UFOs that turned out to be one of the longest and largest press conferences held since World War II. Meanwhile, back in New Mexico, on the day of his speech, a series of daylight sightings were taking place over Los Alamos.

The first sighting occurred at 10 a.m., over Omega Site by an employee at Los Alamos Scientific Laboratory. Says the witness,

I OBSERVED AN OBJECT, WHITE IN COLOR, THAT APPEARED TO BE CHANGING PERSPECTIVE OR GOING THROUGH GYRATIONS. IT HAD A FLUTTERING APPEARANCE... FIVE MINUTES LATER, JETS APPEARED FROM KIRTLAND AIR FORCE BASE.

Several other witnesses observed the event from different locations. One gentleman was standing on a nearby airstrip. As he says,

THE LENGTH OF TIME I OBSERVED THE OBJECT WAS VERY SHORT, ONLY A COUPLE OF SECONDS... THIS OBJECT WAS MOVING ACROSS THE WIND CURRENTS... IT WAS A DISTANCE UP IN THE SKY. THE MAN I WAS WITH WAS USING FIELD GLASSES AND STATED

THAT THIS OBJECT MADE A TURN... AS FAR AS I COULD TELL, THIS HAD HAD NO VAPOR TRAILS TO THE NAKED EYE. AS I SAW IT, IT WAS ONLY A SILVER SPECK IN THE SKY.

A third witness was a mile and a half northwest of the base in his residence. He was outside watching the military jets fly by with his 10-year-old son when they observed a strange object maneuvering through the contrails behind the jet. Says the witness,

[I] SAW A SHINY OBJECT JUST UNDER THE VAPOR TRAILS, TRAVELING IN THE SAME DIRECTION AS THE VAPOR TRAILS, LEAVING NO VAPOR TRAIL. IT SEEMED TO BE TRAVELING SLIGHTLY FASTER THAN THE JETS DID THAT LEFT THE TRAILS.

A fourth witness situated at S Site, Security Station 610, observed the object at 10:57 and was able to discern an actual structure to the craft. Says the witness,

I OBSERVED AN OBJECT APPEARING EGG-SHAPED IN STRUCTURE DIRECTLY OVERHEAD, THE DISTANCE WAS IMPOSSIBLE TO DETERMINE. THE OBJECT WAS MOTIONLESS AND APPEARED TO HAVE NO WINGS. THE OBJECT HAD NO GLARE AND APPEARED LIGHT BROWN IN COLOR. THE OBJECT MOVED VERY FAST WHEN MOVEMENT BEGAN...TAKING ABOUT THREE SECONDS TO DISAPPEAR... THERE WASN'T ANY APPARENT SOUND, ODOR, OR EVIDENCE OF A VAPOR TRAIL."

The witness closed his report saying that he had never seen any object "of this type."
Yet another witness, a member of the Los Alamos Scientific Laboratory said,

I OBSERVED AN INDISCERNIBLE OBJECT, WHITE IN COLOR, APPEARING LARGER THAN A JET AT 30,000 FEET...THE BRILLIANCE OF THE OBJECT UNDERWENT CHANGES AS THOUGH LIGHT REFLECTED VARIABLY WITH THE EXECUTION OF TWISTING OR TURNING MOTION. I VIEWED THE OBJECT FOR APPROXIMATELY TWENTY SECONDS BEFORE THE CANYON WALL OBSTRUCTED MY VIEW. THE OBJECT DID NOT LEAVE A VAPOR TRAIL.

Nearby, a base weather officer and three other weather observers watched several flying disks through a theodolite at Walker (Roswell) Air Force Base. The observers said that the object moved faster than any known conventional craft. The Blue Book intelligence officer concluded his report on the case, writing:

THE SCIENTIFIC EXPERIENCE OF THE WEATHER PERSONNEL MAKING THESE OBSERVATIONS IS SUFFICIENT TO WARRANT CREDENCE IN THEIR SIGHTINGS AND INDICATES AN ACTUAL APPEARANCE OF UNIDENTIFIED FLYING OBJECTS.

Meanwhile, reports came in from the Los Alamos Interceptor Wing where officers observed a "shining metallic" object maneuver for more than thirty minutes over the atomic bomb labs in Los Alamos, at which point it made a 360-degree turn and departed.

Finally, also on July 29, an Air Force reserve colonel (unidentified) observed a fast moving ellipse-shaped light over Albuquerque. According to J. Allen Hynek (who investigated the case in his capacity as consultant to Project Blue Book), there were additional witnesses to the event.

The final sighting of the wave occurred at 9:50 p.m. on August 1, again over Albuquerque. In this case, the witness was *Scripps-Howard* Staff Writer, Doyle Kline. On that evening, Kline observed a fleet of approximately ten glowing objects which he said, "resembled nothing I had ever seen before. Their flight was soundless and graceful." As he watched, the objects shifted formation in a precisely controlled maneuver from a random cluster to a perfect V-shape. A few seconds later, they changed from a V-formation to two rows, with the UFOs in one row spaced evenly between those in the other row. The objects appeared to be about one third the apparent size of a full moon. Kline estimated that they were about 2,500 feet above Albuquerque. He was deeply impressed by the way they moved. Says Kline,

> THEIR SHIFTS IN POSITION WERE INCREDIBLY SWIFT AND FANTASTICALLY VIOLENT — IN TERMS OF OUR EXPERIENCE.

Kline reported his sightings to the 34th Air Defense Division and was then interviewed by intelligence officers who showed interest in how the objects maneuvered. Kline later reported his sighting to NICAP, and says that his experience "made a flying saucer believer out of me... I have witnessed both day and night rocket flights at White Sands...The saucers were something different altogether."

Officials at Los Alamos had, by this time apparently obtained good evidence that the UFOs might be using atomic energy, as illustrated by the following case. On August 14, 1952, a CIA study group from the Office of Scientific Intelligence held a briefing at the base during which they released a report concerning various aspects of UFO reports. One of the entries noted a case involving a UFO that had appeared over Los Alamos precisely "at a time when the background radiation count had risen inexplicably."[27]

BLUE BOOK CASE NUMBER 1961 UNIDENTIFIED

On August 24, 1952, an Air Force colonel was flying his F-84 over Hermanas heading to El Paso, Texas, when he observed two round, silver, disk-shaped objects only six feet in diameter, each of which displayed extreme maneuverability and acceleration. When first observed, the objects were flying abreast, pacing his plane. Suddenly, one of the objects made a right turn and passed directly in front of the colonel's jet. Both objects then darted away over Hermanas. A short time later, they reappeared. At one point, one of the objects darted 3,000 feet straight up in a split-second. The other moved away in a different direction. Blue Book Intelligence officers investigated the case and were apparently impressed enough to label it unexplained, the eleventh such conclusion from New Mexico cases that year so far. (See Blue Book Case #1961)[28]

AIR FORCE OFFICIALLY STUDIES UFOS

In September 1952, newspaper columnist Robert Allen wrote in an article that the Air Force had just finished compiling a "breath-taking report on flying saucers." He wrote that after five years of studying 1,800 reports, the USAF believed that the objects were genuine and originated from sources outside the planet. According to Allen, "the most authoritative and detailed sightings come from atomic plants and military bases and research centers." New Mexico topped the report's list with sightings at Los Alamos, White Sands atomic plant and testing grounds, Albuquerque, Holloman AFB, Kirtland AFB, and Walker AFB. The only other state with an equal amount of activity was California.

In fact, the year of 1952 was such a busy year for UFO activity that of the twenty-eight New Mexico Blue Book reports that were officially declared unidentified, seventeen of them – more than half the total – occurred in that year alone.

One of the last high-profile cases of 1952 occurred in early November. Two observers at the Kirtland Air Force Base control tower saw an oblong-shaped object hover above the airfield. Base radar technicians tracked the object on their scopes. The object appeared to be about fifteen feet tall, and remained totally stationary in the sky. It remained in view for a full six minutes. At this point, an Air Force transport plane flew by and the object veered away and followed the plane for fourteen miles before turning away and disappearing off the radarscope.[29]

UFOS ARE ATMOSPHERIC CONDITIONS"

Hynek's assertions that Blue Book officers appeared to be more interested in debunking UFOs than investigating is illustrated perfectly in the following case, in which intelligence officers put forth a ludicrous explanation to explain away the events. On January 26, 1953, several people in Albuquerque observed a bright red light hanging low on the horizon. The object remained in view for forty minutes, during which time it was allegedly captured on nearby military radar scopes, moving at a speed of about twelve to fifteen MPH, against a prevailing wind. Air Force Blue Book intelligence officers were sent to investigate, but refused to label the case as unexplained. Their explanation was that "gaseous gyrations" of the weather elements could play tricks that not only cause optical illusions, but will also appear on radar. With that, they concluded that the probable cause was "atmospheric conditions."[30]

ASTRONOMERS SEE UFO

The following case is another good example of how Blue Book officers appeared to be biased in their investigations. In 1954, Mr. Schaldach (a former astronomer for Lowell Observatory) was working in a civilian capacity in the Technical Service Unit at White Sands Proving Grounds. His duty involved the camera monitoring of missile launches. At 10 p.m. on the evening of January 25, 1954, he was setting up his ballistic camera to monitor a launch. As he looked at the stars to calibrate his instrument, he noticed a "yellow-white" light moving from the northeast to the southeast in a shallow arc. The object seemed to pulse in brightness at regular intervals.

Meanwhile, seventeen miles southeast of Mr. Schaldach, another White Sands employee viewed the object. Both trained observers, the witnesses quickly performed triangulation measurements and determined that the object was about twelve miles distant, and moving at 12,000 miles per hour. Says Schaldach,

> I HAVE OBSERVED MANY THOUSANDS OF METEORS AND CAN DEFINITELY STATE THAT THIS OBJECT WAS NOT ANY KIND OF METEOR.

Mr. Schaldach worked with famed astronomer Clyde Tombaugh, and quickly alerted him of the sighting. Tombaugh, in turn, encouraged the gentlemen to report their sighting to Project Blue Book, which they did. However, despite the fact that the astronomers insisted that the object was not a meteor, Blue Book investigators wrote in their official conclusion of the case: "Was astronomical (Meteor)."[31]

THREE SIGHTINGS

The year of 1954 proved to be particularly active across the entire United States, including New Mexico. On July 3, 1954, a fleet of nine UFOs were seen from Albuquerque. The objects glowed with green light and were described as "round" in shape. A radar crew on duty observed the objects approach, hover, and then make a 340-degree turn and speed away. The crew tracked the objects on radar at an approximate 2,600 miles per hour.

Another encounter occurred one month later on August 6, 1954, when numerous residents in Santa Fe observed a brilliant white ball of light in the sky for a period of at least fifteen minutes. The object left a long luminous trail, then shot upwards and disappeared into the distance. Lincoln LaPaz reviewed the case and concluded that it was not a meteor. (Dolan, p155)

Two months later, on October 14, 1954 (from 8 p.m. to 9:20 p.m.), witnesses in Hobbs observed five semi-circular-shaped objects move overhead, each of which was bisected by a row of "pearly" lights.[32]

THREE UFOS CIRCLE PILOT

The fact that our military takes UFOs very seriously is highlighted by the following case. On August 13, 1956, an engineer and former Navy pilot was flying his private plane – a Cessna 170 – from Hobbs to Albuquerque at around 8,000 feet altitude when he noticed that his Magnesyn electric compass was revolving and no longer registering the course of his plane. He looked over at his regular magnetic compass. Said the pilot, "It was spinning so crazily I couldn't read it."

He then was shocked to see a tight echelon formation of "three round gray machines" pass directly in front of the cockpit windshield. Each of the objects was identical, gray-colored, like two bowls sealed rim to rim, but with rounded bottoms. They appeared small, about eight feet in diameter, but the pilot admitted they could have been larger. To his shock, they began to circle his plane at an estimated 250 miles per hour. The pilot noticed that the Magnesyn compass pointed directly towards the mysterious objects, which continued to perform tight circles around the Cessna. The regular compass was still spinning crazily. As the object circled around his plane, they left short, wispy contrails. While the pilot's instincts told him to dive and attempt to escape, the objects were so close that he feared he might collide with them, so he tensely waited for them to make the next move.

After a few passes around the plane, the objects suddenly darted off to the rear and disappeared. Both compasses immediately began to function normally. The pilot radioed the nearest airport to report his encounter, but as he did so, an FAA operator interrupted the transmission and ordered the pilot to maintain radio silence.

Says the pilot,

> HE SAID FOR ME TO FLY AT ONCE TO KIRTLAND AFB. WHEN I LANDED THERE I WAS HUSTLED TO AN OFFICE AND INTERROGATED BY AN AF MAJOR – THE BASE UFO OFFICER. THEN HE TOLD ME THAT BEING SO CLOSE TO THOSE OBJECTS I MIGHT DEVELOP RADIATION SICKNESS. HE SAID IF I DEVELOPED ANY UNUSUAL ILLNESS TO LET THE AF KNOW AND GET TO A GOVERNMENT HOSPITAL RIGHT AWAY. HE WARNED ME TO KEEP THIS SECRET FROM EVERYBODY BUT MY WIFE AND TO MAKE SURE SHE KEPT QUIET TOO.

The interrogation took two hours. The officer said that if any illness developed, the Air Force would take care of him. The witness says that this news raised the hair on the back of his neck, and left him and his wife in a state of constant apprehension for the next six months. When it became clear he wasn't going to become ill, the pilot decided it was wrong for the Air Force to conceal the facts about his case. The pilot decided to go public and reported his case to the National Investigative Committee on Aerial Phenomena (NICAP).[33]

EISENHOWER VISITS HOLLOMAN

According to longtime UFO researcher Art Campbell, in February 1955, the press reported that President Dwight D. Eisenhower was going bird hunting in Georgia. Campbell, however, has uncovered evidence and firsthand testimony that Eisenhower was detoured to visit Holloman Air Force Base in New Mexico for the express purpose of viewing UFO evidence. Coincidentally, on that day, the base radar was shut down and two unknown objects were seen coming low over the air base.[34]

UFO COLLIDES WITH PLANE

There are many accounts in the UFO literature in which conventional aircraft have experienced near-misses with UFOs. In a few cases, actual collisions have occurred, usually to the detriment of the conventional aircraft, as in the following case reported by John Keel.

In October 1955, a pilot was in his B-47 over Lovington when something collided with his plane. According to the sole survivor of the accident, the plane struck some unknown solid aerial object. Another witness on the ground said that he saw "a ball of fire" which appeared near the plane just before the accident.[35]

SAUCER HOVERS OVER WALKER AFB

When Emma Baca of Belen began to write a family history, her brother, Louis D. Moya, surprised her by handing her a signed and sworn affidavit detailing a UFO sighting he had had in 1955, while stationed at Walker Air

Force Base. He had often told his family about the UFO sighting. He now revealed the affidavit, which contained the incredible UFO account:

> IN 1955 WHILE ON DUTY WITH OTHER PERSONNEL, WITHOUT WARNING WE NOTICED AN UNIDENTIFIED CIRCULAR OBJECT STANDING IMMOBILE FOR TWO HOURS OVER WALKER AIR FORCE BASE, ABOUT 100,000 FEET HIGH. THE ON-DUTY RADAR CONTROLLER TOLD ME THE OBJECT WAS NOT A BALLOON. HE ORDERED ME TO SAY, IF I WAS ASKED, THAT THE MYSTERIOUS OBJECT WAS NOT A BALLOON.

The affidavit, which was taken in 1995, also included a drawing made by Moya of what he had seen. The drawing shows two officers observing a solid saucer-shaped object, complete with porthole, hovering over the controlling tower. One year after telling his story, Louis Moya died.[36]

NEWSMAN REVEALS CHILDHOOD SIGHTING

In 1994, Santa Fe journalist David Roybal (who writes for the *Santa Fe New Mexican*) wrote in his column that when he was a young teenager back in the mid-1950s (exact date not given), he was witness to an incredible UFO sighting that left him forever convinced of the reality of extraterrestrial visitations. Writes Roybal,

> I'VE GOT TO CONFESS TO HAVING A SPECIAL INTEREST. AS A KID OF 13, I SPOTTED LIGHTS RACING, CIRCLING, BOBBING, DISAPPEARING AND REAPPEARING IN THE NIGHT SKY BETWEEN SANTA FE AND LOS ALAMOS. I NEVER HAD SEEN ANYTHING LIKE IT. NOR HAVE I SEEN ANYTHING LIKE IT SINCE. UNTIL I HEAR A LOGICAL EXPLANATION FOR IT, I CAN'T DISCOUNT THE POSSIBILITY THAT WE'VE BEEN VISITED BY SOMETHING EXTRATERRESTRIAL.

Why were the UFOs hovering over Santa Fe? Roybal points to the many mutilations that have occurred in the area, and adds,

> THEY'D NEED SOMETHING TO DO ONCE THEY ARRIVED. SURELY THE AIRCRAFT I SPOTTED YEARS AGO NEAR SANTA FE'S SOUTH SIDE WEREN'T HOVERING OVER THE YUCCA DRIVE-IN TO GET A FREE LOOK AT FRANKIE AVALON AND ANNETTE FUNICELLO ON THE BIG SCREEN.

Roybal admits that he still has no idea what he saw, and he is okay with that. As he says, "A newspaperman's life, I guess, wouldn't be much fun without mysteries."[37]

NEAR-MISS OVER ROSWELL

At 8:30 p.m. on March 27, 1957, Lieutenant Sondheimer was flying an Air Force C-45 cargo plane near Roswell when he observed three very bright, round objects approach from the left. The three UFOs were tightly bunched together in a fixed formation that Sondheimer said resembled airplane landing lights. Suddenly, he realized that the objects were on a collision course with his own aircraft. He flashed his taxi lights. According to the report on the case,

> ONE OF THE OBJECTS SHOT STRAIGHT UP IN THE AIR ABOVE HIM WHILE THE OTHER TWO CONTINUED ON AND PASSED IN FRONT OF HIS AIRCRAFT. WHEN THE PILOT FLASHED HIS TAXI LIGHTS, THE OBJECTS IMMEDIATELY BLACKED THEMSELVES OUT, THEREBY DISAPPEARING FROM SIGHT.

Researcher Richard Haines Ph.D. points out this case as being a good example of a "CE-V," or an encounter in which the witnesses' actions provoke a response in the UFO.[38]

GRAY SPHERE OVER SANTA FE

Because they are often outside, children are more likely than the average person to see a UFO, as this following case (submitted years later by the witness to MUFON CMS) illustrates. Writes the witness,

> MY SISTER AND I WERE PLAYING OUT IN OUR FRONT YARD. IT WAS A CLEAR DAY IN JUNE [JUNE 14, 1957]. I NOTICED A SPHERE HOVERING IN THE AIR TO THE SW OF OUR HOUSE, AND YELLED AT MY SISTER TO LOOK. WE BOTH LOOKED AT IT FOR ABOUT 30 SECONDS. IT WAS ABOUT 500 FEET AWAY, JUST HOVERING ABOUT 150 FEET IN THE AIR. IT WAS A DULL GRAY AND HAD SEVERAL ROWS OF BLACK SQUARE WINDOWS AROUND IT. IT DID NOT MAKE ANY NOISE THAT WE COULD HEAR. ITS SIZE WAS ABOUT 150 FEET IN DIAMETER.

The witness ran to the porch and screamed for his father to come outside. However, when his father arrived, the object was gone. Both the siblings ran around the house looking for the object in all directions, but it was gone. Writes the witness,

I KNEW THIS WAS SOMETHING UNUSUAL AND I HAVE ALWAYS WONDERED WHAT IT WAS. IT IS STILL A VERY VIVID MEMORY AND I CAN RECALL THE DETAILS TO THIS DAY.[39]

MISSILE FLIGHT SAFETY CHIEF SEES UFO

On July 24, 1957, Nathan Wagner (a missile flight safety chief for the White Sands Proving Grounds) publicly revealed to newspaper reporters that he and his family sighted a UFO while driving south through New Mexico. Wagner's wife was the first to spot the saucer-shaped object, which was heading due east toward the Organ Mountains. When both of Wagner's children said they also saw the object, Mr. Wagner looked and was shocked to see the classic flying saucer shape. He pulled over to get a better look, but by then the object had moved off into the distance. When asked by reporters if he believed he saw an actual UFO, Mr. Wagner replied with the guarded statement,

I DON'T WANT TO START A SCARE, BUT I WOULD SAY IT IS A REASONABLE POSITION TO TAKE TO SAY THAT SUCH A CRAFT MIGHT HAVE BEEN INVOLVED IN SOME INCIDENTS.[40]

ANGEL HAIR OVER PORTALES

In the vast majority of UFO cases, no physical evidence is left behind. In some rare cases, UFOs do land and leave landing traces. In some even more rare cases, UFOs eject a wispy spider-web-like substance known as "angel hair." These types of cases are extremely uncommon, though they continue to turn up, as in the following.

According to the *Associated Press*, on the evening of October 23-24, 1957, enormous quantities of angel hair fell out of the sky over Portales. In this case, no actual UFO was seen. However, the strange substance reportedly covered a very wide area, with strands up to fifty feet long. As in all other cases, the angel hair dissipated very quickly, leaving no traces behind. No explanation for the event was offered.

Almost exactly one year later, on October 9, 1958, there was a repeat performance. Again, the town of Portales reported a large quantity of angel hair falling from the sky. Again, in this case, no actual UFO was seen.[41]

THE INCREDIBLE WAVE OF NOVEMBER 1957

The year of 1957 proved to be extremely active. In fact, what happened in the month of November 1957 changed the way many people viewed the UFO phenomenon, particularly regarding the UFOs' ability to affect electromagnetic machinery.

The first hint of what was to come occurred on October 16, 1957 (twelve days after the launch of Sputnik). At 1 p.m., Miss Ella Louise Fortune was driving adjacent to the north range of the White Sands – Holloman Air Force Base test complex when she saw a large, cigar-shaped white glowing object scoot across the sky, leaving a slight contrail. She quickly snapped a remarkably clear color photograph of the object, as it flew alongside the highway. (See photo section page 297.)

However, events had only just begun. Two weeks later, at 6:20 a.m. on November 1, 1957, a secretary in the Sandia Mountains observed a red, glowing cigar-shaped object hover overhead. After a few moments, it rose out of sight. This sighting marked the first of a series of events across New Mexico (and Texas) involving close-up UFOs that caused vehicles to stall. These series of sightings, researchers later learned, caused great concern among military officials investigating the cases.

The first of the car-stalling cases occurred around 8:30 p.m. on November 2, 1957, when an anonymous motorist driving through Seminole claimed that a light swooped down from the sky ahead of him on the road, dove at his car, causing it to stall briefly and the headlights to fail, at which point the object rose up and zoomed off into the distance. On that same night, at 8 p.m., Odis Echols, owner of Radio Station KCLV, saw an unidentified "yellow object" traveling at high speed over the town of Clovis.

The next day the UFOs were back. At 3 a.m. on November 3, Corporal Glenn H. Toy and PFC James Wilbanks were on Army Jeep Patrol at White Sands when they saw a "very bright light" high in the sky. The object, which was described as egg-shaped and about 100 yards in diameter, then descended to about 100 feet above the old atomic bunker used in the first atomic explosions. After a few moments, the light blinked out. A few minutes later, it flared up again becoming "nearly as bright as the sun." It then began to descend towards the ground at an angle and disappeared. Said Toy, "It looked like a completely controlled landing." A search party was sent to the area, but was unable to find any traces of the object.

About eleven hours later at 1:56 p.m., still on November 3, a test pilot flying from Texas to Roswell, New Mexico landed at Holloman AFB and told Base Operations that he had just encountered a large, oblong, glowing object which had passed over his aircraft. It moved so quickly, that it left what appeared to be a streak of light.

About four hours later, military police at White Sands made a second sighting of a brilliant, vermillion-colored object an estimated 300 feet in diameter, over the range. At the same time, a Deming resident claimed to see a strange glowing object fly overhead.

Finally, at 8 p.m. on November 3, SP 3/C Forest R. Oakes and SP 3/C Barlow were on another two-man Army Jeep patrol at White Sands when they saw a glowing object hover above the test base, again directly over the old atomic bunker. Oakes described the object as being "200 or 300 feet long [and] very bright." They were about two miles away when the object suddenly began to ascend at a 45-degree angle. During this time, its lights pulsated on and off. It moved slowly, sometimes stopping, but continually ascending upward until it had the appearance of a bright star. After a few moments, it became a pinpoint of light and disappeared into outer space. Again, the soldiers concluded that the object made a controlled landing and ascent.

One day after that, at 1:10 p.m. on November 4, 1957, James Stokes (a Holloman AFB high-altitude missile engineer and a Navy veteran) was driving south from Alamogordo near Orogrande at the southeast corner of the Proving Grounds when first his car radio faded and then failed. Seconds later, his car engine stalled. As he rolled to a stop, he noticed that several other cars were also stopped. Some of the drivers were outside of their cars, pointing and looking at something to the northeast. Looking in that direction, Stokes saw a glowing, pearlescent egg-shaped object of "huge proportions" – he estimated about 300-500 feet – performing incredible maneuvers. The object had no visible portholes or external features. As he watched, it passed overhead twice, sending down a strong wave of heat. It performed several dives and sharp turns, finally moving at very high speeds, which Stokes estimated at 2,500 MPH.

Stokes describes what happened in his own words,

> I SAW A BRILLIANT EGG-SHAPED OBJECT MAKING A SHALLOW DIVE ACROSS THE SKY. THEN IT TURNED AND MADE A PASS AT THE HIGHWAY AND CROSSED IT NOT MORE THAN TWO MILES AHEAD. THEN IT MOVED AWAY TOWARDS WHITE SANDS PROVING GROUNDS. AS IT PASSED, I COULD FEEL A KIND OF HEAT WAVE, LIKE RADIATION FROM A GIANT SUN LAMP. THERE WAS NO SOUND AND NO VISIBLE PORTHOLES. WHEN I GOT BACK TO MY CAR AND CHECKED THE ENGINE, I FOUND IT INTACT BUT THE BATTERY WAS STEAMING.

There were also other witnesses, including Allan Baker, who worked at White Sands Proving Grounds and Mr. Duncan, a resident of Las Cruces, who said that when the object appeared, he took photographs of it with his 35 mm camera. The witnesses noticed that as the object maneuvered, the low-level clouds around it dissipated in its path.

After the object departed, everyone's vehicles performed normally, and they departed the scene. Afterwards, James Stokes discovered that his face had been sunburned by the object. He reported his sighting to his military superior at Holloman AFB who told him it was all right to talk publicly about his sighting. Air Force officials did request that Stokes receive a physical examination from the Base doctors.

During a later interview with Coral and Jim Lorenzen, Stokes seemed more reticent to discuss his sighting, and tentatively advanced a theory that perhaps he had seen "some kind of atmospheric phenomenon."

Coral and Jim Lorenzen believed he had been pressured by his military superiors to cover up what happened. Writes Coral Lorenzen,

> IT WAS GENERALLY AGREED LATER THAT STOKES HAD CHANGED HIS STORY SOMEWHAT AFTER HIS INTERVIEW WITH THE MILITARY AUTHORITIES.

They met with Stokes again two months after the incident. By this time, his case had been widely printed in newspapers, and had in some cases, been viciously attacked as a hoax. Stokes told the Lorenzens that he was quite upset about the hoax accusations, and said that if he ever saw anything out of the ordinary again, he wouldn't tell anyone. In a taped interview on station KALG, Stokes did say that what he saw was "definitely a solid object." He refused to elaborate and said only, "I just hope we're ready for whatever it is."

Interestingly, Air Force public information officer, Lieutenant Colonel John McCurdy at the Missile Development Center revealed that he had questioned Stokes extensively regarding the incident and was convinced that Stokes had, in fact, had a genuine sighting.

Later, Coral learned of additional witnesses to the event. One witness was reportedly located by an officer at Holloman, however, the witness declined to come forward. Lorenzen also spoke with a nurse at the local hospital who told her, "I know a couple who were on the highway near Orogrande when that engineer saw that saucer last November." The couple refused to come forward for fear of ridicule, but told the nurse that the thing they saw was a machine of some kind, and a real flying object, not a "natural phenomenon" as some newspapers had reported.

There were also other sightings on the day of Stokes encounter. Albuquerque housewife, Mrs. Dale Van Fleet said that at 7 p.m. that evening, she observed a gold-colored object larger than the full moon hover at 45 degrees elevation in the western sky for about five minutes. A few hours later, at 10:45 p.m., nearby Kirtland AFB was tracking another (or the same) object on radar. (See following.)

One day after the Stokes' sighting, at 4:24 a.m. on November 5, 1957, Don Clarke (an electronics and radar technician employed by a civilian contractor at Holloman) was at his home on east Alamogordo when he saw an orange-red cigar-shaped object hover at 15 degrees elevation in the western sky. The object appeared to be directly over Holloman. He ran to get his camera, but when he returned, the object was gone.

Five minutes later, Lyman Brown Jr. was in his home also in Alamogordo when he saw a yellow-orange light at 45-degrees of elevation. The object moved quickly eastward, then winked out above Dog Canyon in the Sacramento Mountains. Seconds after the object disappeared in the mountains, he saw a powerful searchlight beam rise up and start "looping" where the object had disappeared.

Later that day, two reports came in (which were later reported to NICAP), each involving bright objects that paced motor vehicles down the highway near Hobbs. In each case, the objects passed directly over the cars causing the car lights and engines to fail.

Yet another sighting occurred fifteen minutes later at 7:45 p.m., when bus driver Delbert Boyd observed a mysterious light about five miles southwest of Albuquerque. The light would flare up in brilliance and then become dim, eventually appearing to land outside the city.

On the very next day, yet another car stalling incident occurred to two other witnesses. Just after midnight November 6, 1957, Santa Fe residents J. Martinez and A. Gallegos were driving their car when they saw an egg-shaped object with "red and green and yellow lights" approach them from a low altitude. Although it moved slowly, it was soon directly over their car, illuminating the entire area around them in "a great glow all over." At the same time, it emitted a loud humming noise. As soon as the object was overhead, the car engine suddenly died, and both their clock and wristwatch ceased to function. Seconds later, the object shot off to the southwest and disappeared off into the distance.

Later that day, at 6:15 p.m., an anonymous tourist reported his sighting to policeman Erwin de Oliviera at Tucumcari. The tourist said that he had seen a "huge red object" just outside of Vaughn on U.S. Highway 54.

On the same evening, two additional residents from Santa Fe told police that they saw a "huge ball of fire" which was traveling in a southwest trajectory as they drove through the southwestern section of Santa Fe.

One day later, on November 7, 1957, the UFOs were back. At 1:45 a.m., a group of five airmen (including Bradford Rickets, James Cole, Dennis Murphy, Wayne Hurlburt and Harry Ulrich) were on duty near a salvage yard at the north side of the base when they observed a cigar-shaped object appeared overhead. The object made a whistling noise, and as it moved overhead, it changed from white to orange to red.

About six hours after the above encounter, yet another case involving bizarre electromagnetic effects in automobiles occurred in Orogrande. A mere twenty miles from the above encounter involving James Stokes, Mr. and Mrs. Trent Lindsey and their 22-year-old son, Byron, were driving south on Highway 54. It was exactly 9:20 a.m. when Byron noticed that the speedometer on their 1954 Mercury was behaving strangely. Although the speed of their vehicle was steady, the stick on the dial began to waver erratically back and forth between 60 miles per hour (the speed they were actually traveling) up to the 110 miles per hour mark. Not overly concerned, the three of them discussed the problem and its possible causes. Unable to account for the anomaly, they ignored it until shortly later, when they spotted a strange object in the southwest sky.

Byron Lindsey describes what happened,

THE NEEDLE KEPT SKIPPING BACK AND FORTH BETWEEN 60 AND 110 AND MAKING A CLATTERING SOUND. WHILE THE NEEDLE WAS JUMPING AROUND, DAD POINTED TOWARD THE SOUTHWEST AND SAID, 'I SUPPOSE YOU THINK THAT IS SOMETHING.' AND IT *WAS* SOMETHING. IT WAS CYLINDRICAL IN SHAPE, SILVERY AND MOVING... WE TRAVELED SOME 15 MILES BEFORE THE SPEEDOMETER CORRECTED ITSELF, AND WE HAD NO TROUBLE DURING THE REST OF THE TRIP. STRANGELY THE NEEDLE KEPT WAVERING TO THE SIDE WHERE THE OBJECT WAS INSTEAD OF TOWARD THE ZERO MARK ON THE SPEEDOMETER.

Lindsey described the object as being made of highly polished metal, with sharply defined edges, no visible means of propulsion, no apparent controls and no lights or glows. The object moved in an arcing trajectory at a high altitude towards Organ Mountains to the southwest.

Around this time, so many sightings were being reported that, although the Air Force tried to debunk the sightings, documents now clearly show that they were aware of the situation and contrary to their official statements, were taking the reports very seriously. That same week a group of similar close-up sightings caused numerous cars to stall in Levelland, Texas. By this time, the media was beginning to notice. On November 7, 1957, an article from the El Paso *Times* printed the following editorial:

SOME OF THE NATION'S TOP SCIENTISTS ARE "PRETTY SHOOK UP" ABOUT THE MYSTERIOUS FLYING OBJECTS SIGHTED IN NEW MEXICO AND WEST TEXAS SKIES THIS WEEK, SAID CHARLES CAPEN (A SCIENTIST AT WHITE SANDS). "THIS IS SOMETHING THAT HASN'T HAPPENED BEFORE."

Two days later, at 7:20 p.m. on November 9, a Tularosa housewife, a college student, and several others observed a large, brilliant fast-moving light which approached their car as they drove along U.S. Highway 54 (70 miles north of Alamogordo near White Oaks), causing their vehicle's lighting system to fail. The object approached from the south, flew over their car, then change course to the southwest, accelerating at a high rate of speed into the distance.

At the same time as the above sighting, investigators Jim and Coral Lorenzen were in the area, traveling east on Highway 380, ten miles from Carriozo, when they spotted "a bright light silhouetted against the mountains to the east and which moved erratically until it appeared to move south."

The Air Force was apparently dismayed that a number of their employees were talking freely with the media about their encounters. After the above wave of sightings and subsequent media coverage, the following item was published in the official section of the Holloman AFMDC *Daily*

Bulletin, which is mandatory reading for all base personnel, both military and civilian:

> UNIDENTIFIED FLYING OBJECTS: ON NOVEMBER 7 SIX AIRMEN CLAIMED THEY SIGHTED AN UNIDENTIFIED FLYING OBJECT AND DID NOT REPORT THIS TO PROPER BASE AUTHORITIES. THEY DID, HOWEVER, GIVE THIS INFORMATION TO THE LOCAL PRESS. REQUEST THAT EACH MEMBER OF THE MILITARY AND CIVILIAN EMPLOYED AT THIS CENTER, REFRAIN FROM ANY PUBLIC STATEMENT ON POLITICAL, DIPLOMATIC, LEGISLATIVE OR SCIENTIFIC MATTERS OR ANY CONTROVERSIAL SUBJECTS, SUCH AS UFOS, WITHOUT FIRST CONTACTING THE CENTER INFORMATION SERVICES OFFICER. THIS REQUEST IS IN ACCORDANCE WITH AFR 190-6. DISCIPLINARY ACTION MAY BE TAKEN AGAINST THE OFFENDER.
>
> SIGNED: LT. COL. MCCURDY,
> HDN

Coral Lorenzen writes that this regulation "restricts individuals at Air Force installations in relating the details of UFO sightings" and that "this regulation is a violation of the constitutional rights of civilians and should be challenged."[42]

A RADAR-VISUAL ENCOUNTER

At 10:45 p.m. on November 4, 1957 (the same day as the above James Stokes UFO-car stalling case), two air traffic controllers were on duty in the 100-foot high airport tower at Kirtland AFB in Albuquerque. According to the Blue Book report on the case, one of the controllers was checking cloud conditions when he noticed "a white light traveling east between 150 and 200 miles per hour at an altitude of approximately 1,500 feet."

The controller called the radar station, which confirmed that they had the object on radar. At this point, the unknown object moved across the east of runway 26 in a southwesterly direction and began "a steep descent."

One of the controllers surmised that it was an incoming plane that had become confused about where to land. One of the witnesses then grabbed a pair of binoculars and was shocked to see that it was shaped like "an automobile on end."

As the Blue Book report reads,

> THIS WAS ESTIMATED TO BE 15 TO 18 FEET HIGH. ONE WHITE LIGHT WAS OBSERVED AT THE LOWER SIDE OF THE OBJECT. THE OBJECT SLOWED TO AN ESTIMATED SPEED OF

50 MILES PER HOUR AND DISAPPEARED BEHIND A FENCE AT "DRUMHEAD," A RESTRICTED AREA WHICH IS BRILLIANTLY FLOODLIGHTED. THIS IS APPROXIMATELY ONE-HALF MILE FROM THE CONTROL TOWER.

At this point, the object reappeared moving eastward at an altitude of 200 to 300 feet. One of the controllers now wondered if it might be a helicopter in distress. This theory was discarded when the object "veered in a southeasterly direction, ascended abruptly at an estimated rate of climb of 4,500 feet per minute and disappeared."

The controller described the movement as "like a jet," and definitely faster than any helicopter. According to the Blue Book report on the case,

ALTHOUGH COMPLETELY COOPERATIVE AND WILLING TO ANSWER ANY QUESTIONS, BOTH SOURCES APPEARED TO BE SLIGHTLY EMBARRASSED THAT THEY COULD NOT IDENTIFY OR OFFER AN EXPLANATION OF THE OBJECT WHICH THEY ARE UNSHAKABLY CONVINCED THEY SAW.

Meanwhile, unknown to either of the controllers, the radar operator had watched the object cross the base, slow down, reverse course to the west, and begin to orbit over the Kirtland low-frequency range station. It then took off to the northwest and disappeared from his scope at around ten miles from the station. The visual sighting had lasted about five minutes. However, the radar technician told Blue Book investigators that twenty minutes after the sighting, the object re-appeared.

A plane had just taken off from the airport. The radar technician scanned his scope and was shocked to see the object "over the outer marker approximately four miles south of north-south runway. [The] object flew north at [a] high rate of speed towards within a mile south of east-west runway, where it made an abrupt turn to the west and fell into trail formation with the C-46."

The object then followed the C-46 plane from a half-mile behind for the next fourteen miles. At this point, the radarscope showed that the object turned to the north and hovered for one and a half minutes before suddenly fading from the scope. The technician tracked the object for a duration of twenty minutes.

After reviewing the case, Hynek was shocked by Blue Book's conclusions, which were typically confusing and contradictory. The officers investigating the case concluded that the object:

...MAY POSSIBLY HAVE BEEN AN UNIDENTIFIED AIRCRAFT, POSSIBLY CONFUSED BY THE RUNWAYS AT KIRTLAND AIR FORCE BASE. THE REASONS FOR THIS OPINION ARE:

(1) THE OBSERVERS ARE CONSIDERED COMPETENT AND RELIABLE SOURCES AND IN THE OPINION OF THIS INTERVIEWER ACTUALLY SAW AN OBJECT THEY COULD NOT IDENTIFY. (2) THE OBJECT WAS TRACKED ON A RADARSCOPE BY A COMPETENT OPERATOR. (3) THE OBJECT DOES NOT MEET IDENTIFICATION CRITERIA FOR ANY OTHER PHENOMENA.

Writes Hynek with unabashed exasperation,

THAT IS, THE OBSERVERS RELIABLE, THE RADAR OPERATOR WAS COMPETENT, AND THE OBJECT COULDN'T BE IDENTIFIED: THEREFORE IT WAS AN *AIRPLANE*. IN THE FACE OF SUCH REASONING ONE MIGHT WELL ASK WHETHER IT WOULD EVER BE POSSIBLE TO DISCOVER THE EXISTENCE OF NEW EMPIRICAL PHENOMENA IN ANY AREA OF HUMAN EXPERIENCE.

Hynek, needless to say, was convinced that the case represented a genuine unknown. As he writes,

WHAT, INDEED, CAN ONE SAY OF A RADAR-VISUAL CASE LIKE THIS? THE BASIC AGREEMENT OF THE RADAR AND VISUAL REPORTS AND THE COMPETENCE OF THE THREE OBSERVERS, IN MY OPINION, RULE OUT QUESTIONS OF MIRAGES, FALSE RETURNS ON RADAR, ETC. *SOMETHING* QUITE DEFINITELY WAS THERE. IF IT WAS AN ORDINARY AIRCRAFT, ONE MUST ASK HOW IT WAS THAT THE TWO VISUAL OBSERVERS WITH A TOTAL OF 23 YEARS OF CONTROL TOWER EXPERIENCE, COULD *JOINTLY* NOT HAVE BEEN ABLE TO RECOGNIZE IT WHEN VISIBILITY CONDITIONS WERE GOOD. EVEN IF THERE WERE NO RADAR CONFIRMATION OF THE SLOW AND FAST MOTIONS OF THE OBJECT, OR INDEED JUST OF THE PRESENCE OF AN UNKNOWN OBJECT, THIS QUESTION WOULD STILL HAVE TO BE ANSWERED. THE DESCRIPTION OF THE OBJECT'S APPEARANCE THROUGH BINOCULARS — 'LIKE AN AUTO ON END' — WOULD ALSO DEMAND EXPLANATION.

And so the wave of November 1957 came to an end. Never before or since has there been a rash of UFO car stalling incidents equal to the New Mexico/Texas wave.[43]

1958 SIGHTINGS

Much of the UFO activity in New Mexico continued to focus over military bases. On April 14, 1958, USAF personnel (including an Air Force Staff Sergeant) in Albuquerque witnessed twelve to eighteen gold-colored disks with smaller irregular positioned satellites move overhead in a V-formation. (Flammonde, p436) (Hall, The UFO Evidence, p137)

The Air Force continued its policy of covering up sightings, while at the same time studying the phenomenon in secret, as this next case typifies.

One evening around dusk in July 1958, an unidentified mechanic working at Holloman AFB observed a twenty-five-foot diameter disk-shaped craft with "ball-like landing gear" hovering at a very low altitude over the airport tarmac about 50 yards away. It had a dome-shaped top with several oblong openings which intermittently gave off bright flashes of bluish light. There was also a band of highly polished metal resembling brass around the perimeter of the craft. The shape reminded the witness of a wide thick-brimmed hat. It made no noise whatsoever. As the craft began to retract its gear, the mechanic alerted another mechanic, and they both observed the craft dart away at high speeds.

The two mechanics were interviewed by Air Force Intelligence officers who first interrogated them about the details of the sighting and then showed them a large book containing more than 300 pages of UFO photographs. The mechanics were told to identify the type of craft that they had seen, which they did. The Intelligence officers then told the mechanics that the personnel in the nearby control tower had also observed the object. Finally, the men were told to never discuss the incident and were required to sign statements agreeing to keep the incident a secret.[44]

UFO COMMUNICATES THROUGH CAR RADIO

The ability of UFOs to affect electromagnetic machinery has been exhaustively documented. A large number of such incidents have taken place in New Mexico, usually involving automobiles. The following case (investigated by Coral and Jim Lorenzen of APRO) provides a particularly unusual example.

At 8:30 a.m., on February 25, 1959, Jim Dobbs Jr. was driving on State Road 18 south of his hometown of Dobbs when he saw an egg-shaped object which glowed "like the radium on a watch." The object was about ten degrees above the horizon and moving quickly.

At the time of his sighting, Dobbs had been tuning his car radio into a local station when it was interrupted by a Morse code sound of a steady succession of two dots and a dash. During this time, the object passed overhead and disappeared to the east. As soon as it was out of view, the strange signal stopped and his radio returned to normal.[45]

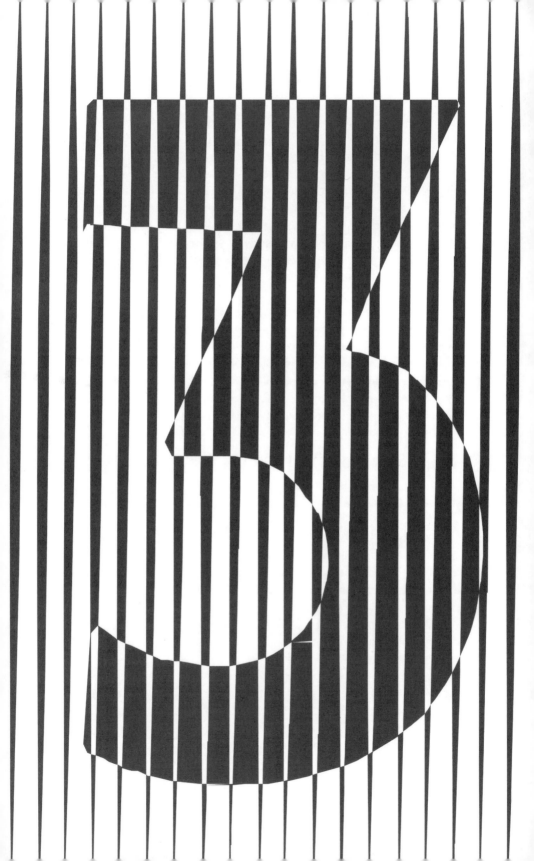

CHAPTER 3

Sightings:1960-1969

The next decade brought a steady stream of UFO encounters over New Mexico. While activity wasn't as intense as the previous decade, it was clear that the UFOs were still active. Also, there was an escalation in their behavior, with more and more cases of landings and humanoids. The sightings also became more dramatic and interactive, including reports of UFO fleets appearing in large displays, more car chases, witnesses being struck by UFO beams or even burned. The physical evidence also grew dramatically in the 1960s, with several radar-confirmed cases, more convincing photographs taken by witnesses and also a nationwide epidemic of UFO-power failure cases. While many of the cases occurred over military bases, there were also an increasing number of civilian cases. Though the reasons for the UFO activity remained a matter of speculation, the cases from the 1960s provided many high-profile sightings.

UFO FLEETS OF 1961

While it is not unusual to see one, two, or even three UFOs during a sighting, much more rare are sightings involving large groups of objects. Beginning at 6:17 p.m. on January 17, 1961, a meteorologist and former weather officer from Holloman AFB was with his friends near the town of Cimarron when they saw a group of lights (ranging in color from yellow to orange) move overhead at an estimated altitude of 30,000 feet. The group of lights flew like "wild geese in a wedge formation" at a speed that seemed "slow for airplanes."

A short time later, the witnesses were watching a bright light which they first thought was Mars when beneath it, a second V-shaped formation of lights appeared. The bright light then winked out and the formation approached. On this occasion, there were eight amber, yellow, and orange lights. The witnesses noticed that the objects "changed position in the formation now and then – first one light would be in the lead, and then another." The mini-fleet of objects veered to the southwest and moved away.

The observers prepared to leave the area when they saw the formation returning. The objects continued to occasionally change positions, only now, they also changed in brightness. Says the witness,

THE GROUP OF OBJECTS FLEW BACK TO APPROXIMATELY THE SAME SPOT WHERE THEY HAD APPEARED FROM THE BRIGHT LIGHT, AND THEN DISAPPEARED. SOME OF THE LIGHTS WOULD PULSATE AS THEY FLEW ALONG AND THEN GREW MOMENTARILY BRIGHTER AND THEN DIM AGAIN.

The Lorenzens, who investigated the case concluded that the case was "well-witnessed" and that "the formation is the typical UFO V formation."

This next case also involves multiple UFOs and also an apparent mother-ship. On September 2, 1961, at 11:40 p.m., a group of witnesses in Albuquerque observed several "circular, silvery objects" moving from east to west with erratic movements. Although it was nighttime, the objects appeared to flash orange light, as if they were reflecting the sun off a brightly polished metallic surface. The objects performed the maneuvers for a period of ten minutes, during which time they twice ejected a group of smaller silver objects, each about 1/16 the size of the larger objects.[46]

A 30-MILE UFO CHASE

It was 2 a.m. on October 21, 1961, and Mr. and Mrs. Dubois (residents of California) were on vacation and returning home from New Mexico. As they traveled along Route 60 near Datil, the highway was completely deserted of other cars. Just as the road led into a dark canyon, the couple observed an extremely bright white ball of light fall down out of the sky, slow down, and pass in front of their vehicle, then turn back and follow alongside. Seconds later, it zoomed back up into the sky and went away.

They breathed a sigh of relief, and told themselves that they must have seen some type of unusual reflection from the moonlight. This theory, however, was discarded when the object returned.

As before, the couple observed the light drop down out of the sky. On this occasion, it approached from behind, raced ahead of the car and then slowed down to let them catch up.

As the couple drove up to the object, it waited for them and then began to pace their vehicle for several miles. During this time, it broke up into four smaller, glowing objects, each of them maintaining an equal distance from their vehicle.

After being followed by the objects for a total of thirty miles, the couple noticed the lights of a service station ahead of them. Greatly relieved, they slowed down and began to stop. As they did, the lights quickly "flashed upward and went out of sight."

These types of cat-and-mouse games are not unusual in the UFO literature and may have something to say about the nature of the phenomenon. Concerning the above case, researcher Richard Haines writes,

> THIS IS A TYPICAL PACING INCIDENT WHERE THE AERIAL PHENOMENA APPROACHES AT HIGH SPEED AND THEN DECELERATES TO PERMIT THE CAR TO CATCH UP WITH IT AND THEN ASSUMES PACING SPEED. THESE UFO MOTIONS REQUIRE PRECISE ENERGY MANAGEMENT (PERHAPS THUS VECTORING), DISTANCE SENSING, AND NAVIGATION IN THREE DIMENSIONAL SPACE. IT IS NOT LIKELY THAT AMERICA HAD SUCH CAPABILITY IN THE EARLY 1960S.

Longtime researcher Richard Hall pointed out this case in particular as being typical of "inquisitive and reaction cases."[47]

CYLINDER OVER ACOMA

On the evening of May 15, 1962, three people were traveling west on Interstate 40 between Albuquerque and Acoma when they noticed a stationary light floating along the horizon. Suddenly it increased in brightness and eventually, they realized the light was actually an object that was flying toward them. Thinking a plane was about to crash, they pulled the car over and got out. Instead of a plane, they watched in awe as the object came directly overhead. The one light now revealed itself to be a cylinder-shaped object lit up with four lights. It moved silently overhead and disappeared to the right. Moments later, they saw it shoot off in a northerly direction. Thirty-five years later, the witnesses remain convinced they saw a genuine UFO.[48]

UFO BUZZES RADAR INSTALLATION

In July 1962, a group of twelve engineers and technicians were at a radar installation located on top of a small mountain called Twin Buttes, adjacent to Holloman Air Force Base. The group was outside during broad daylight when they saw a shiny, silver disk-shaped object approach the radar installation and begin to circle it. The object looked like two bowls put together rim-to-rim, and had no windows or other markings. It appeared to be about fifty feet in diameter, and circled the building only a few hundred feet above.

The job of one of the engineers was to take moving films of missile launches, so he always carried a 35 mm movie camera. He quickly pointed his camera at the object and shot ninety feet of color film. Two days later, officials from the Air Force arrived and confiscated the film.[49]

APRIL ENCOUNTERS

On the evening of April 22, 1964, Marie Morrow and two other people drove westbound, about ten miles east of Lordsbury when, without warning, the entire area around them became illuminated by a brilliant bluish light described "as bright as day." At the same moment, a round object appeared, flying about ten feet above their car, making a loud whining noise. Within seconds, the object darted off to the north and disappeared. The witnesses appear to have been physically unaffected by the experience.

On the morning of April 28, 1964, numerous witnesses in the town of Anthony, (including police officer Paul Arteche), observed a round-shaped reddish object hover at low altitude, and then take off at high speed towards the west. The sighting was later investigated by the National Investigative Committee on Aerial Phenomena (NICAP), and was printed in their monthly journal.

Also on April 28, 1964, businessman Don Adams (age 20) was driving his car on Route 66 between Edgewood and Moriarty when he saw a green-colored object hovering over the road ahead of him. As he drove underneath the object, his car stalled. Suddenly afraid, Adams grabbed his gun, exited the car, and quickly fired six shots directly at the object. There was no apparent effect. He immediately reloaded and fired six more rounds of ammunition. He is certain that his bullets hit the object at least a half-dozen times. Afterwards, the object rose upwards and spun away at high speed into the distance. Researcher Richard Haines Ph.D. calls this case a C-EV because Adams was able to affect the behavior of the UFO through his own actions.

Following the incident, local law enforcement officials were contacted. They said that they had been receiving a series of calls for the past week from people reporting "similar objects" from south of Truth or Consequences to north of Espanola. They told reporters that:

> ALL THE REPORTS ARE SIMILAR IN THAT THEY DESCRIBE OVAL OR EGG-SHAPED OBJECTS, WITH SIZE ESTIMATES RANGING FROM THE SIZE OF A CAR TO ABOUT 30 FEET OR LONGER.[50]

UFO CAUSES UNUSUAL GROWTH

One day after the above case, on April 29, 1964, an extremely unusual encounter occurred in Albuquerque to a young 10-year-old girl named Sharon Stull. As reported in the *Albuquerque Tribune*, Stull was at recess in the Lowell schoolyard when she and several other students noticed an egg-shaped "thing" floating high in the sky above the elementary school. While Stull says that nobody seemed to be paying much attention to the object, she kept her eye on the strange craft, which remained in place during the entire recess period. She said it was the shape of an egg, slightly smaller than an airplane, and had no windows of any kind.

When recess was over, Stull returned to her class. About a half-hour later, her eyes suddenly became red, inflamed, and irritated. She rinsed them out with water but when the symptoms worsened, Stull's teacher excused her and sent her to see the school doctor. The doctor immediately called Stull's mother, who came to the school and rushed Sharon to the nearby Batton Hospital.

Stull's injuries turned out to be severe. Her doctor diagnosed her with "membrane inflammation of both eyes and first-degree burns under the eyes and on the nose."

Doctors treated Stull, but were unable to explain the symptoms. Says Sharon's mother, Mrs. Max Stull,

THEY INSTRUCTED ME TO KEEP HER BLINDS DRAWN TO PROTECT HER INFLAMED EYES AND EYELIDS FROM LIGHT. PART OF MY DAUGHTER'S FACE AND NOSE APPEARED TO BE PUFFY AND RED. SHE CONTINUED TO COMPLAIN OF BURNING PAINS.

Sharon's case became publicized and provoked an official response from Police Chief A. B. Martinez, who issued an unprecedented warning to Albuquerque residents warning them to stay away from any mysterious unidentified objects. Chief Martinez didn't reveal his own views on the subject, other than to say that UFOs "should be treated with respect and caution."

After being treated for her injuries, Sharon was given dark glasses to wear while her eyes healed. For some time following the sighting, she could only read a few paragraphs before her eyes began to hurt. Unknown to the witnesses, eye irritation is one of the most common physiological effects resulting from a close-up UFO encounter. However, what happened next was almost unheard of.

Four months later, the *Albuquerque Tribune* published a follow-up article on Stull's case. According to her mother, Sharon had grown five and a half inches and gained twenty-five pounds in the four weeks following the sighting. As Mrs. Stull told reporters,

A WHILE AGO SHE WAS JUST A CHILD WHO LIKED TO PLAY WITH DOLLS AND CUT-OUTS. NOW SHE IS SUDDENLY MATURE AND GROWN-UP, COOKS MEALS BY HERSELF, CLEANS HOUSE AND TAKES CARE OF THE YOUNGER CHILDREN... NOW SHARON IS

FIVE FEET TWO INCHES TALL AND WEIGHS 110 POUNDS — AND IS STILL GROWING. MY DAUGHTER HAS OUTGROWN ALL HER CLOTHES AND QUICKLY OUTGROWS NEW GARMENTS AND SHOES. I'M SO CONFUSED I DON'T KNOW WHAT TO BELIEVE... I KNOW SHE DEFINITELY SAW SOMETHING IN THE SKY THAT DAY, BUT I DON'T KNOW WHAT. IT HAS BEEN A NIGHTMARE FOR US EVER SINCE — I WISH I HAD KEPT HER INSIDE THAT DAY.

According to Mrs. Stull, Sharon, herself, was unable to account for her sudden growth, saying only, "I just feel funny."[51]

UFOS CAUGHT ON RADAR

Despite the Air Force's assertions that there is no evidence of UFOs, they have been caught on radar on multiple occasions.

On May 15, 1964, between 11:30 a.m. and 12:15 p.m., two UFOs were tracked on surveillance radar and on the FPS-16 radars at Stallion Site. The objects performed "perfect, precise flight maneuvers" including side-by-side flights, separating and then rejoining, and up and down "pogo" maneuvers. Radar operators not only tracked the objects on their scopes but saw them visually, describing them as brown-colored and football-shaped. The objects were flying so low that they disappeared out of sight behind some buildings at the instrumentation site where the radar operator was stationed.

Most disturbing to officials was that the objects appeared to be mimicking the FAA's "recognition signal." This is a pre-determined signal consisting of a series of pulses arranged in a particular sequence that allows tracking ground stations to identify the craft as one of their own. There are two commonly used codes. Officials were concerned because these two UFOs were alternately beaming both of these "recognition signals" while hovering over Stallion Site.

Meanwhile, the UFOs continued to make regular appearances. On May 22, 1964, a UFO was again tracked on radar moving over the White Sands Proving Grounds. Neither case was reported to Blue Book; instead both were filed with the base commander at White Sands Missile Range.[52]

BURNED BY A UFO

One of the most frightening of all New Mexico encounters occurred at 4 p.m. on June 2, 1964, to an 8-year-old child in the city of Hobbs. Charles Keith Davis was playing outside the doorway of the *Deluxe Laundry* while his grandmother, Mrs. Frank Smith, gathered clothes from a washer. She was about three feet away from Charles when she heard a strange sound which she described as similar to that of a whizzing bullet. As she told reporters,

> THERE WAS A WHOOSHING SOUND AND A BLACKISH BALL OF FIRE COVERED CHARLIE.... [HE WAS] COVERED WITH BLACK, HIS HAIR STANDING ON END AND BURNING. CHARLES WAS JUST AS BLACK AS HE COULD BE... HIS HAIR WAS STANDING UP ON TOP HIS HEAD. I GRABBED HIM AND TRIED TO SMOTHER OUT HIS HAIR, WHICH WAS ON FIRE.

Mrs. Frank Smith explained that she just barely had time to see what appeared to be a metallic object that looked like a top, swoop down out of the sky and hang just above her grandson's head, pouring out smoke, soot, and fire. Within seconds, the object darted away.

Employees of the laundry also rushed out of the store and helped extinguish the flames. Charles, however, was badly burned and his face and neck began to swell immediately. There was a strange sooty substance all over his neck and chest. Charles, who had kept his eyes closed during the incident, now asked his grandmother, "Grandma, am I going to die?"

Mrs. Smith comforted him and quickly rushed Charles to Lea General Hospital (or Lee County Hospital). While being treated for second-degree burns on his head and face, the child explained to doctors that while he was playing, he saw a small "black object with flames... A fire that came out of the sky."

Charles also lost some his hair as a result and one of his ears looked, said Mrs. Frank, like a "piece of raw meat." His head and face were so swollen that his eyes had been forced shut and his nose was just barely visible.

The FBI heard about the case. They requested and were sent samples of the boy's burned hair, skin and t-shirt for analysis. Mrs. Smith says she never heard back from the FBI and has no idea if they found anything unusual.

Researcher Coral Lorenzen was able to speak with the doctor who treated Charles. The doctor appeared to believe the story told by Mrs. Frank, but he told Lorenzen that there was "nothing unusual" about

Charles's burns except for one thing: Charles said he suffered no pain from the ordeal. He recuperated in the hospital for five days, during which time he healed from injuries. Again, there was no pain, only "intense itching" which became so severe, Charles had to be sedated.[53]

UFO PHOTOGRAPHED OVER SAN JUAN PUEBLO

The number of photographic cases continued to mount. One afternoon in June of 1964, J. E. Berry was driving through the town of San Juan Pueblo when he sighted a large white circular object moving across the sky, leaving a long white contrail. He quickly grabbed his camera and snapped a clear photograph of the object.[54]

UFO PLAYS CAT & MOUSE WITH MOTORIST

In the summer of 1965, researcher Frank Edwards was approached by a couple who wanted to share their UFO encounter, but only on the condition that they could remain anonymous. Edwards agreed, and the couple revealed an astounding UFO encounter that took place while driving late at night on an empty highway through the deserts of New Mexico.

It was 1 a.m., in March of 1965, and the witness (who was employed as the president of a major bank) and his wife were driving about twenty miles west of Santa Rosa. There were no other cars on the highway. The couple preferred to commute late at night in order to avoid traffic. Looking ahead of them, they saw a bright greenish light swoop down out of the sky and approach their vehicle.

The wife was driving, and when it became clear that the object was unusual, she pulled off the road and stopped the car to get a better look. The object quickly approached to within about 300 feet of the witnesses and about twenty feet above the highway. It was so brilliantly lit that it was blinding to look at.

The extreme brightness of the light and the closeness of the object badly frightened the couple, who quickly locked the doors and ducked down below the dash to get out of the beam. After about three minutes, the light switched off.

The couple regained their composure and pulled back onto the highway to continue their interrupted journey. By the time they had gone a half-mile, however, they realized that the object was pacing their car. It traveled at the same speed about 600 feet to the right of the highway. Every five seconds, it emitted a powerful beam of light onto the ground. At one point, it sent out a white beam and a green-colored beam, both of which struck their car, illuminating the interior for a period of a few seconds.

Without warning, the beams of light shut off and the objects were apparently gone. Writes Edwards,

THE BANKER AND HIS WIFE WERE BOTH BADLY SHAKEN BY THEIR EXPERIENCE. THEY SAID THEY HAD NOT TOLD ANYONE ABOUT IT BEFORE TELLING ME, FOR FEAR OF BEING REGARDED AS A BIT NUTTY.

While the civilian cases seemed to grow in number, the military cases remained steadily strong. As we have seen, Holloman AFB has attracted considerable UFO activity, at least some of which has been caught on radar. Only a few months after the above incident, the Air Force again obtained radar confirmation of unknown objects in the New Mexico skies. Writes researcher Frank Edwards,

IN MAY OF 1965 THE OFFICIALS AT HOLLOMAN AIR FORCE BASE, WHICH GUARDS WHITE SANDS MISSILE RANGE IN NEW MEXICO, REPORTED THAT THEIR RADAR HAD BEEN TRACKING A UFO FOR TWO DAYS, AT INTERVALS.[55]

TENS OF THOUSANDS WITNESS UFOS

Most UFO events are seen (or at least reported!) by only a small number of people. However, the 1960s brought an increasing number of incidents in which UFOs appeared to put on displays, showing themselves to hundreds or even thousands of people. The next cluster of cases is a typical example.

On the evening of August 1, 1965, police officers in Hobbs (near the Texas border) observed a "round white object with an orange tail" which moved overhead from east to west.

Shortly later and sixty-nine miles to the west, a police dispatcher in Carlsbad reported his sighting of a similar object. At the same time, thirty-six miles northwest of Carlsbad, policemen in Artesia received four separate reports of a bright white round object with a red-colored tail which passed overhead northeast of the town.

While this mini wave was spectacular in its own right, the next night proved to be one of the most dramatic events so far. Writes pioneering researcher Frank Edwards,

> ONE OF THE GREAT LANDMARK DATES IN THE UNFOLDING UFO MYSTERY WAS THE MEMORABLE NIGHT OF AUGUST 2-3, 1965.

At that time, the United States was in the midst of a nationwide UFO wave. However, that night proved to be particularly active, with thousands of reports coming from across the central United States, from North Dakota down to New Mexico and Arizona. Writes Frank Edwards,

> TENS OF THOUSANDS OF PERSONS IN THE GREAT PLAINS STATES STOOD OUT ON THAT WARM CLEAR NIGHT AND WATCHED AN AWE-INSPIRING AERIAL EXHIBITION. SOMETIMES THE LIGHTS MOVED IN FORMATION. SOMETIMES IT WAS A SINGLE PULSATING LIGHT. SOMETIMES THEY WENT HIGH; SOMETIMES SO LOW THAT THEY COULD BE PHOTOGRAPHED BY AMATEUR CAMERA OPERATORS. THEY WERE TRACKED ON RADAR — BOTH CIVIL AND MILITARY — ACCORDING TO STATE POLICE REPORTS. THEY CHANGED FORMATION FROM TIME TO TIME; THEY CHANGED SPEED; AND THEY CHANGED COLOR AND SIZE. IT WAS A MAGNIFICENT DISPLAY THAT BROUGHT OUT AN ESTIMATED QUARTER OF A MILLION VIEWERS.

The next morning, the media reported the sightings and turned to the Air Force for an explanation. According to Edwards, the official Air Force conclusion was: "Four stars in the constellation Orion."

The Air Force explanation was widely ridiculed in newspaper editorials. Professional astronomer Dr. Robert Risser pointed out that the cause could not have been Orion as at the time, the constellation was not even visible from the United States!

Frank Edwards says that it was this widespread sighting and the Air Force's weak response that inspired him to write his first UFO book, *Flying Saucers – Serious Business*, which became the first UFO book ever to reach the best-seller lists.[56]

UFO BUZZES CAR

On evening on July 20, 1965, a family of four were driving in the desert, heading west near Albuquerque when they saw a "large, round disk" fly overhead at a low elevation. Says the witness,

THE WHOLE THING WAS LIT UP WITH A WEIRD GREEN COLOR (LIKE PHOSPHORESCENCE). WE LOOKED AT IT, AND AS IT PASSED OVER US, THE TRUCK STOPPED ALL BY ITSELF. IT WOULD NOT START AGAIN UNTIL THE DISK HAD PASSED OVER.

A very similar case took place one evening in 1965. A family was driving along the highway through the New Mexico desert when, up ahead of them, they saw what appeared to be "a glowing dish." As they approached close to the object, their radio began to static. Next their dog reacted and hid under the seat. The object appeared to be 100 to 200 feet across, and had brilliant red, orange, and blue lights coming from the bottom. At their closest approach, the radio was total static and their headlights dimmed. The object remained stationary floating about 200 feet above the highway.

As they passed by, first the headlights came back on, and then the radio. The witness, who was 10 years old at the time, waited more than thirty years to report his sighting.[57]

UFO CAUSES STATEWIDE POWER FAILURE

On December 2, 1965, there was "an unverified report of a UFO" over the area of New Mexico. At the same time, there was a sudden and massive power failure across New Mexico, Texas, and parts of Mexico. Nearly one million people were without electricity. Writes Donald Keyhoe,

THE CHAIN REACTION BLACKED OUT STORES, HOMES, HOSPITALS, AIRPORTS AND ALSO DEFENSE BASES – FORT BLISS, HOLLOMAN AFB, WHITE SANDS PROVING GROUND AND BIGGS AFB.

While the UFO connection in this case is not strong, less than one month earlier, on November 9, 1965, the Great New York Black-Out had occurred, during which there were many well-verified reports of UFOs in the area. In fact, the year of 1965 brought several cases of this type, which some investigators believe were attempts by the ETs to test their abilities to affect the power grid, or were perhaps demonstrations of their ability to do so.[58]

A GIANT ACORN

In 1965, a huge wave of UFO activity swept across the entire nation. Another dramatic case from this year occurred in Deming. The mother of a family went outside to hang out the laundry and rushed back inside to describe an acorn-shaped object that was flying silently at tree-top level. The family rushed outside to watch the object fly about 150 feet from their home.

Shortly afterward, they all observed a "large, round, silver object" which was hovering off to the west. The object appeared to be the size of a football field, and was staying perfectly still in the sky. Says the witness:

> IT WAS AT A STANDSTILL FOR NEARLY THREE TO FOUR HOURS, CLEAR AS CAN BE. IT WAS VERY LARGE, RIGHT IN THE MIDDLE OF DEMING.

The family was dumbfounded that the object wasn't causing more attention. Writes one of them,

> MY FATHER AND MOTHER AND FOUR OF MY SIBLINGS WITNESSED THIS OBJECT FOR HOURS. IT WAS VERY LARGE. I CANNOT UNDERSTAND HOW THIS WAS NOT WITNESSED BY THE WHOLE CITY?

None of them were prepared for what happened next. Writes the witness,

> THREE FIGHTER JETS CAME OUT OF NOWHERE AND BEGAN TO APPROACH THE OBJECT.

To their amazement, the object went from the size of a football field and shrank down until it was the size of a dot and "just vanished." The three jet aircraft flew over the location, then split off in three different directions and left the area.

The witness reported his sighting to NUFORC in the hopes that somebody out there might be able to provide some corroboration.

What might be the same encounter, or another encounter entirely, was reported to MUFON by another witness. One evening around 8 p.m., sometime in the summer or fall of 1965, a 7-year-old boy was playing football with about twelve local friends (all from Deming) when they observed a translucent sphere with a bright red light drop out of the sky to nearly ground-level, and then zipped away. Moments later, they looked up, and about one block away, above Deming's city hall, a giant saucer-shaped craft was hovering. The witness estimates that the object was 1,000 feet wide and hovered at an altitude of 500 feet. It was gray-metallic in color, with a flat bottom and a domed top lined with rectangular portholes. Red, green, and yellow lights flashed around the circumference. It was totally silent and remained in place for a few minutes before suddenly darting at high speed towards Palomas. The witness likened his sighting to the movie *Close Encounters of the Third Kind*, saying that all the children were awestruck and that they did not discuss it among themselves or with their parents.[59]

UFO HOVERS OVER SANDIA CREST

One of the common misconceptions about UFOs is that they are never reported by scientifically trained people. As we have seen, many of the UFO cases in New Mexico involve highly placed scientists and military leaders. A typical case occurred on June 23, 1966.

In this instance, the witness was Julian Sandoval, a former Air Force pilot, and navigator with 7,000 hours of flying time who also worked as an Apollo Space Project flight engineer. At 3:42 a.m. on June 23, Sandoval was driving along Highway 85 near Coralles when he saw a strange-looking object hovering about 12,000 feet above the antenna tower at Sandia Crest in Albuquerque. The object glowed with light and was shaped like a tetrahedron. At one end there were four blue-green lights.

When the object remained in place, Sandoval carefully estimated the size of the craft by using the antenna tower as a reference point and observing the craft through a pair of binoculars. He watched the craft for fifty-one minutes and estimated that it was at least 300 feet long. It would occasionally change position, moving about thirty-five miles per hour, at which time it would brighten considerably.

After some time, the craft descended to an estimated 9,000 feet, then went into a high-speed vertical climb and disappeared. Sandoval estimated that it left at a speed approaching Mach 6, or six times the speed of sound. There were also other witnesses to the event, which to the dismay of the Air Force, earned considerable media publicity.[60]

A UFO-CAR CHASE

Late one evening in 1966, an anonymous gentleman (a Naval Officer on transfer) was driving across the United States, from California to Florida. With him were his wife and two daughters. They were in the middle of New Mexico when the gentleman noticed that something strange was following them down the highway. Says the witness,

IT WAS JUST A SOFT LIGHT...ONE SOFT LIGHT. AT FIRST I THOUGHT IT WAS A CAR OR TRUCK. IT CONTINUED TO FOLLOW ME UNTIL I THOUGHT THERE MIGHT BE SOMEONE WANTING TO HARM US... I TURNED OFF MY LIGHTS TO SEE IF I WAS GETTING A REFLECTION. IT DIDN'T GO AWAY. I PUSHED MY CAR TO 100 PLUS, BUT IT STAYED WITH ME. I SLOWED DOWN TO 25 OR SO, AND IT WAS STILL THERE. I COULDN'T STAND IT ANYMORE, SO I STOPPED AND GOT OUT TO HAVE A LOOK.

IT WAS JUST A SMALL WHITE LIGHT WITH WHAT LOOKED LIKE HORIZONTAL BARS COMING OUT FROM THE SOFT LIGHT. THERE WAS NO SOUND AND IT WAS ABOUT 50 FEET AWAY.

When the object remained in place, the gentleman got back in his car and continued driving east. The object resumed following him for a few more minutes, then suddenly moved off to the left, pacing his car while flying above the westbound lane in the wrong direction. Suddenly, it turned on another light and moved off to the north, disappearing at low level across the desert. The witness reported his sighting to both MUFON and NUFORC, saying in summation, "Believe me, they exist."[61]

DOMED DISK OVER TULAROSA

On February 10, 1967, at around 4:30 a.m., Richard Martinez was driving from his home in Tucumcari to Alamogordo. He was on Highway 54 about twenty-five miles north of Tularosa when he saw it: a round-bottomed metallic object with a domed top. When he first observed the object, it was hovering right beside the highway. It had three lights attached the outer circumference, one of which was green in color and blinking on and off. The object stayed in place for only a moment before lifting up and zooming towards Alamogordo. The witness was deeply impressed by his sighting and reported it to Alamogordo State Police Headquarters.[62]

UFOS AT WHITE SANDS

As we have seen, White Sands at Los Alamos has a list of UFO encounters that rivals any other location in New Mexico.

J. Allen Hynek personally interviewed a gentleman who observed a daylight disk at 8:45 a.m. on March 24, 1967. According to the anonymous witness,

> VERY BRIEFLY, WHAT I SAW WAS A SMALL SILVERY WHITE DISC OF UNKNOWN DIAMETER, UNKNOWN ALTITUDE, BUT DEFINITE PHYSICAL EXISTENCE; IT FIRST APPEARED TO BE STATIONARY, UNDER VISUAL OBSERVATION FOR ABOUT TEN MINUTES. THEN IT MOVED ACROSS THE SKY, VISUALLY PASSING UNDER THE CLOUDS AND FINALLY DISAPPEARING INTO THE WHITE CLOUDS. NO SOUND COULD BE DETECTED. THE WHITE DOT STOOD STILL TOO LONG AND MOVED TOO SILENTLY TO HAVE BEEN AN AIRCRAFT; IT APPEARED TO TRAVEL IN A DIRECTION DISTINCTLY INCONSISTENT WITH THE DIRECTION OF THE CLOUDS SO AS TO PRECLUDE...THAT IT WAS A BALLOON.

Four days later, as investigated by APRO, numerous people in the Las Cruces area reported seeing "lighted objects" over the Organ Mountains.

Two months later, there was another sighting. In this case the witnesses were Dave Adams and his wife (both Mormon Sunday School teachers in Albuquerque) and a group of their students. On May 11, 1967, Adams and his wife decided to treat their pupils to a group picnic. They all drove out to Ponderosa Pines, a development just south of Albuquerque on Highway 10, just past Highway 66. It was just past noon when one of the children saw "a white, bright object in the sky." Everyone turned to watch what they first thought was a plane. Strangely, however, it made no sound. Also, it was glinting very brightly and moving too slowly to be a plane. As it slowly approached their group not far above tree-top level, Mr. Adams grabbed his camera and after quickly focusing it, he began taking pictures.

The object approached closely, then, when it was about to pass overhead, it curved away instead and moved off into the distance. Adams was able to take four photographs before the object was no longer visible.

As the report on the case says:

> THE OBJECT WITNESSED WAS DESCRIBED MUCH AS IT APPEARED IN THE LATER DEVELOPED PHOTOS. IT WAS SEEN AS A BRIGHT WHITE METALLIC DISC-SHAPE VIEWED AT AN ANGLE, WAS QUITE FLAT-APPEARING, DARKER UNDERNEATH AND SEEMED TO BE VERY SMOOTHLY FINISHED. NO DOME, STRUCTURES OR PROJECTIONS OF ANY KIND WERE SEEN. NO OTHER LIGHTS WERE SEEN AND IT LEFT NO TRAIL. THE EDGE OF THE DISC WAS NOT AS SHARPLY DEFINED AS EXPECTED, AND FADED INTO A VERY SLIGHT MIST, HAZE OR HALO. NO OTHER DETAILS WERE NOTED. (SEE PHOTO SECTION ON PAGE 293.)

A month later, the UFOs were back. One morning in June 1967, Edward P. Bedy (a rocket engineer who had overseen more than 850 rocket launches) was standing with nine other people in front of Navy Headquarters, looking east of the White Sands Missile Range. They were waiting for a launch, which was about to take place. The countdown was in progress when somebody shouted out, "Look at that!" and pointed to an object that was flying in a circular pattern above the launch pad.

Says Bedy,

> AT TIMES THE OBJECT JUST APPEARED AS A SMALL BLACK DOT, EXCEPT AT THE RIDGE AND LEFT EDGES OF THE ORBIT IT WOULD REFLECT THE SUN AND APPEAR AS A SHINING OBJECT. THIS IS ASTOUNDING BECAUSE THE WHOLE VALLEY IS COVERED BY NUMEROUS RADARS, INCLUDING THOSE AT HOLLOMAN AFB. THE SKIES OVER WSMR ARE RESTRICTED AIRSPACE, AND IF A PLANE OR OTHER OBJECT FLIES OVER THE RANGE, THE RANGE GOES TO RED STATUS AND NO ONE CAN LAUNCH ANYTHING.

According to Bedy, the radar stations had not registered the object on their scopes and the countdown continued as normal. Seconds later, the rocket took off. Says Bedy,

> WE SAW THE ROCKET RISING FROM THE LAUNCH PAD AND THE ONE-QUARTER-INCH [APPARENT SIZE] DISC WAS PACING ALONGSIDE THE ROCKET, GOING STRAIGHT UP. ALL OF US SAW THIS, AND I KNOW WE DID NOT POSSESS AN AIRCRAFT AT THAT TIME THAT COULD FLY STRAIGHT UP AND PACE THAT ROCKET. I CAN'T EXPLAIN IT.

Bedy was interviewed by UFO researcher Chris Augustin, who convinced Bedy to go public with his account. (Filer, April 2006, p13)

Two months later, on August 15, 1967, three young kids (all Army brats) were chasing lizards behind Speedway Park on the backside of Sandia Base, which they had been told was off-limits. Says one of the kids,

> WE LOOKED UP AND SAW THIS HUGE CIGAR-CYLINDER SHAPED THING HANGING
> UP IN THE AIR. IT WAS GRAY IN COLOR AND DIDN'T MAKE ANY NOISE. IT LOOKED
> LIKE A BLIMP, BUT IT WAS A LOT SKINNIER THAN ANY BLIMP I'VE EVER SEEN. IT SCARED
> THE HELL OUT OF ALL THREE OF US. WE TOOK OFF RUNNING BACK TO SANDIA BASE
> WHERE WE LIVED. WHEN I LOOKED BACK...IT WAS TEARING STRAIGHT UP INTO THE
> SKY AND HAD BECOME VERTICAL."

More than thirty years later, the witness reported his case to NUFORC, saying,

> I HAVE TOLD A COUPLE OF PEOPLE SINCE, BUT IT STILL GIVES ME A CHILL WHENEVER
> I THINK ABOUT IT. SO I TRY NOT TO.

By this time, it was apparently common knowledge that UFOs made regular appearances over the White Sands facility. According to pioneering UFO researchers Ralph and Judy Blum, an employee at White Sands found the following graffiti on a bathroom wall at White Sands Missile Range in 1967:

> I SAW A DISK UP IN THE AIR,
> A SILVER DISK THAT WASN'T THERE.
> TWO MORE WEREN'T THERE AGAIN TODAY —
> OH HOW I WISH THEY'D GO AWAY.[63]

UFO CHASES CARS DOWN HIGHWAY

Three particularly dramatic and terrifying encounters with UFOs took place in 1968, each of which again involved UFOs that chased cars along the highway. In each case, the witnesses were a married couple.

The first case took place at around 2 a.m. on January 20, 1968. Mr. and Mrs. Larry Ferney were driving near Roswell when they saw a UFO drop out of the sky, swooping down about 300 yards, at which point it made a 90-degree turn and headed directly towards the frightened witnesses. The object had three bright lights "like the landing lights of an aircraft." It continued to approach the car until the Ferneys became afraid that it would crash into them. Fifty feet away, it finally leveled out. Maintaining this distance, the object paced the car for the next ten minutes. Mrs. Ferney was reportedly in a state of near hysteria when the mysterious object finally raced upward and out of view.

The second case took place in May or June 1968. Revard N. Vordenbaum, (a businessman and former U.S. Marine from San Antonio, Texas) and his wife, Diane, were traveling eastward along State Highway 10 from San Clemente, California to San Antonio to exhibit their merchandise at a local fair. Revard was driving. At about 2 a.m., they were driving at about 70 MPH along an isolated section of the highway in the New Mexican desert when Diane observed an oval-shaped object pacing their car to the left, about 100 yards north of the railroad tracks that paralleled the road. She pointed it out to her husband, and they both watched the object slow down to about 65 MPH and then pace their car, slowly becoming more distant behind them. After two minutes, the oval light – described as "not large, but not small" – made a sudden 90-degree turn and ascended straight up. Diane Vordenbaum leaned over the backseat and watched it move off into the distance in two seconds. MUFON International Director Walt Andrus reviewed the case and wrote that "the light or object performed a maneuver inconsistent with earthly aircraft or known objects," and that it was "probably a UFO."

The third case also took place in 1968 (exact date not given) to Dr. George Walton (a physicist) and his wife, while driving late at night on a highway through the New Mexico desert. As they drove, two "flying disks" swooped down out of the sky and began to pace their vehicle. Frightened by the sudden appearance of the objects and by their obvious interest in them, the scientist jammed the accelerator to the floor and tried to speed away. For the next three minutes, he drove at speeds in excess of eighty-five miles an hour, frantically trying to escape the objects, which continued to follow them. Fortunately, at this point, the lights of a small town appearance ahead. As the couple raced into the town, the two disks pulled away and climbed up into the sky. By this time, however, the Waltons were left "in a state of shock."[64]

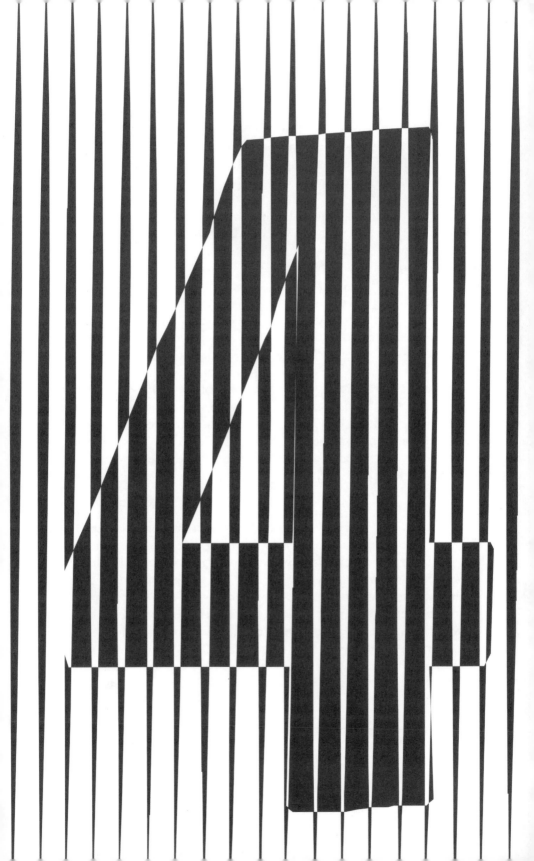

CHAPTER 4

Sightings:1970-1979

While UFO activity in New Mexico in the 1970s remained steady, the intensity of the last two decades had evolved into a smaller scattering of sightings, only a handful of which became well known. Investigators instead were concentrating on more promising cases involving landings and the newly exposed abduction phenomenon. It was the arrival of the cattle mutilations in the 1970s, however, which brought an entire new dimension to the phenomenon, especially as New Mexico was the mutilation hotspot of the United States.

Nevertheless, nearly each year usually brought at least one case high-profile enough to reach the local or national news. These cases typically involved high profile witnesses, large numbers of witnesses or some type of physical evidence. And again, the 1970s brought more cases of sightings over New Mexico military bases.

INTENSELY BRIGHT LIGHTS

According to researcher Linda Kerth, starting on November 15 through December 21, 1970, six separate UFO sightings were reported over the Santa Fe County area. In most cases, the UFOs were described as "intensely bright lights" moving at high speeds, and at other times, hovering in place.

A similar report of bright unexplained lights occurred one year later. On November 19, 1972, an anonymous college professor and several other witnesses observed a group of seven unexplained anomalous lights hovering over the city of Albuquerque.[65]

TRUCKER CHASED BY UFO

As mentioned, New Mexico has generated a large number of UFO-car chases. The following case is a good example. On the evening of January 12, 1973, a 40-year-old married, female truck-driver was driving along Highway 44 southeast of Farmington when she saw a "large bright light" which appeared seemingly from nowhere. Says the witness,

> IT FOLLOWED MY EIGHTEEN-WHEELER FOR ONE TO TWO MINUTES... IT WASN'T A PAIR OF HEADLIGHTS, ONLY ONE LIGHT, AND FAR TOO INTENSE IN BRIGHTNESS. WHEN I FIRST NOTICED IT, IT WAS APPROXIMATELY TWO MILES BEHIND ME. IT APPROACHED ME WITH GREAT SPEED, WITHIN ONE-FOURTH A MILE OF MY TRUCK IN ONE TO TWO SECONDS. THE LIGHT WAS SO WHITE THAT IT SEEMED BLUE.

As quickly as it appeared, the light disappeared, leaving the truck-driver stunned and amazed enough to report her sighting to NUFORC twenty-five years later.[66]

INTRUSIONS AT KIRTLAND AFB

Of all the Air Force Bases in New Mexico, one of the most visited is Kirtland AFB. On November 6, 1973, a security policeman at Kirtland Air Force Base East observed a large glowing object hover over the nuclear weapons inspection facility at Manzano labs. The officer described the object as a flattened sphere about 150 feet in diameter, golden in color, and totally silent. As the object hovered a mere 100 feet over Plant Number Three, the security officer alerted nine other air policemen, each of whom observed the object from various vantage points.

As news of the intruder spread across the base, four F-101 Voodoo interceptors from the 150th Fight Group of the New Mexico Air National Guard were scrambled to chase after the object. However, before the jets could approach, the object moved to the east at treetop level over the Manzano Mountains and into the distance. The incident was later investigated by researcher R. C. Hecker, an investigator for APRO. Writes Hecker,

> I INTERVIEWED ONE OF THE POLICEMEN WHO OBSERVED THE OBJECT. HE RECEIVED WORD OF THE OBJECT'S LOCATION WHEN THE ALARM WAS SOUNDED OVER HIS TRANSCEIVER... HE SAID THAT MILITARY OFFICIALS WERE UPSET BY THE INCIDENT.

Hecker says that the witness demanded anonymity as it was made clear to them that the incident officially had not occurred. The witness also had access to the intelligence briefs on the base and says that all information concerning the incident had been censored from the reports.

One year later, on April 15, 1974, a couple living on the northern edge of the Manzano Laboratory area observed a disk-like object at least 50 feet in diameter. It moved at an altitude of 2,000 feet and appeared to be rotating on its axis. The witnesses heard no sound and saw no visible mean of propulsion.

Just over one month later, the area would experience an apparent UFO crash/retrieval incident.[67]

UFOS OVER CANNON AFB

In 1976, a series of UFO sightings over Cannon Air Force Base in Clovis caused deep concern at high levels. On January 21, 1976, at 4:55 a.m., security police at the base observed two glowing objects hovering near the flight line on the base. The objects were each twenty-five yards in diameter, gold or silver in color, with a blue light on top, a hole in the middle and a red light on the bottom. The Air Force launched an investigation, checking into weather data and any radar evidence. The sighting was eventually reported to the National Military Command Center (NMCC) in Washington, D.C., where it was recorded in a memorandum by Rear Admiral J. B. Morin, the Deputy Director for Operations at the NMCC.

The objects over Cannon were also seen by a large number of Clovis residents. One was Scott Price, a journalism student at New Mexico University who took a photo of a "tubular-shaped craft" that performed strange maneuvers above Clovis.

High School senior Steve Muscato was on the top floor of the Clovis Hotel when he spotted the object.

The next day, on January 22, 1976, the UFOs were back. The strange objects again appeared over Cannon AFB, which scrambled jets to investigate them. The objects reportedly easily evaded the jets, darting at 90-degree angles and accelerating at very high speeds.

On January 23, the UFOs came back for a third night in a row. Shortly after the objects appeared, the Clovis police station received an enormous flood of calls. To police dispatcher Diana Kenemore, it seemed that "nearly everyone" in Clovis called in to report UFOs. Says Kenemore,

> THAT MANY PEOPLE CAN'T BE WRONG. THEY ALL SAW THEM AT THE SAME TIME. PLUS OUR OFFICERS SAW THEM. EVERY CITIZEN THAT CALLED WAS REAL WILLING TO GIVE HIS NAME, ADDRESS AND PHONE NUMBER.

According to the Clovis police, there were more than thirty reports made between nightfall and midnight. Kenemore says that several callers reported seeing a group of twenty objects hovering over the Sandia Elementary School in the north part of the city.

Around the same time, Town Marshall Willie Ronquillo of the nearby town of Texaco received a UFO report, and going outside to investigate, observed an object – totally silent – hovering at an altitude of 900 feet directly above the town. The object glowed with green, yellow, and blue lights. When it moved northward, he chased the object, and heard several other police officers reporting their observations of the same object.

A *Clovis News Journal* staff writer viewed no less than twenty-three objects sliding in and out of formation, moving across the Clovis sky. A group of state police officers reported one of the last sightings of the evening. They observed a single object moving at a high rate of speed, heading towards Tucumcari.

By this time, the objects were front-page news and the talk of the town. Says Steve Muscato,

EVERYBODY WAS EXCITED ABOUT IT. ALL THE MAJOR NETWORKS WERE IN TOWN, AND THEY WERE ALL ON TOP OF HOTEL CLOVIS.

Various UFO groups descended upon the town in hopes of seeing the UFOs for themselves, though it appeared that the mini-wave of activity was over. A spokesman from Reese AFB, 90 miles east of Clovis, said that nothing unusual had been picked up on their radar. Officials from Cannon AFB in Clovis were less forthcoming. Major Bert Rhoton (the command post controller for the day) did tell reporters that the base had received numerous inquiries from citizens about the recent sightings, but that "as far as the military is concerned, it is strictly no comment."

Researcher Brian Vike was later able to interview several servicemen from Cannon AFB who worked there at the time. Each of them reported seeing unknown objects over the base throughout the entire month. One serviceman observed more than a dozen UFOs using a Starlight Scope. The serviceman told Vike,

FLIGHT OPS WAS CONCERNED ENOUGH TO SCRAMBLE TWO F-111's TO GIVE CHASE.

Another serviceman (a Vietnam veteran who worked as an aircraft repairman) reported to NUFORC that he was stationed at Cannon in January of 1976 and was present during the incidents. He watched the jets scrambled after the "bogeys." He spoke with the radar operator. Says the officer,

HE SAID HE HAD NEVER SEEN ANYTHING LIKE THIS. THE BOGEYS WOULD APPEAR AND DISAPPEAR, SEEMING WITHOUT CAUSE AND WOULD OCCASIONALLY MOVE AT INCREDIBLE SPEEDS OVER AND NEAR THE BASE.

Then he made the mistake of calling the radar shack again and asking about the bogeys. A man answered, identified himself as a Captain, and proceeded to threaten and curse at the witness, saying,

THERE WERE NO BOGEYS AND NO SCRAMBLE... WHAT YOU ARE TALKING ABOUT NEVER HAPPENED. YOU ARE A LYING [?!] AND I CAN PROVE IT. I'LL HAVE YOU BUSTED. I WILL BE WATCHING YOUR EVERY MOVE, AIRMAN. YOU ARE NOT TO MENTION A WORD OF THIS TO ANYONE, EVER. AM I CLEAR?!

"Yes, sir," he responded.

Later he researched the name of the Captain, but was unable to find any such person stationed at the base. A few days after the incident, he himself witnessed two "disk-shaped" craft while driving along Highway 60 late at night. He also interviewed a family of five who observed "silver disks" hovering over the behind their Clovis home.

A few days after the main sightings, *Clovis News Journal* reporters discovered that a local rancher had found "an unexplained circle" burned into the ground on his ranch. The rancher also allegedly found a "cylindrical object of unknown origin" in the grass nearby, though nothing is said about what became of this object.

According to a serviceman interviewed by Brian Vike, there were several burned circles found in the rancher's field. He said each of the circles was about thirty feet in diameter and in the center of one, there was a dead cow which had been mutilated. The serviceman said he was interviewed by an agent from Washington, D.C. regarding the events.

Later, UFO researcher Ray Stanford examined the photographs taken by Scott Price and concluded that they showed Saturn, though he admitted that the sightings themselves were likely valid.

When contacted about the incidents thirty years later, the deputy chief of Cannon Public Affairs, 1st Lieutenant James Nichols said that the base had "no information" about the sightings.

Researcher Richard Dolan researched some of the above events and came away convinced of their authenticity. As he writes, "It appears something strange was going on in eastern New Mexico."[68]

SIX 1978 ENCOUNTERS

On the afternoon of April 15, 1978, two sisters were visiting their friend's house in Albuquerque. They were standing in the backyard when one of them saw something red floating in the western sky. She turned to look and noticed it was moving in their direction. Says one of the sisters,

> I COULD TELL THAT IT WAS MAYBE NO LARGER THAN THE HOUSE. IT WAS RED, VERY RED, LIKE IT WAS PULSATING... IT STOPPED ABOVE THE POWER LINES, ABOUT FIFTY FEET ABOVE US. IT WAS THEN THAT MY HALF-SISTER SAW IT AS WELL. I REMEMBER THAT IT JUST HOVERED, AND SEEMED TO MAKE A DULL, LOW THROBBING SOUND.

Her half-sister ran inside to get their parents. Meanwhile, the other sister remained outside gazing at the object, which she felt "seemed to be looking at me." When the others came out to view the object, it zipped back and forth then shot straight up.

Also in April 1978, a family (residents of Farmington) was sitting on their porch after midnight when one of the sisters noticed three circular objects above the foothills behind their home. At the same time, their radio became filled with static. Says one of the siblings,

> MY SISTER TOLD US TO LOOK AT THESE CRAZY THINGS ABOVE THE HILLS. AS WE ALL WATCHED THEM, IT APPEARED AS IF THEY WERE PERFORMING SOME KIND OF ODD BALLET IN THE SKY. THEY KEPT DARTING BACK AND FORTH HORIZONTALLY...BUT WE WERE WONDERING HOW THEY KEPT FROM HITTING EACH OTHER AS THEY SEEMED TO DART IN AND OUT OF EACH OTHER.

They kept watching the object for about ten minutes, at which point the objects began to move to the right and then upwards at a 45-degree angle, disappearing into outer space.

On July 3, 1978, at 12:05 a.m., several Taos residents reported seeing a glowing orange disk hovering at a low altitude over their neighborhood about three miles northwest of Taos. One witness, Mrs. Elias Vargas said,

> I HAD JUST GONE TO BED AND SUDDENLY THE ROOM LIT UP WITH A BRIGHT ORANGE LIGHT... I WENT TO THE WINDOW AND OPENED IT AND I COULD HEAR A KIND OF CRACKLING NOISE. THE LIGHT WAS SO BRIGHT I COULD SEE FOR SOME DISTANCE. AT FIRST I THOUGHT THE NEIGHBOR'S HOUSE WAS ON FIRE, SO I WENT TO THE OTHER WINDOW. I SAW THIS FORM – IT WASN'T A DEFINITE FORM – BUT IT WAS ROUNDISH AND ABOUT AS BIG AS TWO CARS, MAYBE BIGGER. BY THEN IT WASN'T ORANGE ANYMORE; IT WAS SORT OF A GRAY COLOR. IT STAYED FOR ABOUT TWO MINUTES. I RUSHED INTO ANOTHER BEDROOM AND OPENED THE DRAPES, AND IT TOOK OFF TO THE NORTH AND DISAPPEARED IN TWO SECONDS. ALL YOU COULD SEE WAS A RED LIGHT. IT HAPPENED SO FAST I GOT REAL SCARED. I DON'T THINK I WENT TO SLEEP UNTIL FIVE IN THE MORNING.

Mrs. Vargas saw the object hover between her house and the neighbor's home. Unknown to Vargas, the neighbors also saw the object, as did the occupants of another neighboring house. All the witnesses watched the object first hover directly above a 500-gallon fuel tank and then over a pick-up truck. After the object left, a strange powdery residue was found on the truck. Samples collected and sent for analysis showed an abnormally high level of magnesium and potassium.

Later, local Taos rancher Manuel Gomez and cattle-mutilation researcher Gabe Valdez would discover that some of Valdez's cattle had been marked with a similar substance composed of magnesium and potassium, providing a possible link between UFOs and mutilations. (See Chapter Ten on mutilations.)

Less than two weeks later, on July 13, an anonymous woman was driving a half-mile from Canjilon Junction when she saw a huge blimp-shaped object move slowly across the road in front of her at an altitude of about 500 feet. It had a blue light on one end and a red light on the other. About eight portholes or lights lined the circumference. Most odd was the way the object was "hugging" the landscape, moving up and down, as if it had a height governor that kept it at an exact altitude above the ever-changing landscape. The witness was "terrified" by the encounter, and is convinced that she encountered a genuine UFO.

Four months later, on November 17, 1978, four hunters at Ojo Caliente were at their campsite, around 8:45 p.m., when they saw a cigar-shaped object fly at an altitude of 600 feet over the campsite. The object was lit-up with bright orange lights.

Two weeks later, in early December, guide Joe Lucero was on the Jicarilla Apache Indian Reservation when he saw a yellow-orange cigar-shaped object swoop down and hover over Horse Lake. He was able to observe the object through a pair of binoculars.[69]

BEAMED BY A UFO

On the evening of January 15, 1979, a family of four was driving along Interstate 40 near Tijera. They had been on vacation and were now on their way home to Albuquerque. To the left side of the road, they saw a large tower, lit up with lights. As they got closer, they were shocked to see that there were "three spinning flashing lights" circling around the tower.

"Is that a helicopter?" the mother asked.

"Maybe," said the father. "But, what? I don't know. It's too windy. I don't know what it is."

As they got closer, it was clear the object was not a helicopter. It was very windy that day, and yet the object was moving up and down in a perfectly straight line. Nor was there any sound.

Says one of the witnesses (he was nine-years-old at the time),

> As we were passing the tower station, the object leisurely and effortlessly moved and began to follow the highway; particularly our white suburban truck. At this point, my mother began to flip out and begged my father to get off the highway, but we just kept driving.
>
> This is where the events of this night become weird. As we were driving, the craft took up position above our truck and started to flash bright flashes of directed light into our vehicle... They were brighter than any police or emergency vehicle or anti-collision light I have ever seen.

The witness felt the lights were being directed at him, and said that the lights flashed in sequence, including: yellow, red, blue, and green, then, blue, red, green, and blue. After a few moments, the object floated slowly away to the east, then shot straight upward and disappeared out of sight.

More than thirty years later, the witness finally reported his sighting, writing,

> My current vocation is a licensed and soon to be ordained Pastor. There is a big risk for me to even speak out of these events, but they must be told."[70]

LIGHT SHOW OVER STONE LAKE

At precisely 9:30 p.m. on September 12, 1979, residents of Stone Lake on the Jicarilla Apache Reservation observed a "strange light show" put on by several unidentified flying objects. There was a celebration that day, and numerous people observed the lights.

The very next day, also at exactly 9:30 p.m., the lights returned and put on a repeat performance.

Also on that day, two game officers were on duty in search of poachers when their vehicle was targeted by a yellow spotlight coming from an object above them. At the same time, several other residents in the area reported seeing what they thought was a helicopter, except it emitted no sound and had no running lights.[71]

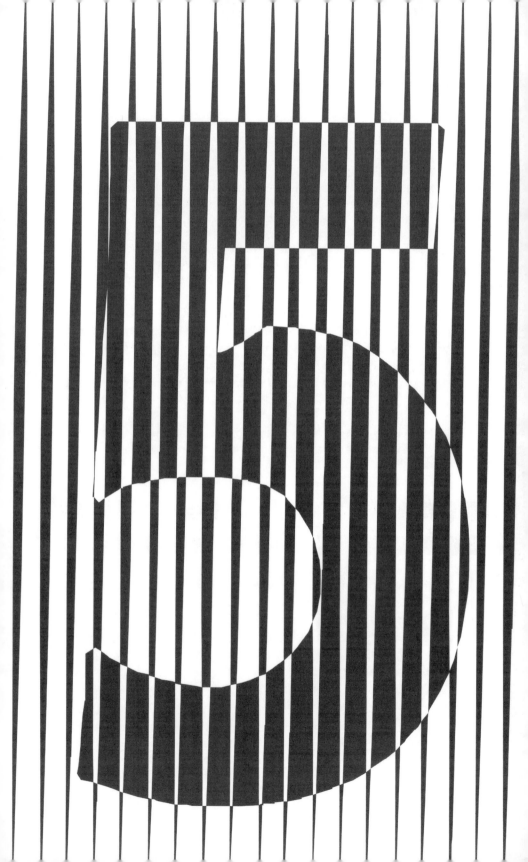

CHAPTER 5

Sightings:1980-1989

The sightings of the 1980s followed the same pattern of previous decades, with a wide variety of reports. Most of the sightings involved what are variously described as unexplained lights. Of course there are the usual UFO-car chases, photographic cases, UFO beams and other regularly reported UFO phenomena. Like the 1970s, the only sightings to receive publicity were those involving numerous witnesses. Even then, the sightings were printed almost exclusively in smaller local newspapers, failing to receive national attention. Again, as in the previous decade, attention had shifted to the rising reports of UFO landings, abductions, and the growing cattle mutilation problem.

UFO PHOTOGRAPHED OVER CARLSBAD CAVERNS

One of New Mexico's most popular tourist attractions are the massive Carlsbad Caverns located in the southern section of the state. In January of 1980, Harold Bordersfeld (a resident of Cleveland, Ohio) was visiting the caverns. He was at the mouth of the caverns and three other couples were coming up the path behind him. Suddenly one of the women shouted out for everyone to look at the sky. Says Bordersfeld, "I looked up and there it was crossing from left to right."

It – the object – appeared to be a classic flying saucer. It was circular, metallic-looking, with a darker circle in the center. It moved "real slow," so Bordersfeld quickly grabbed his camera, re-set the f-stop and snapped a photo.

Says Bordersfeld,

> WE GATHERED IN A GROUP, NOBODY WANTED TO WALK CLOSER.... IT WAS JUST HOVERING THERE, AND THEN IT TURNED RED AND WENT STRAIGHT UP... THE RED BOTTOM GLOW WASN'T THERE AT FIRST, BUT THEN IT GOT REAL BRIGHT. BEFORE I COULD TAKE ANOTHER PICTURE, IT LEFT. STRAIGHT UP.

The group of seven tourists was deeply impressed and went to report their sighting. They soon learned the power of skepticism. Says Bordersfeld,

> VERY EXCITED, WE – SEVEN OF US – FOUND A RANGER TO REPORT WHAT WE SAW. HE SAID IT WAS MOST LIKELY A CLUSTER OF BIRDS. OF COURSE I COULDN'T SHOW HIM THE PICTURE BUT OFFERED TO SIGN A REPORT AND SEND THE PICTURE LATER WHEN I GOT IT DEVELOPED. HE WASN'T AT ALL INTERESTED.

Later, Bordersfeld sent his photo to researchers Ed Walters and Bruce Maccabee, who analyzed the photograph and believe it to be genuine. When analyzing photographs, the researchers required that three qualifications be met for the photograph to be considered for analysis. First, the photo must show that the object has a "structure that is clearly of an unconventional nature." Second, the photo must show the object "interacting with its surroundings." And third, the location of the photograph also gives clues as to its authenticity. Bordersfeld's photo fulfilled all three qualifications.

Writes Walters and Maccabee,

SO WHAT WE HAVE IS AN AMAZING PHOTOGRAPH, ONE IN WHICH ALL THREE OF MY RULES FOR AUTHENTICATION ARE SATISFIED. THE UFO'S SHAPE IS STRUCTURALLY UNCONVENTIONAL. THE UFO'S BLAZING RED POWER SOURCE IS INTERACTING WITH THE ATMOSPHERE. PLUS THE ENTRANCE TO CARLSBAD CAVERN IS AN UNLIKELY IF NOT IMPOSSIBLE PLACE TO FABRICATE A HOAX. BASED ON THE PHOTOGRAPH I HAVE CONCLUDED THAT THIS IS A VERY RELIABLE UFO ENCOUNTER...[72]

LIGHTS OVER ESPANOLA

On February 18, 1980, the State Police in Arroyo Seco received two separate reports of weird lights over Espanola. The first call came at 6:10 p.m. from a woman who said that she had used binoculars to observe a bright yellow light with a red ball on it flying up and down over the city. The witness said the object appeared to be rotating.

An hour and a half later, a second caller reported seeing a "white glowing object" moving in a circular pattern. Patrolman Thomas Vaccarello was sent to investigate, but did not see anything unusual.[73]

UFO FOLLOWS TWO TANKER TRUCKS

In the summer 1980, James Bass (a truck driver) was on a job involving the transportation of hydrochloric acid to an oil field location west of Eunice, New Mexico. He and his partner, George W., (who drove a separate truck) finished loading their 3,000-gallon tankers around midnight. They then set off in convoy down the highway, with George taking the lead.

Because of the delicate nature of their cargo, and because the roads were narrow, they drove at a modest thirty miles per hour. A few hours later found them in the New Mexico desert, about halfway to their location.

Suddenly, George slammed on the brakes to his truck and jumped out, frantically motioning for Bass to do the same.

Bass jumped out, at which point his friend pointed to the sky behind them and said, "Look at that! I saw it in my mirror as I was checking on you. What the hell is that thing?"

Bass looked at where his friend was pointing and saw "a bright pea-green orb hovering motionless about 30 feet above a power-line pole, 100 feet or so away. The object was nearly even with the top of the pole. The light from the ball was so intense the entire area was reflecting a vivid green hue."

The ball had the apparent size of two full moons (Bass estimated about twenty feet in diameter) and was staying perfectly still in the sky. At this point, George W. became frightened and suggested they leave the area.

Both men jumped back into their tanker trucks and raced away from the scene. They increased their speed to forty miles per hour, but to their shock, the green orb followed them, lighting up the highway bright green behind them. Says Bass,

IT WAS PRETTY CLEAR THE THING WAS FOLLOWING US AND GETTING CLOSER.

Was the UFO interested in their cargo? Bass wasn't sure. The truckers increased their speed again. Bass was hesitant to go much faster, for fear of causing the hydrochloric acid to explode. At that point, says Bass,

SUDDENLY, I NOTICED THE SHADOWS INSIDE MY CAB BEGINNING TO GET MORE INTENSE AND THE GREEN LIGHT WAS VERY BRIGHT AROUND ME, MAKING THE ORANGE PAINT OF MY TRUCK APPEAR A GRIM, BROWNISH-GREEN COLOR. I WAS STARTLED WHEN THE GREEN BALL SHOT PAST MY WINDOW AT A SPEED OF SEVENTY MILES PER HOUR... THE OBJECT RAPIDLY OVERTOOK GEORGE'S TRUCK, DROPPING DOWN TO AN ALTITUDE OF ONLY TEN FEET ABOVE THE ROADWAY. IT SLOWED A BIT NEAR HIS TRUCK, SEEMING TO PACE HIM FOR A FEW SECONDS, THEN SUDDENLY CLIMBED AT AN AMAZING RATE OF SPEED, GETTING RAPIDLY SMALLER IN SIZE UNTIL IT WAS COMPLETELY OUT OF SIGHT IN ONLY A FEW SECONDS.

The two truckers continued driving until they reached their destination. They quickly hooked up the hoses and unloaded their cargo into the storage tanks. Neither of the gentlemen discussed the object for some time, and were afraid of being ridiculed. Says James Bass,

AFTER ALL, BOTH OF US COULD HARDLY BELIEVE IT HAPPENED, EITHER. BUT EVER SINCE THEN, I HAVE BEEN A STRONG BELIEVER THAT UFOS ARE REAL AND ARE CONTROLLED BY SOME SORT OF INTELLIGENT ENTITY.[74]

UFOS OVER RADIO TELESCOPE

Located between Magdalena and Datil, along Highway 60, stands the famous VLA (Very Large Array) radio telescope. It consists of 27 dishes, each 82 feet in diameter. Constructed in 1980, it cost more than 78 million dollars.

One afternoon in 1982, Loretta Hargis (an employee of the U.S. Department of Agriculture) was driving west on Highway 60, next to the VLA. Her two children were in the car.

Hargis describes what happened next:

> I LOOKED IN MY LEFT REAR VIEW MIRROR AND I SAW A LARGE SILVER OBJECT OVER THE TREES, SORT OF PARALLEL TO THE HIGHWAY... I COULD SEE IT VERY WELL, A SORT OF BRUSHED STAINLESS STEEL AGAINST A GRAY/BLUE SKY IN THE EAST.

Puzzled, Hargis looked at her mirror again, but the object was gone. Thinking that perhaps a plane was coming in for a crash-landing, she turned around and was surprised to the see the object again. Says Hargis,

> IT WAS NOW CLOSER AND NOT LIKE ANY PLANE I HAD EVER SEEN; NO WINGS, NO TAIL AND NO MOTORS. IT WAS VERY LARGE AND SEEMED TO BE GAINING.

Hargis wasn't sure if the object was following her, as there were other cars on the highway, but the object appeared to pace her car about one block behind. By this time, both her children were watching the object with great excitement.

The area was thick with pine trees. When the road opened up, Hargis pulled over to park. As she and her children exited their vehicle, the drivers of three other cars also pulled over to observe the approaching object. There was a group of nearly a dozen people when the object came alongside them, stopping about one block away, where it remained hovering with a strange "wobbling" motion. The small crowd watched in stunned silence.

Says Hargis,

> IT WAS ONE OF THOSE UFOS... IT WAS ROUND, PERFECTLY ROUND, AND I COULD SEE LITTLE RED LIGHTS UNDER THE RIM...SORT OF LIKE AN INVERTED PIE TIN, DOMED.

She estimates that it was 100 feet in diameter.

After about five minutes the UFO moved slowly to the southwest over the VLA, then accelerated and disappeared from view over Horse Mountain. As far as Hargis knows, none of the witnesses ever officially reported the sighting. Hargis told only family members until being interviewed by researcher Art Campbell.

Says Campbell,

> I CAN PERSONALLY VOUCH FOR THE LADY WHO HAD THE SIGHTING. LORETTA IS A LOCAL PERSON WHO HAS SPENT HER LIFE IN THE AREA AND KNOWS THE MOODS OF THE WEATHER AND OTHER FACTORS THAT MIGHT AFFECT THIS INCIDENT. SHE IS A PERSONAL FRIEND OF MINE, AND EXTREMELY RELIABLE.

Another interesting 1982 sighting occurred in Alamogordo to a gentleman who prefers to remain anonymous. The witness was standing in his front yard looking at the evening sky when he saw a "very fast-moving dark, large cigar-shaped object flying north to south without making a sound."

He estimated that the object was about 2,000 feet high. He describes the object:

> THERE WAS NO VAPOR TRAIL OR TAIL-LIGHT EMISSION, BUT IT SEEMED TO HAVE A ROW OF DIM LIGHTS ALONG ITS CENTRAL AXIS.

The witness was drinking a beer at the time and thought to himself, "This is some potent stuff!" He went inside and didn't tell his wife or 10-year-old daughter.

But the next day, around the same time in the evening, he found himself again in the front yard staring at the sky. This time, his wife and daughter were with him. He told them what he saw the previous night and pointed to the location in the sky. Says the witnesses,

> AS I POINTED TO THE LOCATION WHERE I FIRST SPOTTED THE THING – UNBELIEVABLY – THERE IT CAME AGAIN! SAME DIRECTION, SAME FLIGHT PATH AND ELEVATION, SAME SPEED. ZIP, AND IT WAS OUT OF SIGHT. ALL THREE OF US SAW IT THIS TIME. MY DAUGHTER ASKED ME, 'DAD, WHAT WAS IT?'

"Beat's me," he told her.[75]

UFO OVER CHIMAYO

On April 24, 1984, more than thirty-four people from Medanales to Truchas observed a large unknown object hovering and moving slowly over the mountains near the Rio Grande Valley. The sightings began at 7 p.m. and continued for about twenty-five minutes.

Among the first-known witnesses were Mel and Diane Medina who said the object "looked like a commercial liner coming in for a landing." They said it appeared to move in spurts and would occasionally hover in place. It gave off a low humming noise. They observed the object through binoculars, saying that it was football-shaped and appeared to be "scouting the skies."

Multiple other witnesses up and down the area also saw the UFO as it cruised over Truchas Peaks and disappeared into the distance. Researchers later learned that a KC-135 refueling tanker was flying nearby, but was never actually over Truchas. The identity of the object remains unknown.[76]

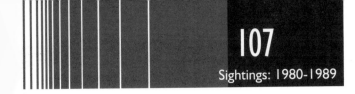

UFO CAT AND MOUSE GAMES

As we have seen, UFOs sometimes play strange cat and mouse games with motorists. The following case is yet another example. On July 15, 1982, a mother and her two daughters were traveling from California to Texas. At around 2 a.m., they were still two hours distant from El Paso, driving through the New Mexico desert. Her daughters were asleep in the back seat.

The mother had been driving for many hours, and was now very tired and struggling to stay awake. Suddenly, she heard a soft whirring/humming noise coming from outside. Says the witness,

> I GLANCED OUT THE WINDOW AND SAW THIS OBJECT HOVERING ABOVE MY CAR, JUST A FEW FEET ABOVE US. THERE WAS A ROW OF LIGHTS ALONG ITS CYLINDRICAL SIDE. THEY WERE SOFT, BLINKING LIGHTS; TWINKLING MORE THAN BLINKING, NOTHING GARISH ABOUT THEM.

The mother was then shocked to see the object take off at a sharp angle, flip on its side and disappear with a soft whooshing sound.

Moments later, it reappeared on the other side of the car. She leaned over and looked at it, and it flipped over to her side of the car again. Says the witness,

> THE AIRCRAFT FOLLOWED MY CAR, PLAYING WITH ME, DASHING FROM ONE SIDE OF THE CAR TO THE OTHER, HOVERING IN FRONT OF ME, AND FOLLOWING ALONG BEHIND, FOR ABOUT 20 MILES. WHEN IT TOOK OFF, I HEARD THE SOFT WHOOSH AND WATCHED AS IT DISAPPEARED IN THE NIGHT SKY.

The witness felt a wave of "sadness" when the UFO left. Strangely, she looked in the back see to find her daughters wide awake and "completely refreshed." They had observed the entire incident. The mother realized she too was no longer sleepy, and the little family drove happily to El Paso. They never felt any fear. Following the sighting, both her daughters lost all memory of the event. The mother, however, says,

> I REMEMBER IT AS CLEARLY AS IF IT HAPPENED YESTERDAY. I WISH I COULD HAVE THANKED THEM.[77]

A MUSICAL UFO

In late 1984, Tammy Standish (not her real name) and her friend were staying together in a roughly hewn cabin located in the wilderness outside of Santa Fe. The cabin had no electricity, no lights, no central heat and no running water. Except for the telephone and the road, it was completely isolated.

Although it was not an easy place to live, both women were in their thirties and enjoyed the experience of living with nature away from all signs of civilization. It was only a few months after they had been living there as roommates when something happened that made them suspect that they weren't as alone as they thought they were.

One evening after dark, near the end of the year, both women saw a strange flash of light outside the cabin, followed by a strange computer-like lyrical noise. Says Tammy,

> MY ROOMMATE HAD BEEN PRESENT IN THE HOUSE WITH ME, AND SHE HEARD IT ALSO. IT WAS REALLY LATE, AND WE HEARD THIS MUSIC, AND WE ALSO SAW A LITTLE FLASH OF LIGHT ON THAT NIGHT…WHAT WE LIKENED IT TO IS A CAR HEADLIGHT. SHE THOUGHT SOMEBODY WAS JOKING WITH US, JUST DROVE A CAR UP. AND I WOULD ALWAYS ARGUE WITH HER, "WELL, HOW COULD THEY JUST DRIVE IT UP AND DRIVE AWAY WITHOUT US HEARING THE AUTOMOBILE?"

"Well, then it was just somebody with a flashlight," her roommate replied.

It was the strange music-like sound, however, that had both of the women mystified. Says Tammy,

> THERE WAS A VERY DISTINCTIVE SOUND WHICH WAS VERY CHEERFUL, VERY COMPUTER-LIKE IN TERMS OF IT SOUNDED LIKE THE NOISES THAT YOU MAKE WHEN YOU PUSH A PHONE BUTTON OR A COMPUTER CALCULATOR. EVEN THOUGH IT FELT KIND OF AUTOMATED, IT WAS VERY LYRICAL, AND VERY PRETTY — A VERY HAPPY SOUND.

After it occurred, Tammy turned to her roommate and asked jokingly, "Did you hear that?"

Her roommate, who was skeptical of all things paranormal just laughed and said, "Ah, it's just, you know…" her voice trailed off.

The more she thought about it, however, Tammy realized the incident was unexplainable. She began to argue with her roommate, saying, "This is an intense thing. This is really weird."

Her roommate just shook her head and said, "No, no, no."

The two roommates agreed to disagree and life continued as normal. Several months later, in September 1985, Tammy's roommate moved out of the cabin. For the next few weeks, Tammy remained completely holed-up in the cabin.

Then, one evening in October 1985, the musical UFO returned. Tammy had just begun to fall asleep when she was woken up by the same computer-like sound she had heard months earlier. Again, it was coming from outside the cabin.

Says Tammy,

> I RECOGNIZED THE SOUND...AND WHEN I RECOGNIZED IT, I IMMEDIATELY WOKE UP, AND SAID KIND OF LAUGHINGLY, "ALL RIGHT, YOU GUYS. I KNOW YOU'RE BACK HERE. WHAT DO YOU WANT?" AND I WAS SORT OF LAUGHING AND TALKING OUT LOUD.

At this point, Tammy rolled over onto her back and looked out the huge picture window at the far side of the room near the foot of her bed. What she saw next shocked her. Says Tammy,

> AT THAT TIME, THE LIGHT REAPPEARED, ONLY THIS TIME, IT WAS NOT A BRIEF FLICKER. IT WAS A VERY INTENSE, FAST-MOVING BRIGHT WHITE LIGHT. IT WAS PROBABLY HEADING SORT OF NORTH, AND IT CAME RUSHING TOWARDS THE WINDOW, AND THEN CAME INTO THE WINDOW AND SORT OF JAMMED ME IN THE SOLAR PLEXUS. I DON'T KNOW HOW ELSE TO DESCRIBE IT EXCEPT TO SAY THAT IT FELT AND LOOKED AS IF IT HAD LITERALLY MOVED THROUGH THE WINDOW AND ZAPPED ME IN THE HEART.

At this point, Tammy says her body slowly became paralyzed and began to vibrate intensely. At first she remained lighthearted and unafraid, but very quickly the vibration began to increase, and she became frightened. Says Tammy,

> AFTER A CERTAIN AMOUNT OF VIBRATION, I BEGAN TO, OF COURSE, BE A LITTLE ALARMED. I DIDN'T FEEL AS IF I WAS IN CONTROL OF THE SITUATION ANY LONGER, AND THAT SOMETHING ELSE WAS CONTROLLING ME. AT THAT MOMENT, I THINK I BEGAN TO EXPERIENCE A LITTLE BIT OF FEAR. THE MINUTE THAT I BECAME AFRAID, IT VANISHED. IT KIND OF EVAPORATED.

After the experience, Tammy appeared to be fine. The object never returned.[78]

A TELEPATHIC SIGHTING

One day just before noon in July 1986, a resident of Las Vegas (in New Mexico) was driving into the town of Mora where he worked when he saw "something shiny in the sky." He pulled over and for a moment, believing he was observing a plane about to crash in the hillside to his right. When he saw that the object had no wings or tail, and that it was glowing, it became clear to him that it wasn't a plane. It fell out of the sky, and then stopped still, hovering at a low altitude in front of the hill.

Says the witness,

> THAT IS WHEN IT GOT REALLY STRANGE. I AM STANDING THERE WONDERING JUST WHAT THE HELL I WAS LOOKING AT WHEN I GET THE FEELING THAT IT IS WATCHING ME BACK. I CAN'T DESCRIBE THIS VERY WELL, BUT I WAS FLOODED WITH A FEELING OF DOING SOMETHING WRONG. THAT THING REALLY WAS LOOKING BACK AT ME! WHAT I REPORT NEXT SOUNDS FABULOUS EVEN TO ME AND I EXPERIENCED IT. I COULD SWEAR I HEARD A CONVERSATION IN MY HEAD BETWEEN TWO OR THREE DIFFERENT PEOPLE.

Voice one said: "We are being observed."
Voice two said: "It is not permitted to be observed."
Voice three said: "We must leave."
Says the witness,

> THEN THE OBJECT SEEMED TO ROTATE AND EITHER SHOT OFF AT AN INCREDIBLE SPEED OR WINKED OUT. IT WAS JUST THERE AND THEN IT SEEMED TO BE GONE IN THE DISTANCE. IT LEFT ME THERE SHAKING IN MY SNEAKERS.

The witness reported his sighting to NUFORC, pointing out that he had served in the army's Presidential Honor guard, and adding, "I am not making this up."[79]

UFO OVER MOUNT ARCHULETA

According to New Mexico-based researcher Linda Kerth, at 7:51 p.m. on October 23, 1988, a party of eight people (including State Police Officer Gabe Valdez and two research scientists) were hiking along the southern slopes of Mount Archuleta, five miles northwest of Dulce, and also the location of a rumored underground alien base. The group was researching these claims when they saw a bright object moving in a straight line from south to north. When the object reached the summit of Mount Archuleta, it suddenly stopped "dead in its tracks," became extremely bright and lit up "at least half the sky." At this point, the object appeared to "fold in on itself" and disappear.[80]

GOVERNMENT INTIMIDATES UFO WITNESS

At around 3 p.m. on February 11, 1989, Richard Sauder looked out the window of his apartment in northeast Albuquerque (a few miles north of Kirtland AFB) to admire the majesty of the nearby Sandia Mountains, whose peaks rise up to 10,000 feet on the outskirts of town. Suddenly, he saw something that looked peculiar moving beyond the mountains.

Says Sauder,

> A PERIODIC TO-AND-FRO MOVEMENT GOT MY ATTENTION. I QUICKLY HURRIED OUTSIDE FOR A BETTER VIEW. I DISCOVERED THAT THE FLASHING WAS CAUSED BY AN ELONGATED OBJECT UNDULATING, OR SCREWING ITS WAY THROUGH THE NORTHEAST SKY AT HIGH ALTITUDE. AS IT APPROACHED THE CREST OF THE SANDIAS I COULD SEE THAT IT WAS A LIGHT METALLIC HUE ON TOP, AND DARKER AND THICKER ON THE BOTTOM.

As the object wobbled, it appeared to change shape, and move closer towards Albuquerque. Suddenly, a much larger and brighter object appeared and followed the smaller flashing object. The two objects began to move overhead when the second larger object suddenly vanished. At this point, the smaller object stopped flashing, and turning eastward, moving at about sixty miles per hour over the Sandias. Again the object appeared to have changed shape. Says Sauder, "[I]t had a dark compact shape that contrasted sharply with its original appearance."

After the object disappeared, Sauder returned inside to call a friend and share his encounter. But events weren't over yet. While he spoke on the phone, two jet fighters from Kirtland AFB roared overhead and raced towards the Sandias.

Sauder looked outside and saw a small cluster of five glowing colored spheres appear over the northern end of the mountains. Says Sauder,

> TWO WERE GREEN, ONE A NICE DEEP BLACK, ONE RED AND THE REMAINING ONE AN IRIDESCENT LIGHT COLOR. THEY WERE CLEARLY VISIBLE AS THEY DELIBERATELY NAVIGATED THE POWERFUL UPDRAFTS THAT SWIRL AROUND THE SLOPES OF THE SANDIAS. THE MOUNTAIN AIR CURRENTS DID NOT DEFLECT THEM FROM A DIRECT COURSE TOWARDS THE SOUTHWEST. THEY DID NOT BOB, OR WEAVE AS BALLOONS DO, BUT SOARED ON TOWARDS METRO ALBUQUERQUE AT A STATELY PACE, GIVING ME AMPLE TIME TO OBSERVE THEIR BEHAVIOR. JUDGING BY THE RELATIVE SIZE OF THE MILITARY AND CIVILIAN AIRCRAFT THAT REGULARLY FLY THROUGH THE SAME AIRSPACE, THESE SPHERICAL OBJECTS, WHICH WERE ALL PRECISELY THE SAME SIZE, WERE ABOUT THIRTY-FIVE FEET IN DIAMETER. WHEN THEY REACHED A

POSITION OVER NORTHEAST ALBUQUERQUE, THE BLACK SPHERE ABRUPTLY VANISHED... WITHIN MOMENTS THE REMAINING FOUR OBJECTS MADE A COURSE CHANGE AND HEADED TOWARDS THE EAST-NORTHEAST AND OUT OF SIGHT OVER THE SANDIA MOUNTAINS.

Sauder was impressed by his sighting and reported it to a local researcher, who told him to call Kirtland AFB and report the sighting. Sauder called the public affairs office at the base and spoke with Sergeant Bernheisel. Sauder reported his sighting, and the sergeant promised to research his case and get back to him, and then encouraged him to also report his sighting to NUFORC. Sauder called NUFORC and left a message.

Some time later following the incident, his phone mysteriously malfunctioned. Says Sauder,

> IT BEGAN MAKING QUIET, ELECTRONIC CLICKING NOISES AGAINST AN ELECTRICAL HUM IN THE BACKGROUND.

Sauder called the phone company and had them fix the problem. Afterwards he called the company and asked them what the problem had been. Says Sauder,

> [I] WAS TOLD THAT THERE HAD BEEN A PROBLEM IN A RELAY THAT HAD CAUSED MY LINE TO BECOME CROSSED WITH SOMEONE ELSE'S.

Sauder wondered if reporting his sighting to Kirtland had caused his phone to be tapped. He called Sergeant Bernheisel to ask about his sighting. Says Sauder,

> WHEN HE CAME ON THE LINE, HE WAS A CHANGED MAN. GONE WAS THE FRIENDLY, OPEN MANNER OF THE PREVIOUS MONDAY. SERGEANT BERNHEISEL INFORMED ME THAT HE HAD DISCUSSED THE MATTER WITH HIS SUPERIORS AND THAT FROM NOW ON THE AIR FORCE POSITION ON THE MATTER WAS THAT IT WAS CLOSED AND WOULD NOT BE DISCUSSED FURTHER.

Sauder says that one week later, two men who identified themselves as police investigators showed up at his door. They were dressed as civilians, but had badges, which they showed to Sauder. They then began to interrogate him about whether or not he was harboring a fugitive. Sauder denied their accusation. Says Sauder,

> AFTER A FEW MINUTES OF POINTED QUESTIONS, THEY STERNLY ADMONISHED ME THAT IF THEY SUBSEQUENTLY DETERMINED THAT I WAS HARBORING A FUGITIVE I WOULD BE SUBJECT TO PROSECUTION FOR A FELONY OFFENSE AND WOULD BE IMPRISONED IN THE NEW MEXICO STATE PENITENTIARY.

Sauder was "puzzled" by the encounter, and wondered if the Air Force was responsible. Then one month later on March 11, 1989, another group of three objects appeared. Says Sauder,

THE OBJECTS, FLYING IN SINGLE-FILE FORMATION, SOARED OUT OF THE NORTH AT ABOUT 150 MPH AND CROSSED OVER EASTERN ALBUQUERQUE'S SUBURBAN SPRAWL AT AN ALTITUDE OF SEVERAL THOUSAND FEET, ON A SOUTHERLY HEADING.

The objects, says Sauder, were shaped like the space-shuttle without wings, though each appeared smaller than a jet-fighter. The objects were dark-colored and totally silent.

Around each of the three objects, says Sauder, were more objects.

THE REALLY UNUSUAL THING, AND THE THING THAT CAUSED MY EYE TO PICK THEM OUT IN THE FIRST PLACE, WAS THAT EACH OBJECT WAS SURROUNDED OR ENCIRCLED BY A SWARM OF DARK, CIRCULAR OR SPHERICAL OBJECTS THAT PACED IT AT THE SAME SPEED AND ALTITUDE BUT REMOVED AT A DISCREET DISTANCE OF ABOUT 30-40 FEET.

Sauder wondered if the objects might be military, and he called Kirtland base again. This time he spoke with Major Rust, who told him that he had no information about the sighting, and that even if he did, he would not be authorized to divulge it.

Sauder is convinced, however, that the objects he saw were not military. As he says,

ONE THING I DO KNOW: NONE OF THESE OBJECTS ARE CONVENTIONAL AIRCRAFT, WHETHER CIVILIAN OR MILITARY.

Sauder continued to research UFOs and related subjects. He later authored the book *UFOs and Underground Bases*.[81]

ORB STRIKES CAR

While extremely rare, there are a small handful of cases in which automobiles have collided with UFOs, such as the following example from 1989. The witness, Eric Eversole, was driving in the middle of the day along an unidentified New Mexico Highway with his girlfriend Tammy. Ahead of him in another car was his friend, Steve. Says Eversole,

> I SAW A METALLIC ORB OR SPHERE THE SIZE OF A BASKETBALL. IT FOLLOWED MY CAR FOR AWHILE… IT WOULD SKIP FROM BUSH TO BUSH, HOVERING ABOVE THE GROUND MAKING NO SOUND. SOMETIMES IT WOULD BE OUT IN THE OPEN. I WATCHED IT FOR ABOUT FIFTEEN MINUTES.

Eversole told his girlfriend Tammy to look at the object, but she thought he was kidding and she kept talking to Steve on their walkie-talkies. Eversole kept watching for the object. Says Eversole,

> AS I KEPT DRIVING THE ROUND METAL ORB SEEMED TO BE COMING TOWARDS MY CAR. ALL OF A SUDDEN, I SAW IT REAL CLEAR. IT KNEW I SAW IT AND I FELT IT IN MY MIND. I YELLED AT TAMMY TO LOOK REAL QUICK ON MY LEFT. BY THE TIME SHE LOOKED, IT HIT MY CAR. IT HIT MY CAR ON THE SIDE… I STOPPED THE CAR. THEN THE ORB WENT AROUND THE CAR AND CONTINUED THROUGH THE DESERT, HOVERING ABOVE THE GROUND. I WILL NEVER FORGET IT. IT PUT A BIG DENT IN MY CAR.

Tammy was shook up. She hadn't seen the orb and she wondered if perhaps a rock had struck their car. Eversole's friend Steve, however, said he caught a quick glimpse of a "round object" that darted in from the desert landscape and struck Eversole's vehicle.
Says Eversole,

> I SAW IT VERY CLEARLY. I KNOW WHAT I SAW. IT HAS BEEN BUGGING ME FOR YEARS.

The witness reported his collision with a UFO to both MUFON and NUFORC, saying that he believed the orb was extraterrestrial technology, and added again, "I will never forget it."[82]

UFO FLEET OVER CHIMAYO

On December 14, 1989, multiple residents across Chimayo reported seeing a formation of unknown aircraft fly at low altitude and slow speed over the city. The sightings began at 8 p.m. and continued for the next hour.

Among the first witnesses was a group of young Christmas carolers who saw "a string of lights, about ten in all" hovering above the city. The lights were totally silent and did not blink. As they watched, the object moved, then aimed a powerful laser-like beam of light into the sky.

At 8:10 p.m., a family from Hernandez observed four or five large triangular-shaped lights surrounded by seven or eight little ones moving overhead. Says the husband, "They looked like Christmas trees."

At 8:15 p.m., a man from Alcalde used binoculars to observe what he concluded were eight jets escorting a stealth bomber. He estimated that they were at an elevation of 2,000 feet over the city. Says the witness, "I saw it do a roll. It was definitely a Stealth bomber."

At around 8:30 p.m., a resident of Chimayo heard a strange wind-like sound, and looking up, saw seven lights moving across the sky. As he told reporters at the *Rio Grande Sun*,

> THEY WERE PRETTY LOW AND IT WAS SILENT, LIKE THE WIND... IT LOOKED LIKE A DARK SHADOW... I JUST WANTED TO CALL TO LET YOU KNOW THAT THOSE GIRLS [THE CHRISTMAS CAROLERS] AREN'T A BUNCH OF LIARS. MY FAMILY, ABOUT EIGHT OF US, SAW IT TOO.

Just prior to 9:00 p.m., Jennie Martinez of Dixon says that she, her daughter, April, and her mother, Irene saw about ten triangular-shaped lights, which they watched for about ten minutes.

Another witness, Virginia X., said she also observed the objects, one of which passed in front of the moon, revealing a shape like a jet.

Newspaper reporters contacted the FAA, and a spokesman said that he was unaware of anything over Chimayo that might be responsible for the UFO reports, other than the fact that there was a meteor shower the night before.[83]

LIGHTS OVER TRUTH OR CONSEQUENCES

Five days after the Chimayo sighting, on the evening of December 19, 1989, the Sierra County Sheriff's station of the town of Truth or Consequences began receiving calls from local residents reporting strange blue flashes of light in the sky. The office dispatcher, Theresa Tabler, said that the police station was flooded with calls for two and a half hours, each from residents reporting the weird blue lights. The calls came from a widespread area, including west of Pietown and Magdalena all the way east to White Sands.

Most reported flashes of light, though some reported that the lights moved across the sky or even hovered. One caller said he saw "something" hovering over Elephant Butte Lake.

After hearing all the calls, deputy Rudy Carey decided to get into a police patrol car and check it out. Says Carey,

> I WAS COMING OUT OF HIGHWAY 151 NEAR THE DAM SITE AND SAW A FLASH OF LIGHTNING. THEN I SAW A BIGGER FLASH WHILE IN MY POLICE VEHICLE SHORTLY AFTER 11 P.M.... [IT] HAD TO BE SOMETHING BIG WAY UP IN THE SKY — LIKE AN ELECTRICAL BLUISH ARC, LIKE LIGHTNING. ALL OF A SUDDEN IT WAS BRIGHT.

Deputy Carey checked out the Elephant Butte area, but didn't see any other strange lights.

However, the strange flashes hadn't stopped, and continued to manifest in other locations. Joe Kowbel was sitting in his Williamsburg home at around midnight when he saw an intensely brilliant blue light flash across the sky. Said Kowbel, "It lit up the sky all the way to Socorro."

Meanwhile, a trucker driver in Williamsburg saw a huge flash of light. Deputy Carey called other police stations and found that a sheriff's deputy in Socorro had also seen the lights.

Carey then made a series of calls to try and solve the mystery of the weird lights. He called the FAA in Albuquerque and they said at first that they had nothing unusual on their radar. He called NASA who denied having anything over the New Mexico skies. He called White Sands and spoke with Public Affairs Specialist Monte Marlin who assured the deputy that no rocket flights or other tests were being conducted. Then, at two minutes after midnight, the FAA called back the Sierra County Sheriff's Station, and said that the lights were meteors.

Deputy Carey, however, was somewhat skeptical of this explanation, and told reporter Bill Johnson, "That's what it could have been, but I'm not sure."

According to Deputy Carey, an FAA official later told him the Albuquerque Tracking Center had, in fact, picked up an object on their scopes which they could not identify, although they were able to track it across the sky.[84]

UFO AT FOUR CORNERS

Starting in the late 1980s, Pat Brown (a therapist from southern California) began having encounters with gray-type ETs. When the encounters continued, she decided to educate herself about the subject. She picked up several books about UFOs and discovered that there were several well-known UFO hotspots located across the United States. One of the books she read said that there

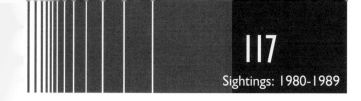

was "an alien space station at Four Corners." Intrigued by the idea of seeing an actual UFO, Pat and her friend Denise decided to drive to the area in the hopes of having an encounter.

In 1993, they headed out to the location. It was late evening when they finally arrived. They were driving along a desert highway in New Mexico when Pat noticed a strange light pacing their vehicle. She pointed it out to her friend, who also saw the light.

Says Pat,

> IT FOLLOWED US FOR ABOUT AN HOUR AND FIFTEEN MINUTES. WE KEPT LOOKING AT IT. IT WAS SPINNING, AND IT JUST FOLLOWED US ALONG THE ROAD. WE DIDN'T PASS A LOT OF CARS, BUT WE DID PASS AN OCCASIONAL CAR. I SAID, "WELL, DENISE, THEY DON'T SEEM TO BE REACTING TO THIS. ARE WE THE ONLY ONES WHO ARE SEEING THIS?"
>
> SHE SAID, "I DON'T KNOW."
>
> BUT NO ONE ELSE STOPPED. NO ONE DID ANYTHING. PEOPLE JUST DROVE NORMALLY. SO AFTER ABOUT AN HOUR, MAYBE AN HOUR AND TEN MINUTES, THE CAR STARTED GETTING VERY HOT. I SAID, "DENISE, I'M GETTING AFRAID."
>
> SHE SAID, "SO AM I!"
>
> I SAID, "WHAT'S HAPPENING?"
>
> SHE SAID, "I DON'T KNOW, BUT I FEEL IT!"

At this point, both Pat and Denise became very frightened. They were convinced that the object was somehow causing a strange heat effect in the interior of their vehicle. Whatever the object was, it was clearly interested in them. However, shortly after they became afraid, the object responded. Says Pat,

> ALL OF A SUDDEN, THE SHIP DROPPED BACK. IT DROPPED BACK TO WHERE – I CAN'T GAUGE THINGS – IT WAS REALLY FAR AWAY, BUT IT STILL FOLLOWED US UP THE ROAD. AND I SAID, "DO YOU THINK IT HEARD US?"

Pat is certain that she and her friend encountered an unconventional object. Says Pat,

> YOU COULD SEE A STRUCTURE AT TIMES... YOU COULD SEE THE FORM. YOU COULD TELL IT WASN'T REALLY LARGE. AND THE LIGHT MOVED AROUND, LIKE CIRCULAR, BUT THERE WAS ALSO THIS PANEL OF LIGHTS...SO EVERY NOW AND THEN, THE LIGHTS WERE CONSTANT, BUT EVERY NOW AND THEN, YOU WOULD SEE THIS SPINNING.

Following the encounter, Pat and Denise went back home. They had fulfilled the purpose for their trip. Pat was amazed by their success and wondered if the ETs had placed an implant in her body (during her earlier encounters) and were therefore able to track her wherever she went.[85]

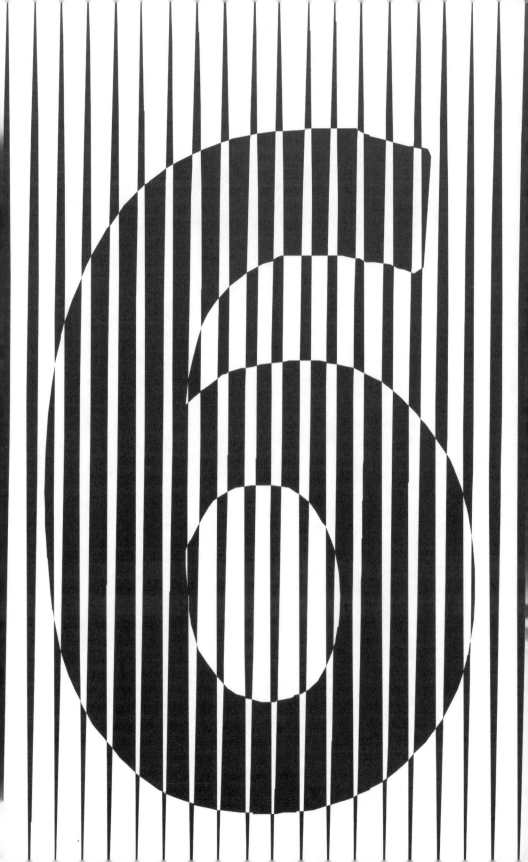

CHAPTER 6

Sightings:1990-1999

The 1990s brought a new batch of high profile cases, some of which received national media attention, while others received almost no publicity at all. The accounts of animal mutilations continued. And a new phenomenon – the Taos hum – manifested itself. Otherwise, the pattern exhibited in previous decades repeated itself with a steady stream of landings, abductions, and about a dozen prominent sightings. The second half of the decade produced most of the reports, a few of which eventually became very well known not only in the UFO community, but also in the mainstream press. Of course, the actual number of sightings is likely in the hundreds or even thousands as only a small minority of UFO witnesses ever report their sightings.

SHIPROCK PHOTOGRAPH

In 2007, UFO hunter Chris Miller was going through his old photographs from 1993 when he was surprised to come upon one that he had taken of Shiprock. To his amazement, he saw the photo contained a clear image of a white glowing sphere apparently swooping down at high speeds, darting across the sky. Miller calls the photo "an incredible capture, a one of a kind shot...simply fantastic." Miller had been taking photographs of UFOs for some time. From 1995 to 2000, he claims to have captured a total of 37 different sightings on video. In 1999, his footage appeared on the Fox Network television premiere of *UFOs: The Best Evidence Caught on Tape 2*. After discovering the Shiprock photo in 2007, he became inspired enough to send a copy of the photo to MUFON CMS. (See photo section on page 296).[86]

UFO PROBES TEENAGERS

On April 25, 1994, two junior high school students were standing in the backyard of one of their parents' houses at around 2 a.m. Says one of the friends,

OUT OF THE CORNER OF MY LEFT EYE I SAW A BALL OF LIGHT PERHAPS THE SIZE OF A BASKETBALL RAISE UP OVER THE FENCE. I TURNED QUICKLY TO FACE IT, BUT ALL I SAW WAS THE TRAIL OF LIGHT IT HAD LEFT BEHIND AS IT CAME TOWARDS US. I LOOKED BACK TOWARDS ADAM. HIS ARMS WERE RAISED...AND HE WAS LOOKING DOWN. I LOOKED DOWN AND I SAW THE TRAIL OF LIGHT THIS SPHERE HAD LEFT BEHIND AS IT MADE A FIGURE EIGHT AROUND US. WE ARE NOT SURE IF IT MADE THE FIGURE EIGHT AROUND US ONCE OR TWICE. WE THINK IT SHOT OFF ACROSS THE YARD AFTER THAT AND OVER THE FENCE TOWARDS THE PARK. THE OBJECT WAS MOVING SO FAST, IT WAS REALLY SOMETHING ELSE. THE ENTIRE EVENT TOOK TWO-THREE SECONDS.[87]

UFOS VIDEOTAPED OVER MIDWAY

On March 5, 1994, video producer Jose Escamilla was at his sister Becky's house in Roswell when she phoned him from the family home in Midway. She told Jose that she and their brother Manuel were observing what appeared to be an entire fleet of UFOs darting back and forth across the daylight sky over their property.

Jose was shocked. Over the past years, Becky had often told her family that she had seen UFOs darting around in the night sky over Midway. Her first sighting was in 1972 at age eight. She claims to have seen them regularly ever since. Jose, however, was skeptical and just assumed his sister was "wacko" and was seeing things. Now here she was, telling him to come over and see the objects for himself.

Jose, who was in the middle of filming a video, grabbed his camera and rushed back to Midway. When he arrived, he looked up and was amazed to see that his sister was right. A small group of glowing disk and dome-shaped objects were performing darting movements overhead. He quickly ruled out birds or planes. Says Jose, "This stuff is hauling way too fast."

He aimed his video camera at the objects and proceeded to tape seventeen minutes of footage. Much of the footage is blurry and unclear, however, several frames clearly show what appears to be unconventional flying craft darting back and forth across the sky. Jose believes that the objects are genuine UFOs, but stops short of calling them alien craft. As he says, "There's something up there. I just don't know what it is."

Becky Escamilla speculates that the display was not accidental. Says Becky, "Whoever they were, they wanted to be seen and they wanted to be captured on tape."

Over the next few months, the UFOs returned on several occasions. The Escamillas kept their video-cameras rolling for up to sixteen hours a day, eventually capturing more than 100 UFOs on film. After analyzing their videotape, some analysts estimated that the objects were moving at 2,000 miles per hour.

On July 14, 1994, the UFOs returned. The Escamilla family was in their home in Midway when somebody shouted out that a UFO was hovering overhead. Grabbing his video camera, Manuel Escamilla rushed outside and videotaped a "giant marble-shaped sphere" as it hovered overhead. Later that evening, the Kelly sisters (residents of Roswell) observed what was apparently the same object dart across the sky. The Escamilla footage was later aired on numerous television programs including local and national news stations, *Sightings, Hard Copy, Encounters* and more.[88]

A NATIONWIDE FLAP

Over a six-week period in October and November 1994, a wave of low-level UFO sightings swept across the United States. During that time, the National UFO Reporting Center received more than 500 telephone calls from people reporting objects from Alaska to Maine and everywhere in-between including several from New Mexico.

On September 1, an anonymous resident of Clovis said that he observed a small glowing object for a period of about forty minutes. At times the object "appeared to respond" to his actions.

On September 14, 1994, Toby and Maida Martinez were in their backyard in Taos when they looked up and saw a very large bright white light accompanied by about a dozen smaller lights drift slowly over their home at a very low altitude. Maida Martinez said she could hear a strange humming noise as the light traveled about twenty feet above the treetops and her neighbor's trailer. Says Maida,

> IT WAS THE MOST SPECTACULAR THING I HAVE EVER SEEN. IT WAS ABOUT AS BIG AS MY LIVING ROOM... THERE WAS A ROUND LIGHT AND A SERIES OF RED LIGHTS, ABOUT 12 OR 15. WE DID NOT HEAR THE ENGINE OF A JET. AS THE OBJECT GOT CLOSER TO OUR HOME, WE HEARD A HUM — THAT IS THE ONLY THING WE HEARD. IT WAS SO CLOSE TO THE EARTH THAT IT WAS A LITTLE TOO CLOSE FOR COMFORT. IT WAS LIKE WATCHING A SCIENCE FICTION MOVIE IN REAL LIFE. I GUESS BECAUSE IT WAS MOVING, WE WEREN'T AFRAID.

On the same night as the Martinez sighting, a tourist was also traveling through town and observed the object. He later told friends that he had been "scared" by the sight of the object.

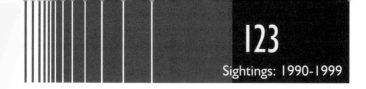

Also in September 1994 (exact date unknown), Eric Tafoya observed a very unusual object over the Taos skies. At the time, Tafoya lived only two miles away from the Martinez residence, in the Upper Ranchitos subdivision. One evening in September he went outside to lock his car for the night when he saw a weird blimp-like object with a big belly "like fish are when they're pregnant."

The object was covered with more than a dozen white lights. It entered into a cloud and made the entire cloud glow brilliantly. It approached slowly and went directly overhead from east to west. Says Tafoya,

> IT WAS LIKE NOTHING I'VE EVER SEEN. IT WAS RIGHT ON TOP OF ME, MAYBE 400 OR 500 FEET UP THERE. BUT IT WAS HUGE, WHATEVER IT WAS. IT MADE A NOISE, BUT IT DIDN'T MAKE A NOISE OF ANY OTHER AIRCRAFT I'VE HEARD. IT WAS LIKE A RUSH OF WIND MORE THAN ANYTHING ELSE.[89]

TELEPATHIC CONTACT IN TAOS

It is not unusual for witnesses to report telepathic communication with a UFO or its occupants. In March of 1995, an anonymous Taos woman revealed to a local UFO group that she had an experience (date not given) during which she made telepathic contact with a UFO that hovered outside her home. According to the witness, she was cleaning the window in her son's bedroom when she saw a round metallic object with red and blue twinkling lights flying very low. Says the witness,

> I KNEW IT COULDN'T POSSIBLY BE AN AIRPLANE. AS I CONTINUED STARING, I WAS WISHING THAT IT WOULD COME CLOSER SO I COULD GET A BETTER LOOK. RIGHT ON CUE, IT CAME CLOSER, BUT STILL FAR ENOUGH WHERE I COULDN'T GET THE BEST VANTAGE POINT. I BECAME EXTREMELY EXCITED. "WHAT IF IT REALLY IS A SPACE SHIP?" I THOUGHT. "WHAT SHOULD I DO? SUMMON IT? LEAVE WITH IT?"

The anonymous witness was shocked at what happened next. As she says,

> A VERY TIRED FEELING OVERCAME ME. I FELT COMPELLED TO LIE DOWN ON THE BED. WHAT'S MORE, I FELT A WEIGHT RIGHT OVER MY CHEST PUSHING ME DOWN.

She fought to remain conscious, but was unable to do so. Instead, she began having a very strange dream. Says the witness,

> I KEPT SEEING ROWS AND ROWS OF GREEN NUMBERS. AFTER A LONG TIME, THE NUMBERS STARTED CHANGING COLOR. THEY BECAME GREEN ON TOP AND ORANGE ON THE BOTTOM.

The witness says she tried to wake up, but was "powerless to do so." The stream of colored numbers continued for several moments then finally stopped. The witness got up, feeling strangely dazed. As she says,

> I TRIED TO SEE THE FLYING CRAFT, BUT THE SKY LOOKED LIKE A BLUR TO ME. I WONDERED HOW LONG THE ENTIRE THING LASTED, BUT I WAS TOO DISORIENTED TO CHECK IT OUT.

The witness says that she felt a "strange numbness" for two days following the incident, and often had recurring dreams about it. She now feels that the object that was hovering outside her window somehow tried to make telepathic contact with her. Says the witness,

> IT FELT LIKE I WAS EXPERIENCING A BRAIN RAPE.[90]

NORAD CONFIRMS PILOT SIGHTING

Perhaps the most significant sighting of the decade, on May 25, 1995, the crew of an America West Airlines flight was flying from Tampa, Florida, to Las Vegas, Nevada, when they had a dramatic encounter with a large unknown object which raced by their plane. Piloted by Captain Eugene Tollison and First Officer John Waller, America West Flight 564 was at 39,000 feet over north Texas when – at 10:25 p.m. – the pilots observed a strange-looking craft just below them at 30,000 feet. The object appeared to be about 400 feet long. It was thin, cylindrical, and had blinking pulsating strobe-lights flashing in sequence along its length. As Flight 564 was just about to enter New Mexico, they radioed Albuquerque Air Traffic Control and asked them if there was any other traffic in their area. The following conversation ensued:

Albuquerque: Cactus 564, say again.

Flight 564: I said, there's nothing on the radar on the other centers at all in that particular area, that object that's up in the air?

Albuquerque: It's up in the air?

Flight 564: Affirmative.

Albuquerque: What's the altitude about?

Flight 564: I don't know, probably right around 30,000 or so. There's a strobe, it starts from going counter clockwise. And the length is unbelievable.

Flight 564 reported that the object flew by them and off into the distance over New Mexico. As the object was not appearing on their radar, Albuquerque controllers decided to contact Cannon AFB radar operations in Clovis, New Mexico. The following conversation ensued between Cannon AFB and Albuquerque:

Cannon AFB: Cannon, go ahead.

Albuquerque: A guy at 39,000 says he sees something at 30,000. The length is unbelievable and it has a strobe on it.

Cannon AFB: Uh-huh.

Albuquerque: This is not good.

Cannon AFB: What does that mean?

Albuquerque: I don't know, it's a UFO or something. It's that Roswell crap again.

The only other known traffic in the area at the time – other than Flight 564 – was an Air Force F-117A Nighthawk stealth-fighter jet from the 49th Fighter Wing at Holloman AFB. Immediately after Captain Tollison made his report, controllers alerted the fighter pilot of the situation. The following conversation ensued between Albuquerque and the Nighthawk stealth-fighter:

Albuquerque: Hawk 85, in the next two to three minutes, be looking off to your right side. If you see anything about 30,000 feet, one aircraft reported something. It wasn't a weather balloon or anything. It was a long white-looking thing with a strobe on it. Let me know if you see anything out there.

Nighthawk: You got any traffic off our left wing right now?

Albuquerque: I've got something passing off your 9 o'clock in about 12 at 31 westbound.

Nighthawk: It actually looks like something about a little lower than us...just went off our left wing.

The object sped by the Nighthawk and disappeared off into the distance. A few moments later, Flight 564 radioed Albuquerque again and told them that the UFO was back, only this time it began to approach dangerously close to the airplane.

Flight 564: We're all huddled up here talking about it. With the lightning, you could see the dark object. It was like a cigar shape from the altitude we could see it and the length is what got us sort of confused because it looked like it was three to four hundred feet long. So I don't know if it's a wire with a strobe on it, but the strobe starts going left then goes right counterclockwise, and it was a pretty eerie sight.

At this point, the object accelerated off into the distance and was gone. However, Albuquerque control was concerned about the unidentified craft, and decided to contact NORAD to see if they had any information about the incident. The following conversation ensued between NORAD and Albuquerque Air Traffic Control.

Albuquerque: I've got something unusual, and I was wanting to know if you all happened to know of anything going on out here. I had a couple of aircraft reported something 300- to 400-foot long, cylindrical in shape with a strobe.

NORAD: Oh?

Albuquerque: At 30,000 feet.

NORAD: We don't have anything going on up there that I know of.

Albuquerque: This guy definitely saw it run all the way down the side of the airplane. It's right out of the *X-Files*. It's a definitely UFO or something like that.

NORAD: And...oh, you all are serious about this?

Albuquerque: Yeah, he's real serious about it too and he looked at it...saw it.

NORAD: Holy *shit*!

NORAD denied knowing anything about the craft. However, thirteen minutes later, Albuquerque control called NORAD again to see if they were able to locate the unidentified craft. NORAD replied:

NORAD: We had someone call earlier about a pilot spotting an unidentified flying object?

Albuquerque: Yep, that's us.

NORAD: Okay, well, hey... We're tracking a search-only track kind of up where that might have happened. We've been tracking it for about three or four minutes now.

When UFO researchers later obtained copies of the live recordings of the conversations from Albuquerque, they contacted NORAD who – on December 16, 1995, responded with an official letter denying that they had any information about the incident. They claimed that there was no correlation to any space debris. They wrote that they had "no reports and no recordings" of the alleged incident and then asked investigators not to attempt to use the FOIA to get records from NORAD, as they were exempt from the FOIA.[91]

FOLLOWED BY A UFO!

On December 4, 1995, a gentleman was moving from Georgia to California and had rented a U-Haul truck to move his stuff. Late in the afternoon, he was driving along Interstate 10 just west of Las Cruces when he saw "an unknown object, silver in color" pacing his vehicle. As he says,

I KNOW IT SOUNDS STRANGE BUT IT SEEMED TO BE PURPOSELY FOLLOWING MY VEHICLE AT A DISTANCE OF ABOUT A HALF MILE ON MY LEFT... IT CONTAINED AT A CONSTANT HEIGHT LESS THAN 1,000 FEET ABOVE THE GROUND.

The object, says the witness, constantly changed shape, looking alternately like a crushed aluminum can, a crumpled piece of paper, and a flat sheet. At times, it disappeared behind trees or hills but always returned, still pacing the witness's car. For the next hour, he traveled at sixty miles per hour, past Deming, and still being followed by the object. Finally, says the witness, 'It suddenly lifted up and out of sight at a very fast speed."[92]

ALIEN SPACECRAFT OR IRRIGATION SYSTEM?

Between 5:15 a.m. and 5:45 a.m. on January 31, 1996, several people traveling north into Roswell, near the Midway area observed what they believed to be a flying object. Coincidentally, nearly all the witnesses were employees of the Nova Bus Company, and were driving to work in separate vehicles when they saw the object.

Says one employee, Kay Lykins,

I WAS COMING INTO WORK AND THERE WAS THIS BLUE LIGHT FLASHING. AT FIRST I THOUGHT IT WAS THE AIRPORT, BUT THEN I REALIZED IT WAS COMING TOWARD ME. ALL OF A SUDDEN IT WAS RIGHT BESIDE ME. I LOOKED AT IT TO SEE WHAT IT WAS, BUT THEN I HAD TO TURN FROM IT BECAUSE IT WAS SO BRIGHT. WHEN I LOOKED BACK IT WAS GONE... WHEN I WAS LOOKING DOWN THE ROAD, IT LOOKED LIKE A ROADBLOCK LIGHT. BUT THEN WHEN IT WAS BESIDE ME, IT WAS SO BRIGHT THAT I COULDN'T EVEN TELL ABOUT [THE SIZE.]

Another witness was Tom Gomez, who saw the object at around 5:40 as he drove to work. He first noticed a light at about telephone pole height, moving at high speed adjacent to the highway. Says Gomez,

> I SAW A BLUE LIGHT FLASHING. I COULDN'T TELL WHAT IT WAS. EVERY TIME IT BLINKED IT WAS MOVING BY ABOUT 2,000 YARDS PER BLINK OR BETTER. IT WAS PRETTY FAST.

A third Nova Bus employee, Jesus Chavez, was also on his way to work when he saw the strange light. Says Chavez,

> IT WASN'T LIKE AN AIRPLANE THAT YOU CAN FOLLOW ITS PATH. IT WOULD BLINK AND THEN SUDDENLY BE SOMEWHERE ELSE. I DON'T KNOW WHAT IT WAS, IT WAS TRAVELING TOO FAST FOR A JET, AND IT WAS FLYING TOO LOW.

A fourth Nova Bus employee, Larry Vandenbout, also saw the object, but wasn't as impressed as the other witnesses. Says Vandenbout,

> I REALLY DIDN'T THINK MUCH ABOUT IT UNTIL EVERYBODY STARTED TALKING ABOUT IT.

As talk of the sighting spread, the witnesses learned that more than fifteen Nova Bus employees claimed to have seen the unexplained light. The sighting caused a sensation, even appearing in local newspapers.

However, one week later, a few of the witnesses concluded that the UFO was not a spacecraft, but rather an irrigation system. Local farmer Fred Schrimser had set up a mobile irrigation system in the area. It stood about ten feet high and had a row of blue lights on top which remained lit while the device rolled back and forth across the fields. Vandenbout is convinced that the sprinkler system is responsible for the sighting. At least one other witness agrees with Vandenbout, saying that from a distance, the irrigation system does look very strange.

However other witnesses remain convinced that they encountered a genuine UFO. Say Lykins,

> THERE ARE STILL SOME OF US THAT SAY *THAT* IS NOT WHAT WE SAW. I SAW THAT [IRRIGATION SYSTEM] ON THE SAME MORNING THAT I SAW THAT OTHER THING [THE UFO], AND IT SIMPLY WASN'T THE SAME THING. I KNOW WHAT I SAW. I

KNOW WHERE IT WAS AT. THE SPRINKLER SYSTEM WASN'T IN THE FIELD WHERE IT [THE UFO] WAS WHEN IT WAS BESIDE ME.

Lykins added that she saw the object move from one side of the road to the other, which the irrigation system doesn't do.

After the article came out in the newspaper, another witness stepped forward to say that she had seen an unusual light in the same area two days later. Rebecca Valasco said that she and a friend were driving in the area around 9 p.m. when they saw a blue light appear ahead of them on the road. Says Valasco,

> IT WAS LITTLE AND IN A MATTER OF SECONDS IT JUMPED RIGHT FOR US. EVERYTHING WAS REALLY BLUE. IT LOOKED LIKE A BIG ROUND TRAMPOLINE.

Valasco says that as they raced past the object, she looked back and watched the object circling the area. She feels certain that the object was not the irrigation system. Says Valasco,

> WHERE WE SAW IT WAS PAST THE IRRIGATION, AND IT CAME TOO CLOSE TO US TO HAVE BEEN THAT.[93]

LIGHTS OVER DEMING

Later that year, in late July 1996, three different people reported seeing strange lights in the sky over Deming.

One of the witnesses, Greg Granado, was on the front porch of his family's home on East Maple Street at 12:30 a.m. when he saw "a ball of fire, red in the middle and orange around the outside" fly across the sky from east to west. Says Granado, "I was just amazed by its speed."

Granado says the object moved much faster than a plane, in a level trajectory from horizon to horizon and disappeared. Says Granado,

> IT SHOCKED ME WHEN I SAW IT. I DIDN'T KNOW WHAT IT WAS, AND I STILL DON'T KNOW WHAT IT WAS, BUT IT WAS SO STRANGE THAT I CALLED THE POLICE.

Granado's family teased him, however, after the story of his sighting appeared in newspapers, two additional witnesses came forth saying they also saw strange lights on that night.

Around the same time as Granado's sighting, Jerry Hernandez and his brother Steve Kucera were driving home along Highway 180 when they saw what they first assumed were "truck headlights on bright." The mystery was, the lights were northeast of them, about a half-mile off the highway where there was no road. Says Hernandez, "I didn't think anything of it until I realized they were too high to be a truck."

The brothers discussed the lights. Kucera wondered if it might be a truck on a hill, but his brother pointed out that there were no hills in that area.

As they watched, the lights suddenly banked and turned. Shortly later the brothers drove past the lights and continued on their drive. It wasn't until the paper came out a few days later and they read about the other sighting that they wondered if they had seen something unusual. Says Hernandez,

> THIS ISN'T THE FIRST TIME I'VE SEEN SOMETHING NORTH OF TOWN THAT I THOUGHT COULD BE A UFO, OR MAYBE AN EXPERIMENTAL AIRCRAFT.[94]

UFOS LINKED TO CATTLE MUTILATIONS

Starting in July 1996, numerous residents around Gallina Canyon reported seeing strange colored lights hovering in the sky. Recently, several ranchers had lost several head of cattle to mutilations. Two days after one such mutilation, rancher Jesse Gonzales observed anomalous lights hovering over the area of the mutilation. Says Gonzales,

> I SAW THESE VERY WEIRD LIGHTS, BLUE AND RED, THREE OR FOUR OF THEM HOVERING OVER GALLINA CANYON.

Gonzales soon learned that several other people in the area were also seeing the lights. Other witnesses include Gonzales' sister and her husband who both watched a glowing red light "as big as the moon" hover on the far side of the Rio Grande Gorge. The couple became frightened when the hovering object suddenly "took off like a comet" and disappeared from view.

On July 30, Anthony Garcia of Arroyo Seco said he watched two glowing spheres "one red, white and blue, the other white and greenish-blue" hover over Valdez for about twenty minutes at around 2:30 a.m. Garcia is convinced that the objects were unusual. As he says,

> THEY WEREN'T PLANES. THEY WERE TOO LOW AND THEY WEREN'T MAKING ANY NOISE.

In early August, another report came from two Arroyo Hondo residents and one Arroyo Seco resident, each of who said they observed red, white, and blue lights hovering over the canyons.

A few weeks later, on August 31, Jenny Meadowcraft woke up just before dawn to see three globes floating in the sky. Again, they were red, white, and blue. Says Meadowcraft,

> I FIGURED THEY WERE PART OF ONE CRAFT. THEY TOOK OFF, MOVING SOUTH VERY FAST AND DISAPPEARED... THAT WAS THE FIRST UFO I'VE EVER SEEN. I'LL NEVER FORGET IT... IT WAS BEAUTIFUL. I WAS AWED AND AMAZED. I WASN'T AFRAID.

Another local resident (who prefers to remain anonymous) says that he has seen the strange glowing lights on several occasions. He reports that they are all different colors, and hover low in the sky. Says the witness, "I kind of got used to them."

One month prior to the prior cluster of July sightings, two cows had been found mutilated in Arroyo Hondo. Many of the ranchers feel that there could be a connection between UFOs and the mutilations. (See Chapter Ten on Mutilations)[95]

LIGHTS OVER SANTA ROSA

On October 5, 1996, Santa Rosa city employee Edward Salazar was doing his rounds spraying insect poison when he saw strange lights hovering above the Truckstops of America and the Cinnamon Ridge Apartments.

At the same time, Santa Rosa resident Davy Delgado woke up and looking outside saw "a light as bright as the moon above Mockingbird Hill west of the truck stop and Cinnamon Ridge." He at first assumed it was the moon until he saw it move across slowly across the sky followed by "a stream of smaller lights."

There was also an anonymous report from someone who called the newspaper, but declined to give his name.[96]

HELICOPTER UFO CHASE

At around 11 a.m. on the morning of June 15, 1997, Gulf Breeze researcher Mike Hawkins had arrived early in Roswell for the upcoming 50th anniversary UFO convention two weeks later on July 4. He was thinking of moving to the area and had traveled to a small piece of property for sale about one mile east of Roswell to take some photos. To his amazement, a UFO showed up. As the report on the case reads,

> HE WAS WALKING OVER THE GROUND WITH CAMERA READY TO GET SNAPSHOTS, WHEN HE HEARD THE SOUND OF A SMALL HELICOPTER OVERHEAD. LOOKING AROUND, HE SAW THAT THE HELICOPTER SEEMED TO BE INTERESTED IN A SMALL SILVERY-WHITE FLYING DISC WITH A LITTLE CUPOLA ON TOP AND ANOTHER SMALLER ONE ON THE BOTTOM. HE RAISED THE CAMERA AND STARTED TAKING PICTURES. HE GOT FIVE GOOD PHOTOGRAPHS OF THE DISC WITH THE HELICOPTER IN THE SAME FRAME, AS BOTH SHIPS MANEUVERED ABOUT OVER THE OPEN FIELD. THE DISC-SHAPED CRAFT WAS SILENT DURING THIS WHOLE EPISODE, UNTIL THE HELICOPTER BROKE OFF AND LEFT THE AREA. (SEE PHOTO SECTION ON PAGE 297.)[97]

UFO OVER WHITE SANDS

On the evening of July 7, 1997, a gentleman was driving his car along the White Sands Missile Range. He had just reached the curve at Launch Complex 32 when he saw what appeared to be "an orange ball of fire" floating down the mountain. He kept his eye on it, trying to figure out what it was. As it got closer, the object suddenly turned white and turned directly toward him, approaching until it was less than a block away.

Says the witness,

> IT STARTED TO DESCEND AND I THOUGHT IT WAS GOING TO LAND, BUT IT DID NOT. IT CAME WITHIN ABOUT 15 FEET OF THE GROUND AND I WAS WAITING TO SEE SAND KICK UP AROUND IT, BUT THERE WAS NONE. IT WAS ABOUT THE SIZE OF A VW BEETLE SHAPED LIKE AN ORDINARY LIGHT BULB. THIS OBJECT JUST STOPPED IN MID AIR AND DIDN'T FLOAT AROUND OR WOBBLE, BUT STAYED IN ONE PLACE.

The object was so bright, the witness wondered how anybody inside could see through the light. He stopped his car and faced his headlights on the object. It immediately became extinguished. A few moments later, it lit up again.

The witness then flashed his headlights three times, then twice, then once. The object reacted by slowly moving away in the same direction it had come from. He watched it travel to the top of the mountain where it briefly joined another identical-looking object and a blinking red light. All three lights then moved off in opposite directions and disappeared.[98]

ROSWELL FIREBALL

On June 16, 1998, the Chaves County Sheriff's Department received a call from a gentleman who stated that he and ten others had just observed a glowing red ball of light fall from the sky.

Moments later they received another call from Linda Ortiz, who said that she was heading southeast on Old Dexter Highway when she and several others with her saw it. Says Ortiz,

> WE SAW THIS BIG RED BALL, BUT IT WASN'T ON FIRE BECAUSE THERE WAS NO STREAK. IT WAS REAL BRIGHT AND RED AND I SAW IT LAND, NO EXPLOSION OR NOTHING LIKE THAT. IT JUST LANDED AND IT TURNED OFF.

When she arrived home, Ortiz's children said they had seen the light, which was so bright it made the cows look pink from the brilliance of it. Said Ortiz's daughter, Josie Herrera,

> IT LOOKED LIKE A BIG RED BALL AND IT JUST LANDED.

The sightings received newspaper coverage, and reporters converged upon the family, who refused all further interviews. The State Police received no calls, and officials at White Sands and Holloman denied having any military activity in the area at the time of the sighting.[99]

POLICE OFFICER SEES FLYING BOOMERANG

In June of 1998, Gabe Valdez, a state trooper in northern New Mexico, was giving a French UFO researcher a tour of the local area around Mount Archuleta, near Dulce. By this time, Valdez had become one of the state's leading researchers on cattle mutilations. Because one of the theories to explain cattle mutilations was UFOs, Valdez had become somewhat knowledgeable about local UFO activity, and had, in fact, seen strange orange lights on a few occasions. On this particular day, he had a close-up dramatic sighting.

Says Valdez,

> IT LOOKED LIKE A BOOMERANG SHAPE. IT LEFT A LIGHT BLUISH-GREEN STREAK. IT WAS FLYING SO FAST IT LOOKED LIKE A FLASH. IT CAME BY REAL FAST. IT JUST POPPED OUT OF THE SKY.[100]

A SKY-QUAKE

Just after 11 p.m. on October 19, 1998, residents across Roosevelt County heard a massive explosion, which seemed to be centered over the Pep-Dora area but was heard over a much wider location.

Dora residents Henry and Deana Forrer were woken up by the explosion. Says Deana Forrer,

> IT WAS SO LOUD, IT SHOOK THE WHOLE HOUSE AND NEARLY KNOCKED US OUT OF BED.

Forrer says that it was powerful enough to literally shake the ground itself.

Four miles east of Pep, Charlie Carmichael (a columnist for the *Portales News-Tribune*) heard the big boom. Twelve miles southeast of Dora, Karl Cox Jr. also heard it, and rushing outside, failed to see anything that might have caused it.

Residents of Causey, ten miles away from Dora, also heard and felt the boom.

Whatever caused the explosion, however, remained a mystery. An investigation failed to turn up any leads. Nearby Cannon Air Force Base denied any knowledge of the event. The National Weather Service in Albuquerque said that there was no thunderstorm activity. The U.S. Geological Survey was contacted and said that there was no seismic activity in the area which might account for the explosion. And so the mystery remains.[101]

GLOWING ORBS OVER TALPA

According to the *Taos News*, on December 31, 1998, Talpa resident Margaret LaValley went outside her apartment to retrieve her dog. Looking up, she saw a round, white, lighted object move from the northeast to the southeast toward Mora. Seconds later, another one followed the same path. LaValley was shocked, and thought to herself, they're traveling in pairs. She couldn't believe what happened next. Says LaValley,

THEN CAME A WHOLE FLOCK OF THEM, DIFFERENT SIZES.

LaValley ran and got a pair of binoculars and observed additional globes of light travel across the sky for the next ten minutes. Says LaValley,

THEY WERE ALL SILENT, NOT BLINKING. I COULDN'T MAKE OUT ANY DETAILS. THEY WERE JUST BRIGHT, GLOWING ORBS.[102]

UFO OR MINUTEMAN MISSILE?

At 7 o'clock p.m. Pacific time on October 2, 1999, an unarmed Minuteman-2 Intercontinental missile was launched from Vandenburg Air Force Base in southern California. As the missile soared westwards over the Pacific ocean, an interceptor rocket was launched from the Marshall Islands. As officials had planned, the interceptor rocket successfully targeted and destroyed the Minuteman missile. Meanwhile, calls came in from across the western United States, as far east as Iowa, from witnesses who observed the aerial display. The test was judged a huge success, and showed the military's ability to protect the country from foreign attack.

At the same time of this missile test, numerous people in the Gallup area reported a UFO. Despite the fact that the missile was airborne at the time of their sightings, they are convinced that what they saw was not a missile.

The Gallup sightings began at 9 p.m. Mountain time when two Navajo police officers, Sergeant Tommy Rogers and Officer El Reno Henio observed a circular disk-shaped object hovering at low altitude in the north McKinley County area. The disk projected a bright cone-shaped beam of light directly onto the ground. The officers approached the object in their patrol vehicle, at which point it took off and eluded them. The object would then appear to stop and wait for them. The officers continued to chase it, but each time they got close, it would dart away. They chased it for two hours before it finally moved off and disappeared.

While the officers were chasing this object, numerous calls were received by police dispatchers from witnesses in nearby Crownpoint, Becenti, Dalton Pass, Standing Rock, and Window Rock.

Despite the fact that a missile launch seemed to be the cause, many witnesses were not convinced, and believed their sighting was a genuine UFO. The next day, Don Gonzales of KGAK radio conducted a call-in show taking calls from numerous witnesses who also said that the UFO would dart away from them when they tried to approach it. Other witnesses also described the cone-shaped beam, saying that the smallest and brightest part of the cone was at ground level. The radio show was jammed with callers and people lined up outside the station to tell their stories. Gonzales let the show run an extra forty-five minutes because it was so popular.

Meanwhile, investigators from the National Institute for Discovery Science (NIDS) converged on the scene to interview witnesses and to determine if the sighting was related to the missile launch or not. True to the conservative nature of the organization, they made no solid conclusions. Whatever the case, however, NIDS investigators were impressed by the similarity of witness descriptions.[103]

FLEET OF TRIANGLES OVER ARTESIA

One day following the above sighting, on the evening of October 3, 1999, an Artesia couple claimed to witness a dramatic display involving a fleet of triangular-shaped objects. Joyce Booker-Cole and her husband, David, stepped out of their Artesia home at around 10:30 p.m. when they saw a large round-shaped object covered with lights move overhead and then drop out of sight at the horizon. Shortly after, a group of six white, glowing, huge triangular-shaped objects traversed the sky in single file from the northeast to the southwest. This was followed by a second round object moving from the northwest, which was followed by five additional white triangular objects. Joyce Booker-Cole said the sighting gave her chills.

THEY WEREN'T HIGH ENOUGH TO BE AIRPLANES. THEY MADE NO NOISE.

At first she hesitated, but upset by what she had seen, she decided to call the local police. The police told her they had not received any calls. Booker-Cole spoke with reporters who also did some investigating. They contacted Tom McKenzie, an on-duty Albuquerque air traffic controller who told them he knew of no military aircraft flying at that time in that area. One possible explanation, he said, was a balloon launch from Fort Sumner which had taken place that morning at 7 a.m.[104]

UFO STOPS TRUCK

Early in the morning of December 19, 1999, a man was driving his old Ford pick-up truck along 84-285 towards Santa Fe when he had an encounter he won't soon forget. Says the anonymous witness,

ON MY RIGHT, ABOVE MY HEAD, COMING FROM THE LOS ALAMOS AREA, APPEARED THE BIGGEST THING I HAD EVER SEEN IN THE AIR. IT FLOATED RIGHT OVER ME, FROM THE PASSENGER SIDE TO THE DRIVER SIDE AND KEPT GOING. IT WAS TOTALLY SILENT BUT HAD A LUMINESCENCE. AS IT WENT OVER ME, MY OLD FORD TRUCK STOPPED.

The witness said that the light seemed extremely bright, but at the same time, it failed to cast much illumination onto the ground. The object slowly passed overhead and went away.

Afterward, the radio was still working, so the man switched it off and attempted to re-start his vehicle. Unfortunately, it would not restart, so he called for a tow-truck on his cell phone and had it towed to his long-time mechanic.

He later called his mechanic to find out what was wrong with his truck. The mechanic told him, "You've got to come see this to believe it. I've been a mechanic for forty years and I've never seen this happen."

The witness went to the mechanic shop to examine his car and the mechanic told him that his distributor had exploded. He said, "I've seen distributor caps crack, but I've never seen an entire distributor pulled out and exploded."

Says the witness, "He opened the hood, and there – magnetized and stuck to the top of my hood – were the pieces of my distributor!"

The mechanic asked him, "How did this happen?"

The witness said, "You don't want to know!"[105]

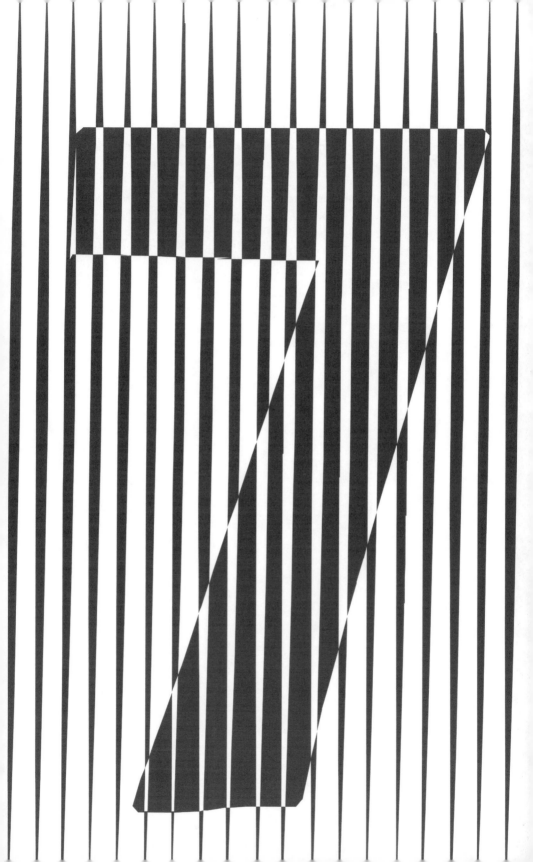

CHAPTER 7

Landings AND HUMANOIDS

UFO sightings are interesting, but they usually involve only limited interaction with the environment and the witnesses. Among the most compelling of all types of UFO encounters are landings and reports of humanoids. Unlike sightings, these objects are often seen very close up, virtually removing the possibilities of misperception or misidentification. Before the 1940s, UFO landings were practically unheard of. While there are many cases that pre-date the modern age of UFOs, it wasn't until the 1950s that accounts of landings were reported in large enough numbers to get attention. The first cases of New Mexico landings and humanoids (excluding crashes) began in the 1950s and continued regularly ever since. As with sightings, the reports were most numerous in the 1950s and 1960s, and then dropped off. While most of the cases failed to gather much media attention or public notice, a few became extremely well known. One case in particular – the 1964 Socorro UFO landing – became the single most famous UFO case of that year and is today considered by many researchers to be one of the best verified UFO landings on record.

The more than twenty cases below represent only a small sampling of the actual number of these types of encounters, which is likely many times greater, especially in an area as active as New Mexico.

UFO LANDING AT LAS CRUCES

One evening in June or July of 1952, Hilda McAfee (age, late 50s) and her elderly mother were driving from Las Cruces to their home in Deming. They were about twenty-three miles east of Deming on Interstate 10 when they saw a blinding blue light ahead of them in their lane.

McAfee slowed down and pulled around and alongside the object. As they drove by, the women were shocked to see two strange-looking figures standing directly underneath a brightly lit object. The figures were five and a half feet tall, muscular-looking, and wore identical bulky, pale-blue uniforms with helmets, gloves, wide belts, and calf-length boots.

The figures paid no attention to the women as they drove by. One had his back turned to them and appeared to be working on something. The other stood in a rigid, stiff posture. The women also saw three black five-inch-thick rods next to the two figures.

After they passed the object, the women looked behind them and were shocked to see that the object had extinguished its lights. They speculated that the lights had been turned on to prevent them from colliding into the object.

Following the incident, both women suffered strange symptoms including pains in their chest, arms, and bones. At first they kept their encounter a secret. It was only after the Travis Walton abduction on November 5, 1975, in Snowflake, Arizona, that McAfee decided to reveal their encounter. It turns out that McAfee was the landlady of Chaney Rogers, brother to Mike Rogers who was one of the witnesses in the famous Travis Walton abduction case. It was this connection that finally prompted McAfee to go public with her own experience.[106]

UFO LANDING IN SANTA FE

On October 25, 1953, at around 9:30 p.m., sixteen-year-old Jim Milligan was driving his car through a park in Santa Fe when he saw a strange object fall out of the sky and move so closely across the road in front of him that he feared a collision. He slammed on the brakes and watched in amazement as the object slowed down and landed in the bushes off the side of the road. Milligan then exited his vehicle and approached the object on foot. He walked right up to it and was amazed to see a metallic craft, the color of dull gray gun-metal. The object was shaped like two ship hulls glued together. It was nine feet long and six feet wide, nearly the same size as his own vehicle. There were no other markings. Summoning up his courage, Milligan reached out and tried to touch the surface of the object. However, before he could do so, it lifted up and flew away in a steep ascent towards Santa Fe. The teen-ager arrived home "shaking and white in the face."

When the case received publicity, nearby White Sands was contacted for information. Brigadier General G. C. Eddy, then commanding officer of the depot denied that the object had anything to do with White Sands, saying, "I know nothing whatever about this incident."[107]

UFO LANDING AT WALKER AFB

The following case was reported to both NUFORC and MUFON by the daughter of an Air Force Air Policeman stationed at Walker AFB (Roswell) in the 1950s. Her father worked nights on the flightline. One morning (between 1952-1954, exact date unknown), he came home from work, excited and frightened about something that had happened on the flightline that evening. He told them that everything about it was classified and that if he spoke about it, he would be prosecuted.

However, the man was apparently felt it was important enough that he later did tell his family what happened. Writes the man's daughter,

> HE SAID A LARGE UNIDENTIFIED CRAFT LANDED DIRECTLY ON THE FLIGHTLINE THAT NIGHT. THEY HAD SURROUNDED IT FOR SEVERAL HOURS. THERE WAS NO CONTACT BETWEEN THE OCCUPANTS AND THE BASE OFFICIALS. FINALLY, JUST AS SUDDENLY AS IT LANDED, IT TOOK OFF AND WAS GONE. EVERYONE WHO HAD BEEN PRESENT FOR THE EVENT WERE TOLD THAT THE INCIDENT WAS TO BE CLASSIFIED TOP SECRET AND THAT THEY WOULD NOT SPEAK OF IT TO ANYONE.

According to the father, the entire base security had responded to the incident. Not only had they surrounded the craft, they photographed it non-stop.

Later there was another incident with apparently the same craft, which was seen to hover over the base and briefly follow one of the AP vehicles.[108]

LANDING TRACES AT LAS CRUCES

According to Harold T. Wilkins, he received a report from two women (Mrs. Weiss and Mrs. Sanders), who stumbled on what appeared to be landing traces from a UFO outside the town of Las Cruces. According to Wilkins, on May 7, 1954, the U.S. Army and officials from White Sands AFB examined and were puzzled by the markings, which appeared at Kilburne Hole, the location of an extinct volcano. The markings took the form of four concentric circles, with a dot in the center and two straight lines at either end. At the end of the lines, four deeper impressions "like pads" appeared on the ground. According to the report, there were more than thirty of the markings which varied in diameter, but no larger than two feet across. According to the report, "They seem to have been formed by a metallic object."

When the women first examined the strange tracks, they also observed yellow and red mysterious lights a few miles away, which winked at irregular intervals.[109]

UFO LANDING AT CANNON AFB

On May 18, 1954, a UFO landing occurred directly on a New Mexico military base. Two people were on the grounds of Cannon Air Force Base when they saw a lens-shaped object the size of a house swoop down out of the sky and land next to the railroad tracks. As it landed, it disturbed the local environment, causing a minor sand storm around it. After the dust settled, one of the witnesses decided to approach it. However, as he got closer, he became overwhelmed in fear and ran away. Shortly later, the object departed.[110]

UFO LANDING AT WHITE SANDS

Around 8 a.m. on a September morning in 1956, numerous witnesses observed a disk-shaped object with a dome on top land along the highway. The object landed within the White Sands Proving Grounds, twelve miles west of Holloman AFB, right alongside U.S. Highway 70. As it set down, the engines of all the cars within its vicinity failed and the cars rolled to a stop. At the same time, their radios and other electrical equipment failed. Traffic on either end of the highway quickly backed-up for several miles as the strange craft remained on the ground for about ten to fifteen minutes. Dozens of the witnesses were actually employees of Holloman. The closest witnesses were about seventy-five feet away from the craft. These witnesses reported hearing a whirring sound coming from the craft as it landed.

Meanwhile, numerous witnesses on the base itself, including two USAF colonels, two sergeants and at least ten other men also observed the landed craft. Finally, the craft took off with a "whirring" sound. Within a few hours of the incident, officials arrived from Washington, D.C. The base personnel who had observed the craft were assembled in a hangar and sworn to secrecy. The secrecy order came not from the Air Force, but from the CIA, who told the personnel that their conclusion was that the UFO's origin was unknown.[111]

ANOTHER WHITE SANDS UFO LANDING

As we have seen, White Sands has shown itself to be very attractive to UFOs. Yet another landing occurred there on November 3, 1957. On this occasion, an army patrol jeep observed an orange glowing object hovering at about 150 feet altitude. After about three minutes, the object came down out of the sky, "apparently controlled," and then landed at Stallion Site, at the northern end of the testing grounds and adjacent to the location of the first atomic bomb explosion. The two witnesses described the object as being very bright, like the sun. After a short period of time, the object departed.

According to researcher Donald Keyhoe, shortly after the first incident, another sighting occurred during which other military police observed a second UFO hovering 50 feet above the ground. Says Keyhoe,

IT WAS DESCRIBED IN AN OFFICIAL ARMY STATEMENT AS A CONTROLLED CRAFT MORE THAN 200 FEET LONG.

According to Keyhoe, when news of these encounters reached Air Force Headquarters in Washington, they moved swiftly to debunk the case. Writes Keyhoe,

IN THE FIRST WHITE SANDS INCIDENT, THE OBJECT THE MPS HAD SEEN LANDING WAS EXPLAINED AS THE PLANET VENUS. IN THE SECOND WHITE SANDS CASE, THE UFO WHICH HOVERED AT FIFTY FEET WAS EXPLAINED AS THE MOON.[112]

LANDING AT LAKE BONITA

Late at night on August 20, 1959, four young girls decided that they would sneak out of the house and hide inside the station wagon (which belonged to one of the girl's parents), so that they could see how late they could remain awake. At some point, they all fell asleep. However, around 3 a.m., they woke up when a bright light like a fireball appeared overhead. Looking up, they watched the object land on the side of the mountain, not far from where they were. The entire area of the mountain was "lit like day." The girls became even more frightened when figures – apparently from the object – approached. Writes one of the girls,

WE SAW SOME SORT OF PEOPLE WALKING. THEY HAD LIGHTS, AND WHERE THEY SHINED THEM IT WAS LIKE DAYLIGHT. IT WAS SO SCARY.

The figures walked by the car and shined their lights on it. The girls ducked down. Says the witness,

INSIDE THE CAR WAS LIKE DAYLIGHT. WHEN THEY FINALLY WENT ON DOWN THE ROAD, WE CLIMBED OUT OF THE CAR.

The girls crept quietly back to the cabin where the parents of one of the girls were. By the time they made it back to the cabin, one of the girls had become hysterical with fear. Forty years later, at least one of the witness was impressed enough by her encounter to report it to NUFORC.[113]

LANDING AT HOLLOMAN AFB

This next case is among the most controversial of any New Mexican encounter. The reason for the controversy is because of the location of the event, the extensive nature of the case, and the high level of the witnesses involved. There are differing versions of the event, but most accounts agree that it involved a face-to-face meeting with gray-type ETs and military leaders, and may have been the source of the widespread rumor that our military made some type of nefarious deal with ETs in order to acquire their technology.

On April 2, 1964, a crew at Holloman Air Force Base was preparing for a missile launch. At some point prior to the launch, radar technicians in the airport tower detected three unidentified blips on their scopes. The blips showed that the objects were approaching through restricted airspace directly towards the base.

Officials attempted to contact the objects by radio, but were ignored. Soon the three craft were in view. Suddenly, one of the craft broke away from the other two and landed on the tarmac. The entire event was captured on film by two separate camera crews who were there to film the upcoming missile launch.

However, the encounter wasn't over yet. When the disk-shaped object remained on the tarmac, the Holloman base commander, two officers, and two Air Force scientists approached the landed craft. As they arrived, a door opened up in the craft and there they saw three blue-gray skinned ETs with wide-set eyes, prominent noses (according to one account), tight-fitting suits, and strange rope-like headdresses. The beings spoke in mental telepathy.

The purpose of the alleged visit was the negotiated release of some of the alien bodies from the Roswell crash, and also, officials agreed to allow the aliens the right to experiment on certain selected human civilians in exchange for some of the aliens' technology.

While the story has yet to be confirmed by a firsthand source, the rumor that the United States military has acquired ET technology with some sort of exchange program has originated from a number of different sources and has now become a firmly entrenched belief within the UFO community.[114]

THE SOCORRO INCIDENT

Next to the Roswell UFO crash, perhaps the most famous UFO incident in New Mexico history is a landing that occurred outside the small town of Socorro on April 24, 1964. Unknown to many, there were a few sightings immediately prior to the event.

At around 5 p.m., on April 24, Paul Kies and Larry Kratzer were about one mile southwest of Socorro driving east on Highway 60 when Kratzer (who was driving) saw a strange black cloud of dust or smoke on the ground about one mile ahead of them to the right of the road. He pointed it out to Kies, and both watched as a bright shiny "reflection" appeared within the smoke. Kies wondered if the object was emitting an actual light or if it was just a reflection. He speculated that maybe a junk yard was on fire. Only after he heard about later sightings in the area did he wonder if what he had seen was a UFO.

Kratzer, however, remembers the story differently from Kies. He recalls seeing the black smoke and pointing it out to Kies, at which point a round or egg-shaped object ascended vertically from the smoke, leveled off and then moved towards the southwest, still emitting black smoke. He said that the object appeared to be shiny silver with a row of round "darker mirror-like windows" with a strange "red Z" marking on the right end of the object. He then wondered if it was some type of secret experimental vertical-lift aircraft. They then headed through Socorro, where they bought some gas, told their story to the gas-attendant, and continued on their way.

It was 5:45 p.m., and Opel Grinder, the gas station attendant at the local Socorro gas station remembers the incident. He was assisting a customer. The customer excitedly explained that he had just seen a strange egg-shaped craft fly overhead as he drove northward on Highway 85. The customer told Grinder that the object was heading west and disappeared behind a mesa. Moments later Grinder saw a speeding police car race by. (Investigators are unsure whether or not this customer was Krazter or another unidentified witness.)

At that time, Socorro police officer Lonnie Zamora was in pursuit of a speeding motorist when he heard a loud roaring sound. Looking towards the source of the noise, he saw a bright flaming object descend behind a small hill, near the location of a dynamite shack. Concerned that the shack had exploded, he drove to the top of the hill. To his shock, he saw a small "shiny-type object" landed near the road and two short figures standing next to it. They appeared to be working on the object. He first assumed that there had been an auto accident and he radioed headquarters that an accident had, in fact, occurred. He continued to a drive towards the object, approaching within about 100 feet.

As Zamora wrote in his notes following the incident,

> IT LOOKED AT FIRST LIKE A CAR TURNED UPSIDE DOWN. THOUGHT SOME KIDS MIGHT HAVE TURNED IT OVER. SAW TWO PEOPLE IN WHITE COVERALLS VERY CLOSE TO THE OBJECT. ONE OF THESE PERSONS SEEMED TO TURN AND LOOK STRAIGHT AT MY CAR AND SEEMED STARTLED — SEEMED TO QUICKLY JUMP SOMEWHAT. AT THIS TIME I BEGAN MOVING MY CAR TOWARDS THEM QUICKLY WITH THE IDEA TO HELP… OBJECT WAS LIKE ALUMINUM — WAS WHITISH AGAINST THE MESA BACKGROUND, NOT CHROME. SEEMED LIKE OVAL IN SHAPE, AND I AT FIRST GLANCE, TOOK IT TO BE AN OVERTURNED WHITE CAR. CAR APPEARED TURNED UP LIKE STANDING ON RADIATOR OR TRUNK, AT THIS FIRST GLANCE.

"The only time I saw these two persons," Zamora continues, "was when I had stopped for possibly two seconds or so to glance at the object… Those persons appeared normal in shape – but possibly they were small adults or large kids."

As Zamora drove closer, a small hill hid the object and figures from view. He drove to the top of the hill and jumped out of his car to approach on foot. As he crested the hill, the figures were no longer visible. The craft sat there on what appeared to be landing gear. Seconds later, he heard two thumping sounds and a loud roar. The craft then rose upward, emitting a blast of flame. Zamora jumped behind his car for protection, hitting the fender and knocking off his glasses. The craft barely cleared the dynamite shack. The flame then became extinguished, the roar stopped and a whining sound began, and the craft flew away in a bobbing motion at a very low altitude towards the southwest. As it left, Zamora observed a strange red-colored arrow-like symbol (about two and a half feet high and two feet wide) on the side.

Moments later, state police Sergeant Sam Chavez arrived. He and Zamora both discovered landing traces where the craft had rested. There were four deep indentations in the earth, a burnt mesquite bush, and charred grass. The rock where the craft had sat also appeared to be melted and fused.

Within forty-five minutes, military personnel were on the scene. They reportedly took away samples of the melted rock, burned soil, and vegetation.

Lonnie Zamora, it turned out, was a friend of Dr. Lincoln La Paz, so it wasn't long before officials heard about his sighting. Air Force investigators converged on the scene. One of them was J. Allen Hynek, who investigated the incident shortly after it occurred. By measuring the placement of the landing marks, Hynek determined that the center of gravity of the object corresponded exactly to the location of the burned foliage. At the time, Hynek was still somewhat skeptical of UFOs, but after investigating this case, he came away baffled, and later wrote that it was one of the "major UFO sightings in the history of the Air Force's consideration of the subject."

The object landed very near the local Socorro Airport. Hynek was surprised that the object was not caught on the airport radar. Jim and Coral Lorenzen, however, also investigated the case and learned that all airport radar had been shut down at 4 p.m., shortly before the incident occurred. However, the fact that military officials showed up within hours of the incident has caused investigators to speculate that perhaps the nearby White Sands facility were tracking the object on radar.

The Air Force and the FBI also conducted investigations into the incident. Captain Richard T. Holder was accompanied by FBI agent D. Arthur Byrnes in a joint investigation, though only on the condition that no mention be made of FBI interest in the case. The officials interviewed Lonnie Zamora firsthand. Zamora told them his theory that the craft was a secret government experimental craft. Captain Holder suggested that he might have been the victim of a hoax.

Despite Holder's comment, it is clear from declassified documents that FBI agent D. Arthur Byrnes took the case seriously. Researcher William Moore later obtained documents using the FOIA which contained Byrnes' written report on the case. Byrnes wrote that he examined the landing traces, and that Zamora was a "well-regarded, industrious, and conscientious officer and not given to fantasy."

The landing traces left by the Socorro incident are among the most impressive in UFO history. These landing traces also include metal fragments. The craft landed in an area of sharp volcanic rock. In the holes made the craft's landing gear, there were "metal streaks" left by the craft.

Stanton Friedman and Dr. James McDonald both interviewed Mary Mayes, who, at the time of the incident was working on her Masters degree in "radiation biology" at New Mexico University. Mayes told researchers that she was asked by the University to investigate the landing traces. She visited the site, confirmed the melted sand and the burning vegetation. She took samples of the latter, which she studied in a lab. She found no evidence of radiation; the plants were scorched, and there were also "two organic substances" which she was unable to identify. After her investigation, she was ordered to turn in her report and all samples, and to "keep quiet" about the case.

Says Hynek,

THE SOCORRO CASE WAS BASICALLY A SINGLE-WITNESS SIGHTING (ALTHOUGH SEVERAL OTHER MORE DISTANT WITNESSES TO THE OBJECT WERE REPORTED), BUT THE WITNESS WAS A POLICEMAN WHOSE CHARACTER AND RECORD WERE UNIMPEACHABLE. PHYSICAL TRACES WERE LEFT ON THE GROUND; AND, AS I PERSONALLY OBSERVED, SOME OF THE GREASEWOOD BUSHES IN THE VICINITY HAD BEEN CHARRED. EVEN MAJOR QUINTANILLA, THEN HEAD OF BLUE BOOK, WAS CONVINCED THAT AN ACTUAL PHYSICAL CRAFT HAD BEEN PRESENT... MAYBE THERE IS A SIMPLE EXPLANATION FOR THE SOCORRO INCIDENT, BUT HAVING MADE A COMPLETE STUDY OF THE EVENTS, I DO NOT THINK SO. IT IS MY OPINION THAT A REAL, PHYSICAL EVENT OCCURRED ON THE OUTSKIRTS OF SOCORRO THAT AFTERNOON OF APRIL 24, 1964.

Later Major Quintanilla did try to explain away the incident as a test flight of a secret lunar module. However, the Socorro incident became the only case involving occupants that Blue Book officials labeled unidentified. (See Blue Book Case #8766)

By this time there had been so many landings in the area that investigators Jim and Coral Lorenzen wondered if the ETs had some kind of agenda. As they wrote,

THE SOCORRO CASE HAD BEEN PRECEDED BY SOME UNEXPLAINED, AND IN SOME CASES TERRIFYING INCIDENTS ON AND AROUND WHITE SANDS PROVING GROUND – HOLLOMAN AIR FORCE BASE INTEGRATED RANGE. WE HYPOTHESIZED IN THE APRO BULLETIN THAT THIS WAS AN INTELLIGENCE OPERATION OF SOME SORT. THE MILITARY CASES (THE FEW WHICH WE WERE ABLE TO OBTAIN) WERE NOT, NATURALLY PUBLICIZED... WE CONJECTURED THAT IF THE OBJECTS WERE, AS WE THOUGHT, INTERPLANETARY, THEY MIGHT HAVE BEEN ATTEMPTING TO FIND OUT IF MILITARY ORGANIZATIONS TENDED TO WITHHOLD INFORMATION ON CASES

TAKING PLACE WITHIN THE CONFINES OF MILITARY INSTALLATIONS... IN THE CASE OF THE CONCENTRATION OF SIGHTINGS AT HOLLOMAN, WHITE SANDS, AND THE SURROUNDING TERRITORY, IT WOULD BE EASY FOR AN INTELLIGENT SPECIES TO MONITOR RADIO FREQUENCIES AND DETERMINE THAT MILITARY SIGHTINGS WERE NOT PUBLICIZED, WHEREAS CIVILIAN CASES WERE.

In 2003, Zamora was contacted by Socorro-based newspaper reporters and asked if he would consent to an interview. Zamora, long since retired, declined, saying only, "I just don't talk about it anymore."

Recently, another witness to the incident has come forth. Sally Haigler, (a Socorro Chamber of Commerce Volunteer), says that she saw the same object between her home on Lopez Road and the 'M' Mountain. According to Haigler, Hynek told her that about *400* other witnesses had also seen the same phenomenon along the mountain. In the year 2009, Lonnie Zamora passed away.[115]

UFO LANDING AT LA MADERA

On April 26, 1964, a mere two days after the Socorro Incident, the UFOs were back. On that day, La Madera resident Orlando Gallegos observed an object described as bright, metallic, and egg-shaped land on the ground about 200 feet away. A bright ring of blue flames circled the base of the craft, which was totally silent. After a few moments, the craft took off.

UFO researcher Jacques Vallee personally investigated the case. He spoke with Police Captain Martin Vigil who had been called to the scene. According to Vigil, scorch marks and imprints were found where the witness said the object had hovered. While the description of the craft is similar to the one at Socorro, it is not known if they were the same or different craft.[116]

THE SOCORRO CRAFT LANDS AT HOLLOMAN

According to APRO investigators, on April 30, 1964, the pilot of a B-57 bomber from Holloman AFB radioed the control tower that he had an "egg-shaped, white" object with markings that were identical to the one observed at Socorro, less than one week earlier. The pilot was on a routine bomb test mission over Stallion Site. He continued to watch the object, and to his amazement, it landed directly on the base.

Little is known about what happened next, except that Jim and Coral Lorenzen, who first uncovered the case, said that they had three "entirely independent unconnected sources of information" confirming the event.

According to one source, a nearby ham radio operator, he was able to monitor the exchange between the pilot and the control tower. The pilot reportedly shouted out, "I'm not alone up here."

Control asked, "What do you mean?"

"I've got a UFO," the pilot replied.

The controller asked, "What does it look like?"

The pilot replied, "It's egg shaped and white."

"Any markings?" the controller asked.

"The same as the one at Socorro. I'm going to make another pass."

A few seconds later, the pilot shouted out, "It's on the ground!"

At this point, there was a message about photo crews being asked to stand by and then the radio transmission ceased.

While investigating the incident, Coral Lorenzen learned of yet another separate landing. In this case, a guard was on duty on the range at night when he came upon a landed UFO on the base. According to Lorenzen, the guard became distraught as a result of the encounter and afterwards required sedation and hospitalization.

As an aftermath, a few days after the April 30, 1964 incident, an Air Force airman walked into an Alamogordo clothing store and blurted out to people that there was a UFO being held under heavy security at Holloman AFB. Later, he returned to the store and said that he was mistaken. However, by then it was too late; the story was out. Writes Brad Steiger,

LOCAL NEWS MEDIA PERSONNEL WERE BUZZING WITH THE RUMOR THAT A UFO HAD BEEN CAPTURED ON THE GROUND AND WAS BEING KEPT IN A HOLLOMAN AIR FORCE BASE HANGAR UNDER HEAVY GUARD.

Researcher Brad Steiger says that he learned from an inside source that the UFO wasn't so much captured as given. One of his informants said of the incident:

THE UFO LANDED AT HOLLOMAN OF ITS OWN ACCORD. IT WASN'T "CAPTURED" AT ALL. IT WAS JUST ANOTHER OF THE CARROTS THAT THE GRAYS DANGLED ON A STICK TO KEEP THE MJ-12 BOYS HAPPY WHILE THE ALIENS WERE FOLLOWING THEIR OWN SECRET AGENDA.

Writes researcher Kevin Randle,

AN AIR FORCE CREW WAS THERE TO FILM THE SEQUENCE, AND A NUMBER OF PEOPLE CLAIMED TO HAVE SEEN THIS FILM. SUPPOSEDLY THIS FILM WAS INTENDED TO BE USED AS PART OF A DOCUMENTARY TO ANNOUNCE THE PRESENCE OF ALIENS ON EARTH. CLIFFORD STONE, A RESEARCHER LIVING IN ROSWELL, NEW MEXICO, CLAIMED THAT AS AN ARMY ENLISTED MAN, HE SAW THE FILM UNDER STRICT SECURITY.[117]

A SAUCER WITH PORTHOLES

Late in the evening of August 8, 1965, a family in Tularosa was woken up by their aunt screaming in terror. Looking outside, they saw a bright blue light flashing through the window. They went to the window. Says one of the witnesses,

I SAW A SAUCER HOVERING ABOUT FIFTY FEET OFF THE GROUND AND ABOUT EIGHTY YARDS AWAY. IT HAD LIGHT AROUND ITS CENTER AND SEVERAL PORTHOLES. I COULD SEE THE INTERIOR OF THE CRAFT, BUT WITH NO REAL DETAIL. MY SISTER SAID SHE SAW A MAN.

Other than the portholes and a series of lights set around its circumference, the object had a smooth metallic surface with no other markings of any kind. After a few moments, it suddenly picked up speed and disappeared.[118]

A SEVEN-FOOT-TALL ORANGE GLOWING ET

In the summer of 1967, twelve-year-old Chris Brethwaite of Albuquerque had an experience involving UFOs and aliens that he would never forget. At the time, he lived with his family on Tivoli Avenue, directly across the street from the Hoover-Aspen Elementary School in the Northeast Heights section of Albuquerque. The whole experience began when his neighbors began reporting UFOs.

Says Brethwaite,

ON TWO SUCCESSIVE NIGHTS, IN THE SUMMER OF THAT YEAR, PEOPLE ON MY STREET SAW A NEBULOUS BALL OF WHITE LIGHT FLY NORTH OVER THE CITY, TURN TO THE NORTHEAST, PERFORM A SERIES OF ZIGZAG MOVES AND DISAPPEAR OVER SANDIA CREST. THE OBJECT RETURNED FOR A THIRD NIGHT. HOWEVER, AFTER PERFORMING THE ZIGZAG MOVES, IT STOPPED DEAD IN THE AIR. FOURTEEN OF US STOOD IN MY NEIGHBOR'S DRIVEWAY WONDERING WHAT IN THE WORLD THE THING WAS. MINUTES LATER, MY NEIGHBOR WALKED OVER TO ME AND SAID, "CHRIS, I JUST SAW AN ORANGE MAN ON THE SCHOOL ROOF." I KNEW WHAT HE WAS IMPLYING, BUT REMARKED THAT MAYBE IT WAS THE SCHOOL JANITOR IN ORANGE COVERALLS.

I THEN WALKED OVER TO THE CURB WITH HIM AND ASKED HIM TO POINT OUT WHERE HE HAD SEEN THE ENTITY. I STOOD THERE LOOKING FOR SEVERAL MINUTES, BUT ALL I SAW WAS THE BLACK OF NIGHT. I WAS JUST GETTING READY TO TURN AND WALK AWAY, WHEN RIGHT WHERE I WAS LOOKING, APPEARED A SEVEN-FOOT-TALL LUMINOUS ORANGE MAN. HE WAS HUMAN IN SHAPE, THOUGH HIS HEAD WAS SLIGHTLY MORE ELONGATED. HE ALSO HAD SOME KIND OF A BLACK SPECKLING THAT IS HARD TO ARTICULATE BECAUSE I CAN'T EQUATE IT WITH ANYTHING I'M FAMILIAR WITH. TWO SECONDS LATER, HE WAS GONE. BUT I HAVE NO DOUBT AS TO WHAT I SAW — SOMEBODY WHO WAS NOT FROM THIS PLANET. A SHORT TIME LATER, THE UFO RESUMED ITS FLIGHT AND DISAPPEARED OVER SANDIA PEAK. WE LOOKED FOR IT FOR A FOURTH NIGHT, BUT IT DID NOT RETURN.

Brethwaite, who now lives in Kansas City, Missouri, remains convinced that he saw a genuine extraterrestrial. As he says,

[I] GOT TO FIND OUT FIRSTHAND THAT ALIENS REALLY DO EXIST! THANKS TO AN EXPERIENCE I HAD WHILE LIVING IN ALBUQUERQUE IN 1967, I KNOW WE ARE BEING VISITED.[119]

UFO LANDINGS AT ALBUQUERQUE

In May of 1974, numerous people throughout a wide area of Albuquerque reported seeing UFOs. At the time, there was little publicity of the incidents, though researchers were later able to locate and interview numerous witnesses.

Researcher Linda Moulton Howe spoke with several witnesses who reported seeing UFOs, and a few who reported a much more extensive encounter.

Around noon on May 28, 1974, three men (age 20), were camping high in the Sandia Mountains when they observed two craft landed on the ground. One was a silvery-white disc, and the other was a triangular-shaped craft, with strange symbols on one side. Using binoculars they determined the exact location: a section between Menaul and Copper on the trail side of Tramway Boulevard.

The men reported their encounter and were later taken by officials to a military detainment center at Kirtland AFB where they were interrogated by intelligence agents, who seemed particularly interested in the symbols that the witnesses had seen. Following the interrogation, the agents told the witnesses that they had seen a "Soviet incident" and told them that they were never to speak about what happened. To back up this threat, they told the witnesses that they would be monitored at all times.

According to NICAP, on May 28, 1974, during the daytime, a local resident observed a large glowing object traverse the western side of the Sandia Mountains. The witness was unable to see any structure as the light was too bright. He opened his window, but heard no sound. As he watched, the object landed on a nearby hillside, staying there for about an hour, at which point it took off and departed.

Later in the afternoon, a married couple in Albuquerque observed a flattish-round craft move first northward and then eastward at an elevation of 2,000 feet. They said the object was about 50-75 feet in diameter, and was flat, "like viewing a coin on end."

Linda Moulton Howe uncovered another incident which occurred later that evening. An Albuquerque family saw a football-shaped object at around 9 p.m., moving north towards the Sandia Mountains, as if coming in for a landing. Intrigued, they hopped in the car and followed it down Tramway Boulevard, until they hit a roadblock. A state patrol officer told them that they could not proceed any further. According to the family, however, behind the officer, the family was able to observe the craft which was now hovering alongside the rocky hill, surrounded by military personnel.

Researcher Richard Dolan describes this incident as "startling" and writes, "Was this a recovery – or operation – of one or more UFOs?"[120]

TOUCHDOWN AT TAOS

It should be obvious that most UFO landings receive little or no publicity. For example, this next case remains virtually unknown. On March 25, 1979, a deputy sheriff in Taos, and his friend, saw a multi-colored object "about the size of a car" fly across the sky. Suddenly the object descended to the ground. Afterwards a glow came from the area, which was apparently inaccessible by vehicle. After an undetermined time, the object left.[121]

UFO LANDINGS AT KIRTLAND AFB

The pathway of UFO research is a tricky one, as this next case illustrates. On November 14, 1982, a television documentary produced by Ron Lakis called *The UFO Experience* aired on nationwide television. UFO researcher Barry J. Greenwood viewed the program and was shocked to see the screen flash a U.S. government document about a series of UFO events at Kirtland AFB in August of 1980.

Greenwood was an active member of the special interest group, Citizens Against UFO Secrecy (CAUS), founded by Peter Gersten. Both Gersten, Greenwood, and others had used the Freedom of Information Act (FOIA) to wrestle declassified UFO documents from the United States government.

On November 23, 1982, Greenwood filed an FOIA request with OSI Headquarters in Washington, D.C., attempting to get the documents he had seen. In most cases, requests resulted in flat denials, so Greenwood and his associates were shocked when on December 9, the AFOSI released the document stamped "identifiable with your request."

The file is seven pages long and is titled, "Kirtland AFB, NM, 8 Aug – 3 Sep 80, Alleged Sightings of Unidentifiable Aerial Lights in Restricted Test Range."

This official government document goes on to list no less than four UFO *landings* which took place in the Coyote Canyon Manzano Weapons Storage Area at Kirtland AFB.

According to the document, the first encounter occurred on August 8-9, 1980, to three security policemen identified as Sergeant Stephen Ferenz, Area Supervisor Martin W. Rist, and AMN Anthony D. Frazier. The three policemen were each interviewed by Major Commander Ernest E. Edwards, and all revealed the same story. Just before midnight, on August 8, a "very bright light" appeared over the east side of Manzano. Writes Major Commander Edwards,

> THE LIGHT TRAVELED WITH GREAT SPEED AND STOPPED SUDDENLY IN THE SKY OVER COYOTE CANYON. THE THREE FIRST THOUGHT THE OBJECT WAS A HELICOPTER, HOWEVER, AFTER OBSERVING THE STRANGE AERIAL MANEUVERS (STOP AND GO), THEY FELT A HELICOPTER COULDN'T HAVE PERFORMED SUCH SKILLS. THE LIGHT LANDED IN THE COYOTE CANYON AREA. SOMETIME LATER, [THE] THREE WITNESSED THE LIGHT TAKE OFF AND LEAVE PROCEEDING STRAIGHT UP AT HIGH SPEED AND DISAPPEAR.

Commander Edwards later learned that another security guard also saw the object land, but was afraid to report it for fear of harassment. The guards contacted Central Security Control, who in turn alerted all of Sandia Security.

The next UFO event revealed in the document occurred shortly later, at 12:20 a.m. A Sandia security guard who requested anonymity was driving east on the Coyote Canyon access road to perform a routine security check on an alarmed building. Edwards writes,

> AS HE APPROACHED THE STRUCTURE HE OBSERVED A BRIGHT LIGHT NEAR THE GROUND BEHIND THE STRUCTURE. HE ALSO OBSERVED AN OBJECT HE FIRST THOUGHT WAS A HELICOPTER. BUT AFTER DRIVING CLOSER, HE OBSERVED A ROUND DISK-SHAPED OBJECT. HE ATTEMPTED TO RADIO FOR A BACK UP PATROL BUT HIS RADIO WOULD NOT WORK. AS HE APPROACHED ON FOOT ARMED WITH A SHOTGUN, THE OBJECT TOOK OFF IN A VERTICAL DIRECTION AT A HIGH RATE OF SPEED. THE GUARD WAS A FORMER HELICOPTER MECHANIC IN THE U.S. ARMY AND STATED THAT THE OBJECT HE OBSERVED WAS NOT A HELICOPTER.

Meanwhile, the three other security guards who had originally observed the UFO land, also watched the object now race straight upwards toward outer space.

The third incident occurred the next evening on August 10, 1980. On this occasion, the object was not witnessed by security guards inside the base, but by a New Mexico State Patrolman who observed the object land in the Manzano Mountains between the cities of Belen and Albuquerque. The patrolman reported the sighting to Kirtland AFB Command Post, who responded by telling the officer to report the event through his own agency, and that the USAF "no longer investigates such sightings unless they occur on a USAF base."

The fourth and final incident occurred on August 22, 1980. Three new security policemen observed "the same aerial phenomena described by the first three." Writes Edwards, "Again the object landed in Coyote Canyon."[122]

THE OWL-MAN

Although rare, there are a small number of cases in which people have seen unidentified entities flying through the air unaided by any apparent mechanical devices. The Mothman sightings in Virginia are a good example. New Mexico, however, has its own equivalent: the Owl-man. One evening in early May 1984, country-western guitarist, Hayden Scott (pseudonym) was driving home along Interstate 25 to Albuquerque after performing at a gig. He had just passed the Las Lunas exit and was passing through the Isleta Reservation when he noticed a "faint glow" in the sky above the canyon pass, northwest of his location. There were no other cars on the highway. He assumed the light was a plane or helicopter, or perhaps the train which comes west into Belen. But to his surprise, it was coming towards him and it wasn't anything he had ever seen before.

Scott describes what happened next:

I WATCHED THE OBJECT MOVE TOWARD ME FOR A MINUTE OR SO, THEN I BECAME MORE INTERESTED, AS IT APPEARED TO MOVE IN AN INTERSECTING PATH WITH MY VEHICLE... I WATCHED IT APPROACH AND THEN I BECAME VERY PERPLEXED AS IT SEEMED TO BE GLOWING SOMEWHAT LIKE A FLUORESCENT BULB, NOT LIGHTING

THE AREA AROUND IT, BUT GLOWING SORT OF WITHIN ITSELF. IN THE SECOND IT FLEW DIRECTLY OVER MY VEHICLE, I LOOKED UPWARD OVER THE STEERING WHEEL TO SEE THAT THE OBJECT WAS ACTUALLY A LIVING BEING, GLOWING WHITE. AND AT THE LAST SPLIT SECOND I LOOKED UP, IT TURNED ITS HEAD SLIGHTLY AND LOOKED DOWN DIRECTLY AT ME... I COULD NOT MAKE OUT MUCH DETAIL EXCEPT TO NOTICE THAT IT HAD TWO HUGE BLACK EYES. NO WINGS WERE VISIBLE.

Scott immediately tried to rationalize what he had just seen. Perhaps it was just a very large Great Snowy owl, he thought, on a migratory path. The explanation failed, however, as the creature was moving much too fast to be an owl. Also, its flight path was "mechanical" and didn't waver like a bird's does. Furthermore, the creature was "self-illuminated" and he didn't see anything resembling wings. Whatever it was passed a mere 100-200 feet above his car.

For the next two weeks he tried and failed to come up with a rational explanation. And then, two weeks after the first encounter, he saw it again. And this time he wasn't alone. On this occasion, he was driving alone, but his other band-members were in two other cars driving behind him. They had just come in convoy over the mountain pass from Magdalena toward Socorro. Suddenly, Hayden saw something flying above his car.

"I watched in amazement for a few short seconds," he says, "as the same being was again coming towards me...only this time it was significantly lower, possibly only fifty feet above the car. I again peered upward over the steering wheel at the last split second, and again the thing turned its head and looked at me with its big black eyes. Even though it was a lot closer this time, I still could not make out much detail, except to say that the body seemed to be almost trapezoidal, with it tapering toward the head."

When they arrived in Socorro, Scott asked his band-mates in the other vehicles if they had seen anything fly over his car at the mountain pass. The rhythm guitar-player and his wife said that they had seen "some kind of big bird or something" move very fast over Scott's car.

Scott was stunned by this confirmation. The chances of seeing a weird creature like that on two different nights in two different locations seemed remote. Says Scott,

I STARTED TO BECOME A BIT PARANOID ABOUT THIS FACT, AND BEGAN TO FEEL 'TARGETED' OR 'STALKED' BY WHATEVER THIS THING WAS.

Two weeks after the second encounter, the band was practicing at the home of two of the members in south Belen. Scott had brought along his five-year-old son, James, and his three-year-old daughter, Amy. The two children stepped outside of the studio and then came running back inside with an incredible story. Says Hayden,

> "BOTH OF THE KIDS CAME RUNNING INSIDE THE STUDIO DOOR, SCREAMING AT THE TOP OF THEIR LUNGS. MY SON JAMES EXCITEDLY TOLD ME THAT HE SAW A 'CREATURE' ABOVE THE DOOR... HE SAID IT HAD A PAIR OF ARMS, WINGS, AND CLAWED FEET BIG DARK EYES AND BIG EARS. IT BENT OVER THEM AS THEY APPROACHED THE HOUSE AND PUT ONE OF ITS HANDS UP TO ITS MOUTH...SAYING, "SHHH, BE QUIET!" PROMPTING JAMES AND AMY TO RUN INTO THE HOUSE.

Everybody immediately ran outside, but by then the creature was gone. Says Scott,

> AFTER THIS INCIDENT I WAS SURE I WAS BEING TARGETED. BUT I ALSO BEGAN TO FEEL ANGRY AS THIS WAS SOMEHOW INVOLVING MY FAMILY.

June passed uneventful, but on July 4, 1984, the creature made its fourth and final appearance. The band had finished performing a gig for the annual Independence Day ball at Mountainair. Hayden was talking about his recent encounters with the drummer of the band when a "weird feeling" overcame him that he would see it again that very night.

He hitched a ride with the rhythm guitarist and his wife, sitting in the backseat with their daughter. As the trip progressed, the wife suddenly screamed out, "What is it?"

"It's just an owl," said the guitarist.

Scott, who was dozing, instantly woke up. As he says,

> I LOOKED OUT THE FRONT OF THE CAR SEEING A LARGE WHITE THING SWOOP DOWN TOWARD THE CAR, HEAD BACK UP SLIGHTLY, THEN DIVE RIGHT TOWARD THE WINDSHIELD. AS THE ENTIRE WINDSHIELD BECAME TOTALLY BRIGHT WHITE, THE WIFE TOOK BOTH HER HANDS OFF THE WHEEL TO SHIELD HERSELF FROM THE "INEVITABLE" BREAKING OF THE WINDSHIELD. LUCKILY [HER HUSBAND] GRABBED THE STEERING WHEEL AT THE LAST SECOND... IN AN INSTANT, THERE WAS NOTHING AHEAD OF THE CAR EXCEPT TOTAL BLACKNESS OF NIGHT. WE DROVE HOME, ALL OF US SHAKEN UP FROM WHAT JUST HAPPENED.

Scott has no idea why he was targeted by the creature, what it was, or what it wanted. He never saw it again after that.

However, a few years after the series of sightings, his neighbor told him a frightening story. Says Scott,

A NEIGHBOR OF MINE IN BOSQUE, NEW MEXICO, WHERE I LIVED FOR A SHORT TIME, RELAYED A STORY OF HOW HE SHOT AT A CREATURE WHO WAS FLYING FROM LIMB TO LIMB ON A NEARBY TREE — NEXT TO MY PROPERTY — AND HE WAS UNABLE TO HIT IT WITH HIS SHOTGUN AS IT WAS MOVING TOO FAST.

The witness was so impressed by his encounters that he later reported it in detail to MUFON, writing,

TO THIS DAY, I STILL DON'T KNOW WHAT THE HECK I SAW OUT IN THE DESERT, AND I AM STILL AT TIMES A BIT UNNERVED BY THE IDEA THAT I WAS THE APPARENT TARGET OF THIS THING'S INTEREST. [123]

UFO LANDING AT DULCE

One evening in July 1984, officers from the Jicarilla Apache Tribal Police in Dulce were called the residence of an elderly woman. She revealed to one of the officers that she had just been visited by two gray-type ETs who had appeared at the foot of her bed and held a "box-type object" at her, which emitted a red light in her eyes. Says the officer,

THEY [THE BEINGS] WERE FITTED IN A SKIN TIGHT SILVER/GREY ONE PIECE SUIT. ALL HER DOGS WERE QUIET AND WERE FOUND SHAKING BY THE HOUSE IN THE MORNING ALONG WITH THE HORSES. NO BIRDS WERE EVEN CHIRPING. I WAS IN TOTAL AWE OF THE SIGHT I SAW. AND OF COURSE, I AM A TRAINED OBSERVER.

The officers had checked on her all night as they were on the graveyard shift. They visited her again after the sun came up and after exiting her house, observed three "saucer-shaped craft" take off from behind a group of pine and juniper trees. From their distance of sixty yards away, the officers heard no noise and saw no disturbance on the ground. The craft were fiery orange in color. After lifting off the ground, they became bright white and took off towards Chama where they were observed by the Chama Marshall and State Police Dispatchers.

The officer anonymously reported his sighting to NUFORC. [124]

HEALED BY ETS

An anonymous nursing home worker from Deming says that in 1989, she was suffering badly from dizziness as a side effect of medication she was taking. The dizziness was so bad that for three months, she could only walk by holding onto furniture.

Around that time, she was laying down in her bedroom when she had a dream-like experience during which she saw four men, each four feet tall wearing coveralls and hoods over their faces. They were holding a "mysterious box." The witness then found herself slammed back onto her bed, and the entities were gone. She was left alone, sweating profusely in her bed. She got up and went to the bathroom. That's when she discovered that she was no longer dizzy. After she returned from the bathroom, the witness heard a heavy object strike the roof of her home and then run across it. She now believes that she experienced an ET visitation and that they were there to help her. Says the witness,

I THINK THOSE LITTLE MEN TOOK AWAY MY DIZZINESS. I AM GRATEFUL FOR THAT. I THINK THAT THEY WILL COME WHENEVER I NEED THEM.

The witness also says that she has had several UFO sightings in the past, however, as far as she knows, she has not been abducted.[125]

UFOS DISAPPEAR INTO THE GROUND

On March 19, 1993, a Los Alamos employee and fourteen of his co-workers were working on a high plateau overlooking Pojoaque, the location of a Native American reservation, when they had an incredible sighting. Says the witness,

MY CO-WORKERS AND I SUDDENLY WERE STOPPED IN OUR TRACKS WHEN WE SAW THREE EXTREMELY LARGE DISKS – AT LEAST A HALF MILE IN DIAMETER – EMERGE FROM NOWHERE AND ENTER INTO A VERY WIDE OPENING IN THE GROUND. WE WERE AT LEAST FIFTEEN MILES FROM THE LANDING SITE. EACH ONE OF THE DISKS ENTERED THE OPENING, ONE AFTER THE OTHER, THEN THE EARTH CLOSED.

Strangely, the witness says that he was the only one who remembered the sighting. He later tried to find and visit the landing site, but was unable to trespass onto the reservation lands.[126]

UFO LANDING AT ALBUQUERQUE

As reported to NUFORC, a man and his wife were driving through Bernalillo, a suburb of Albuquerque. It was around 1:30 a.m. in mid-July 1998. Only a few cars were on the highway when the wife shouted out, "What the [censored!] is that?"

Says the husband,

> COMING DIRECTLY UP FROM THE GROUND WAS A BALL OF GREEN LIGHT. IT LOOKED SOMEWHAT LIKE A ROMAN CANDLE, BUT THIS WAS FAR TOO BIG TO BE ANYTHING LIKE THAT. IT FLEW STRAIGHT FROM A SPOT WE COULD NOT SEE NEAR THE GROUND, STRAIGHT UP IN THE AIR BEFORE VANISHING. IT WAS VERY LARGE AND MOVING EXTREMELY FAST... OUR FIRST THOUGHT WAS "SHOOTING STAR" EXCEPT THAT IT WAS AN INTENSELY BRIGHT GREEN, AND OBVIOUSLY METEORS DON'T MOVE UPWARDS FROM THE GROUND.

The area where the object had taken off from was Pueblo tribal land, containing a small number of livestock. They were only 1,000 yards away when the object took off.

The witness was so impressed, he reported his sighting to NUFORC, writing,

> WE BOTH SAW IT VERY CLEARLY... IT WAS A BIT UNNERVING.[127]

WEIRD CIRCLE IN MIDWAY PASTURE

In early May 2001, Midway resident Glenn Graves (then 75 years-old) was walking across his property when he discovered a large oval-shaped depression "cut" about six inches into the ground. The circle was twenty-nine feet across in one direction and forty-three in the other. The center was devoid of vegetation. Outside the circle, the soil was normal, hard-baked clay. However, inside the circle, the soil was rich, dark and loose, like potting soil. Graves is certain that the strange oval-shaped mark wasn't there the day before. As he says,

> IT'S A CURIOSITY... I GUESS I STOOD THERE AND JUST STARED AT IT FOR SEVERAL MINUTES.

Graves thought about calling authorities, but afraid of ridicule, he hesitated. Says Graves,

> BUT WITH ALL THE TALK ABOUT UFOS AND THE LIKE, I WAS AFRAID PEOPLE WOULD THINK I WAS CRAZY.

In the next two weeks, there were some heavy rains, causing vegetation to grow inside and along the circumference of the circle. Still bothered by the "oddity," Graves finally called the Chaves County Sheriff's Department, who sent down a deputy to take a look. The deputy, however, declined to file a formal report.[128]

SILVER-SUITED ETS ON THE HIGHWAY

As reported to NUFORC by his wife, on July 27, 2004 at 1:10 a.m., an anonymous truck-driver was driving south along Interstate 25 near Exit 138 when he saw a bright light "like a blue laser" about a half mile ahead, right along the exit ramp. Says the wife,

> AS HE CAME NEARER THE RAMP HE SAW TWO FIGURES APPROXIMATELY THREE TO FOUR FEET TALL. EACH WAS EITHER HOLDING A BLUE LIGHT OR THE LIGHT WAS COMING FROM THEIR HEAD AREA. HE COULDN'T TELL FOR SURE.

The figures were looking out towards the side of the road until he approached. Says the wife,

> THEY LOOKED TOWARD HIS TRUCK AS HE WENT BY. THE FIGURES SEEMED TO HAVE ON LOOSE FITTING BRIGHT SILVER SUITS, SIMILAR TO "HAZ-MAT" SUITS. HE COULDN'T TELL IF THEY WERE WEARING HELMETS.

There were no vehicles in the area. The truck driver drove by intending to turn around, but the next exit was more thirty miles down the highway.

The wife admits that, as truck-drivers, they had both seen weird lights on many occasions, "but nothing as strange as this."[129]

A BALD BABOON?

Many UFO encounters occur to people who are driving along highways late at night. In this case, just after midnight on August 14, 2008, a truck-driver was driving through the New Mexico desert along Interstate 10. He had just passed a rest stop when he saw something very strange. As he says,

I SAW A WHITE CREATURE THAT LOOKED LIKE A BALD BABOON WITH LARGE ALMOND-SHAPED EYES. IT WAS SQUATTING AT THE EDGE OF INTERSTATE 10. I SLOWED THE VEHICLE TO SEE WHAT I WAS LOOKING AT. THE CREATURE STOOD UP ON TWO LEGS AND TURN AND LOOKED. I SAW IT HAD SPIKES RUNNING DOWN ITS BACK... I COULD SEE HIS HAND AND IT WAS PRIMATE-LIKE. THE FACE HAD THE LOOK OF A BABOON AS WELL.

The truck-driver was on a tight schedule and kept driving. However, four days later, he was doing another haul through the same area when he saw that the area was swarming with black vans covered with antenna and other sensing devices. There were also men dressed in black searching the area and a group of helicopters circling overhead. Shocked, the truck-driver counted no less than twenty-four black vans. Says the witness,

THEY WERE DEFINITELY LOOKING FOR SOMETHING ON THE GROUND. MIGHT BE THE CREATURE I SAW?

NUFORC investigators interviewed the witness over the telephone, and he assured them that his report was both "accurate" and "serious-minded."[130]

MORE WEIRD CIRCLES

On May 29, 2010, Dee Gragg (the assistant director of the New Mexico chapter of MUFON) revealed the results of a month's-long investigation into a series of apparent UFO landing sites that were found in the mountains of northern New Mexico. The landing sites were found in an empty pasture in Moreno Valley near the town of Angel Fire.

At least six sites were found, ranging in diameter from five feet to twelve feet. They appear to be foot-wide circular rings where no vegetation will grow.

The owner of the property, Mr. Piper, had no explanation and cooperated in the investigation into the circles.

Although no solid conclusions have been forthcoming, Gragg says,

> MY GUESS IS THAT THIS WAS A LANDING SITE FOR QUITE A LONG TIME.

Investigator Janet Sailor says,

> THIS IS PROBABLY THE MOST SIGNIFICANT THING TO HAPPEN IN THIS AREA. BUT WE NEVER HAD ANY PROOF OF THESE THINGS. NOW WE DO. (SEE THE PHOTO SECTION ON PAGE 304.)[131]

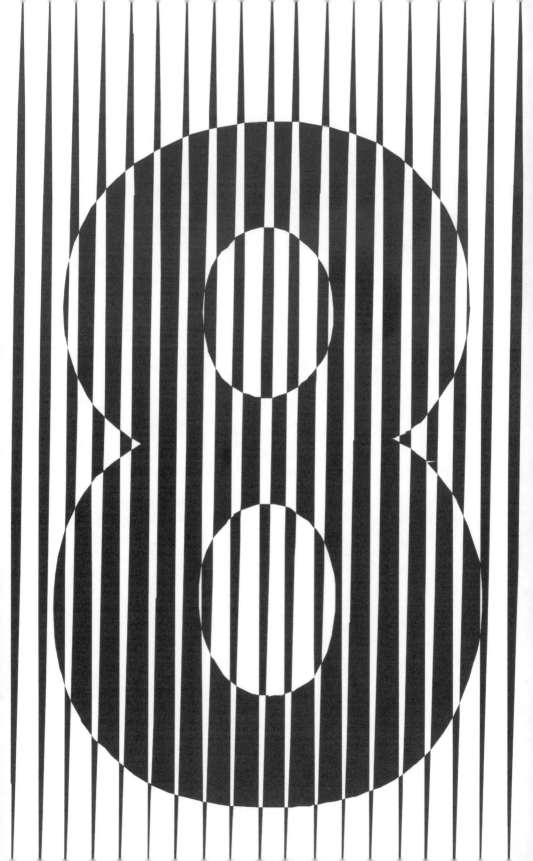

CHAPTER 8

Onboard**ENCOUNTERS**

Perhaps the most controversial aspect of the UFO phenomenon are the many accounts from people who claim to have been taken onboard UFOs. Exactly how many people have had this experience is hard to say. While some UFO researchers believe it is very rare, a Roper Poll conducted by the Bigelow Research Organization found that one in fifty people exhibit the "markers" associated with UFO abduction experiences. If true, this would mean that at least 250,000 New Mexicans have been onboard a UFO.

Most researchers agree that the vast majority of UFO abduction accounts go unreported. While some cases are uncovered through hypnotic regression, others are experienced consciously. In other cases, the witnesses spontaneously recall what happened to them during their period of missing time without the aid of hypnosis. Whatever the case, what follows is only a small representative sample of onboard UFO experiences in New Mexico.

THE CONTACTS OF APOLINAR VILLA, JR.

Born September 24, 1916, Apolinar Villa (a farmer and mechanic from Albuquerque) was also a contactee with friendly human-like aliens. His contacts began when he was only five years old and continued throughout his life. Unlike many contactees, the ETs in Villa's case often posed for him, allowing him to take literally hundreds of very clear photographs of their craft. Throughout the 1960s and 1970s, Villa continued to meet with the ETs and take startling photographs of their craft in various locations across New Mexico.

Villa's first contacts were telepathic. His first face-to-face contact occurred in 1953 in Long Beach, California. He was approached by a seven-foot tall man who led him to a craft floating in the water off the coast. They told him that the universe was incredibly more vast than we here on Earth could imagine. They said they were on a friendly mission to help our people and that they planned to make more appearances in order to increase public awareness of their existence. He was told that they had bases on the moon, and that many countries on earth were experimenting with nuclear power.

On June 16, 1963, Villa was telepathically guided by the ETs to a location outside of Albuquerque, near Peralta. When he arrived, he came upon a landed saucer about seventy feet in diameter. Nine human-looking ETs exited, four men and five women, each ranging in height from seven to nine feet. They told him they come from a different galaxy which we call Coma Berenices, many light years away. They spoke to him in Spanish but told him they were able to converse in many different languages. After the contact, they allowed him to take a series of photographs of their craft as it hovered below treetop level and maneuvered around the field. Researcher Brad Steiger says of these photographs:

AMONG THE CLEAREST UFO PHOTOGRAPHS EVER TAKEN, CONTROVERSY OVER THEIR AUTHENTICITY HAS RAGED FOR DECADES.

Two years later, on April 18, 1965, Villa was telepathically guided to a location near Bernalillo. The ETs showed up and again allowed him to take a series of photographs. At one point, the craft landed and the beings disembarked. Villa talked with them for about two hours. They hoped that humans would rise above their warlike inclinations and told him that love is the most powerful force in the Universe.

Later that month, Villa had another contact and took another series of photographs of Albuquerque near the Volcano Mountains.

On June 19, 1966, he photographed the UFOs near Algodones. On this occasion, the UFOs were small "remote-controlled" craft, a mere three to six feet in diameter.

Villa kept a low profile about his contacts and sought no publicity. However, his startling photographs caused a great deal of attention. He had his mail stolen on more than one occasion, and more and more people began to ask him about the photographs, with some people accusing him of hoaxing them. As a result, he became increasingly private and reluctant to share his information. He moved twice, living most of his life in a small home in Las Lunas. Nevertheless his contacts continued.

On September 24, 1972, Villa was driving his pickup when he saw a group of silvery objects in the distance. Suddenly one of them dropped out of the sky and began circling his truck. He snapped a series of photographs as the UFO – a bright silver disk-shaped object – hovered only a few feet away, again clearly posing for him.

One day in late June 1977, at around 11:30 a.m., Mr. Apolinar Villa was washing dishes in his kitchen. Suddenly he heard a crashing sound. Looking out through the kitchen window, he saw that a truck-bed in front of his home had just fallen off its blocks. Then, looking above the truck, he was shocked to see something else: a small, silver chrome-like flying saucer. It was flat on the bottom with a domed top, and appeared to be about ten to twenty feet in diameter. Villa quickly grabbed his 127 Instamatic camera and rushed out into the yard. He quickly snapped a series of eleven photographs as the object circled over his yard and then darted away. Villa's son also saw the entire event occur.

While Villa's photos have been attacked, nobody has been able to prove a hoax or even reveal any evidence of one. Photographer and researcher Gabriel Green took a set of photos to MGM studios for analysis. The pictures were enlarged and printed in light and dark, and high and low contrast looking for evidence of suspension lines or other trickery. No such evidence was found.

Villa died in September 1982 of stomach cancer. Many of his photos, including those allegedly showing his trip to another planet, have never been published and are now missing. (See the photo section on page 297.)[132]

THE ONBOARD UFO EXPERIENCES OF DR. DANIEL FRY

THIS IS A TRUE STORY OF AN UNIQUE EVENT... BELIEVE IT OR NOT, ON THE EVENING OF JULY 4, 1950, I HAD THE EXPERIENCE OF SEEING, TOUCHING AND RIDING IN AN UNMANNED, REMOTELY CONTROLLED SPACE CAPSULE WHICH LANDED NEAR THE WHITE SANDS PROVING GROUNDS OUTSIDE THE CITY OF LAS CRUCES, NEW MEXICO.

So opens Daniel Fry's controversial book, *The White Sands Incident*, in which he presents his experiences with UFOs and a being named "A-lan."

At the time, Dr. Daniel Fry worked for an aero-jet group as a missile engineering executive at White Sands Proving Grounds. He and his group helped to develop many guided missiles on the base. On the evening of July 4, Fry planned to join the fireworks celebration in Las Cruces. However, he missed the bus, and instead decided to take a walk around the base. He walked along a two-mile dirt road that ended at the base of the Organ Mountains.

As he walked, Fry noticed that the bright stars above him were becoming occulted by a large silent object. With alarm, Fry realized that it appeared to be approaching him. When it was a few hundred feet away, he was able to discern a shape. Says Fry,

FINALLY I COULD SEE WHAT IT WAS. AT THE SAME TIME, I REALIZED WHY I HAD NOT BEEN ABLE TO SEE IT SOONER. ITS COLOR APPEARED TO BE NEARLY IDENTICAL TO THE COLOR OF THE NIGHT SKY SO THAT, EVEN WHEN IT WAS QUITE CLOSE, IT WAS DIFFICULT TO MAKE OUT ANYTHING BUT THE OUTLINE.... ITS SHAPE WAS AN OBLATE SPHEROID ABOUT THIRTY FEET IN DIAMETER AT THE EQUATOR OR LARGEST PART.

To Fry's shock, the craft landed quietly on the ground about seventy feet away. His first thought was that it was "something secretly developed by the Soviet Union." However, as he inspected the craft, he quickly rejected that explanation. It was sixteen feet tall and thirty feet in circumference. Says Fry,

A CLOSER INSPECTION SHOWED THAT THE HIGHLY POLISHED METAL SURFACE WAS SILVERY IN COLOR, WITH A SLIGHT VIOLET IRIDESCENCE. I WALKED COMPLETELY AROUND THE CRAFT WITHOUT SEEING ANY SIGN OF OPENING OR SEAMS.

Fry's first instinct was to return to the base and get more witnesses. However, afraid that the strange craft would depart, he decided to remain. He approached the craft and touched it. Says Fry,

IT WAS ONLY A FEW DEGREES ABOVE THE AIR TEMPERATURE AND INCREDIBLY SMOOTH. IT'S DIFFICULT TO DESCRIBE THE DEGREE OF SMOOTHNESS. IF YOU WERE TO RUN YOUR FINGER OVER A LARGE PEARL WHICH HAD BEEN COVERED WITH A THIN SOAP FILM YOU MIGHT RECEIVE A SENSATION SOMEWHAT SIMILAR TO THAT WHICH I FELT WHEN I TOUCHED THE METAL OF THE SHIP.

At this point a voice said, "Better not touch the hull, pal, it's still hot!" Fry fell back, astonished. The voice then told Fry not to fear, that he was among friends.

So began Fry's contact with "A-lan" or Alan. The voice first explained to Fry that it was dangerous to approach too closely to the craft because of the radiation given off by the ship. Alan told Fry that it was his assignment to "become" an American and live undetected among humanity. He said he had spent the last two years studying the English language, and would spend the next four years going through various procedures to adapt him to Earth's atmosphere, gravity, and germs and bacteria.

Alan told Fry that "one of the principal purposes" of his expedition was to determine how adaptable people's minds were to the idea of their presence, and that previous expeditions centuries ago met with "almost total failure in this respect."

He said that one of their main purposes was "to stimulate a degree of progress which will eliminate the reasons for war on Earth..."

Finally, Alan invited Fry aboard the craft which he called "a remotely controlled cargo carrier."

A door opened, and Fry was surprised to find the craft empty. Inside was a very sparse room with four chairs mounted to the floor, each facing the same direction and forming two rows. Later he would notice that the seats were imprinted with the well-known symbol of "the tree and the serpent." Fry entered inside and, following Alan's instructions, sat in the seat.

Alan asked Fry where he would like to go, and then suggested New York City. Fry was skeptical, but agreed. There were no windows in the craft, so Fry was surprised when suddenly the wall in front of him became clear as "the finest type of plate glass or Lucite window."

Alan then provided a lengthy scientific explanation concerning how they are able to turn metal transparent by creating "a field matrix between the atoms."

Fry watched in amazement as the ground fell beneath him. Says Fry,

> THE LIGHTS OF THE ARMY BASE AT THE PROVING GROUND, WHICH HAD BEEN HIDDEN BY A SMALL HILL, SPRANG INTO SIGHT INSTANTLY AND BEGAN DRAWING TOGETHER LIKE A FLOCK OF BABY CHICKS WHEN CALLED BY THE MOTHER HEN. A FEW SECONDS LATER THE LIGHTS OF THE TOWN OF LAS CRUCES CAME INTO VIEW IN THE LOWER LEFT HAND CORNER OF THE WINDOW, AND I KNEW THAT WE HAD RISEN AT LEAST A THOUSAND FEET IN THOSE TWO OR THREE SECONDS... I WAS ALSO ABLE TO SEE THE HIGHWAY FROM LAS CRUCES TO EL PASO, A NARROW BUT BRILLIANT RIBBON ILLUMINATED BY THE HEADLIGHTS OF THE MANY CARS ON IT.

The craft continued rising until it was, according to Alan, thirteen miles above the surface of the earth. The craft then began moving at 8,000 miles per hour towards New York City. During this time, Alan continued to provide Fry with detailed explanations regarding the propulsion methods used by the craft. He told Fry that they do plan on landing on Earth and publicly revealing themselves when humanity becomes more evolved. He explained that they often travel to earth on mining expeditions as there are materials on earth in great abundance which are scarce elsewhere.

Alan explained that they communicated with Fry, not through telepathy, as he thought, but through a technology that allows them to modulate the nerves in the ear drum to simulate speech. He said that they have the ability to look into people's minds and examine their memories, thoughts, and feelings. He then told Fry that it was no accident that he had been contacted. They had searched through the minds of many scientists, including Fry's, but found that most were too skeptical. When they found that he was open-minded to new ideas, Alan was allowed to establish contact.

Several moments later, the craft was over New York City, at a height of twenty miles. Fry says that the lights of the city were incredibly beautiful and that "the entire city was a seal of pulsing, shimmering luminescence."

Fry asked if he would be able to take a short tour of their mother ship. Alan replied that this was an impossibility due to their atmospheric conditions on their ship. Alan explained that they didn't live on a planet like humans, but permanently inhabited the mothership, which was much larger than any human-made construction.

When Fry noticed the serpent symbol on the seat, Alan then explained that their race and humanity have common origins. He said that tens of thousands of years ago, Alan's people lived on Earth on a small continent called Lemuria. During that time, the civilization Atlantis existed. The two cultures, Alan explained, became very scientifically advanced and then destroyed each other through greed and abuse of power.

By this time, the ship had returned to White Sands, and Fry was told to exit the craft, and that they would meet again. Fry stepped out of the craft and watched with amazement as it left. As he says,

THE DOOR HAD CLOSED BEHIND ME AND AS I TURNED, A HORIZONTAL BAND OF ORANGE COLORED LIGHT APPEARED ABOUT THE CENTRAL PART OF THE SHIP AND IT LEAPED UPWARD AS THOUGH IT HAD BEEN RELEASED FROM A CATAPULT… I MANAGED TO KEEP MY EYES ON THE CRAFT WHILE THE BAND OF LIGHT WENT THROUGH THE COLORS OF THE SPECTRUM, FROM ORANGE TO VIOLET. BY THIS TIME, IT WAS SEVERAL THOUSAND FEET IN THE AIR AND, AS THE LIGHT PASSED THROUGH THE VIOLET BAND, THE CRAFT DISAPPEARED FROM SIGHT.

Fry immediately felt a strong sense of depression. As he says,

I FELT AS THOUGH MY WORK AND MY LIFE HAD LOST ALL ITS SIGNIFICANCE. A FEW HOURS BEFORE, I HAD BEEN A RATHER SELF-SATISFIED ENGINEER SETTING UP INSTRUMENTS FOR THE TESTING OF ONE OF THE LARGEST ROCKET MOTORS EVER BUILT… NOW I KNEW THAT THE MOTOR FOR THOSE ROCKETS WAS PITIFULLY INEFFICIENT AND MIGHT SOON BE OBSOLETE. I FELT LIKE A SMALL AND INSIGNIFICANT COG IN A CLUMSY AND BACKWARD SCIENCE, WHICH WAS MOVING ONLY TOWARDS ITS OWN DESTRUCTION.

Four years later, on April 28, 1954, in Oregon, Alan contacted Fry for the third time, charging him with a mission to "avert the holocaust which is otherwise inevitable." They asked Fry to go public with his story of contact.

Fry asked Alan why they don't just land on the White House lawn. Alan explained that such a maneuver would seriously disrupt our civilization. He said that tens of millions of people would go to great lengths to deny or disprove their existence, and if forced to accept them, thirty percent would end up worshipping them as Gods and the remaining seventy percent would consider them tyrants. He also explained that our military forces would feel threatened and would immediately surround and attempt to take over their craft, and then cover-up the event.

Alan explained that material science has advanced too quickly on Earth, and that because humanity has not evolved spiritually or socially, we were on the pathway to imminent self-destruction. Alan told Fry,

WHETHER OR NOT YOUR CHILDREN HAVE ANY FUTURE TO LOOK FORWARD TO, WILL DEPEND LARGELY UPON THE SUCCESS OR FAILURE OF YOUR OWN EFFORTS.

If we succeed in coming together in peace, said Alan, we will have a "Golden Age" of progress for all humanity.

After the third contact, the ETs promised to contact Fry again. Fry's book, *The White Sands Incident* reveals no other contacts. However, at some point, Fry was able to take moving films of their ships.

At first, Fry kept his experiences a guarded secret. He feared ridicule and saw no reason to expose himself to it. However, in 1954, under increasing pressure from those who knew of his account, he went public and began to lecture about his encounters. Ten years later, his book was published. Says Fry,

NO PUBLIC REPORT WAS MADE OF THIS EVENT AT THE TIME IT OCCURRED; PARTLY BECAUSE THE UNITED STATES MISSILE PROVING GROUND, WHERE I WORKED, OPERATED UNDER A TIGHT "SECURITY COVER"... UNFORTUNATELY, FACTORS INVOLVING THE RULES OF MILITARY SECURITY PROHIBITED THE PUBLICATION OF A LARGE AMOUNT OF THE SPECIFIC DATA I RECEIVED.

Why did he write the book? Says Fry,

THIS IS THE GREATEST AND MOST EXCITING EVENT IN MY LIFE, AND I CAN'T KEEP IT ENTIRELY TO MYSELF.

He later wrote a second book, *Alan's Message to Men of Earth* in which he elaborated upon the importance of social and spiritual progress and the dangers of abusing technology.

Says Fry to skeptics,

> REALITY HAS NO BOUNDARIES. IT IS NOT SMALL NOR LIMITED — IT IS INFINITE. PEOPLE DRAW A CIRCLE AROUND WHAT THEY CONSIDER TO BE REAL, BUT ALL THAT CIRCLE SHOWS IS THE LEVEL OF CONSCIOUSNESS THEY HAVE REACHED.

While Fry did receive some ridicule and disbelief, he also had many believers, including UFO researchers Bryant and Helen Reeve. In April of 1955, the Reeves visited Fry in his home to determine the nature of Fry and his claims of extraterrestrial contact. Writes the Reeves,

> IN OUR OWN PRIVATE RESEARCH, WE HAVE APPLIED OUR OWN METHODS OF COORDINATION AND COMPARISON TO OUR STUDY OF THIS CONTACT. WE HAVE EVEN STUDIED THE HISTORY OF VARIOUS EFFORTS WHICH WERE MADE TO RIDICULE IT. WE ONLY WISH THAT IN OUR REPORTING WE COULD SOMEHOW CONVEY TO OUR READERS SOME OF THE QUALITIES OF DANIEL FRY HIMSELF, ESPECIALLY HIS HUMILITY AND SINCERITY. WHILE OUR OWN IDEAS MAY NOT BE TOO IMPORTANT FOR OTHERS, FOR THE SAKE OF THE FEW WHO MAY WISH TO KNOW — OUR OWN STUDY INDICATED TO US THAT THIS WAS A *PHYSICAL CONTACT* AND WE FEEL THAT THE INFORMATION GAINED WILL IN TIME EMERGE AS AN HISTORIC LANDMARK IN MAN'S EFFORT TO UNDERSTAND AND MASTER OUTER-SPACE.

Today, while many contactee accounts have been dismissed as fanciful hoaxes, Fry's story continues to generate interest among some UFO prominent researchers (including Timothy Good) who maintain that his case is genuine.[133]

THE ABDUCTIONS OF SARA AND DANIEL

Sara X. is today a special education teacher. She has been married to her husband, Daniel, for more than thirty years. Sara grew up in "the back country of New Mexico" and had always known that there was a great deal of unusual activity going on in her area. As her husband, Daniel, says,

> STRANGE SOUNDS, CATTLE MUTILATIONS, ODD SIGHTINGS AND OTHER INSTANCES OF THE UFO PHENOMENON WERE QUITE COMMON IN THE AREA AND IT DIDN'T

TAKE LONG BEFORE HER FAMILY JOINED THE SURROUNDING RANCHERS IN SEEING THEIR SHARE OF STRANGE THINGS IN THE SKIES. THE PEOPLE WHO LIVE IN THAT AREA DON'T MAKE MUCH OF WHAT THEY'VE SEEN AND ARE TYPICALLY UNWILLING TO SPEAK OF WHAT THEY'VE SEEN TO OUTSIDERS. IT'S BOTH BECAUSE THEY DON'T WANT TO BE TROUBLED WITH THE CURIOUS OR SKEPTICAL AND BECAUSE THEY THEMSELVES AREN'T TERRIBLY INTERESTING. THEIR LIVES ARE A FAR MORE SERIOUS STRUGGLE FOR ECONOMIC SURVIVAL THAN MOST OF US MIGHT IMAGINE AND THERE'S LITTLE TIME FOR THE RED LIGHT MR. DAVIS SAW OVER HIS BARN THE OTHER NIGHT.

The activity in Sara's household sometimes became very intense, though the subject was rarely talked about. Says Daniel,

ODD BEEPING NOISES, ROARING NOISES LIKE THAT OF HUGE JET ENGINES OVERHEAD, STRANGE BLUE LIGHTS IN THEIR BEDROOMS, EVEN VEHICLE SIGHTINGS IN THE NIGHT AND OCCASIONALLY DAYTIME SKIES, WERE ALL TAKEN IN STRIDE AND SOON BECAME PART OF THE WEB OF INSIDE FAMILY JOKES AND STORIES — TO BE DISCUSSED ONLY WITH OTHER FAMILY MEMBERS IF AT ALL — AND MOSTLY IGNORED.

Sara's first memory of an actual UFO abduction occurred around the early 1960s (exact date not given). Sara was visiting home on spring break from college. She was driving with her sister and mother, on their way home from a visit to the local town. Their ranch was located at the end of a twenty-three-mile dirt road. They were heading down the dirt road towards the ranch when Sara saw "a huge, black object in the sky."

She looked at it in amazement. Says Sara,

IT WAS LONG, BIG AND BLACK. IT REMINDED ME OF THE X-15. THERE WERE SOME THINGS STICKING OUT OF IT.

Sara turned to her mother and said, "Look at that! I wonder what that is."

"What is the government up to now?" her mother jokingly replied. At this point, the object suddenly disappeared and the three women continued their journey safely home.

It was only much later – during meditation – that Sara began to recall that she had been abducted during this trip. All memories of the experience had been somehow suppressed. Without ever going under hypnosis, however, Sara spontaneously and consciously recalled an extensive abduction scenario.

She recalled driving towards the ranch with her mother and sister. As the strange black object made its closest approach, the engine in their pick-up suddenly died. She asked her mother, "What's going on?"

Her mother replied in fear, "I don't know" and tried to comfort Sara's younger sister, who was crying. Sara then felt a strange paralysis creep over body.

Sara describes what happened next.

> I SAW THREE TALL GRAYS APPROACHING THE TRUCK, DRESSED IN UNIFORMS, APPROACHING FROM THE DRIVER'S SIDE. THE UNIFORMS WERE SILVER IN COLOR, LIKE SILVER CLOTH, BUT NOT LIKE ALUMINUM FOIL. I THINK THERE WAS A BELT.

Without any transition, Sara found herself lying on a table in a white sterile-looking circular-shaped room with three different gray-type ETs standing around her. Her mother and sister were nowhere to be found. Says Sara,

> I WANTED TO GET BACK TO MY MOTHER AND MY SISTER. I WAS VERY ANXIOUS, ALMOST TO THE POINT OF BEING SICK, ON THE VERGE OF THROWING UP. THEY REASSURED ME THAT EVERYTHING WAS ALL RIGHT. THEY DIDN'T SPEAK, THE MESSAGE WAS MORE OF A FEELING. THEY SEEMED VERY CURIOUS ABOUT WHY I WAS SO UPSET ABOUT BEING KEPT AWAY FROM MY MOTHER... THEY KEPT ASKING ME QUESTIONS ABOUT WHY I WAS SO UPSET. I TOLD THEM THAT I LOVE MY MOTHER, THAT WE'RE CLOSE, AND THAT I WANTED TO GET BACK TO MY FAMILY AND OFF THIS SHIP.

Sara says that she can remember very little else about the encounter. She remembered that it reminded her of when she had gone to the hospital to have her tonsils removed, and being separated from her mother prior to the surgery. She spoke with her mother about the abduction experience. Her mother confirmed that she too remembered "some of the details" which confirmed Sara's own memories.

Following the experience, Sara returned to college. She later married her husband, Daniel, and moved to Texas, where both she and Daniel continued to have encounters.

Daniel, like his wife, has a long history of UFO encounters. In Daniel's case, they stretch back to around age four. Most of these occurred in their Texas home. However, at least one occurred in what appears to be the same exact location as Sara's earlier abduction.

It was around the early 1980s (exact date not given) and Daniel and Sarah were driving on the way to her parents' house. It was a very dark night so Daniel had no warning when he came around a bend in the road to find a strange cylindrical-shaped object sitting in the road. The object was about twenty feet long, metallic, and had four landing-struts holding it up. Daniel swerved to avoid the object and skidded to a stop.

At this point, his memory becomes confused. In one memory, he recalls getting out of the car and waiting for Sara who had apparently wandered off somewhere. After a few moments, she returned and they drove home with only a vague memory of seeing the object.

Later, under hypnosis, a different scenario emerged. Daniel recalled seeing the object, nearly colliding with it and skidding to a stop. The next thing he realized, Sara was gone from the car. He remained inside the car. The engine was turned off but the headlights remained shining.

He then felt a hand reach out from behind him and rest on his shoulder. Says Daniel,

> I DON'T FRIGHTEN EASILY, BUT I'M TERRIFIED OF THIS THING, TERRIFIED ENOUGH TO WANT TO RUN AND HIDE. BUT I DON'T MOVE. I CAN'T SAY IF IT'S BECAUSE I CAN'T MOVE OR I SIMPLY DON'T MOVE.

Daniel is convinced that the figure was an ET, and that it was implanting a screen memory in his mind that he was outside the car, pacing and waiting for Sara to return from going to the bathroom alongside the road. After many minutes, Sara suddenly reappeared, got into the car and buckled her seat belt.

Still terrified, Daniel started the car and tore away from the scene. He later told Sara about the incident. She had no memory of it. Immediately afterwards, says Daniel, neither of them discussed it and the amnesia settled quickly into place. Says Daniel,

> PERHAPS THE STRANGEST ASPECT OF MY EXPERIENCES...IS A TENDENCY TO EXPERIENCE SOMETHING BIZARRE, FOLLOWED BY AN UTTER LACK OF CURIOSITY ABOUT WHAT HAPPENED.... A MOTHER AND HER TWO DAUGHTERS ARE STOPPED BY A UFO ON A COUNTRY ROAD, AND NOTHING IS SAID ABOUT IT FOR NEARLY FIFTEEN YEARS. MY WIFE AND I NEARLY COLLIDE WITH A UFO SITTING ON THE MIDDLE OF THAT SAME ROAD, AND WE DON'T DISCUSS IT, OR EVEN REMEMBER MORE THAN A SNIPPET OF THE EVENT FOR MUCH THE SAME LENGTH OF TIME. THE FIRST SIGN OF AN ABDUCTEE IS, IN MY OPINION, A BIZARRE EVENT UTTERLY IGNORED.[134]

MISSING TIME IN CARLSBAD

It was either 1964 or 1965 when a group of teenagers including a young lady, her two brothers, her future ex-husband and one of his friends all decided to drive to the foothills outside of Carlsbad. They were passing time doing an activity they called "coyote calling" which was just hanging out and having fun, howling at the coyotes. It was around 10 p.m. Says the young lady of the group,

> WE WERE DRIVING DOWN ONE OF THE DIRT ROADS WHEN ALL OF A SUDDEN IT GOT LIGHT ALL AROUND US. YOU COULD SEE THE PLANTS AND ROCKS LIKE IT WAS DAYLIGHT. THE PICKUP DIED, AND THEN MY NEXT MEMORY IS THAT I WAS SO AFRAID THAT I WAS ON THE FLOORBOARDS OF THE PICKUP.

It was dark at this point. But then suddenly, the area around them lit up again and then became dark. The pickup now started, but the teenagers no longer recognized the area where they were. Frightened, they drove home. They believed that they hadn't been out for much longer than an hour, but their parents disagreed, and they were grounded for being out so late.

Following the incident, nobody ever discussed it. Many years later, after one of the witnesses had died, the young lady brought up the incident with some of the other witnesses. They discussed the incident and remembered the details, including the light, being very frightened, and also one other strange detail: Each of them remembered that, following the event, they all had to go to the doctor to have a metal object removed from their legs. They also wondered why they never discussed the strange event, which should have been the topic of conversation for years.[135]

UFO ABDUCTS JET FIGHTER OVER ROSWELL

In June of 1965, 16-year-old Jim Cumber and his family were on vacation, visiting the Bottomless Lakes State Park, just east of Roswell. As they camped at the location, they could see the lights from Roswell and Walker Air Force Base to the west. Cumber was an amateur astronomer and owned a 3-inch Newtonian reflector telescope. However, because he was on vacation, all he had with him was a pair of 7x50 binoculars.

He was searching the sky for something to look at with his binoculars when he saw what appeared to be a satellite moving in his direction. Says Cumber,

> AS IT PASSED DIRECTLY OVERHEAD, I ZEROED IN ON IT WITH MY BINOCULARS.
> I CONTINUED TO WATCH AS IT MOVED DIRECTLY BETWEEN TWO SMALL STARS AND
> STOPPED DEAD BETWEEN THEM! IT DIDN'T SLOW; IT JUST STOPPED AND HUNG THERE,
> DEAD STILL, FOR SEVERAL SECONDS. THEN IT WENT OUT, AS IF SOMEONE HAD TURNED
> OFF A LIGHT SWITCH.

Puzzled, Cumber realized the object couldn't have been a satellite. Then,
fifteen minutes later, four pairs of jet fighters appeared and began to perform
a grid pattern over the area where the object had been. Cumber watched
through the binoculars as one of the pairs reached the exact area where the
strange object had disappeared.

Says Cumber,

> AS THIS PAIR OF AIRCRAFT PASSED THROUGH WHERE THE UFO HAD DISAPPEARED, THE
> WINGMAN (TO THE RIGHT REAR OF THE ELEMENT LEADER) FLEW DIRECTLY THROUGH THE
> POINT WHERE THE UFO HAD VANISHED, AND HE VANISHED AS WELL! I WAS WATCHING
> THROUGH THE BINOCULARS, AND THE WINGMAN DISAPPEARED AS IF SOMEONE HAD
> FLIPPED A SWITCH – NO NAVIGATION LIGHTS AND NO ENGINE EXHAUST! THE ELEMENT
> LEADER FLEW ON FOR PERHAPS ONE OR TWO MILES BEFORE HE (APPARENTLY) NOTICED
> HIS WINGMAN WAS GONE. THEN HIS AFTERBURNERS BLOOMED AND HE DOVE STRAIGHT
> FOR WALKER AIR FORCE BASE AT FULL BURNER, STRAIGHT IN, WITH NO APPROACH
> CIRCLE! I LOOKED UP AND SAW ALL SIX OF THE OTHER AIRCRAFT DO EXACTLY THE SAME
> THING. THEY LIT THEIR BURNERS AND DOVE DIRECTLY FOR WALKER AFB. FORGET THE
> APPROACH PATTERN! WITHIN FIVE MINUTES THERE WASN'T A PLANE LEFT IN THE SKY!

Cumber continued to observe the area to see if the missing jet fighter
would re-appear. It never did.

The incident sparked a lifelong fascination in Cumber with UFOs and aircraft.
He later became the MUFON State Section Director of Utah. Says Cumber,

> WHAT HAPPENED TO THAT AIRCRAFT NEAR ROSWELL IN 1965? OCCASIONALLY,
> EVEN NOW, MORE THAN 30 YEARS AFTER THE INCIDENT, I WAKE UP AT NIGHT WITH THAT
> VERY BURNING QUESTION IN MY MIND. SEEING A JET FIGHTER SIMPLY VANISH BEFORE MY
> EYES IS SOMETHING I'LL NEVER FORGET.[136]

MISSING TIME IN LOVINGTON

In early March of 1967, a family of five was driving near Lovington on
their way to visit their grandparents, a trip which usually took about one

hour and a half to complete. The road they drove on was isolated and it was around dusk. No other cars were visible when the family suddenly noticed a "bright object" to the right of their car. Says one of the children, Anthony (pseudonym), who was fourteen-years-old,

> I NOTICED A BRIGHT OBJECT TO THE RIGHT OF THE CAR AND MENTIONED IT. IMMEDIATELY THIS OBJECT WAS DIRECTLY ABOVE THE CAR. AT THE SAME TIME THE RADIO WENT TO STATIC AND WE HEARD THE SPEEDOMETER CABLE BREAK, AND IT ACTUALLY FELT LIKE THE HAIR ON MY HEAD WAS STANDING UP. THERE WAS NO SOUND, BUT THERE WAS LIGHT EVERYWHERE.

Anthony was sitting in the back seat of the car with his other two brothers. He said the object was so large that he could see the edge of the craft extending past the front of their car as it hovered overhead. The perimeter of the craft was lined with colored lights. At the same time, the interior of the car itself was flooded with light.

Writes Anthony,

> I HAD NEVER BEEN SO TERRIFIED IN MY LIFE AND I JUST FROZE WHERE I WAS. MY MIDDLE BROTHER WAS CLIMBING BETWEEN THE FRONT AND BACK SEATS, AND MY YOUNGEST BROTHER WAS ONLY THREE, SO HE DIDN'T SEEM TO REACT.

Suddenly Anthony became terrified when he saw "a huge black eye staring at me from the window beside me... It was a translucent black teardrop shape."

Anthony's next memory was their car moving down the highway and heading for a ditch. His father jerked the steering wheel and managed to keep the car on the road. Writes Anthony,

> WE WERE ALL SO TERRIFIED THAT ALL OF US WERE COMPLETELY SILENT.

When they arrived at their destination, their grandparents were frantic. Anthony's grandfather said, "What happened? I was just about to call the state police to look for you. What took so long?"

Anthony doesn't recall their answer, only that all of them were still in a state of terror. Even now, Anthony is still traumatized by the incident. He reported his experience to the MUFON CMS, saying,

> I AM 54 YEARS OLD NOW... I CAN FEEL MY HEART BEATING RAPIDLY AS I RECALL THIS EVENT, EVEN THOUGH IT HAS BEEN 40 YEARS... I HAVE HAD NIGHTMARES THROUGHOUT THE YEARS, ALTHOUGH THEY HAVE LESSENED WITH TIME. I AM STILL

VERY AFRAID OF BEING ABDUCTED, AND MY HEART RACES EVERY TIME I THINK ABOUT IT.

Once, in Fallon, Nevada, Anthony thought he saw a UFO. Says Anthony, "I prayed that it wasn't what I feared." Thankfully it turned out to be just a star. Prior to reporting his case to MUFON, Anthony had revealed his experience to only about twenty people. "Strangely," he says, "almost everyone seems to believe me. I would like to know what happened, but at the same time, I am too terrified to know any more."[137]

MISSING TIME IN ALBUQUERQUE

On September 22, 1967, a young man was sitting watching the news in his apartment next to his parents' home when he heard his dogs barking furiously. Then suddenly, all barking noises stopped. Curious, he went outside and checked the area. Nothing seemed out of place.

He went back inside, reclined on his bed and continued watching the news. About one minute later, he heard a "somewhat mechanical-sounding" voice say, "I want you to come with me."

Thinking there was an intruder, he grabbed his .38 pistol and went outside. Nothing seemed different, but again the voice said, "I want you to come with me."

Meanwhile, his dogs were hiding on the edge of the property, growling at the shed, but refusing to come closer. The voice kept repeating the same message, "I want you to come with me."

Scared, the witness went back inside and called his dad next door. They both met outside and searched the property again. Says the young man,

WE CHECKED THE HOUSE, THE SHRUBS AROUND THE PROPERTY AND THE SHEDS. WE FOUND NOTHING... THERE WERE SOME BAREFOOT PRINTS IN THE DUSTY GROUND AROUND THE PLACE. THEY DID NOT LOOK LIKE HUMAN PRINTS, AND DIDN'T LOOK LIKE ANY ANIMAL PRINT I HAD HUNTED OR SEEN. THEY WEREN'T VERY CLEAR BECAUSE IT WAS REAL DRY AND QUITE FINE SILTED SOIL. THERE WERE SOME STRANGE SOUNDS LIKE A HIGH-PITCHED WHISTLE THAT CAME AND WENT AS MY DAD AND I WERE MOVING FROM THE SHRUBS INTO THE SHEDS. BUT WE DIDN'T SEE ANYTHING.

I HAVE NO MEMORY OF ANYTHING AFTER THAT. NOT GOING BACK INTO THE HOUSE, NOT GETTING BACK INTO BED OR SAYING GOOD NIGHT TO MY DAD. HE HAS NO MEMORY OF ANYTHING BEYOND OUR CHECKING THE SHEDS. MORE THAN AN HOUR PASSED FROM THE TIME I WENT OUTSIDE THE FIRST TIME AND THE TIME I CAME BACK INSIDE. THE NEWS WAS OVER AND JOHNNY CARSON WAS ON TV WHEN I CAME BACK. THE PROPERTY INSPECTION NORMALLY TOOK ABOUT FIVE MINUTES TO DO.[138]

MISSING TIME IN ROSWELL

It was September 1972 when Steven T. Roney arrived at the New Mexico Military Institute in Roswell, where he planned to study for the next two years. He was a brand new cadet and along with the other freshmen, was assigned to the third level of the Hagerman barracks. He had only been there three days when he had an experience that would haunt him for many years to come.

Roney had just cleaned his uniform and polished his shoes in preparation for an inspection that afternoon. Prior to the inspection, he was supposed to meet his squad leader, Sergeant Peebles, who would make sure that Roney's uniform was properly prepared for the inspection. Not wanting to be late, Roney decided to meet Peebles a few minutes early. The Sergeant's room was on the floor level of the Hagerman barracks, only a minute or two away from Roney's room.

Carrying his newly shined shoes in one hand and wearing socks on his feet, Roney stepped out of his room and went down one set of stairs. He was at the top of the second set of stairs when he saw it hovering in the sky: a "pie-plate, metallic object just hanging there."

Roney identified the object immediately as a UFO. It looked very much like a UFO that he had seen in a photograph taken by Ralph Ditter in Zanesville, Ohio back in 1967.

Says Roney,

MY THOUGHT AT THE TIME WAS, "OH, LOOK! THAT MUST BE ONE OF THOSE SO-CALLED FLYING SAUCERS." I THOUGHT I HAD WATCHED IT ONLY A MINUTE OR TWO, THEN CONTINUED ON MY WAY TO SGT. PEEBLE'S ROOM BELOW. WHEN I GOT DOWN THERE, SGT. PEEBLES SAID, "HEY, F$%#ER, GET IN HERE! YOU'RE TWENTY MINUTES LATE!" HE TOLD ME TO STAND AGAINST THE WALL, WHICH I DID. HE HAD ME SO SCARED MY HEAD WAS SHAKING BACK AND FORTH AGAINST THE WALL. HE READ ME THE RIOT ACT AND I JUST STOOD THERE SHAKING. I TRIED TO TELL HIM WHAT I HAD JUST SEEN AND THE REASON I WAS LATE. IT WAS LIKE I

WAS TALKING TO A CONCRETE WALL. HE DIDN'T SAY ANYTHING OR ACKNOWLEDGE THAT I SAID ANYTHING.

Roney decided to keep the experience to himself. However, as time went on, he became more curious about his sighting. Years later, after learning about the phenomenon of missing time in conjunction with UFOs, he sought out a hypnotist who regressed him back to the time of the incident. The session failed to bring back any new information, however, Roney was impressed by how vivid the memory became while under hypnosis. As he says,

I REACTED THE SAME WAY I DID THEN. MY HEAD SHOOK BACK AND FORTH, SIMILAR TO HAVING A SEIZURE.

More than thirty years later, Roney still wondered about the incident. In January 2004, he wrote a letter to *Fate* magazine in which he detailed his story and asked any possible additional witnesses to his sighting to contact him.[139]

THE ABDUCTION OF A HOBBS FARMER

It was a warm September day in 1974. An anonymous farmer was driving his pickup, and had just approached his home in the town of Hobbs. At that moment, a huge "disc-shaped" object descended over the fields about 500 feet over his barn, and almost directly above the farmer. Amazed, the farmer leaned out of his window and looked up at the object.

Watching from the farmer's home were his wife, daughter and a neighbor. Writes Leonard Stringfield, who first revealed the case,

SUDDENLY, BEFORE THEIR EYES, THE PICKUP TRUCK WITH THE FARMER IN IT WAS LIFTED VERTICALLY FROM THE GROUND AND VANISHED INTO THE UNDERBELLY OF THE DISC. HYSTERICALLY, THE FARMER'S WIFE CALLED THE POLICE.

The unfortunate farmer, however, was *not* returned by the UFO, and was never seen again. Despite the fantastic nature of this case, Stringfield says that it came from a reliable source. Writes Stringfield,

THE FACTS OF THIS CASE, STILL INCOMPLETE, ARE IN THE CONFIDENTIAL FILES OF THE INTERNATIONAL UFO REGISTRY. THE INVESTIGATOR IN THIS CASE, A RADIO NEWSMAN, PREFERS ANONYMITY. THROUGH A GOOD SOURCE HE GOT THE BASIC INFORMATION ABOUT THE INCIDENT FROM AN OFFICER ONLY ON THE BASIS THAT THE NAMES AND MOST OF THE DATA BE KEPT CONFIDENTIAL UNTIL THE VICTIM WAS FOUND, DEAD OR ALIVE.

One year after the incident, the body of a man was found in "unusual circumstances" in the town of Ruidoso, about 150 miles from Hobbs. The body turned out to not be the farmer, but of *another* missing Hobbs resident. The investigator of the case told Stringfield that he was still working with the authorities on the case, hoping that the abducted farmer will be found.

Writes Stringfield,

THE MYSTERY OF MISSING PERSONS LINKED TO THE UFO IS A SENSITIVE SUBJECT, MUCH LIKE ANIMAL MUTILATIONS. MOST PUBLICIZED CASES INVOLVING MISSING PERSONS AND UFOS TURN OUT TO BE CULTISH SHENANIGANS. OCCASIONALLY, ONE LIKE THE HOBBS CASE TAKES ON SERIOUS OVERTONES.

Two years later, Stringfield would investigate another similar case involving an entire family that disappeared following a UFO encounter. (See the following.)[140]

THE ABDUCTION OF SERGEANT CHARLES MOODY

On the evening of August 13, 1975, USAF flight mechanic Charles Moody (who worked at Holloman AFB), decided to watch the Perseid meteor showers, which were active that evening. He left his home in Alamogordo and drove outside of town to watch the stars. After seeing several shooting stars, he was shocked to see one of them drop out of the sky in front of him and stop. It was not a shooting star.

In a later interview, Moody described what happened:

I OBSERVED A DULL METALLIC OBJECT THAT SEEMED TO JUST DROP OUT OF THE SKY AND START TO HOVER WITH A WOBBLING MOTION, APPROXIMATELY 100 FEET IN FRONT OF ME.

As the object moved towards him, Moody tried to start his car, but the engine mysteriously died. The object approached closely and Moody heard a high-pitched whining sound coming from the craft. Looking up, he saw oddly shaped windows, behind which were two or three human-looking forms. Says Moody,

> AT THIS TIME THE HIGH-PITCHED SOUND STOPPED, AND A FEELING OF NUMBNESS CAME OVER MY BODY. THE FEAR THAT I HAD BEFORE LEFT ME, AND I FELT A VERY PEACEFUL CALMNESS. THE OBJECT LIFTED VERY FAST. IT MADE NO SOUND.

After the object had departed, Moody's car started easily. As he drove home, he looked at his watch and saw that it was 2:45 a.m., at least one hour and twenty-five minutes later than it should have been.

Afterwards Moody suffered from lower back pain and a strange rash on his lower body. Concerned about the missing time and his symptoms, Moody discretely contacted APRO researchers, Jim Lorenzen and Wendelle Stevens, who interviewed him about the incident. Moody was concerned that the Air Force would hear about the incident.

Apparently they did, because a few weeks later, Moody was transferred overseas, something Jim Lorenzen had predicted would happen. Before he left, however, Moody wrote a letter to Lorenzen, explaining that his memory of the incident had returned naturally over the past few weeks, and that he now consciously recalled almost everything that had occurred and that he had been taken onboard the craft.

Moody says that after hovering in front of him, the craft landed on the road. Two men dressed in tight-fitting suits approached his car. Moody attempted to shoot at them with his revolver but suddenly felt powerless as the two strange figures pulled him out of the car and dragged him into the craft.

Says Moody,

> THE BEINGS WERE ABOUT FIVE FEET TALL AND VERY MUCH LIKE US, EXCEPT THEIR HEADS WERE LARGER AND NO HAIR; EARS VERY SMALL, EYES A LITTLE LARGER THAN OURS, NOSE SMALL, AND THE MOUTH HAD VERY THIN LIPS. I WOULD SAY THEIR WEIGHT WAS MAYBE BETWEEN 110-130 POUNDS. THERE WAS SPEECH BUT THEIR LIPS DID NOT MOVE.

The beings were dressed in featureless black skin-tight suits, except for one of the figures whose suit was silver-white. Moody was taken to a room where one of the figures (who Moody perceived to be the leader) placed a "rod-looking device" around his body. Says Moody,

> HE SAID THERE HAD BEEN A SCUFFLE WHEN THEY FIRST MADE CONTACT WITH ME, AND HE ONLY WANTED TO CORRECT ANY MISPLACEMENT THAT MIGHT HAVE HAPPENED.

Moody was impressed by the interior of the craft, which he described as having indirect lighting and being "as clean as an operating room."

The beings were telepathic and answered Moody's questions as he formulated them in his mind. Says Moody,

> I WAS THINKING TO MYSELF, "IF ONLY I COULD SEE THE DRIVE UNIT OF THE CRAFT, HOW WONDERFUL THAT WOULD BE." THE ELDER OR LEADER PUT HIS HAND ON MY SHOULDER AND SAID TO FOLLOW HIM. WE WENT TO A SMALL ROOM THAT HAD NO FIXTURES AND WAS DIMLY LIT... THE FLOOR SEEMED TO GIVE WAY LIKE AN ELEVATOR. I GUESS WE WENT DOWN ABOUT SIX FEET AND WHAT I SAW THEN WAS A ROOM ABOUT 25 FEET ACROSS, AND IN THE CENTER WAS WHAT LOOKED LIKE A HUGE CARBON ROD GOING THROUGH THE ROOF OF THE ROOM; AROUND THE ROD WERE THREE WHAT LOOKED LIKE HOLES COVERED WITH GLASS. INSIDE THE GLASS-COVERED HOLES OR BALLS WERE WHAT LOOKED LIKE LARGE CRYSTALS WITH TWO RODS, ONE ON EACH SIDE OF THE CRYSTAL. ONE ROD CAME TO A BALL-LIKE TOP, THE OTHER CAME TO A "T" TYPE TOP. I WAS TOLD THIS WAS THEIR DRIVE UNIT, AND THAT I COULD UNDERSTAND IT IF I TRIED.

The beings told Moody that the craft was only a small observation craft, and that they had a much larger craft which was about 400 miles above the earth. Moody asked if he could see the main craft and was told that time was too short. He was told that limited contact with humans would be made in the future, but only over a gradual period of time. They said that they are concerned about the radiation tests being conducted. They told him that the radar interferes with their ability to navigate, and also that there were currently several different alien races working together. The beings then told Moody that he would not remember what had happened this evening, but that his memory would return over a period of time. Finally that told him that could find him whenever they wanted and that "they would see me again."

Moody was not contacted again, or at least has not revealed any contact. His case later became very well known and is today considered a classic case of an onboard UFO experience.[141]

FAMILY ABDUCTED AND NEVER RETURNED

The following case, investigated and first revealed by researcher Leonard Stringfield, took place on May 26, 1976, in Albuquerque. Writes Stringfield,

A FAMILY OF THREE — WIFE HUSBAND, AND A TEENAGE SON — WAS LAST SEEN MAY 26, 1976, VANISHING WITHOUT LEAVING A TRACE. QUIET INVESTIGATION IS CONTINUING BY THE AUTHOR, WORKING WITH DENNIS HAUCK, DIRECTOR OF THE IUFOR, AND WITH OTHER MEMBERS OF THE CONCERNED FAMILY WHO PREFER ANONYMITY. ONE MAJOR CLUE IS THAT THE MISSING WIFE TOLD HER MOTHER, PRIOR TO DISAPPEARING, THAT SHE HAD ESTABLISHED CONTACT WITH AN ALIEN BEING ABOARD A UFO NEAR THE SANDIA CREST. ACCORDING TO THE MOTHER, HER FRIGHTENED DAUGHTER PREDICTED, "YOU'LL NEVER SEE US AGAIN."

The prediction turned out to be correct. The anonymous family disappeared without a trace. Stringfield heard about the case three months after it occurred. No further information has been forthcoming. This is at least the third case in New Mexico in which people have been abducted by a UFO and never returned.[142]

THE ABDUCTION OF TOM MURILLO

One evening in 1976, Tom Murillo (then a 39 year-old heavy equipment operator) got into a family quarrel and decided to drive out onto the prairie southwest of the small New Mexico town where he lived. He parked his truck and left the radio on as he walked around his truck to cool down. And some point, he heard a rustling sound in the surrounding sagebrush.
Says Murillo,

I LOOKED UP TO SEE A TALL FIGURE. I CALLED OUT AND GOT NO ANSWER, TO WHICH I STARTED CALLING HIM BAD WORDS.

The figure backed out of view. Murillo sensed that something was wrong and started to get back into his truck. He didn't make it. Says Murillo,

> I HEARD THIS WHIRLING NOISE ABOVE ME TO WHICH I COULDN'T MOVE AT ALL. AS AN ELEVATOR FORMED, A TUBE ENGULFED ME AND I WAS RAISED UP INTO THE SPACECRAFT WHERE I WAS INSERTED INTO SOME KIND OF TUBE-LIKE SPACE. I FLOATED THROUGH SOME KIND OF PASSAGE WHICH TOOK ME TO A BIG ROOM WHERE I LANDED ON A GLASS-LIKE TABLE.

Murillo lay on the table unable to move any part of his body except his eyes. Shortly later, four seven-foot-tall, gray-skinned aliens walked in. They had hands with three fingers and were wearing a "flexible armor-type suit" with "strange helmets" that covered their faces.

The four ETs first observed Murillo. They then undressed him and began a physical examination using a scanning device that formed a ring around the table and his entire body. Says Murillo,

> ALL THE DATA PICKED UP BY THE SCANNING DEVICE WAS FED INTO A STRANGE-SHAPED GRAY SCREEN WHERE I WAS FORTUNATE TO SEE MY INSIDES. MY HEART, MY STOMACH AND OTHER PARTS. I JUST LAY THERE AS THEY EXAMINED ME. I FELT SCARED BUT SENSED THAT THEY WERE NOT OUT TO HARM ME. I COULD PICK UP SOMEHOW SOME THOUGHT WAVES OF A FRIENDLY NATURE... [THEY] WERE FRIENDLY.

The ETs expressed "real interest" in the fact that Murillo had ten fingers and toes and during the examination, repeatedly returned to re-examine his digits. Although the ETs seemed friendly, Murillo says that his "frightened state" allowed very little communication.

After the lengthy physical examination, the ETs conversed among themselves. They then lifted Murillo from the table, quickly dressed him in his clothes and then inserted him back into the same tube-like elevator that they had used to draw him into the craft. Seconds later, Murillo found himself "set free on solid earth to find myself with no sense of direction whatsoever."

Having no idea where he was, Murillo looked around and saw he was in the same prairie where he had parked his truck. He then saw the moonlight glinting off the windshield. Says Murillo,

> I THEN BROKE TO PIECES AS MY WHOLE BODY SHOOK UNCONTROLLABLY. I CRIED, "OH, GOD, WHY ME?" I COULDN'T CALM MYSELF AS I CRIED LIKE A BABY...I WAS STILL SHAKING A LOT, BUT FINALLY STARTED MY TRUCK. IT DIED ON ME SEVERAL TIMES TILL I STARTED CRYING AGAIN. I FINALLY HALF-CONTROLLED MYSELF AND STARTED THE TRUCK AND MADE IT HOME. I DON'T KNOW, BUT I DID GET HOME.[143]

THE ABDUCTIONS OF
BONNIE HAYNES

Bonnie Haynes grew up in Taos. She's not sure when her alien encounters began, but her first clue was a series of strange dreams (date not given, late 1970s?). The dream was always the same: She would be forcibly taken from her bed by what she called "horrible-looking humanoid creatures."

Researcher Tom Dongo investigated her case. As he writes,

> THESE BEINGS TAKE HER, HOLD HER DOWN AND INSERT SOMETHING INTO HER MID-SPINAL AREA. IN THE DREAM, SHE REALIZES WHAT IS GOING ON, SO SHE FIGHTS. SHE KICKS VIOLENTLY TO TRY TO DEFEND HERSELF, BUT THE CREATURES CONTINUE IN A COLD, MECHANICAL MANNER AS IF THEY SIMPLY HAVE A JOB TO DO AND THEY ARE GOING TO FINISH IT. THEY SEEMED TO HAVE NO REGARD WHATSOEVER FOR HER EMOTIONAL WELL-BEING.

According to Dongo, the week after she had the first "dream," she had such severe and debilitating pain in the middle of the back that she had to seek medical attention.

In another "dream," a group of beings took her seven-year-old daughter away, telling Haynes that her daughter would not be harmed and would be returned. In the dream, Haynes became very emotional and screamed at them, objecting loudly.

At this point, there was a flash of white light and an angelic-looking female figure appeared, turned to the beings and ordered them to give the child back, which they did.

Haynes' unusual experiences have not been limited to just dreams. On a few occasions, she was led to isolated locations to view what appeared to be an abnormally large and beautiful golden eagle. Dongo has remarked on the possibility that the eagle was a "screen memory." He is now persuaded that there is enough evidence to conclude that Haynes is having apparent encounters with extraterrestrials. Writes Dongo,

> THE SIMILARITY BETWEEN BONNIE'S "DREAMS" AND DOCUMENTED UFO ABDUCTION CASES IS DISTURBING.[144]

THE ABDUCTIONS OF GLORIA ANN HAWKER

One of the few UFO abductees to write a book about her own experiences (and perhaps the only New Mexican to do so), Gloria Hawker was born and raised in Albuquerque. For much of her life she was skeptical of UFOs and aliens. It wasn't until September 20, 1988, when she experienced a particularly dramatic encounter that she began to realize that something strange was happening to her. Five years later, she finally accepted that she was, in fact, a UFO abductee. Eight years after that, her autobiographical book, *Morning Glory: Diary of an Alien Abductee* was published.

Her first clue that UFOs might be real occurred on the evening of September 20, 1988, when she saw a "large, bright white light" hovering in the sky to southeast, a short distance away from her home. Thinking it was a hot-air balloon coming in for a landing, she called her 15-year-old son and 12-year-old daughter to watch.

Hawker grabbed a pair of binoculars and was amazed to see the bright light transform into five or six smaller lights in a circular pattern. When the lights remained in the sky, Hawker called several people, including the local news station and airport, but was unable to receive any confirmation. When she looked outside again, there was another object blinking blue, orange, green, and purple. At one point, planes and helicopters showed up and began to circle the lights. By then, it was so late that Hawker went to bed. Later, however, she would discover that other people also witnessed UFOs in the same area on that night.

Three days later, in the middle of the night, gray-type aliens came through the wall of Hawker's bedroom and approached her where she lay in bed. Wondering if she was dreaming or hallucinating, Hawker screamed. She felt paralyzed as the strange figures surrounded her. One of them placed a hand on her head, while two others seemed to be doing something to her legs, which had been recently injured. At some point, she lost consciousness.

Not knowing about aliens, Hawker didn't know what to think of her experience. She didn't have to wait long for an answer. One month later, she had another sighting of strange lights outside her home. That evening, she woke up and saw a small ball of light inside her bedroom, whizzing around the ceiling.

A few days later, the UFOs were back again. On this occasion, her husband and daughter were also witnesses. They all used binoculars, but were still unable to identify the strange lights.

Over the next few months, Hawker witnessed anomalous lights on several other occasions. Seemingly related, she also experienced a rash of paranormal events, including being pushed by an invisible force, and a long list of premonitions and precognitive dreams.

Then one morning, both Hawker and her daughter woke up to find identical triangular-shaped burn marks on their hands. Says Hawker,

IT APPEARED TO BE A BURN, BUT IT DID NOT HURT LIKE A BURN. WHAT AMAZED ME MOST WAS ITS TRIANGULAR SHAPE.

Hawker received another incredible shock when she went to visit the doctor to examine how her legs had healed from a recent injury. Two doctors told her that x-rays of her foot revealed that it had been subjected to surgery. However, Hawker had never had surgery on her foot.

Meanwhile, she began having dreams in which she recalled being surrounded by gray-type beings inside small rounded rooms. She also recalled seeing hybrid babies.

As time went on, Hawker's experience became more intense and dramatic. In 1993, she was driving near her home when she saw "two silver-colored discs…two spaceships, sitting there, side by side, in a high canyon."

Moments later, a being came through the roof of her car and sat briefly in the back seat before disappearing.

One evening in spring of 1994, she was woken up by a short caped-figure who came into her bedroom. Says Hawker,

I DON'T KNOW IF MY BRAIN WAS ABLE TO COMPREHEND WHAT HAPPENED NEXT. I FOUND MYSELF ON OUR BALCONY, NOT KNOWING HOW I GOT THERE. I WAS STANDING IN FRONT OF A SMALL BLACK VEHICLE THAT HAD ONLY TWO SEATS IN FRONT OF IT. ONE SEAT WAS LOCATED DIRECTLY IN FRONT OF THE OTHER. THE BACK SEAT WAS RAISED UP HIGHER THAN THE FRONT SEAT. THERE WAS A PANEL IN FRONT OF THE FORWARD SEAT. THE PANEL HAD A COUPLE OF RED AND YELLOW LIGHTS ON IT.

Hawker and the being sat in the craft which whisked upward over Albuquerque. She watched the lights below her shrink down and disappear, and a field of stars grow bright before her when she lost consciousness.

In May of 1994, she had an experience during which a gray-type being apparently healed her leg.

Today, Hawker has had literally dozens of face-to-face encounters and onboard encounters with the gray-type ETs. Each member of her family has also had encounters and can corroborate many of Gloria's experiences. Her gripping book delves into great detail and reveals what it is really like to live the life of an alien abductee.

Hawker believes that the ETs promised to one day reveal themselves to everybody.

> THIS IS WHAT I'VE BEEN TOLD, THAT IN A CERTAIN YEAR, A CERTAIN MONTH, THEY'RE GOING TO LET THE HUMAN POPULACE KNOW THAT YES, THIS SPECIES — AND NOT JUST THE GRAYS, THERE ARE OTHER SPECIES: THE NORDICS, THE REPTILIANS, THE PRAYING MANTISES — WILL LET US KNOW THEY ARE HERE... THERE IS A FEDERATION OF THESE SPECIES. BUT HUMAN BEINGS HAVE NOT BEEN ASKED TO BE IN THAT FEDERATION. WE CAN'T EVEN GET ALONG WITH ONE ANOTHER HERE ON EARTH. ONCE WE CAN ALL GET ALONG AND COOPERATE, AND BE ONE HUMAN SPECIES AND ACCEPT ONE ANOTHER AND NOT BE CRUEL TO ONE ANOTHER, THEN YES, WE WILL BE INCLUDED. AND THAT'S WHEN THEY WILL MAKE THEMSELVES AVAILABLE TO US.[145]

THE ABDUCTION OF MYRNA HANSSEN

On May 5, 1980, Myrna Hanssen was driving with her 8-year-old son near the town of Cimarron. Suddenly they were shocked to see two UFOs appear overhead, possibly more. One object was larger, oval-shaped and about twice the size of a Goodyear blimp. The other was a smaller triangular-shaped craft. At this point, all they could remember is leaving the area. They were missing more than an hour of time.

A few days later on May 11, Myrna Hanssen was hypnotized by UFO researcher Leo Sprinkle. Under hypnosis, she recalled a harrowing abduction scenario.

She saw that the UFOs landed in the pasture along the highway and abducted a cow. Moments later, she and her son were also abducted into the craft where they were forced to watch the surgical mutilation of the cow. The operation was conducted by gray-type ETs who told her that it had to be done.

Next, Hanssen and her son were both physically examined. At some point, a strange "jaundiced-looking" man approached and apologized to her, saying that the abduction was a mistake and those responsible would be punished.

At this point, Hanssen's story gets even more bizarre. She recalled that she and her son were taken to a hidden elevator in the New Mexican desert. Going underneath the ground, they found themselves in an underground "city." Here she saw large numbers of human beings working alongside gray-type extraterrestrials.

At one point, the beings separated Hanssen from her son. She became enraged and managed to escape her captors and run into another room. Looking around she was shocked to see vats of various human body parts suspended in bubbling liquid.

The beings then rushed in and took her to another room where they proceeded to implant her with several devices. Following the experience, Hanssen had several CAT scans done, which allegedly verified the presence of these apparent implants.

Finally, she was taken to another room with her son, and both were subjected to strange flashes of light which had the effect of erasing their memory of the incident. They next found themselves being taken into a UFO which took off and deposited them back at the location of their abduction. They were placed back into their car and left with almost no conscious memory of what had just occurred.

According to Air Force officer Richard Doty, the Hanssen case is valid. He says that Hanssen was later hypnotized by an Air Force psychologist. Under hypnosis, she was able to describe and draw one of the facilities at Manzano in great detail.

Hanssen's case was also investigated by Paul Bennewitz, a scientist and UFO researcher, who would later become the victim of an extensive government-sponsored disinformation campaign.[146]

MISSING TIME IN VAUGHN

One afternoon in September 1988, a father dropped his two sons off at Albuquerque Airport and began the drive back to his home in Roswell. He stopped for dinner in Vaughn, and then got back on the highway. At some point, he believes that he must have somehow dozed off or lost consciousness. Says the witness,

> I WOKE UP SURROUNDED BY FLASHING GREEN, RED AND YELLOW LIGHTS THAT SEEMED TO BE SPINNING AROUND MY CAR... I THINK THE LIGHTS WOKE ME UP. I DROVE BACK ONTO 285 AND CONTINUED ON TO ROSWELL AND HOME!

The witness is certain that he lost time as he arrived home much too late for the drive, around 11 p.m.[147]

MISSING TIME IN TULAROSA

On July 12, 1990, a retired Navy man (41-years-old) was working a mine claim outside of Tularosa. At around 11 a.m., he decided to sit down for an early lunch. Says the witness,

> I WAS EATING MY LUNCH [AND] THE NEXT THING I KNOW I WAKE UP FACE DOWN IN THE DIRT. I WAS VERY SCARED. IT WAS AS IF I HAD BEEN PUT UNDER FOR AN OPERATION.

It was now 2:30 a.m., nearly sixteen hours later. The witness jumped into his four-wheel-drive vehicle and drove "like a madman" out of the canyon where his mine was located. A half hour later, he arrived in his home at Alamogordo. His 68-year-old mother was still awake, wondering where he had been. He told her that he took a nap.

He went to take a shower and found that his boots were on the wrong feet.

In the days and weeks following the incident, the witness suffered from apparent post-traumatic stress syndrome. As he says,

> MY MIND WAS NOW BLANK ABOUT MISSING CLOSE TO SIXTEEN HOURS OF TIME. I BECAME SCARED TO GO TO THE DESERT ALONE. WHEN I WOULD GO, I WOULD TAKE A MACHINE GUN WITH ME. I THEN STOPPED GOING TO MY CLAIM NOT LONG AFTER.

Then there were the dreams.

> I HAVE HAD DREAMS WHERE I AM ON A WEIRD-LOOKING TABLE, NUDE, FACE-DOWN. I AM TRYING TO LOOK TOWARDS MY BACK. I SEE A THING WITH WEIRD EYES. [IT] HAS THREE FINGERS AND A THUMB. IT TOUCHES MY BACK AND I AM NO LONGER SCARED. I WAKE UP SHAKING.

The witness reported his experience to NUFORC, adding that he has also seen green fireballs in the same area where he had the missing time.[148]

THE ABDUCTION OF DR RICHARD BOYLAN PH.D

In early 1992, leading UFO abduction researcher Richard Boylan Ph.D. decided to take car trip across the United States in order to visit some of the nation's most secret and heavily guarded installations which have been identified by multiple inside sources as working with extraterrestrial technology.

August 12, 1992 found Boylan driving north on U.S. 180 between Deming and Silver City. Says Boylan,

> IT WAS AT ABOUT 11:20 P.M., I VAGUELY NOTICED A PATCH OF WHITENESS SHINING IN THE MOONLIGHT ON A RISE OVER THE LEFT, ABOUT 200 YARDS OFF THE ROAD.

Boylan was puzzled and wondered if the patch of white could have been snow, except there was no snow at this low of an elevation. Around this time, Boylan saw a "huge luminous cloud of smoke stretched across the highway…a solid curtain across the highway."

Unsure if it was smoke or fog, he slowed down and drove into the mass. At this point, the smoke-fog became so thick that he was forced to stop the car. He exited his vehicle and stepped towards the edge of the road. At this point, he suddenly found himself paralyzed. Says Boylan,

> I COULD NOT MOVE MY BODY. I SENSED THE APPROACH OF TWO PERSONS, WHO GOT ON EITHER SIDE OF ME AND PLACED A FIRM GRIP ON MY FOREARMS. I CANNOT RECALL VIEWING THEM. THEIR FINGERS WERE LONG AND DIDN'T FEEL LIKE HUMAN FINGERS. THEY DID NOT HAVE ARTICULATED BONES, BUT FELT LIKE CONTINUOUS CARTILAGE INSIDE WITH A PADDED, FLESHY EXTERIOR.

Boylan was led by the creatures towards "a metallic vehicle." Says Boylan,

> IT WAS SHAPED LIKE A FLATTENED ARCH WITH ROUNDED ENDS. THE BOTTOM SEEMED MORE FLAT, BUT THAT MAY BE BECAUSE IT WAS PARTIALLY SUNK INTO THE SAND. IT LOOKED METALLIC, ABOUT THE COLOR OF AIRSTREAM TRAILERS, ONLY NOT SO BRIGHT.

Boylan estimates that the craft was about 35-50 feet long and 10-12 feet high. A rectangular opening appeared and he was led inside and placed into a chair in a small room. After a short time, the ETs appeared around him. Only then did he get a good look at one of them. As he says,

> HE HAD A ROUNDISH, OVAL FACE WITH TWO LARGE, HORIZONTALLY OVOID BLACK EYES THAT DID NOT SLANT OR WRAP AROUND THE SIDE. HIS EYES WERE BLACK ALL THE WAY ACROSS, WITH NO IRISES OR PUPILS. I DID NOT NOTICE A NOSE, AND GOT MORE OF AN IMPRESSION THAN A VIEW OF THE MOUTH.

The ET, says Boylan, was about five feet tall and had a thin torso and skinny limbs. After a few moments, he was taken into another room and placed into a dentist-type chair. While in the chair he felt strange sensations, including "a sense of pressure in my nose, as if a small object was being introduced into my nasal passages or even a little higher." He felt strange buzzing feelings in his head, and the sensation of a force-field holding his limbs in place.

After several moments, Boylan was released from the chair. His next memory was "being outside the craft in the night, floating horizontally towards my vehicle."

He was then placed back into the driver's seat. He suddenly found himself driving out of the dissipating fog bank and up U.S. 180 toward the Gila National Forest campground, where he camped for the night. Most of his memory of the event (except for driving into the fog and exiting the car) had been vanquished from his mind.

The next morning, he had a headache and soreness in his nasal passage. He also noticed two small scoop-marks on the top of his right big toe. Only then did he realize that he had arrived at least an hour later than he should have the night before.

Being an abduction researcher himself, he began to wonder, could he have been abducted by aliens? He remembered driving into the fog bank and then driving out of it. In-between there, however, his memory was hazy. He vaguely remembered stopping the car and being pulled out of his vehicle.

A few weeks after he returned home from his trip, Boylan sought out a hypnotist and underwent hypnotic regression. Under hypnosis, the above abduction scenario emerged.

In the weeks following his experience, Boylan found that his attitude towards the ETs had shifted to one of benevolence. He also noticed a dramatic increase in paranormal and psychic events, and would have further dramatic sightings and encounters in both California and Nevada.[149]

THE ABDUCTION OF WILLIAM SHELHART

At around 3 a.m. on April 22, 1994, William Shelhart (a retired Navy officer and letter-carrier) pulled off the highway into the small town of Clovis, New Mexico. He had been driving all night and he wanted to get some gas and coffee and call his wife. Because he had to drive all the way to California, he made his stop short, and quickly got back on the highway, heading towards Fort Sumner.

Later, as he approached the exit, something strange happened. Says Shelhart,

> UPON APPROACHING THE EXIT, I SLOWED DOWN PREPARING TO TURN AND FOR SOME REASON UNKNOWN TO ME, I OVERSHOT THE EXIT AND KEPT GOING. I WAS PUZZLED AS TO WHAT HAPPENED, BUT DECIDED IT WAS NO BIG DEAL AS I COULD CATCH THE NEXT EXIT AT VAUGHN, NEW MEXICO.

Shelhart continued towards the next exit.

> THE ROAD I WAS TRAVELING WAS A MOUNTAIN ROAD, ONLY TWO LANES AND HILLY... ABOUT A HALF-HOUR LATER, I CAME UP THIS HILL. AND WHEN I HEADED DOWN, I COULD SEE FAR OFF IN THE DISTANCE, A HUGE BRIGHT WHITE LIGHT. MY FIRST THOUGHT WAS IT HAD TO BE A HUGE TRUCK COMING, BECAUSE THE LIGHTS WERE SO BRIGHT. THEN A FEW SECONDS LATER, THIS LIGHT STARTED MOVING IN DIFFERENT DIRECTIONS – UP, DOWN, SIDEWAYS, FORWARD... THEY STARTED DANCING...AND I THOUGHT, "MY GOD, WHAT IS THIS?"

Shelhart felt like the light was trying to get his attention. As he got closer, the light suddenly moved from the center of the road to the right, zoomed forward and stopped. At this point he became concerned. As he says, "I had no idea what I was looking at."

He slowed down his car to twenty miles per hour and drove up to the object. Just before he arrived, the light moved back to the middle of the road, came straight for his car and went straight up into the air. He stopped his car and looked upwards through the windshield. Says Shelhart,

> AT THAT POINT, I RECEIVED THE SHOCK OF MY LIFE. THAT'S WHEN I SAW IT. IT WAS A SAUCER-SHAPED VEHICLE AT ABOUT 50-75 FEET IN THE AIR, AND NOT MOVING. THE ONLY LIGHT VISIBLE WAS AN ORANGE HUE OVER THE DOME. THE SURFACE WAS

A DARK GRAY COLOR AND ROUGH-LOOKING. THE ROUND SAUCER UNDER IT WAS EASY TO SEE. THE CRAFT WAS NOT LARGE, MAYBE 36 FEET IN DIAMETER.

Suddenly, Shelhart became consumed with fear. He leaned back in his seat and accelerated away from the area. Looking in his rearview mirror, he saw that the object was following. Shelhart later wrote about the incident,

AT THAT POINT, I WENT INTO A TOTAL PANIC. EVERY MUSCLE IN MY BODY FROZE. I COULD FEEL MY FOOT ON THE ACCELERATOR TRYING TO PUSH IT THROUGH THE FLOORBOARD AND MY HANDS WERE GLUED TO THE STEERING WHEEL. I GLANCED AT THE SPEEDOMETER. IT SHOWED OVER 90 MILES PER HOUR.

After seeing the speedometer register 90 mph, he became concerned because the road had suddenly become dangerous and hilly. And yet, he was more frightened of whatever seemed to be chasing him down the road. Says Shelhart,

OF COURSE I WAS FRIGHTENED. I DIDN'T KNOW WHAT WAS GOING ON. I WASN'T LOOKING FOR UFOS. I MEAN, I HAD NEVER SEEN ONE IN MY LIFE. IT JUST SCARED THE LIVING HELL OUT OF ME.

His next memory was of looking in the rear view mirror and watching the light move off in another direction and go away. He breathed a sigh of relief and headed towards the next exit. At this point, however, events became even more bizarre.

Shelhart started to feel disoriented and frightened. The road and the environment did not seem familiar. There were lots of hills and trees, and the road was different. There were no other cars on the road, and he couldn't figure out where he was.

Next he saw something which scared him badly – what appeared to be an extremely thick cloud bank came roiling towards his car like an enormous landslide. He had no choice but to drive directly into it. Says Shelhart,

I'VE NEVER SEEN ANYTHING LIKE THAT IN MY LIFE — IT WAS JUST LIKE A BIG ROLLING THING… WHEN I HIT THOSE CLOUDS, AND THEY STARTED ROLLING IN ON ME…I FELT I WAS IN THE CAR. I FELT I WAS DRIVING… AND EVEN THOUGH I FELT I WAS DRIVING ON THE ROAD, A SENSATION OF BEING IN THE CLOUDS OVERCAME ME.

A few seconds after driving into the fog, he popped out on the other side and found himself driving north on the I-40. He was shocked. Only a short time earlier, he had been more than 50 miles away. Says Shelhart,

> It seemed like such a short time to cover 50-plus miles... See, that's the funny part of it. The road that I was traveling was about an hour and a half to get up to I-40, which would take me straight into Albuquerque. And I swear to the God Almighty, I made that in such a short time. It's true I was traveling fast, but I wasn't traveling *that* fast, that I could have covered that in say, 30 minutes.

After finding himself on the I-40, he pulled immediately into a rest-stop and parked between two large semi trucks, as he did not want to be alone. When he woke up a few hours later, one of the semis was being towed away. Shelhart asked the driver what was wrong with his truck. The truck-driver said that all his batteries were completely dead. Shelhart checked his own vehicle and was puzzled to find that his own car had suffered a blown-fuse.

When he returned home later, his wife greeted him with a strange story of her own. Shortly after her husband had phoned her from Clovis, she was watching television when it started changing channels by itself. She turned the TV off, but then it came on by itself. She turned it off again, and again, it turned back on.

A few years later, William and his wife experienced a close-up UFO sighting and missing time in Arizona. Under hypnosis, they recalled an extensive onboard UFO experience. At that time, William was also hypnotized to recall what happened during his 1994 trip in New Mexico. Unfortunately, he was not able to recall anything.

Nevertheless, he believes that he was probably abducted. He feels certain that he experienced a period of amnesia, and he also is unable to explain how he got onto the I-40 so quickly. But the clincher came about two years later, when Shelhart drove the same route again. As he says,

> Two years [after] my original encounter, I got on that road...and what shocked me is there wasn't a tree, and there wasn't a hill. And that first night, that's all I saw, was hills and trees. Now I don't know, but that blew my mind. Two years later I travel the same road, and all of a sudden, it's flat, straight and no trees. I can't even explain that. I mean, I was totally, totally shook up from that because I know what I saw that first night. I remember going up and down hills. I remember seeing trees. That is strange, isn't it, so help me God.[150]

GROUP ABDUCTION IN SANTA FE

In the Spring of 1997, a Native American woman (a peer counselor who ran A.A. meetings and held traditional "talking circles" for other Native American students) was participating in a school dance event, at the school where she worked.
Says the anonymous witness,

I WAS SINGING WITH THE OTHER SINGERS WHEN ONE OF THE DRUMMERS POINTED TO THE NORTHWEST AND SAID, "OH, MY GOD! LOOK AT THAT!" WHEN I TURNED AND LOOKED, I THOUGHT WE WOULD BE CRUSHED IN A FEW SECONDS BY THE ENORMOUS SHIP WE SAW. IT SEEMED TO BE LANDING. IT WAS SO ENORMOUS I CAN ONLY SAY THAT IT LOOKED LIKE A LARGE METROPOLIS. IT MADE NO SOUND BUT HAD A STRANGE ENERGY THAT YOU COULD "SENSE OR FEEL." IT HAD MILLIONS OF LITTLE LIGHTS ALL OVER IT AND IN MANY COLORS. IT WAS LIKE A CITY BECAUSE IT WAS NOT A UNIFORM SHAPE. IT HAD MANY APPENDAGES AND PARTS TO IT. IT WAS SO BIG IT SEEMED TO BLOCK OUT THAT PART OF THE SKY. I WAS STANDING THERE AND JUST COMPLETE SHOCK HIT ME. THIS IS ALL I REMEMBER.

WHEN WE "CAME TO" OR BECAME CONSCIOUS AGAIN, I FELT DAZED. AND THE MEMORY OF IT WAS FADING SO QUICKLY THAT I HAD TO MEDITATE QUICKLY TO HOLD IT IN MY MIND. EVERYONE ELSE SEEMED TO JUST GO BACK TO WHAT THEY WERE DOING AND WHEN I TRIED TO GET THEM TO TALK ABOUT IT OR EVEN COME WITH ME TO GO SEARCH FOR IT, THEY SEEMED LIKE ZOMBIES.

Finally, she convinced one witness – the psychologist who worked with her – to go search for the object. They drove around for two hours looking for it and never found it. They did see military jets circling the area, and later heard that calls reporting a UFO had come into local radio and police stations.

She is convinced that she and several others who were at the school event all had missing time and amnesia of the event. Strangely, a few days after it occurred, she completely forgot about the event. As she says,

FOR ABOUT FIVE YEARS, I COULD NOT REMEMBER IT.

One day, somebody brought up the subject of UFOs and the entire incident spontaneously flooded back into her mind. Says the witness,

I WAS OVERWHELMED AND THAT SAME SHOCKED FEELING CAME OVER ME. I STILL DON'T REMEMBER WHAT HAPPENED THOUGH BETWEEN THE TIMES I SAW IT LANDING AND THEN THE NEXT SECOND "POOF" IT WAS JUST GONE, COMPLETELY VANISHED.

The witness reported her missing time encounter to NUFORC, writing,

I THOUGHT IT WAS TIME TO TELL THE STORY... I AM A NATIVE AMERICAN AND MY TRIBE BELIEVES IN ALIENS COMPLETELY. I DO TOO, ESPECIALLY NOW.[151]

ABDUCTEE ATTEMPTS SUICIDE

A close encounter, particularly an abduction, can be extremely traumatic, and beyond the abilities of some to cope with. On July 20, 2000, state police officer Billy Cunningham of Grants went to investigate a report of an abandoned Jeep Cherokee in Cibola County. He and a sheriff's deputy arrived on the scene and spotted blood inside the vehicle. Further investigation revealed a trail of blood leading away from the scene. The two officers followed the trail of blood for two miles for five hours to the top of a remote mesa where they found the victim, an unidentified woman from California. The woman had slit her wrists in her car and then hiked up to the mesa where she first fired a flare pistol into the ground (apparently a failed suicide attempt), and then cut her throat with a rock. When the officers found her, she was dazed and bleeding heavily. Says Officer Cunningham,

SHE JUST TOLD ME SHE HAD BEEN IMPREGNATED BY AN ALIEN...THAT SHE DIDN'T WANT TO HAVE AN ALIEN BABY. SHE CUT HER THROAT WITH A ROCK.

The officers rescued the woman who was rushed off to Cibola General Hospital for emergency surgery. No other information was forthcoming on the case.[152]

MISSING TIME IN RIO RANCHO

On June 18, 2003, a woman (who prefers to remain anonymous) returned to her home from work around 6:15 p.m. She opened the door and, as suddenly, there was a period of missing time and she found herself looking up at a craft directly over her head. Says the witness,

> I SAW A SHIP HOVERING ABOVE MY BACK PATIO JUST MISSING THE TOP OF OUR MIMOSA TREE IN THE BACK YARD. THE OBJECT WAS APPROXIMATELY 30 FEET BY 30 FEET BUT WAS NOT A SILVER DISK... IT HAD ATTACHMENTS, PLATES AND BOLTS, AND THERE WERE ANTENNAE STICKING FORWARD IN THE FRONT. AS I STOOD THERE I HEARD A LOW HUM, ALMOST TOO LOW TO HEAR, RESONATING FROM THE OBJECT.

The witness walked into the back yard to see the other side of the craft. She stood twenty feet below it and saw that it had "three equal rectangle areas on back that glowed red."

The object then began to move, floating over to the neighbor's yard, circling the tree, and then zooming upwards until it appeared to be only a tiny dot in the sky. Then it was gone.

The witness returned inside to go tell her husband what she had seen. To her shock, it was 9 p.m., and she was missing nearly three hours of time.[153]

THE ABDUCTION OF LINDA AND ANNE X

On March 21, 2004 at around 5:45 p.m., Linda and Anne (sisters) were driving from Santa Rosa to their home in Clovis. They were heading down Route 60/84 about two miles past Fort Sumner when they saw a triangular formation of lights, which appeared to be train-lights. However, a few minutes later, the road seemed to change. They knew the road well, so when it suddenly began to narrow and veer to the left in an apparent spiral, both women became concerned and disoriented. The road in this area, they knew, was supposed to be wide and straight. Also, there were no other cars on what was normally a busy road.

At this point, they noticed twelve to fifteen strange lights, about four feet high, spaced in a circle ahead of them. At this point, Anne became increasingly disoriented and dizzy, while Linda (who was driving) felt that the experience was "somehow unreal, not really happening."

Suddenly, the spiral of lights un-winded and flashed past their car on the right side. As soon as the lights moved past their car, the scene returned to normal. The road became straight and wide and other cars became visible ahead and behind them.

They kept driving and fifteen minutes later arrived in Melrose. It was now 7:45 p.m. They later realized that they could not account for more than an hour of time.

That evening Linda felt ill and did not sleep well. She later noticed that she had somehow received a small cut in the middle of her lower back. Anne also noticed a mysterious bruise or indentation which had appeared on her left shoulder after the incident.

MUFON field investigator Donald R. Burleson Ph.D. investigated the case. He returned to the site with the witnesses and even took radiation readings, which came up negative. Burleson concluded,

BASED ON THE ACCOUNTS GIVEN, I WOULD SUGGEST THAT IT WOULD NOT BE UNREASONABLE TO ASSOCIATE THE EVENT WITH UFOS... THE PHYSICAL ANOMALIES, LINDA'S SMALL CUT ON HER BACK AND ANNE'S TENDER INDENTATION ON HER RIGHT SHOULDER, ARE THE SORT OF THING THAT RAISES THE POSSIBILITY OF ABDUCTION, ESPECIALLY THE LOST TIME ELEMENT.[154]

MISSING TIME IN DULCE

On September 16, 2008, a husband and wife, residents of Dulce, decided to drive to Pagosa Springs, Colorado for an early dinner. They took a short cut along a little-traveled dirt road. To their dismay, they came upon two horses lying dead along the side of the road. Getting out of the car, the husband observed that the horses were missing various body parts including the flesh from their cheek area, their ears, and all their legs from the knees down. Three other dead horses were also visible farther out in the field – presumably in the same mutilated condition.

They left the area and continued towards Pagosa Springs where they enjoyed their dinner. Later that evening, they returned home to Dulce along the same route. As they approached the area long the dirt road where they had seen the horses, they slowed down. However, when they arrived, the horses were gone.

"Look at that! In the sky!" the wife said.

Says the husband, "I leaned down toward her lap to look out her window. I could see a dim white light to the north toward Archuleta Mesa."

As they watched, the light moved, south, then east, and then north, completing a full circle around their car. It then passed directly in front of the moon. Says the husband,

> I COULD CLEARLY SEE THE SHAPE OF THE CRAFT. IT LOOKED LIKE A LONG CYLINDRICAL BUTANE TANK. IT WAS FOLLOWED BY WHAT I THOUGHT WERE TWO SMALLER BLACK OBJECTS, ALMOST FLYING IN FORMATION.

"Let's just get out of here," his wife said.

The husband agreed and started to accelerate. "The object then descended," he says, "and circled directly behind and above our car. I looked up through our sunroof and saw that the object/light was right above us and slightly behind. The last thing I remember is looking through my sunroof at the light. Then we were just driving like nothing had happened."

When they got home, they were shocked to see that it was 10:10 pm. They should have arrived home around 8 or 8:30 p.m., which meant there were two hours that they couldn't account for. Not only were they missing time, both were confused by how they lost sight of the object, and why they felt no emotion as they drove away. Says the husband, "It just does not add up."

Realizing that what happened to them, the husband reported their experience to MUFON.[155]

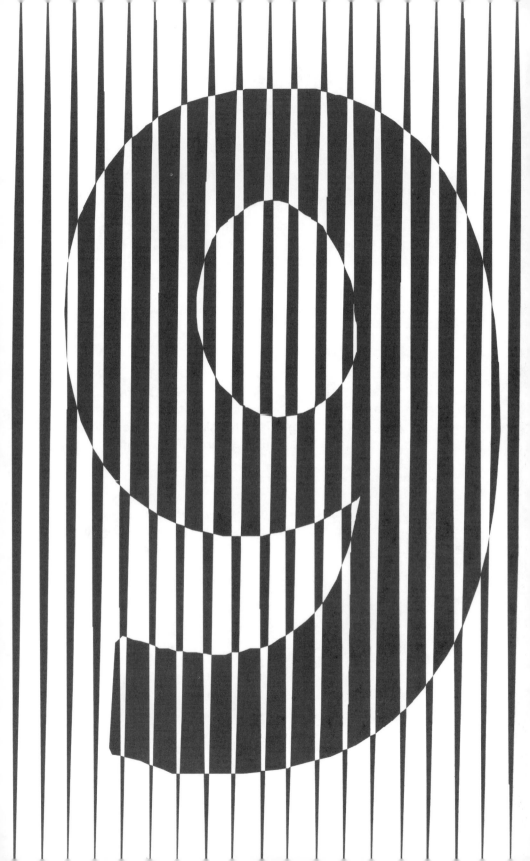

CHAPTER 9

ufoCRASHES

In June of 1945, the world's first atom bomb was exploded in the New Mexican desert. Within two years, the world was engulfed in a gigantic UFO super-wave. It wasn't long before one or more of these craft either crashed or were shot down by the United States military. The 1947 Roswell incident is by far the most famous, but it is not unique. UFO researchers have uncovered scores of accounts from across the United States and the world. New Mexico, with more than a dozen cases, has had perhaps more UFO crashes than anywhere in the United States, if not the world.

The reason for so many crashes in a state that is comparatively sparsely populated remains a matter of speculation. The advanced research into atomics, primarily at Los Alamos Labs, and the surrounding areas, would seem to be the major factor. For whatever reason, the state of New Mexico has produced an abnormally large number of crashes, more so than any other state by several magnitudes.

As with sightings, researchers have likely only touched the tip of the iceberg. The following dozen or so cases probably represent only a small portion of the actual number. Because UFO crashes involve hard physical proof of extraterrestrial reality, the United States military has taken extraordinarily severe measures to keep these accounts secret. While researchers have uncovered mountains of circumstantial evidence in the form of documents and eye witness testimonies, landing traces and more, the actual UFO hardware remains elusive and beyond the domain of the public.

UFO CRASH AT SAN ANTONIO

In August 1945, two young boys, Jose Padilla and Remegio Baca, were working on the Padilla Ranch outside of San Antonio when they stumbled upon a crashed UFO complete with live occupants. According to Baca, they were actually looking for a lost cow when they came upon the crashed UFO. Says Baca,

> WHAT WE SAW WAS A LONG, WIDE GASH IN THE EARTH, WITH A MANUFACTURED OBJECT LYING COCKEYED AND PARTIALLY BURIED AT THE END OF IT, SURROUNDED BY A LARGE FIELD OF DEBRIS. WE BELIEVED THEN, AND BELIEVE TODAY, THAT THE OBJECT WAS OCCUPIED BY DISTINCTLY NON-HUMAN LIFE FORMS WHICH WERE ALIVE AND MOVING ABOUT ON THEIR ARRIVAL MINUTES AFTER THE CRASH.

The witnesses approached the site. The area around the craft was littered with pieces of "thin, shiny material" which reminded them of tinfoil. Baca picked up one piece to examine. As he says,

> IT WAS FOLDED UP AND LODGED BENEATH A ROCK. WHEN I FREED IT, IT UNFOLDED ALL BY ITSELF. I REFOLDED IT, AND IT SPREAD ITSELF OUT AGAIN.

Through a gash in the side, Baca and Padilla observed the humanoid creatures move in quick darting movements while making weird squeaking sounds "like a jackrabbit in pain."

Padilla (who was nine years old) wanted to approach and examine the craft, but Baca (who was younger) became afraid. As it was getting late, they returned home.

The boys returned to the ranch on their horses to tell the owner of the ranch, Faustino Padilla, what had happened. Faustino agreed to check it out. He believed it was probably a military experiment. He contacted state policeman Eddie Apodaca, who agreed to help investigate. Two days later, Faustino Padilla, Apodaca and the two boys returned to the site of the craft. Once there, however, they discovered that the site had been largely swept clean of debris and that the beings were now gone. Only the large nearly intact body of the craft itself remained, though it had been covered with dirt and debris as if to disguise it.

The craft was too big to move, so after observing it for several minutes, the witnesses returned to their ranch. Shortly later, a man showed up at the ranch, saying that his name was Sergeant Avila and that an "experimental weather balloon" had come down on their property. He requested permission to remove one of their fences so they could bring in some heavy equipment to remove it. Faustino Padilla agreed.

On August 20, a crane and a low-boy trailer were brought in, and were used to lift the craft and carry it away. The entire operation took five days and was observed by the two boys from a secret vantage point on their property. First, all surrounding debris was collected. Then the large craft was lifted up onto the flatbed truck, covered with a tarp and hauled way.

Jose Padilla claims that they recovered some of the metallic debris, which remained on the ranch for several years. Today only two pieces remain. Both have been sent for metallurgical tests, which revealed that both samples were composed of aluminum. Dr. Smith, who examined the samples, says that the aluminum has an unusually high percentage of carbon, and that the metal had a strange structure. Says Baca,

THERE IS CERTAINLY SOMETHING UNUSUAL ABOUT THAT METAL... IT APPARENTLY DOES NOT MELT WHEN SUBJECTED TO THE 2,000-DEGREE FLAME FROM AN OXY-ACETYLENE TORCH FOR UP TO TWO MINUTES, DESPITE THE FACT THAT ALUMINUM SILICATE WOULD BE EXPECTED TO MELT AT ABOUT 700 DEGREES... A BLEND OF CARBON AND SOME OTHER TRACE MATERIALS IS USED WHICH DRAMATICALLY INCREASES THE CONDUCTING POWER, ELIMINATING THE RESISTANCE TO ELECTRICITY, WHILE AT THE SAME TIME A TRANSFERENCE OF HEAT TAKES PLACE. THERE APPEARS TO BE THE POTENTIAL FOR HEAT SHIELDING, OR COMPUTER-CHIP MANUFACTURING.

Remigio Baca and Jose Padilla have co-authored a book about their experience titled, *Born on the Edge of Ground Zero, Living in the Shadow of Area 51*.[156]

WHITE SANDS SHOOTS DOWN A UFO?

There are many reports of the military attempting to shoot down UFOs. One early report occurred few days before the Roswell crash, on May 29, 1947, at White Sands Proving Grounds. According to researcher and former Republican State Representative C. Jon Kissner, radar technicians at White Sands observed one or more unidentified radar targets hovering to the south west of the WSPG Launch Row. At 7:15 p.m., one surface-to-air missile with a 674-pound atomic warhead was fired at one of the radar targets. Five minutes later, the warhead exploded at an elevation of 60,000 feet.

Meanwhile, witnesses in Las Cruces (including the editor of the *Las Cruces Sun News* and his neighbors) saw the rocket climb into the sky and move towards two star-like objects high in the sky and then explode.

Apparently the tactic worked. Following the explosion, the target was tracked on radar moving south. Ten minutes later, it impacted the earth about thirty miles to the south, outside the town of Juarez, Mexico. Although U.S. officials attempted to go to Mexico and retrieve the object, the town of Juarez had already been closed-off by Mexican officials, who refused to allow anybody inside the area. According to Kissner, whatever had crashed, however, had been largely vaporized upon impact.[157]

THE ROSWELL UFO CRASH

Of all recorded UFO crashes, the Roswell incident remains unparalleled. Several hundred testimonies now support a story that for more than twenty years remained virtually unknown. It wasn't until 1971, when UFO researcher Stanton Friedman interviewed Major Jesse Marcel, an intelligence officer who was stationed at Roswell in 1947 and was a firsthand eyewitness that the story of the UFO crash finally came to light.

Friedman began to seek out other witnesses. He also contacted other researchers who located additional witnesses. The first book on the case, *The Roswell Incident*, by William Moore and Charles Berlitz, which was based largely on Friedman's research, broke the floodgates. More researchers now began to work on the case, including Kevin Randall, Don Schmitt, Tom Carey, and many others. Before long, hundreds of additional witnesses had been located, covering virtually every aspect of the incident.

Researchers have interviewed everybody from the radar operator who first saw the craft on radar, witnesses who saw it plummeting to the ground, the rancher who discovered the wreckage, the officers who were called to the scene, the soldiers who guarded it, the pilots who flew the wreckage, the people who examined the bodies, the scientists who attempted to study the craft, and so on. Today the crash has been so thoroughly researched that there are several dozen books focusing solely on the subject, including one by the Air Force who continues to insist that the object was a then secret Mogul weather balloon, a theory most researchers have dismissed as ludicrous.

What makes the Roswell crash different from every other crash/retrieval case is that researchers have been able to confirm the details of the event virtually from start to finish. Where most UFO crash reports rest on the testimony of a small handful of witnesses, the Roswell case involves so many people, it has become impossible to dismiss. Many researchers consider it to be the single greatest UFO case of all times.

While it has taken many years, we now have a fairly complete picture of what happened on the fateful evening of July 4, 1947.

There was a severe lightning storm over the Roswell area that night. A large, metallic craft, somewhat disk-shaped, and piloted by four short humanoid beings had somehow become disabled. Apparently unable to remain aloft, the craft fell downward and crashed onto the ground of a ranch north of Roswell. It created a long gouge in the earth and then took off again. It traveled a few miles of distance and landed on the neighboring sheep ranch owned by Mac Brazel. After several moments, it took off again, leaving an area of the ground burned and fused by high temperature. However, it only traveled a short distance when it malfunctioned again. This time it crashed violently into the ground, exploding and disintegrating the outer shell of the craft. It bounced several times, digging a shallow gouge in the earth and showering considerable debris along a quarter mile stretch. Around that time, Brazel heard a strange explosion and decided to check the next morning at daylight. The craft then took off again, flying over the nearby Capitan Mountains. Another rancher watched it bounce down briefly on a hilltop, sheering off the tops of trees and scattering more foil-like debris, before taking off again. Other witnesses watch it fly over the mountains, reporting that it was being accompanied by two other craft.

By this time, the Roswell craft had lost all control and appeared to be on fire. It lost altitude as it crossed over the mountains and headed for the desert floor.

William Woody and his father were driving through Roswell when they saw the flaming object fly overhead crash to the ground in the distance. They attempted to drive to the location to look for it, but were turned back by a military cordon blocking the road.

At the same time, a small group of archeologists saw the crash, and thinking that it was a normal aircraft accident, they waited until daylight to hike to the location.

Also witnessing the actual crash were Jim Ragsdale and his girlfriend Trudy Truelove. They were camping when they saw the craft crash on the desert floor not far from them. They also assumed it was a normal aircraft accident.

Sheriff George Wilcox received a call about an aircraft accident at his station, so he phoned Dan Dwyer at the local fire department and informed them of the approximate location. Dwyer prepared to travel to the area.

Meanwhile, radar operators at Roswell Base had been tracking the object, and watched as it flared up and disappeared off the screen. One of them, Steve Mackenzie, was part of a small group of Roswell officers who were dispatched to locate the craft.

The archaeologists arrived first, walking around the craft. Shortly later, prospector Barney Barnett stumbled upon the craft. Ragsdale and Truelove were hiking to the location and saw the military from Roswell Base arriving. They retreated to the hidden safety of their campsite and moved away slowly.

The Roswell officers first on the scene acted quickly. All non-military personnel were ushered off the scene and told it was their patriotic duty to remain silent. A perimeter was set up, and roadblocks. MPs were ordered to stand guard. Others were ordered to pick up loose debris.

Roswell fireman Dan Dwyer showed up around this time and was shocked by the scene before him. In the confusion, he was at first overlooked, but it wasn't long before he too was ordered away from the scene.

Meanwhile photographic experts were brought in. After everything was photographed, the craft and bodies were recovered and taken to the base. The entire scene was thoroughly cleaned of any debris. It's around this time that mortician Glen Dennis began receiving calls from the base inquiring about how to preserve bodies. He decided to drive out to the base to see if he can help.

Meanwhile, rancher Mac Brazel woke early the next morning and, exploring his property along with the son of his neighbor, they came upon the now famous Roswell debris field. Brazel was dismayed as his sheep would not cross the debris field, and whatever it was, there was so much of it that it would take him days to clean up.

The debris consisted of three main types. Most numerous was a thin foil-type of material, apparently metallic but which could not be torn or burned. Some of the foil was thicker and could be bent but would always resume its original shape. A second type included fragments of I-beams, tan or brown in color with pastel purple hieroglyphic-like symbols along the edge. It was similar to balsa wood in weight, but could not be broken, burned, or dented. Also among the debris were strange wire-like filaments, like fiber optics, and other miscellaneous debris.

Realizing it was unusual, Brazel picked up a small piece of the balsa-wood type material and showed it to his neighbors, the Proctors. They talked about the possibility that it was from a flying saucer, many of which had been seen in the area recently. He tried to get them to view the debris field, but the Proctors declined.

Another neighbor of Brazel, also a rancher, looked at his own field and saw a large mysterious gouge and flattened area. Not knowing anything about a crashed UFO, he didn't think much of it.

By now, the bodies and wreckage had arrived at the base. Glenn Dennis arrived just in time to glimpse the wreckage and the bodies. He was able to gain access to the hospital, and speak briefly with a nurse friend of his who was shocked to see him there and urged him to leave, telling him that he was in danger. At this point, the military police intercepted him, and then threatened to kill him if he revealed anything that he had seen.

The next morning, July 6, Brazel collected some of the debris and drove it to the sheriff's station in Roswell about seventy-five miles away. Sheriff George Wilcox was impressed and called the base. Intelligence officer Major Jesse Marcel was sent to investigate. While waiting for Marcel, Wilcox sent out two deputies to the ranch to view the wreckage. They returned unable to find it, but instead said that they came upon a circular burned area on the ranch, where the sand appeared melted because of extremely high temperatures.

At the same time, the local radio station called and reporter Frank Joyce interviewed Brazel over the telephone. Brazel revealed what he had found at his ranch.

Major Marcel arrived at the police station, and impressed by what Brazel had found, took some of the wreckage back to the base and showed it to Colonel Blanchard. Also impressed, the Colonel ordered Marcel and counter-intelligence agent, Sheridan Cavitt to go investigate the site.

Marcel and Cavitt returned to the sheriff's station, found Brazel and followed him back to his ranch. It was evening by the time they arrived, so they spent the night and investigated early the next morning, July 7.

It was quickly clear to them that the material was not from any conventional aircraft or weather balloon. The two men collected as much as they could fit into their jeep and car and returned back to the base.

Marcel, however, stopped first at his home to show his wife and son the debris, which had not yet been classified or identified, so technically, he wasn't breaking any rules. It was the middle of the night, but waking up his son to show him bits of a flying saucer seemed like it would be worth it. His wife and son were suitably amazed. After a short while, he returned to the base with the wreckage.

The next morning, July 8, Colonel Blanchard examined the wreckage and held a high level meeting. He ordered the ranch to be immediately cordoned off and the roads to the area blockaded. Once on the actual ranch and crash site, he ordered a group of MPs to guard it, facing outwards, and another group to pick up the debris and place it inside vehicles that had been brought to transport the debris. Early that day, he ordered the base's Public Information Officer, Walter Haut to issue the now famous Roswell press release, telling the entire world that the army had done the unbelievable: recovered an actual flying saucer! As the press release reads:

> THE MANY RUMORS REGARDING THE FLYING DISC BECAME A REALITY YESTERDAY WHEN THE INTELLIGENCE OFFICE OF THE 509TH BOMB GROUP OF THE EIGHT AIR FORCE, ROSWELL ARMY AIRFIELD, WAS FORTUNATE ENOUGH TO GAIN POSSESSION OF A DISC THROUGH THE COOPERATION OF ONE OF THE LOCAL RANCHERS AND THE SHERIFF'S OFFICE OF CHAVES COUNTY.
>
> THE FLYING OBJECT LANDED ON A RANCH NEAR ROSWELL SOMETIME LAST WEEK. NOT HAVING PHONE FACILITIES, THE RANCHER STORED THE DISC UNTIL SUCH TIME AS HE WAS ABLE TO CONTACT THE SHERIFF'S OFFICE, WHO IN TURN NOTIFIED MAJOR JESSE A. MARCEL OF THE 509TH BOMB GROUP INTELLIGENCE OFFICE.
>
> ACTION WAS IMMEDIATELY TAKEN AND THE DISC WAS PICKED UP AT THE RANCHER'S HOME. IT WAS INSPECTED AT THE ROSWELL ARMY AIR FIELD AND SUBSEQUENTLY LOANED BY MAJOR MARCEL TO HIGHER HEADQUARTERS.

Haut contacted the local radio stations and gave them the press release, which would appear the next day in the *Roswell Daily Record*. The press release would go off like an atom bomb, generating interest from across the world.

Meanwhile, Brazel was hiding in the house of Walt Whitmore, a reporter for KGFL in Roswell. Whitmore interviewed Brazel and planned to air it as soon as possible. Unfortunately, before he had the opportunity to do so, he was contacted by government officials and told in no uncertain terms that he was not to broadcast the interview.

British officer Major Hughie Green was driving through New Mexico around this time, and was shocked to hear several stations talking about the crash of a flying saucer. All the stations were buzzing about the encounter, and details of the story were developing as he drove along the highway.

After leaving Whitmore's house, Brazel reported to the base, where he was held incommunicado for at least three days. Military officers proceeded to question him and convince him not to go public with his story.

Whitmore was contacted and told not to air the interview with Brazel. Instead Brazel returned, and gave a watered-down version, discarding any public mention of a flying saucer.

The rest of the debris was gathered up, and the military began the process of plugging any leaks in the cover-up, starting with a press conference explaining that the debris described in the press release was not from a flying saucer, but was from a secret weather balloon.

Meanwhile, mortician Glen Dennis contacted the nurse, and she described the bodies in detail, drawing sketches for him. The beings were described as short, slender, with oversized heads. The nurse said she was so sickened by the smell, that she had great difficulty working. She was reportedly killed in a plane crash a few weeks later. Her identity has never been verified.

As the wreckage began to come into the base, excitement mounted. According to Ruben Anaya, he and Senator Joseph Montoya (then New Mexico's lieutenant governor), were both present on the base at the time of the incident. Anaya says that Montoya was "very, very scared" and told him that he had seen "four little men." He said they were hairless, their skin was white, and they wore tight-fitting one-piece jumpsuits. He told Anaya,

> I TELL YOU THAT THEY'RE NOT FROM THIS WORLD.

Montoya has made no comment regarding Anaya's revelations.

On July 7, Lydia Sleppy, administrator at KOAT radio in Albuquerque says that at 4 p.m., local reporter Johnny McBoyle called their station to reveal that a flying saucer had crashed near Roswell. McBoyle said he had been to the site and seen the craft which looked like a crumpled dishpan. McBoyle was sending his report through the teletype machine when the machine suddenly stopped. Sleppy says that McBoyle seemed very excited. Then suddenly, McBoyle left the phone for a moment to talk to someone else. When he returned to the phone, the teletype printed out to "stop communication immediately." McBoyle then told Sleppy,

> FORGET ABOUT IT. YOU NEVER HEARD IT. YOU'RE NOT SUPPOSED TO KNOW. DON'T TALK ABOUT IT TO ANYONE.

Several other civilians were threatened to remain silent.
Writes Kevin Randall, a leading Roswell researcher,

> IF NOTHING EXTRAORDINARY HAPPENED AT ROSWELL, WHY THE EXTRAORDINARY EFFORTS TO KEEP IT SECRET?

Researcher Stanton Friedman agrees:

THE UFO CRASHES IN NEW MEXICO LAUNCHED THE U.S. GOVERNMENT ON A
LONG-TERM, ELABORATE, AND HIGHLY SOPHISTICATED CAMPAIGN OF CONCEALMENT
AND DISINFORMATION THAT HAS YET TO BE RELAXED.

Meanwhile, the wreckage and bodies were being shipped out to various locations for study.

Reportedly, one of the ETs survived the crash. According to rumors and unverifiable sources, the ET was able to communicate with humans and told a history of the human race that is allegedly very different from what most people believe.

Also, some of the wreckage and bodies were shipped to Fort Riley where Lt. Colonel Philip Corso pried open a crate and viewed one of the bodies. Corso claims he was later given a locker filled with debris and given the task to see if it could be made useful. Corso says that the Roswell debris was eventually used to help develop various technologies including night-vision goggles, Kevlar, the integrated circuit, fiber-optics, lasers, and more.

Over the next two years, Bill Brazel continued to find bits of wreckage. He had amassed nearly a dozen pieces when one day the military showed up and asked to have it. Brazel handed it over. And so the Roswell UFO crash story continues. The story has taken more than sixty years to unfold, and it shows no signs of stopping. We have not heard the last of Roswell. Unfortunately, as time marches on, the number of living witnesses becomes smaller every day. Fortunately, researchers have acted quickly enough to gather the testimony of enough witnesses to convince any skeptic.

What follows are quotes from some of the well-known witnesses of the world's most famous UFO crash.

LORETTA PROCTOR

THE DAY FOLLOWING THE CRASH, MAC BRAZEL TRAVELED TO HIS NEIGHBORS,
FLOYD AND LORETTA PROCTOR TO SHOW THEM A PIECE AND ASK THEM TO TAKE A
LOOK. SAYS PROCTOR, "HE DID BRING A LITTLE SLIVER OF A WOOD-LOOKING STUFF
UP BUT YOU COULDN'T BURN IT OR YOU COULDN'T CUT IT OR ANYTHING. I GUESS
IT WAS JUST A LITTLE SLIVER OF IT, ABOUT THE SIZE OF A PENCIL AND ABOUT THREE
OR FOUR INCHES LONG...IT WAS KIND OF BROWNISH TAN...IT LOOKED LIKE PLASTIC,
OF COURSE, THERE WASN'T ANY PLASTIC THEN BUT THAT WAS KIND OF WHAT IT
LOOKED LIKE."

BILL BRAZEL.

THE SON OF MAC BRAZEL, BILL ALSO VIEWED AND HANDLED PIECES OF THE ROSWELL UFO CRAFT, SOME OF WHICH HE PICKED UP IN THE MONTHS FOLLOWING THE INCIDENT. AS HE SAYS, "IT WEIGHED ALMOST NOTHING... THESE WERE LIKE BALSA WOOD IN WEIGHT, BUT A BIT DARKER AND MUCH HARDER... THERE WERE ALSO SEVERAL BITS OF METAL-LIKE SUBSTANCE, SOMETHING ON THE ORDER OF TINFOIL EXCEPT THE STUFF WOULDN'T TEAR AND WAS ACTUALLY A BIT DARKER IN COLOR THAN TINFOIL — MORE LIKE LEAD FOIL, EXCEPT VERY THIN AND EXTREMELY LIGHTWEIGHT. THE ODD THING ABOUT THIS FOIL WAS THAT YOU COULD WRINKLE IT AND LAY IT BACK DOWN AND IT IMMEDIATELY RESUMED ITS ORIGINAL SHAPE."

BESSIE BRAZEL

THE DAUGHTER OF MAC BRAZEL, BESSIE WAS 12 YEARS OLD WHEN THE UFO CRASHED ON HER FATHER'S RANCH. SHE VIEWED THE WRECKAGE WHICH SHE DESCRIBED AS "SO MUCH DEBRIS SCATTERED OVER PASTURELAND. THERE WAS WHAT APPEARED TO BE PIECES OF HEAVILY WAXED PAPER AND A SORT OF ALUMINUM-LIKE FOIL. SOME OF THESE PIECES HAD SOMETHING LIKE NUMBERS AND LETTERING ON THEM...LIKE PASTEL FLOWERS OR DESIGNS... IT WAS ALL VERY LIGHT IN WEIGHT BUT THERE SURE WAS A LOT OF IT.

"WE WERE TOLD NOT TO TALK ABOUT THIS AT ALL. BACK IN THOSE DAYS WHEN THE MILITARY TOLD YOU NOT TO TALK ABOUT SOMETHING, IT WASN'T DISCUSSED."

INTELLIGENCE OFFICER MAJOR JESSE MARCEL

MARCEL WAS THE FIRST MILITARY OFFICER TO EXAMINE THE WRECKAGE ON MAC BRAZEL'S RANCH. SAYS MARCEL, "I SAW A LOT OF WRECKAGE, BUT NO COMPLETE MACHINE... IT WAS DEFINITELY NOT A WEATHER OR TRACKING DEVICE, NOR WAS IT ANY PLANE OR MISSILE. WHAT IT WAS WE DIDN'T KNOW. WE JUST PICKED UP THE FRAGMENTS. IT WAS SOMETHING I HAD NEVER SEEN BEFORE, OR SINCE, FOR THAT MATTER. I DIDN'T KNOW WHAT IT WAS, BUT IT CERTAINLY WASN'T ANYTHING BUILT BY US AND IT MOST CERTAINLY WASN'T ANY WEATHER BALLOON.

"THERE WAS ALL KINDS OF STUFF — SMALL BEAMS ABOUT THREE EIGHTHS OR A HALF INCH SQUARE WITH SOME SORT OF HIEROGLYPHICS ON THEM THAT NOBODY COULD DECIPHER. THESE LOOKED SOMETHING LIKE BALSA WOOD, AND WERE OF ABOUT THE SAME WEIGHT, EXCEPT THAT THEY WERE NOT WOOD AT ALL. THEY WERE VERY HARD, ALTHOUGH FLEXIBLE, AND WOULD NOT BURN. THERE WAS A GREAT DEAL OF AN UNUSUAL PARCHMENT-LIKE SUBSTANCE WHICH WAS BROWN IN COLOR AND EXTREMELY STRONG, AND A GREAT NUMBER OF SMALL PIECES OF METAL LIKE TINFOIL, EXCEPT THAT IT WASN'T TINFOIL."

JESSE MARCEL JR.

MARCEL'S SON, JESSE JR. WAS 11 YEARS OLD WHEN HIS FATHER BROUGHT HOME PIECES OF THE DEBRIS TO SHOW THEM. SAYS JESSE JR., "THE MATERIAL WAS FOIL-LIKE STUFF, VERY THIN, METALLIC-LIKE, BUT NOT METAL, AND VERY TOUGH. THERE WAS ALSO SOME STRUCTURAL MATERIAL TOO — BEAMS AND SO ON... IMPRINTED ALONG THE EDGE OF SOME OF THE BEAM REMNANTS THERE WERE HIEROGLYPHIC-TYPE CHARACTERS."

JIM RAGSDALE

RAGSDALE WAS CAMPING WITH HIS GIRLFRIEND WHEN THEY SAW THE ROSWELL CRAFT CRASH. THE NEXT MORNING, THEY APPROACHED AND VIEWED THE WRECKAGE AND BODIES. REGARDING THE OBJECT, RAGSDALE SAID, "YOU COULD STILL SEE WHERE IT HIT... ONE PART WAS BURIED IN THE GROUND, AND PART OF IT WAS STICKING OUT OF THE GROUND."

HE SAW PIECES OF WRECKAGE WHICH LOOKED LIKE FOIL. SAYS RAGSDALE, "YOU COULD TAKE THAT STUFF AND WAD IT UP AND IT WOULD STRAIGHTEN ITSELF OUT."

REGARDING THE ALIENS, HE THOUGHT AT FIRST THEY WERE MIDGETS. AS HE SAYS, "THEY LOOKED LIKE BODIES. THEY WEREN'T VERY LONG, FOUR OR FIVE FOOT LONG AT THE MOST."

SERGEANT ROBERT ROBBINS

ROBBINS WAS STATIONED AT THE BASE AS AN AIRCRAFT SHEET METAL REPAIRMAN. ACCORDING TO HIS WIDOW, ANN, HE TOLD HER THAT HE WAS ON THE SECOND SITE AND SAW THE CRAFT AND BODIES. HE SAID THE OBJECT LOOKED LIKE TWO SAUCERS PUT TOGETHER AND THAT ON THE TOP LAYER THERE WERE OBLONG WINDOWS AROUND THE PERIMETER. HE SAID THE ENTITIES HAD LARGE PEAR-SHAPED HEADS, LARGE BLACK EYES, NO APPARENT NOSE OR MOUTH, AND BROWNISH SKIN. ONE WAS STILL ALIVE.

AT FIRST, ROBBINS REFUSED TO REVEAL ANY INFORMATION TO HIS WIFE, BUT HE FINALLY RELENTED, SAYING, "WELL, I GUESS YOU MIGHT AS WELL KNOW. IT'S GOING TO BE IN ALL THE PAPERS. A UFO CRASHED OUTSIDE OF ROSWELL."

STEVE MACKENZIE

MACKENZIE WAS STATIONED AT THE RADAR STATION AND WATCHED THE ROSWELL CRAFT DISAPPEAR FROM THE SCOPES. HE WAS ONE OF A SMALL GROUP OF MEN SENT TO RECOVER THE ACTUAL CRAFT. THEY WERE STUNNED BY THE SIGHT OF THE CRAFT AND BODIES AND NOT SURE WHAT TO DO. SAYS MACKENZIE, "WE WERE ALL SMOKING CIGARETTES AND TALKING ABOUT HOW THE HELL WE WERE GOING TO HANDLE THIS THING. WE WERE ALL CONCERNED AND A LITTLE SCARED."

MACKENZIE SAW THE BODIES WHICH HE DESCRIBED AS SLENDER, FIVE FEET TALL WITH OVERLY LARGE HEADS AND LARGE EYES. HE OBSERVED TWO DEAD BODIES LAYING ON THE GROUND AND TWO OTHERS INSIDE THE CRAFT. ONE WAS ALIVE, SITTING NEARBY. SAYS MACKENZIE, "THAT'S THE ONE THAT I CANNOT FORGET. IT HAD THIS DAMNED SERENE LOOK ON ITS FACE...LIKE IT WAS AT PEACE WITH THE WORLD."

MACKENZIE SAYS THAT THE BODIES WERE QUICKLY REMOVED. "WE HAD A SPECIAL GROUP COME IN WHO WERE WELL COVERED... [THEY] PUT THEM IN BODY BAGS."

WILLIAM BLANCHARD EASLEY

ANOTHER MEMBER OF THE 509TH BOMB GROUP WHO WAS SENT TO THE SECOND SITE, EASLEY SET UP THE PERIMETER GUARD AROUND THE CRAFT AND ORDERED A SECOND GROUP OF MPS TO PICK UP THE LOOSE WRECKAGE. SAYS EASLEY, "THE SECOND GROUP [OF MPS] SCANNED QUITE A LARGE AREA LOOKING FOR DEBRIS... IT WAS LOADED ONTO A TRUCK AND THEN ONTO A PLANE, AND IT TOOK OFF. WHATEVER THEY FOUND WAS JUST ODDS AND ENDS."

EASLEY WATCHED AS THE PROFESSIONAL PHOTOGRAPHERS RECORDED EVERYTHING. SAYS EASLEY, "ONE WAS A TECH SERGEANT AND THE OTHER A MASTER SERGEANT... REAL PROS [WHO] KNEW THEIR BUSINESS...TOOK STILLS AND THEY TOOK MOVIES OF THE AREA...RECORDED EVERYTHING THEY SAW, ANYTHING UNUSUAL."

FRANKIE ROWE

ROWE IS THE DAUGHTER OF DAN DWYER, A ROSWELL FIREFIGHTER WHO WAS ON THE SCENE ON THE SECOND SITE AND OBSERVED THE BODIES. SAYS ROWE, "THERE WERE APPARENTLY THREE PEOPLE IN THE CRAFT BECAUSE HE SAW TWO BODY BAGS AND HE SAW ONE LIVE PERSON...A VERY SMALL BEING ABOUT THE SIZE OF A 10-YEAR-OLD CHILD...HE SAW [IT] WALKING. HE DIDN'T THINK IT SUFFERED ANY INJURIES."

ROWE SAYS THAT SHE AND THEIR ENTIRE FAMILY WERE THREATENED WITH PHYSICAL VIOLENCE, TOLD BY MILITARY OFFICERS THAT THEY WOULD "DISAPPEAR INTO THE DESERT" IF THEY REVEALED WHAT THEY KNEW ABOUT THE INCIDENT. SAYS ROWE, "THE AIR FORCE OR THE ARMY OR THE MILITARY CAME UP TO OUR HOUSE AND TOLD US WE COULD NEVER TALK ABOUT THIS. AS FAR AS WE WERE CONCERNED THE WHOLE INCIDENT NEVER HAPPENED... THEY BASICALLY THREATENED US. THEY WERE GOING TO TAKE MOTHER AWAY AND THEY WERE GOING TO TAKE DADDY AWAY."

MAJOR LEWIS RICKETT

RICKETT WAS ONE OF TWO COUNTER-INTELLIGENCE OFFICERS WHO VISITED BOTH SITES. OF THE WRECKAGE, RICKETT SAYS, "THERE WAS A SLIGHTLY CURVED PIECE OF METAL, REAL LIGHT. IT WAS ABOUT SIX INCHES BY TWELVE OR FOURTEEN INCHES. VERY LIGHT. I CROUCHED DOWN AND TRIED TO SNAP IT. MY BOSS LAUGHS AND SAID, 'SMART GUY. HE'S TRYING TO DO WHAT WE COULDN'T DO.' I ASKED, 'WHAT IN THE HELL IS THIS STUFF MADE OUT OF?' IT DIDN'T FEEL LIKE PLASTIC AND I NEVER SAW A PIECE OF METAL THIS THIN THAT YOU COULDN'T BREAK."

LATER RICKETT AND LINCOLN LAPAZ WORKING TOGETHER WERE ABLE TO DETERMINE THAT THERE WERE IN FACT, MULTIPLE TOUCH-DOWN SITES. SAYS RICKETT, "THE BEST WE COULD FIGURE OUT, THIS ONE WAS IN TROUBLE. MAYBE THE GUIDANCE SYSTEM ON IT HAPPENED TO FAIL."

MAJOR HUGHIE GREEN

A MEMBER OF THE BRITISH RAF (AND A FAMOUS RADIO PERSONALITY), GREEN WAS DRIVING THROUGH NEW MEXICO ON JULY 5, 1947, AND HEARD SEVERAL RADIO REPORTS ABOUT THE CRASH. SAYS GREEN, "AS I DROVE THROUGH NEW MEXICO FROM EAST TO WEST, I KEPT HEARING THESE REPORTS ABOUT A DOWNED SAUCER ON THE LOCAL STATIONS AS I CAME WITHIN THE RADIUS OF EACH ONE... THE RADIO STATIONS I WAS LISTENING TO WERE SO ON EDGE THAT THEY KEPT INTERRUPTING THEIR REGULAR BROADCASTS TO GIVE THE LATEST DEVELOPMENTS. I AM CERTAIN THAT ONE OF THE NEWS BROADCASTS COMMENTED ON THE FACT THAT THE SHERIFF AND HIS MEN WERE PROCEEDING TOWARDS THE FIELD OF THE CRASH WITHIN SIGHT OF THE WRECKAGE."

GLENN DENNIS

A CIVILIAN MORTICIAN IN ROSWELL, DENNIS RECEIVED A SERIES OF CALLS ABOUT PRESERVING SMALL BODIES. HE DROVE TO THE BASE AND OBSERVED WRECKAGE AND LATER SPOKE TO A NURSE OBTAINING A DESCRIPTION OF THE BODIES.

OF THE WRECKAGE, HE SAYS, "WHAT I SAW REMINDED ME OF THE FRONT PART OF A CANOE...ABOUT THREE FEET LONG AND LYING UP AGAINST THE SIDE...THERE WERE INSCRIPTIONS ON [A] BORDER AROUND PART OF IT... IT REMINDED ME OF EGYPTIAN INSCRIPTIONS."

ROBERT J. SHIRKEY

AN ASSISTANT GROUP OPERATIONS OFFICER FOR THE 509TH BOMB GROUP, ROBERT J. SHIRKEY SET UP THE FLIGHT PLAN FOR THE B-29 THAT TRANSPORTED WRECKAGE FROM THE ROSWELL TO FORTH WORTH, TEXAS. SAYS SHIRKEY, "I SAW PIECES OF METAL FROM THE CRAFT. I SAW THE I-BEAM WITH THE STRANGE MARKINGS ON IT.

"THOSE OF US WHO WERE INVOLVED IMMEDIATELY KNEW WE'D BETTER KEEP OUR MOUTHS SHUT." IN 1999, SHIRKEY RELEASED A BOOK ABOUT HIS INVOLVEMENT CALLED *ROSWELL 1947: I WAS THERE*.

CAPTAIN O. W. "PAPPY" HENDERSON

ACCORDING TO HIS WIFE AND CHILDREN, CAPTAIN O. W. "PAPPY" HENDERSON (WHO WAS STATIONED WITH THE 509TH BOMB GROUP AT ROSWELL), TOLD THEM THAT THE ROSWELL CRASH WAS TRUE, AND THAT HE FLEW THE WRECKAGE TO WRIGHT PATTERSON AFB IN OHIO. HE TOLD THEM THAT THE ETS WHO PILOTED THE CRAFT WERE LITTLE PEOPLE WITH EXCEPTIONALLY LARGE HEADS. HENDERSON NEVER SPOKE OF THE INCIDENT FOR YEARS, UNTIL THE STORY BECAME POPULARIZED IN THE MEDIA. HENDERSON TOLD HIS WIFE, "I'VE BEEN DYING TO TELL YOU FOR YEARS, BUT COULDN'T. IT WAS TOP SECRET." HENDERSON REFUSED TO DESCRIBE THE WRECKAGE ITSELF, SAYING ONLY, "IT WAS STRANGE."

COLONEL THOMAS JEFFERSON DUBOSE

DUBOSE WAS ORDERED BY MCMULLEN IN WASHINGTON TO MAKE SURE THAT COLONEL BLANCHARD DELIVERED THE WRECKAGE TO WASHINGTON. DUBOSE CONFIRMED THAT THE WEATHER BALLOON STORY WAS A COVER STORY. ALTHOUGH HE DIDN'T VIEW THE ACTUAL WRECKAGE, HE SAW AN EARLY SAMPLE BEING LOADED ON A PLANE TO FORTH WORTH, BOUND FOR WASHINGTON. SAYS DUBOSE, "I ONLY SAW THE CONTAINER, AND THE CONTAINER WAS A PLASTIC BAG THAT I WOULD SAY WEIGHED FIFTEEN TO TWENTY POUNDS. IT WAS SEALED... THE ONLY WAY TO GET INTO IT WAS TO CUT IT."

SERGEANT ROBERT E. SMITH

SMITH WAS ANOTHER OFFICER WHO WAS ORDERED TO LOAD THE WRECKAGE ONTO AIRCRAFT TO SHIP OUT TO OTHER LOCATIONS. ACCORDING TO SMITH, ALTHOUGH THE CRATES CONTAINING THE WRECKAGE WERE SEALED, EVERYONE KNEW WHAT WAS IN THEM. ONE OF HIS FELLOW OFFICERS HAD HELPED PICK UP THE WRECKAGE AND HE ADMITTED THAT HE HAD ACTUALLY SNEAKED OUT A PIECE. SAYS SMITH, "HE SAID HE'D BEEN OUT THERE HELPING CLEAN THIS UP. HE DIDN'T THINK TAKING A LITTLE PIECE WOULD MATTER. IT WAS JUST A LITTLE PIECE OF METAL OR FOIL OR WHATEVER IT WAS. JUST SMALL ENOUGH TO BE SLIPPED INTO A POCKET. I THINK HE JUST PICKED IT UP FOR A SOUVENIR... IT WAS FOIL-LIKE, BUT IT WAS A LITTLE STIFFER THAN THE FOIL WE HAVE NOW. IN FACT, BEING A SHEET METAL MAN, IT KIND OF INTRIGUED ME, BEING THAT YOU COULD CRUMPLE IT AND IT WOULD FLATTEN BACK OUT AGAIN WITHOUT ANY WRINKLES SHOWING UP ON IT. OF COURSE WE DIDN'T GET TO LOOK AT IT TOO CLOSE BECAUSE IT WAS SUPPOSED TO BE TOP SECRET. HE JUST POPPED IT OUT THERE REAL QUICK AND LET US FEEL IT AND SO FORTH WHILE EVERYBODY WAS DOING SOMETHING ELSE."

BRIGADIER GENERAL ARTHUR E. EXON

EARLY IN HIS CAREER, EXON WAS STATIONED AT WRIGHT PATTERSON ASSIGNED TO THE AIR MATERIAL COMMAND HEADQUARTERS WHEN THE ROSWELL DEBRIS CAME IN. EXON CONFIRMS THAT THE MATERIAL WAS TESTED EXTENSIVELY, AS HE SAYS, "EVERYTHING FROM CHEMICAL ANALYSIS, STRESS TESTS, FLEXING. IT WAS BROUGHT INTO OUR MATERIAL EVALUATION LABS. I DON'T KNOW HOW IT ARRIVED, BUT THE BOYS WHO TESTED IT SAID IT WAS VERY UNUSUAL... [PARTS] COULD BE EASILY RIPPED OR CHANGED... THERE WERE OTHER PARTS OF IT THAT WERE VERY THIN BUT AWFULLY STRONG AND COULDN'T BE DENTED WITH HEAVY HAMMERS... IT WAS FLEXIBLE TO A DEGREE.

"SOME OF IT WAS FLIMSY AND IT WAS TOUGHER THAN HELL, AND THE OTHER WAS ALMOST LIKE FOIL, BUT STRONG. IT HAD THEM PRETTY PUZZLED... THEY KNEW THEY HAD SOMETHING NEW IN THEIR HANDS. THE METAL AND MATERIAL WAS UNKNOWN TO ANYONE I TALKED TO... A COUPLE OF GUYS THOUGHT IT MIGHT BE RUSSIAN, BUT THE OVERALL CONSENSUS WAS THAT THE PIECES WERE FROM SPACE."

COLONEL PHILIP J. CORSO

IN HIS BOOK, *THE DAY AFTER ROSWELL*, CORSO REVEALED THAT IN HIS CAPACITY AS A RESEARCHER AND EVALUATOR OF WEAPONS SYSTEMS AT THE FOREIGN TECHNOLOGY DESK IN THE PENTAGON, GENERAL TRUDEAU PRESENTED HIM WITH A BOX OF ARTIFACTS FROM THE ROSWELL CRAFT, AND INSTRUCTED CORSO TO MAKE USE OF IT. WRITES CORSO, "BUT HIDDEN BENEATH EVERYTHING I DID, AT THE CENTER OF A DOUBLE LIFE I LED THAT NO ONE KNEW ABOUT, AND BURIED DEEP INSIDE MY JOB AT THE PENTAGON WAS A SINGLE FILE CABINET THAT I HAD INHERITED BECAUSE OF MY INTELLIGENCE BACKGROUND. THAT FILE HELD THE ARMY'S DEEPEST AND MOST CLOSELY GUARDED SECRET: THE ROSWELL FILES, THE CACHE OF DEBRIS AND INFORMATION AN ARMY RETRIEVAL TEAM FROM THE 509TH ARMY AIR FIELD PULLED OUT OF THE WRECKAGE OF A FLYING DISK THAT CRASHED OUTSIDE THE TOWN OF ROSWELL IN THE NEW MEXICO DESERT... MY BOSS, GENERAL TRUDEAU, ASKED ME TO USE THE ARMY'S ONGOING WEAPONS DEVELOPMENT AND RESEARCH PROGRAM AS A WAY TO FILTER THE ROSWELL TECHNOLOGY INTO THE MAINSTREAM OF INDUSTRIAL DEVELOPMENT THROUGH THE MILITARY DEFENSE CONTRACTING PROGRAM. TODAY SUCH ITEMS AS LASERS, INTEGRATED CIRCUITS, FIBER-OPTICS NETWORKS, ACCELERATED PARTICLE BEAM DEVICES, AND EVEN THE KEVLAR MATERIAL IN BULLETPROOF VESTS ARE ALL COMMONPLACE. YET THE SEEDS FOR THE DEVELOPMENT OF ALL OF THEM WERE FOUND IN THE ALIEN CRAFT AT ROSWELL..."

CORSO DESCRIBES SOME OF THE ARTIFACTS: "FIRST THERE WERE THE TINY, CLEAR SINGLE-FILAMENT, FLEXIBLE GLASSLIKE WIRES TWISTED TOGETHER... THEY WERE NARROW FILAMENTS, THINNER THAN COPPER WIRE. AS I HELD THE HARNESS OF STRANDS UP TO THE LIGHT FROM MY DESK, I COULD SEE AN EERIE GLOW COMING THROUGH THEM..." IT WAS THIS THAT CORSO SAYS, SPARKED RESEARCH INTO FIBER-OPTICS.

OF THE BIRTH OF THE INTEGRATED CIRCUIT, CORSO DESCRIBES ANOTHER ROSWELL ARTIFACT: "THEN THERE WERE THE THIN TWO-INCH-AROUND MATTE GRAY OYSTER CRACKER-SHAPED WAFERS OF A MATERIAL THAT LOOKED LIKE PLASTIC BUT HAD TINY ROAD MAPS OF WIRES BARELY RAISED/ETCHED ALONG THE SERVICE."

AND OF THE ORIGIN OF NIGHT-VISION TECHNOLOGY, CORSO WRITES, "I WAS MOST INTERESTED IN THE FILE DESCRIPTIONS ACCOMPANYING A TWO-PIECE SET OF DARK ELLIPTICAL EYE PIECES AS THIN AS SKIN. THE WALTER REED PATHOLOGISTS SAID THAT THEY ADHERED TO THE LENSES OF THE EXTRATERRESTRIAL CREATURE'S EYES AND SEEMED TO REFLECT EXISTING LIGHT, EVEN IN WHAT LOOKED LIKE COMPLETE DARKNESS..."

CORSO SAYS THAT, PRIOR TO WORKING WITH THE ROSWELL TECHNOLOGY, HE ALSO VIEWED ONE OF THE ROSWELL BODIES, WHERE IT WAS PACKAGED IN A GLASS OR PLASTIC CONTAINER AT FORT RILEY. OF THE BODY, CORSO SAYS, "AT FIRST I THOUGHT IT WAS A DEAD CHILD THEY WERE SHIPPING SOMEWHERE. BUT THIS WAS NO CHILD. IT WAS A FOUR-FOOT HUMAN-SHAPED FIGURE WITH ARMS, FOUR-FINGERED HANDS – I DIDN'T SEE A THUMB, THIN FEET, AND AN OVERSIZED INCANDESCENT LIGHT BULB-SHAPED HEAD THAT LOOKED LIKE IT WAS FLOATING OVER A BALLOON GONDOLA FOR A CHIN."

CORSO FURTHER DESCRIBED THE BODY AS HAVING GRAY SKIN, OVERSIZED ALMOND-SHAPED EYE-SOCKETS, A TINY NOSE, A SLIT FOR A MOUTH, AND NO HAIR. HE SAID THE EYES, NOSE, AND MOUTH WERE ALL PLACED TIGHTLY TOGETHER IN A VERY SMALL AREA, FORMING A "CLEARLY NONHUMAN FACE."

Again, the Roswell case is not over and researchers continue to make strides in their research. It has now become an open conspiracy. The majority of Americans believe it to be true. Key witnesses are speaking publicly about the event without repercussions from the government. And yet, it was only a series of coincidences that the case was revealed at all. The entire event came very close to being covered up completely. And it also came just as close to being busted wide open.

Researcher Gray Barker says that he was able to obtain an interview with a man by the name of Baron Nicholas von Poppen, who was an expert in the field of photographic metallurgical analysis. Von Poppen told Barker than he was offered a top secret assignment in the late 1940s, during which he was taken to Los Alamos to photograph a flying saucer.

Whether this was the Roswell craft or another is difficult to say. However, von Poppen recalls that the object was thirty feet in diameter. It had a main cabin with four small seats facing a control board "covered with push buttons and tiny levers."

Still strapped in the seats were four dead aliens described as having white skin, wearing shiny black jumpsuits, and soft tiny hands with neatly trimmed nails. Von Poppen was ordered to ignore the bodies and concentrate on photographing the metallic surfaces. He took hundreds of pictures over a period of several days. Before returning to Los Angeles, von Poppen was told that the craft was due to be shipped to Wright-Patterson. The baron says he tried to take pieces of the craft with him, but was unable to do so. He says he did manage to keep one photograph, which he promised to reveal upon his death. Poppen died in 1975, just short of 90 years old. The photograph has never been revealed.

Another person who has confessed his involvement in shipping the wreckage is Robert R. Porter. Porter learned through rumors that the flight he was on allegedly contained the wreckage of a flying saucer, which would explain what seemed to be excessive security concerning their cargo. Porter asked others on the flight if the cargo really was wreckage of a flying saucer. Porter says he was told, "That's just what it is, and don't ask any more questions."

Many years after the UFO crash, Bill Brazel Jr. was working on a job in Alaska, and was talking with his co-workers when the subject of UFOs came up. Brazel Jr. told the story of his father's discovery. One of the men, Mr. Lamme then revealed that he was involved with the recovery of the saucer itself, which was found largely intact in a desert area. Inside were creatures about three to four feet tall, two of which were still alive. Both were taken to California and kept alive for only a short time.

Consider the following report which was submitted to NUFORC on June 15, 2004. The reporter of the case wrote that his great uncle worked with the Army Air Corps Judges' office. On July 11, 1947, he was sent to Roswell to represent an officer who was being charged with the crime of stealing thousands of dollars worth of Army Air goods. According to the nephew, his great uncle arrived at Roswell and "once there he reported to the Military Police station and told them he was there to interview the prisoner. The MP officer on duty knew that my great uncle was from Wright-Patterson and escorted him to a section of the stockade. This section had only one way in and one cell. My great uncle believed he was to see the prisoner. [He] was shocked by what he saw. He told me that he saw a little man (believing the man to be a midget) dressed in a silver-gray flight suit. The man was very pale, as if he was not out in the sun much, with white hair. The guard told my uncle the prisoner refused to eat. My great uncle realized that this was not who he was sent to see. [He] left quickly and returned to the MP station." (NUFORC)

Many documents have now surfaced that apparently validate the UFO crash at Roswell. First, it is important to remember that the entire story was dormant for many years, until researcher Stanton Friedman interviewed Jesse Marcel Sr. in the late 1970s.

The first book *The Roswell Incident* was published in 1980. Since, then, events have unfolded very rapidly.

One of the most controversial aspects of the case involves a set of government documents called "the MJ-12 papers." These controversial documents were leaked to various researchers in the late 1980s. The documents have been widely attacked by skeptics, while at the same time several high-profile investigators claim that they are authentic.

For example, one such document dated November 18, 1952, actually provides a detailed description of the Roswell UFO crash. This particular document was studied in detail by Dr. Roger Wescott, director of the linguistics department at Drew University in Madison, New Jersey, a graduate of Princeton, a 1948 Rhodes scholar and the author of 400 articles and 40 books on linguistics. These impressive credentials made Dr. Wescott the ideal candidate to determine the authenticity of the questioned document. In a 1988 interview with the *Roswell Record,* Dr. Wescott revealed that after studying the document, he has concluded that it is, in fact, authentic. Dr. Wescott was reluctant to reveal further details and only confirmed this conclusion after the results of his study were revealed by Robert Bletchman, a Massachusetts attorney who had originally given him the document to study.

Another odd development in the Roswell story was the so-called "Alien Autopsy" footage which was aired as a television special in 1992. The footage showed a body lying face up on a table. The head was large and hairless. There were six fingers. An autopsy followed, during which strange-looking organs were removed. The footage was grainy and unedited. Also shown was the wreckage, which included metallic-looking panels that appeared to be very light in weight judging from how they were being held for the camera.

The footage was provided by the camera man, who says that the military never asked for it back as it was a back-up reel. So he kept it. Today, the alien autopsy has been largely dismissed as a hoax, though some researchers have speculated that it might be a clever disinformation ploy, containing elements of truth. And some still claim that it's exactly what it purports to be: an alien autopsy.

Repercussions from the Roswell crash were still being felt nearly fifty years later. In 1993, the office of New Mexico Congressional Representative Steven H. Schiff was flooded with letters from constituents requesting an investigation into the incidents at Roswell. Schiff agreed to begin an investigation. However, from the very beginning, Schiff reports that what should have been a "routine" investigation was effectively stone-walled at every juncture. The Defense Department, the Pentagon and the National Archives, all claimed to have no information whatsoever about the incident. Says Schiff, "I thought the whole thing was entirely routine. I simply asked where the existing documents were."

In response, the Air Force sent Schiff a "rather terse letter" referring him to the National Archives. Says Schiff,

> IT WAS SURPRISING THAT A GOVERNMENT AGENCY SAID, "GO AWAY AND DON'T BOTHER US."

It was this brush-off from the Air Force that prompted Schiff to contact the GAO and request a federal investigation. As Schiff told reporters,

> I WAS GETTING PRETTY UPSET AT ALL THE RUNNING AROUND... THE ISSUE IS WHETHER THE GOVERNMENT IS BEING FORTHRIGHT WITH THE AMERICAN PEOPLE, AND THAT IS A SERIOUS ISSUE FOR ME.

This bold move pushed the Roswell incident back onto the front pages of newspapers across the country. The UFO community held its collective breath as it seemed for the first time that there might be an actual official governmental investigation in the Roswell incident.

Schiff says that he believes the crash could have involved "a weather balloon" but that more likely it was "some kind of military experiment." In a March 1993 letter to Defense Secretary Les Aspin, he stated that the testimony from the many witnesses suggests that "the balloon explanation was a cover story," and that it appeared that "federal authorities sought to intimidate witnesses and their families into silence."

Unfortunately, Schiff was never able to obtain any documentary proof of the Roswell incident. While he did succeed in bringing considerable attention to the subject, the alleged cover-up remained locked tightly in place. A few years later, on May 25, 1998, Representative Steven H. Schiff died in his home at age 51 from an aggressive squamous-cell skin cancer. He had announced in January that he would not seek re-election because of his illness. He was elected in 1988. He made headlines in 1994 when he asked for a Federal investigation into the Roswell incident, requesting that the General Accounting Office locate Air Force documents related to the case.

The Roswell story continued to have new developments. In 1998, J. Bond Johnson launched an investigation into a very famous photograph which he took on July 8, 1947, days after the Roswell crash. At the time, Burt was a photographer. He was at the press conference in which Brig. Gen. Roger Ramey and Jesse Marcel Sr. posed with a weather balloon to explain away the incident. However, in Ramey's hand there was a memo with writing on it.

Using photo technology, researchers were able to obtain close-ups of the memo, the results of which were explosive. Much of the writing remained illegible, however, there were several phrases that were intriguing such as "...and the victims of the wreck..." and "in the 'disc' they will ship..."

Still the Roswell story continues to unfold. In 2008, Lawrence R. Spencer released a book, which he edited, titled *Alien Interview*. The book contains the notes of Roswell Senior Master Sergeant Matilda O'Donnell Macelroy (retired.) In the book, Macelroy says that she was at Roswell in July 1947. She says she was enlisted in the U.S. Women's Army Air Force Medical Corp and was assigned to the 509th Bomb Group as a flight nurse. When news of "a crash" reached the base, Macelroy said she was ordered to accompany Sheridan Cavitt to the scene. At the scene, they found the craft, three dead occupants and one live one. She was told to examine the living occupant for injuries. At this time, she started receiving a telepathic communication from the ET.

Nobody else appeared to be able to communicate with the ET, so, after a brief consultation among the top officials at the site, Macelroy was told that she would accompany the ET back to the base. This simple consultation changed Macelroy's life forever. As she says,

> As NO OTHER PERSON PRESENT COULD PERCEIVE THESE THOUGHTS, AND THE ALIEN SEEMED ABLE AND WILLING TO COMMUNICATE WITH ME, IT WAS DECIDED, AFTER A BRIEF CONSULTATION WITH A SENIOR OFFICER THAT I WOULD ACCOMPANY THE SURVIVING ALIEN BACK TO THE BASE. THIS WAS PARTLY DUE TO THE FACT THAT I WAS A NURSE, AND COULD ATTEND TO THE PHYSICAL NEEDS OF THE ALIEN, AS WELL AS SERVE AS A NON-THREATENING COMMUNICATOR AND COMPANION. AFTER ALL, I WAS THE ONLY WOMAN AT THE SITE, AND THE ONLY ONE WHO WAS NOT ARMED. I WAS THEREAFTER ASSIGNED PERMANENTLY TO SERVE AS "COMPANION" OF THE ALIEN AT ALL TIMES.

So began two months during which Macelroy communicated with the ET on the Army's behalf, learning its history, its intentions, and other details. The alien, says Macelroy, had a non-biological body. It claimed its species was very numerous throughout several galaxies, and were part of an organized society a trillion years old called "the domain." It called the earth a prison planet, and said that they were investigating the planet because of recent atomic explosions. Again the full story is told in the book *Alien Interview* and provides another controversial piece to the ongoing Roswell puzzle.[158]

UFO CRASH AT SAN AUGUSTINE

Confusing and deepening the mystery of the Roswell UFO crash are the many rumors and reports that there was *another* UFO which crashed on or around the same day as the Roswell incident. The UFO crash on the Plains of San Augustine rests primarily on the testimony of U.S. Conservation Corps soil engineer Grady "Barney" Barnett. Some researchers have tried to match his account up to the Roswell crash, while other researches point to inconsistencies in the location which would seem to separate the two incidents. Many researchers now treat the incident as a separate event. Some have even speculated that the Roswell craft and the San Augustine craft struck each other, causing both to plummet to the ground. Still others insist that the two crashes are, in reality, just one incident and one craft.

Whatever the case, Barnett's testimony is compelling because he sought no publicity; he had a good reputation as an upstanding citizen, and the details of his testimony were given before there was any media attention given to the crash.

Barnett says that he came upon the craft along with a group of archaeologists. The craft was intact, though the bodies of silver-suited small humanoid bodies lay outside it. Barnett and the group of students had only examined the craft and bodies for a short time when the military arrived, cordoned off the area and warned Barnett and the other civilians not to speak of the incident.

Before he died, Barnett told his friend Vern Maltais what the bodies looked like. Maltais revealed these details in an interview with researcher Stanton Friedman. "They were like humans," explained Maltais, "but they were not humans. The heads were round, the eyes were small, and they had no hair. They eyes were oddly spaced. They were quite small by our standards and their heads were larger in proportion to their bodies than ours. Their clothing seemed to be in one piece, and gray in color. You couldn't see any zippers, belts or buttons. They seemed to be all males and there were a number of them."

Further confirmation of the incident comes from the testimony of Gerald Anderson, who claims that he and his family were actually the first on the scene. In an interview with Stanton Friedman, he explained how they first thought the object was a blimp, and that the bodies were dolls. Only after closer examination did they understand that it was a flying saucer. Anderson said that he looked inside the craft and saw strange components, some of which had weird writing. He also said that one of the ETs was still alive.

Some researchers attacked the credibility of Anderson when it was discovered that the diary recording the incident was written on paper that dated much later. Anderson, however, explained that multiple copies were written and the original diary has not been tested.[159]

THE AZTEC UFO CRASH

Perhaps one of the most controversial UFO crashes, the Aztec UFO crash has been summarily dismissed by many researchers as a hoax that was unintentionally perpetrated by UFO author Frank Scully in his best-selling book, *Inside the Flying Saucers*. Today, however, many researchers feel that the Aztec crash was, in fact, valid, and have pointed out that Scully's book was the first to reveal the fact that the U.S. military was in possession of extraterrestrial craft.

In 1977, researcher Leonard Stringfield wrote,

> SOME RESEARCHERS HAVE NEVER GIVEN UP AND BELIEVE THAT SCULLY WAS THE VICTIM OF OFFICIAL COUNTERACTION AND THAT HIS SMEARED BOOK WAS ACTUALLY TRUE.

Leonard Stringfield was a pioneering investigator of UFO crash/retrieval incidents. In 1978, Stringfield wrote that the backlash from the publication of Scully's book actually slowed the progress of research into UFO crash/retrievals. Says Stringfield,

> AT THAT TIME, ACTIVE RESEARCHERS, INCLUDING MYSELF DID LITTLE MORE THAN SCOFF. WE THOUGHT WE HAD GOOD REASON. OUR COLLECTIVE "SCOFFING" WAS THE RESULT OF AN ALLEGED GRAND HOAX. HERE I REFER TO A BOOK, *BEHIND THE FLYING SAUCERS* BY THE LATE FRANK SCULLY... INVESTIGATION REVEALED THAT SCULLY'S SCIENTIST WAS A FRAUD. WITH THE BOOK'S SUBSEQUENT EXPOSURE AS A HOAX, WHICH GOT A LOT OF PUBLICITY, IT BECAME UNFASHIONABLE TO WRITE OR TALK ABOUT CRASHED UFOS AND THEIR ALLEGED "LITTLE MEN."...SO COMPLETELY WAS SCULLY'S RETRIEVAL STORY PUT DOWN THAT SOME RESEARCHERS TODAY WONDER, IN RETROSPECT, IF THE BOOK AND/OR ITS EXPOSURE WERE CONTRIVED... WE MUST NOW TAKE A NEW AND HONEST LOOK AT THE OLD RUMORS. AND WE MUST ALSO TAKE A NEW LOOK AT THE POSSIBILITY OF A GRAND OFFICIAL COVER-UP AND WHY.

Leading researcher Timothy Good is one of many researchers who are taking a new look at the incident. Writes Good,

> ACCORDING TO A NUMBER OF SOURCES, THE MOST IMPORTANT CASE INVOLVING THE RECOVERY OF AN ALIEN CRAFT TOOK PLACE OUTSIDE THE LITTLE TOWN OF AZTEC, NEW MEXICO IN 1948.... [A] GREAT DEAL OF TECHNICAL AND OTHER INTELLIGENCE RESULTED FROM THIS RECOVERY, INTELLIGENCE WHICH GAVE THE AMERICANS A GIANT LEAP FORWARD IN TECHNOLOGY AND WEAPONRY UNPARALLELED IN HUMAN HISTORY.

Researcher Linda Moulton Howe is also convinced and says,

> I HAVE INTERVIEWED SOME OF THE PEOPLE WHO ARE STILL ALIVE, WHO SAW IT IN MARCH OF 1949...AZTEC IS A VERY IMPORTANT PIECE BECAUSE OF THE TECHNOLOGY RECEIVED THERE.

Mrs. Scully says that both she and her husband were visited by Captain Edward Ruppelt. During the visit, Ruppelt made a startling revelation about Scully's book, telling them,

> CONFIDENTIALLY OF ALL THE BOOKS THAT HAVE BEEN PUBLISHED ABOUT FLYING SAUCERS, YOUR BOOK WAS THE ONE THAT GAVE US THE MOST HEADACHES BECAUSE IT WAS CLOSEST TO THE TRUTH.

The Aztec story began on March 8, 1950, when Silas M. Newton (who claimed to be a Texas oil millionaire) gave a public lecture at the University of Denver saying that the military was in possession of an actual flying saucer, which had been found in the New Mexico desert. Newton said that his friend, "Dr. Gee" was one of the scientists brought in to study the craft and the occupants.

Frank Scully was a highly respected entertainment columnist. His 1950 book, *Behind the Flying Saucers*, was one of the first UFO books published in the United States. Much of the book was devoted to the Aztec story.

Scully claimed that Dr. Gee didn't exist and was actually a combination of several scientists to whom he had spoken about the incident. Scully's informants claimed that the craft had been found outside Aztec, on February 13, 1948, [some sources now say March 1948 or 1949] completely intact, except for a small hole in one of the portholes. The craft was exactly 99.99 feet in diameter. It was composed of a metal so light that only a few men could lift the entire craft.

Most puzzling, the scientists studying the craft were unable to find any method of entrance. It took the Air Force several days to open the craft, which was finally achieved by sticking a stick through the hole and turning a latch which opened a door. Inside they found sixteen (some reports say twelve) small gray-type ETs, all dead, apparently from explosive decompression. Also inside they found hieroglyphic-type writings and small wafers which were apparently food.

The craft was then dismantled and carted away for study.

While Scully's claims remained largely uncontested for years, the story became tarnished when it was learned that Silas Newton and the mysterious "Dr. Gee" (now identified as Leo GeBauer) were actually con-men who defrauded investors out of thousands of dollars by claiming they had an instrument based on alien technology which could detect oil underground.

Both Newton and GeBauer were convicted of their crimes and were jailed and fined. Researcher William Steinman, however, has studied the entire court case in detail and has raised a convincing case that the whole affair was an attempt to discredit Scully and the entire Aztec UFO crash by providing real information mixed with disinformation, coming from a less than credible source. In his book, *UFO Crash at Aztec*, Steinman recounts the entire story and includes the testimony of several new witnesses.

As further possible confirmation, a newspaper article about the crash appeared in the *Farmington Daily Times* following the incident. Several witnesses claim to have seen this article, however, researchers have not been able to locate a copy.

Meanwhile, the Aztec story continues to unfold as more researchers continue to uncover further confirmation.

One new witness has recently been discovered. In 1952, Bill Devlin (who worked for a radio and television servicing company) says that he befriended a soldier and got to talking about UFOs. The soldier revealed that he had personally been involved in a UFO crash incident in Aztec. The soldier told Devlin that he was one of three drivers who delivered the remains of the saucer from Aztec to Fort Riley. The soldier said that there were 16 tiny bodies, all dressed alike in tight jumpsuits. They had, he said, yellowish skin, human-like features (including teeth), and a light peach-fuzz on their skin.

Further confirmation comes from a witness interviewed by researcher Chuck Oldham. The witness, known to Oldham, was a former military officer with a very high security clearance. At the base where he was stationed was a library that was restricted to officers with a high security clearance like his. Looking for something to read, the officer stumbled upon a UFO file which described the Aztec case in detail, and even included photographs.

The officer described one photo,

> THERE WAS A PERFECT INTACT, CIRCULAR SHAPED CRAFT AND IT WAS LYING SOMEWHAT TILTED TO ONE SIDE ON THE GROUND IN THE DESERT. THERE DID NOT APPEAR TO BE A CRATER OR GROUND DISTURBANCE IN THE PHOTOGRAPH THAT WOULD INDICATE A CRASH, BUT I COULDN'T TELL FOR SURE... THE MATERIAL OF WHICH THE CRAFT WAS COMPOSED WAS METALLIC, AND RESEMBLED BRUSHED ALUMINUM.

There was a written report which explained the crash and the craft in detail. Says the officer,

> IT STATED THAT THE CRAFT WAS RETRIEVED SOMEWHERE NEAR FARMINGTON, NEW MEXICO, PRIOR TO 1950. IT STATED IN THE REPORT THAT THERE WERE PORTHOLES ON THE CABIN PART OF THE CRAFT, BUT THEY WERE NOT MADE OF ANY TYPE OF GLASS... THIS PORTHOLE HAD A PUNCTURE THAT WAS THE DIAMETER OF A PENCIL; THAT WAS THE ONLY DEFECT DISCOVERED ON THE ENTIRE SHIP. OUR PEOPLE TRIED DIAMOND DRILLS, AN ACETYLENE TORCH — EVERYTHING THEY COULD COME UP WITH ON THE PORTHOLE WHERE THIS OPENING WAS LOCATED, BUT NOTHING WOULD BREAK THROUGH IT. THEY COULDN'T ENLARGE THE HOLE, EITHER; THE MATERIAL WAS TOUGHER THAN ANYTHING WE WERE FAMILIAR WITH ON EARTH. BUT THEY EVENTUALLY GOT INTO THE CABIN.[160]

UFO CRASH IN SAN MIGUEL COUNTY

This case first came to light in an official declassified document from the AFOSI at Tinker AFB which contained a letter written by a Mr. McLean of Friona, Texas. In spring of 1952, Mr. McLean (a retired farmer) and his wife, residents of Friona, were camping in the mountains in the eastern part of San Miguel County. One evening, they saw a dim light "circling around up high." The strange object performed a mile-wide circle, slowly descending. When it reached a low altitude, it suddenly turned green and exploded, "showering lighted objects in all directions."

Says Mr. McLean,

SEVERAL OF THOSE FIERY OBJECTS LANDED CLOSE TO ME. MOST OF THEM WERE
BURIED IN THE GROUND, BUT I GATHERED UP THREE THAT WERE ONLY PARTLY BURIED
AND BROUGHT THEM HOME WITH ME.

He broke open one of the strange rocks and says,

IN THE CENTER WAS A ROUND HOLE OR VACUUM FILLED WITH FINE POWDER.

McLean says he informed the Pentagon, who didn't respond. He wrote
a letter to Senators Lyndon Johnson of Texas and Clinton Anderson of New
Mexico. Both Senators responded, asking that McLean send samples of
the material for analysis. McLean complied and says that the analysis came
back as "meteors." He says that he was later visited by a Russian scientist
who bought one of the objects and told McLean that the object was made
of uranium and other materials.

McLean later told researchers (despite the official AFOSI document)
that he had *not* seen the objects fall to earth. Instead he said he had found
them while driving through the area. He also said he had never sold any of
the material to a Russian scientist, but did remember being visited by an
individual from the Russian Consulate in Amarillo, Texas who expressed
interest in the samples.

The case, like many UFO crash cases, contains little other information.
Writes UFO crash/retrieval researcher Bob Wood,

MORE THAN A HALF CENTURY ON, AND WITH THE KEY PLAYER IN THIS CASE LONG
DEPARTED, THIS EVENT REMAINS INTRIGUINGLY UNRESOLVED.[161]

RADAR SPECIALIST VIEWS FILM OF UFO CRASH

Researcher Leonard Stringfield interviewed a gentleman who, in 1953
(at the age of 20) was a radar specialist at Fort Monmouth, New Jersey.
While stationed there, he was given a secret security clearance. Later, he
and a small group of radar specialists were summoned to view a special 16
mm film at the base theater.

The witness says that the film opened with a desert scene. Immediately
apparent, says Stringfield, was a "silver disc-shaped objects imbedded in
the sand with a domed section at the top. At the bottom a hatch or door
was open."

The scene shifted to show a group of ten to fifteen military personnel standing around the craft, which appeared to be about twenty feet in diameter. The hatch appeared to be about three feet tall and one and a half feet wide.

The film then showed the interior of the craft which had only "a panel with a few simple levers" and "muted pastel colors."

The next scene showed three dead alien bodies on tables inside a tent. Writes Stringfield,

> MR. T. SAID THE BODIES APPEARED LITTLE BY HUMAN STANDARDS AND MOST NOTABLE WERE THE HEADS, ALL LOOKING ALIKE, AND ALL BEING LARGE COMPARED TO THEIR BODY SIZES. THEY LOOKED MONGOLOID, HE THOUGHT, WITH SMALL NOSES, MOUTHS AND EYES THAT WERE SHUT. HE DIDN'T RECALL SEEING EARS OR HAIR. THE SKIN, HE SAID, WAS LEATHERY AND ASHEN IN COLOR. EACH WORE A TIGHT-FITTING SUIT IN A PASTEL COLOR.

The movie ended without any credits. It had been only five minutes long and seemed filmed by an amateur. The officer in charge told the radar technicians to "think about the movie" and "don't relate its contents to anyone."

The witness told nobody, not even his wife. Shortly after viewing the film, two top security officers told him that a UFO (presumably the one he viewed in the film) had been shot down somewhere in New Mexico in 1952.

Two weeks afterwards, the witness was approached by an Air Force Intelligence officer who told him, "Forget the movie you saw; it was a hoax."

Later, he revealed his account to researcher Leonard Stringfield. At that time, he was no longer employed by the Air Force and held a "high technical" position in civilian life. Says Stringfield,

> CONSIDERING THE CREDIBILITY OF MY INFORMANT, I BELIEVE HE SAW THE MOVIE AND DESCRIBES THE SUBJECT MATTER TO THE BEST OF HIS RECOLLECTION. REGARDING THE SUBJECT MATTER, HE BELIEVES THAT THE CRASHED CRAFT AND THE DEAD BODIES WERE BONAFIDE. IT WOULD HAVE BEEN DIFFICULT, EVEN BY A MAJOR HOLLYWOOD STUDIO, TO HAVE MADE DUMMY BODIES LOOK SO REAL FOR USE IN AN OTHERWISE SO MAKE-SHIFT FILM.[162]

UFO CRASH AT WHITE SANDS

According to highly respected researcher Todd Zechel, an anonymous Army helicopter pilot who served as aide to an Air Force General told him that a "crashed saucer" of ovoid shape (about eighteen by thirty feet), along with four, four-foot-tall bodies of ETs were retrieved near White Sands in 1953, and then later shipped to Langley AFB in Virginia.

According to the witness, Air Force personnel found the craft in perfect condition with the doors wide open. All four occupants were dead, though no cause of death could be found. The bodies were reportedly hairless, but otherwise, very human-looking.

Because of his association with the general, the witness rode along with him and viewed the bodies and the craft. Inside, there was no visible means of controlling or propelling the craft. They were also shown three other UFO craft that had been recovered. These craft were about twenty-five feet long and thirteen feet wide.

According to the witness, despite many years of intense research, leading scientists have been unsuccessful in discovering the means of propulsion of the recovered craft.

In 1977, researcher Richard Hall spoke with a Lieutenant Colonel who confirmed the incident, saying that he had seen the four bodies at Langley AFB and was told that they had been "recovered from a crash in 1953 near White Sands, New Mexico."[163]

UFO CRASH AT WALKER AFB

In early 1954, "K. A." completed his basic training at Sampson Air Force Base in Geneva, New York. He was then immediately sent to Walker Air Force Base near Roswell where he began "special training in the Sikorsky H-19 helicopter...in relation to desert search and rescue operations."

K.A. told researchers Fred Schaefer, Gerald Miskar, and Linda Robinson that on the evening of April 12, 1954, he and his crew were told to launch a search and rescue mission for "a crash in the desert."

The crash-site was located about twenty-five miles distant from Walker, out into the desert wilderness. Says the witness,

AS WE FLEW OVERHEAD, AT AN ALTITUDE OF ABOUT 40 FEET, WE COULD PLAINLY SEE BELOW US THE OUTLINE OF A ROUND SILVER OBJECT... AT THIS POINT, THE "STRANGER" IN THE COCKPIT GAVE THE ORDER TO TURN ON THE SPOTLIGHT. WHEN THE LIGHT WAS TURNED ON, WE SAW BELOW US A ROUND, METALLIC, SAUCER-LIKE OBJECT, APPROXIMATELY 40-50 FEET IN DIAMETER. THE CRAFT APPEARED TO HAVE CRASHED EDGEWISE INTO THE SAND.

There were four small (4½-feet-long) bodies dressed in dark blue, tight fitting uniforms scattered outside the craft, each of which had "extremely large heads which were out of proportion with the rest of their bodies." K.A. was ordered to photograph the bodies, which he did, though he was not allowed to approach any closer than 40 feet. He reports that an overpowering stench came from the bodies, which caused one of the ground crew to vomit. He talked to another member of the ground crew and learned that there were two more bodies inside the craft. He was then removed from the scene.

What followed, says, K.A., was a "living hell." He was interrogated for the next three days straight regarding the incident, being alternately asked what happened, then told that he did not see anything. One day after being released from interrogation, he was flown back over the crash-site, which appeared as it had been "gone over with a fine-toothed comb." One of the interrogating intelligence officers told him, "See, I told you guys that you didn't see anything."

Rumors on the base were that the craft and bodies had been recovered and secreted at the base. Later, K.A.'s superior's accused him of having leaked the incident, which he denied. K.A. was then accused of going AWOL, and was summarily dismissed from the Air Force, having served for less than four months.

K.A. says that stories about "Hangar 18" stem from this incident as the craft was stored in Hangar 18, after which it became "top security" and "no one but top brass could enter or leave the area." K.A. says that the hangar was totally reconstructed. He was able to speak with one of the construction workers who told him that it was expanded "to a height of nine stories and a depth of eleven stories," and that heavy equipment, radars, and large computers were installed.

K.A. also heard that another UFO crash occurred only a few weeks later, on April 24, 1954 near Bandelier, New Mexico. After speaking with researcher Leonard Stringfield, K.A. continued to receive threats and warnings not to talk about his role in the incident. K.A. has suffered from nightmares ever since the ordeal occurred, and he and his wife continue to fear government reprisals.[164]

UFO CRASH AT CLOVIS

In the summer of 1957 or 1958, a former Air Force Officer was traveling through New Mexico when he heard that "a crash of some kind" involving an unusual aircraft had occurred on a ranch about thirty miles southwest of Clovis. Being in the military at the time, he was intrigued. So he and two "Air Force buddies" trekked to the scene in hopes of examining the craft. Upon arrival, they saw numerous military vehicles in the area, which was scattered with small pieces of "unusual lightweight wreckage." The witnesses could see evidence that "something large" had hit the ground. However, before they had a chance to get closer and examine the scene, the witness and his friends were approached by military personnel, and were ordered to leave and remain silent about the incident.[165]

UFO CRASH AT PORTALES

As revealed by the brother-in-law of a retired Air Force Lieutenant General, an apparent UFO crash/retrieval took place northeast of Portales. According to the Lt. General, in January of 1960 (while he was stationed at Cannon Air Force Base), a disk-shaped craft "went down" in an unidentified lake near Portales. It was retrieved and taken to a "black" hangar at Cannon AFB. The Lieutenant General told his brother that other UFO craft from across the western United States had been sent there in the past, and each was shipped either to Groom Lake in Nevada or Wright-Patterson AFB in Ohio. In this case, however, something unexpected happened. Writes the General's brother-in-law, (himself a pilot):

> AFTER SOME PRELIMINARY STUDY, BEFORE IT WAS SENT OUT, THE DISC SUDDENLY FLEW OUT OF THE HANGAR AND OUT OF SIGHT.

No further information about the case was revealed, however, the brother-in-law did confirm another well-known UFO crash. Says the brother-in-law,

> MY BROTHER-IN-LAW, ALTHOUGH NOT DIRECTLY CONNECTED TO THE MOST FAMOUS INCIDENT IN NM, DID CONFIRM TO ME THE ESSENTIALLY ACCURATE PORTRAYAL OF THE ROSWELL INCIDENT.

The brother-in-law is currently seeking further confirmation of the Portales retrieval. He reported the case to the MUFON CMS system, detailing the events and in closing made the following request:

IF ANYONE READING THIS CAN SHED LIGHT ON THE 1960 INCIDENT, PLEASE REPORT ON THIS [MUFON CMS] SITE.[166]

THE HOLLOMAN UFO CRASH

According to UFO researcher Robert D. Barry, on June 12, 1962, officials at Holloman Air Force Base tracked a UFO that appeared to be having flight difficulties across two southwestern states. When the object came over New Mexico, military jets were sent up to intercept it.

At this point, the circular craft seemed to lose control and began to descend. Moments later, it impacted, bottom-first, into the sands at an estimated ninety miles per hour.

According to Barry,

THE CRAFT WAS 68 FEET IN DIAMETER AND 13 FEET IN HEIGHT...TYPICALLY CIRCULAR. THE TWO BEINGS DISCOVERED INSIDE THE CRAFT WERE 42 INCHES IN HEIGHT. EACH BEING WAS DONNED IN A ONE-PIECE SUIT THAT CONTAINED NO BUTTONS OR ZIPPERS.

According to researcher Kevin Randle, the craft was dull aluminum in color and had skidded for a distance, leaving a trench.

Barry's source said that the heads of the ETs were abnormally large, the eyes larger than normal, with small thin lips and only an ear-hole for an ear. Their skin color was a gray-pink. The creatures were believed to have died upon impact. They were immediately removed and placed in a secret location for study.

The craft, the witness learned later, was an "exploratory" craft. It was also removed and taken to a secret location for study. Barry's source writes that only twenty individuals were involved in the retrieval and investigation, and that three of them had died.

According to Randle, the craft was taken back to Holloman AFB, with sections being distributed to Los Alamos and other research installations.

Leonard Stringfield investigated the case. He writes,

THERE ARE MORE AND STRONGER DATA CONCERNING THE 1962 NEW MEXICO CRASH WHICH ARE NOT PUBLISHABLE AT THIS WRITING.

Stringfield never did reveal this data, but did say,

THE 1962 CRASH SITE WAS NEAR HOLLOMAN AFB IN NEW MEXICO. THE INCIDENT IS KNOWN BY AN ASTRONAUT WHO PREFERS ANONYMITY.[167]

UFO CRASH AT SANTA ROSA

In early 1963, an anonymous medical technician (age 24) was working in a hospital in the small town of Santa Rosa. Although she was not a registered nurse, it was her job to do the x-rays and ride with the patients in the ambulance. The hospital was very small with only one doctor and a few rooms. Because the town and hospital were so small, things were usually very quiet and slow. Therefore, when accidents occurred, they were considered big news and generated considerable gossip for weeks after.

One particular incident, however, was different. It started out normally when the hospital received a call from the town's only police dispatcher that there had been "a crash with fatalities."

She and the ambulance driver raced eighteen miles to the scene of the accident. When they arrived, there were two police cars and two State Troopers on the scene. On the ground were three bodies, each three and a half feet tall – and very badly burned. The witness assumed they were children and asked the State Trooper, "Where are the parents?"

He replied, "I don't think they have parents. This is something unusual we have here."

"What is this?" she asked him.

He replied, "I'm going to have to notify the Air Force. I don't know what this is."

Ten feet away from the bodies was the vehicle which looked like "a pile of wreckage of metal" about the size of one or two cars.

The witness checked for signs of life with her stethoscope and found no signs of life. Thinking that they might still be alive, she and the ambulance driver put the bodies on gurneys and loaded them onto the ambulance. She said that the bodies oozed some kind of brownish-colored fluid.

They returned to the hospital, and the witness immediately took the bodies to the x-ray room and x-rayed them. She was eager for the doctor to examine them because they looked so strange, with very thin bodies and large heads, reminding her of photos she had seen of children dying of famine in Africa.

The doctor came in and after examining the bodies, pronounced them dead. While he was filling out the reports and signing the necessary paperwork, an Air Force colonel stormed into the hospital and demanded that the bodies be removed.

He then proceeded to remove "every single thing he could that bore on this trip."

"Do you have any notes?" he asked the witness.

She said yes and he took them away. He unhooked the x-rays which were hanging up on a wire drying. She said, "You can't take those; they're still wet."

He replied, "I'm taking the x-rays." After removing the bodies and everything associated with them, the Air Force colonel and his associates descended upon the ambulance and retrieved the evidence from there. Writes researcher Budd Hopkins, who uncovered the case and interviewed the main witness says,

> [THE AIR FORCE] TOOK EVERY SINGLE THING THEY COULD OUT OF THE BACK OF IT: THE SHEETS, ANY OBJECTS, ANYTHING MOVABLE, CLEANED OUT THE WHOLE THING. SHE SAID, "WE WERE NEVER PAID FOR ANYTHING."

After removing all evidence of the event, the Air Force colonel approached the witnesses and threatened them not to talk, saying,

> THIS DID NOT HAPPEN, YOU ARE NEVER TO SPEAK ABOUT THIS. AND REMEMBER THIS: THE GOVERNMENT HAS A LONG ARM.

Says the witness,

> WHAT WAS SO STRANGE WAS THAT WHENEVER WE HAD A FATALITY, A WRECK, A CRASH, WE WOULD ALL BE DOWN IN THE CAFÉ, GOING OVER THE DETAILS AND TALKING ABOUT IT, AS IT WAS A BIG EVENT IN OUR AREA. BUT NOBODY EVER MENTIONED THAT; THERE WAS SOME KIND OF UNDERSTANDING OR FEAR NOT TO MENTION IT... I HAVE NO IDEA WHAT IT WAS WE HAD THERE.

The witness is now convinced that the bodies were not human, and that they had become unwitting participants in a UFO crash/retrieval. The witness remained silent for years, finally contacting researcher Budd Hopkins, who revealed details of the case in the November 14-16, 2003 UFO Crash Retrieval Conference in Laughlin, Nevada.[168]

THE MANZANO MOUNTAINS
UFO CRASH

According to APRO researcher R. C. Hecker, at 10:22 p.m. on May 17, 1974, a gentleman who worked at Kirtland AFB East's Manzano Labs monitoring electrical scanning instruments noted that the sensors had observed an unexplained burst of energy in the range of 250 megahertz. The blast was so intense that it threw all the instruments off-scale. The source was quickly traced to an object in a certain location in the Earth's upper atmosphere. A trajectory was plotted which showed that the object had just descended down in the east side of the Manzano Mountains, about thirty miles southwest of Albuquerque.

The employee later learned that the object crashed just outside the town of Chili. A team was sent out to locate it. After being found, the craft was immediately surrounded and cordoned off. Within hours, the object, which was described as metallic, circular and about sixty feet in diameter, was dismantled, and secretly moved into an unidentified hangar at the base.

Hecker interviewed the gentleman who worked on the base. Writes Hecker,

> THIS INDIVIDUAL HAS GIVEN ME LEADS TO SIGHTINGS IN THE PAST WHICH HAVE ALWAYS PROVED VALID... AFTER BEING TOLD OF THIS INCIDENT, I WAS STOPPED BY A MAN WHO IDENTIFIED HIMSELF AS A KIRTLAND AFB OFFICER. HE ORDERED ME TO FORGET EVERYTHING I HAD BEEN TOLD ABOUT THIS INCIDENT.[169]

As can be seen, New Mexico leads the nation in the sheer number of UFO crash/retrieval incidents. And if even one of these reports are true, it points to a cover-up of monumental proportions. And as we have seen, many witnesses and investigators have paid a high price for revealing these stories. A case in point is that of UFO researcher, Sergeant Clifford Stone. For many years, Stone had investigated UFO crash/retrieval incidents, and was a vocal critic of U.S. military policies regarding UFOs. On June 21, 1987, a news article about Stone's research appeared in the *Roswell Daily Record*. According to Stone, immediately following the publication of this article, his supervisors at the New Mexico Military Institute (where he was assigned) began to treat him differently. His "efficiency ratings" which had always been excellent, began to receive lower scores. He was relieved of his position as an administrative non-commissioned officer, and was assigned to low-level filing duties. He was then sent to Fort Bliss for a psychological evaluation, which found that he was normal.

Nevertheless, the harassment continued, so on February 1, 1988, Stone filed an affidavit with the Fourth ROTC Region inspector general alleging that he was being wrongfully forced to retire from the army. While Army officials have refused to comment on his case, Stone says that he believes that officials are displeased with the fact that he has sent numerous letters to New Mexico's Republican Senator, Pete Domenici, questioning various UFO incidents. Today, Stone remains a vocal critic of the U.S. Military's handling of the UFO situation.[170]

UNDERGROUND ALIEN BASES

On the fringe of UFO research, more incredible perhaps than UFO crash/retrieval cases, are those reports of alleged underground bases established and inhabited by the various ET races currently visiting our planet. While these types of reports are normally rare, New Mexico seems to have more than its fair share of these rumors. FBI investigator Kenneth Rommel is not convinced. I don't think there's a secret alien base anywhere in New Mexico," he told reporters at the Santa Fe New Mexican, adding that, "but that's just my opinion."

One of the most bizarre stories to come out of New Mexico is that there is an underground base being run by aliens beneath Dulce, near the Four Corners section of the state.

One of the leading proponents of this base comes from anonymous conspiracy writer, Commander X., who writes that Dulce is home to a population of 18,000 gray-type extraterrestrials who are actually native to our planet and have lived here for thousands of years, and are working for the Reptilians. According to Commander X, the base is being used largely as a genetics laboratory, and that the grays are conducting grotesque experiments involving crossbreeding humans with animals, or transplanting souls between bodies.

Another proponent of the existence of an alien base was physicist and electronics expert, Paul Bennewitz. In 1980, Bennewitz, whose home was adjacent to the top secret Sandia Military Reservation, used advanced electronic equipment in his home to detect strange electromagnetic signals which were coming from the Dulce area. His own personal investigation into the bizarre abduction of Myrna Hanssen helped to convince him that there was an underground base beneath Dulce.

At this point, the story becomes murky. While Bennewitz felt that he was receiving coded electronic messages from UFOs, researcher William Moore says that Bennewitz was actually receiving signals from terrestrial Air Force technology. He says that Air Force officials approached Bennewitz and asked him to cease his efforts to intercept the signals. Bennewitz allegedly refused, believing the signals to be evidence of UFOs being covered up by the government. It was only then, Moore says, that Bennewitz became the target of a carefully coordinated program of disinformation. Moore states that he cooperated with the Air Force Office of Special Investigations (AFOSI) to supply Bennewitz with false information about UFOs and evil aliens designed to undermine his credibility and drive him towards a nervous breakdown.

The Air Force's plan apparently worked and Bennewitz reportedly had a nervous breakdown and was forced to give up his attempts to monitor the goings-on at Sandia Military Reservation.

Another area often named as involving strange underground activity is the alleged base located in the Manzano Mountains. The base is said to be adjacent to Kirtland Air Force Base, which is also the location of a large nuclear-weapons storage area. One of the first clues to leak to the public regarding this base came from UFO abductee Christa Tilton.

Researcher Timothy Good has revealed that he also received confirmation of the existence of the Manzano alien base. According to Good, there was, allegedly, a conflict between humans and extraterrestrials there, which resulted in retaliation on the part of the aliens. Writes Good,

ON AN UNDISCLOSED DATE, TWO CREATURES WHO HAD SURVIVED A CRASH OR CRASHES, WERE KILLED BY AN AIR FORCE POLICEMAN OUTSIDE KIRTLAND, PROVOKING A PHENOMENAL RESPONSE BY THE CREATURES' COLLEAGUES, WHO DEMONSTRATED THE EASE WITH WHICH THEY COULD CONTROL LOCAL WEATHER. COMMUNICATIONS WERE ESTABLISHED. THE ALIENS INSISTED ON THE RETURN OF THE TWO CORPSES AND, I WAS TOLD, CONTACT WITH THE U.S. MILITARY, REPRESENTED BY AN AIR FORCE MAJOR, WAS INITIATED AT AN UNDISCLOSED LOCATION IN THE SOUTH-WEST DESERT.[171]

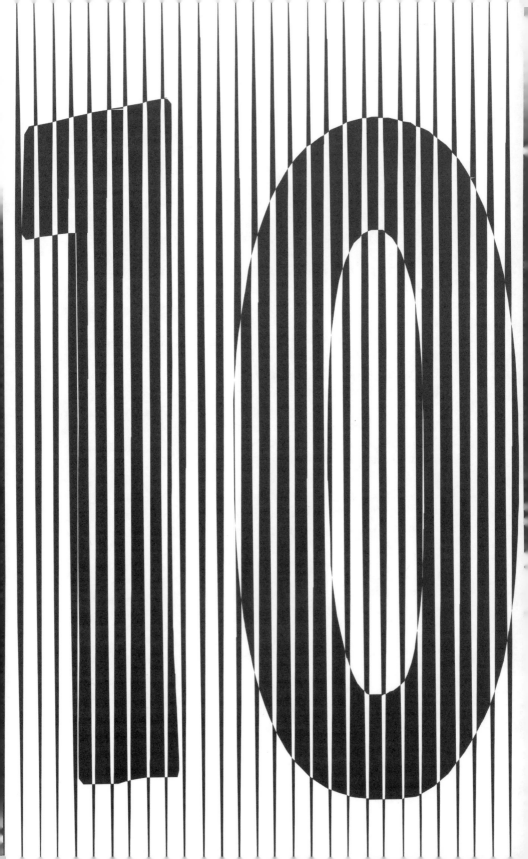

CHAPTER 10

THE**Cattle**MUTILATIONS

One of the strangest and least understood aspects of the UFO phenomenon, cattle mutilations, emerged in the mid-1970s, seemingly out of nowhere. Linda Moulton Howe's award-winning documentary film, *A Strange Harvest* (1980), was the first in-depth look at the mystery. Forty years later, we are no closer to solving it.

The phenomenon first appeared apparently only in the Midwest, primarily in New Mexico and Colorado, which is not surprising considering that these states are leaders in cattle farming. Currently, researchers have discovered that mutilations occur to multiple different species across the world. Initially, however, cattle appeared to be the primary target.

In a typical case, a cow or bull is found dead, with eyes, tongue, rectum, and sex organs removed, apparently surgically, and with no blood spilled on the scene. There is usually no evidence of any struggle.

In some cases, the mutilations are directly associated with UFO activity. In other cases they are associated with unmarked black helicopters, leading to speculation that our own government may be responsible.

Write researchers Lawrence Fawcett and Barry Greenwood say,

> THE CONNECTION BETWEEN HELICOPTERS, UFOs, AND MUTILATIONS IS BECOMING MORE DISTINCT, BUT WHAT IS THE ULTIMATE PURPOSE BEHIND THIS SEEMINGLY INCONGRUOUS ASSOCIATION?

The official explanation offered by skeptics is that the mutilations are the work of predators and natural causes, or perhaps Satanic cult activity. However, among the leading researchers, aliens and government agents remain the prevailing theories. Whatever the case, New Mexico has been particularly hard-hit by the phenomenon.

THE BEGINNING

In New Mexico, the first cases were not understood and were believed to be caused by predators. However, it didn't take long before events escalated to the point where they could no longer be ignored. The year of 1975 produced dozens of helicopter-mutilation incidents. On October 21, 1975, residents of Union County observed five unmarked helicopters buzz a herd of cattle on the Kennann Ranch near Seneca. One week later, numerous helicopters were observed hovering over the Heinmann Ranch and other areas in Union County.

On November 2, 1975, residents of two ranches in Quay County watched a helicopter flashing colored lights, and also sending down beams of white light to the ground. Over the next two weeks, at least thirty unidentified helicopters were seen over Union and Quay counties. During this time, at least four cattle mutilations were reported.

By this time, there were so many complaints coming into the FAA that they launched an official investigation. On November 7, 1975, the *Tucumcari News* said that the FAA was investigating the sightings of unknown aircraft over northeastern New Mexico and was taking depositions from eyewitnesses.

Unfortunately, the results of the investigation were never revealed and the FAA has subsequently denied the existence of any such investigation. FOIA requests to FAA office regarding the affair were met with blanket denials.

Around this time, a New Mexico Livestock Board investigated the mutilations and concluded that there was "possible involvement of clandestine Satanic groups."

According to the *Taos News*, on May 13, 1976, a mutilated cow was found near Pot Mountain. Exactly one month later, on June 13, Gabe Valdez, a state police officer from Dulce, was called to the scene of another apparent mutilation at a local ranch owned by Manuel Gomez.

The instant he saw the dead animal, Valdez was impressed. As he says,

> IT WAS VERY STRANGE. IT WAS WHAT WE CALL A CLASSIC MUTILATION. THE TONGUE, THE EARS, THE SEX ORGANS HAD BEEN REMOVED.

A veteran butcher who examined the carcass says the injuries appeared surgical, and that he was unable to duplicate the precision of the wounds. Gabe Valdez agreed, saying,

> I'VE BEEN AROUND CATTLE ALL MY LIFE, AND I'D NEVER SEEN ANYTHING LIKE IT.

Equally strange were odd fourteen-inch circular imprints found adjacent to the animal and scorched grass. Valdez was puzzled.

Soon he had reason to be concerned. Within a year, he was called to investigate more than thirty similar cases in the Dulce area. He soon became an expert on such cases, and would continue to investigate cases for decades to come.

In 1978, researcher Gabe Valdez was informed that mutilated cows were being marked by an unknown substance which caused the skin on the victims to fluoresce under ultraviolet light. On July 5, 1978, Valdez and cattle rancher Manuel Gomez decided to put Gomez's cattle through an experiment. They penned up 120 cattle and moved them through a "squeeze chute" under a series of ultraviolet lights. Five cattle were found to have a fluorescent substance on their neck, ear and right leg. Samples were collected and analyzed by Schoenfeld Clinical Labs in Albuquerque and the Los Alamos Scientific Labs. They showed high proportions of magnesium and potassium levels at more than seventy times above normal. Dr. Robert Schoenfeld at Schoenfeld Labs believed that the substance was not naturally-occurring and "highly suspicious." He speculated that Gomez's cattle may have been "marked for future taking." Between 1975 and 1980, Gomez had lost at least fifty cattle to mutilations, the most recorded by any single ranch. Interestingly, the marks found on the cattle were exclusively on one particular breed, which had been heavily hit by the mutilations.

On September 11, 1978, rancher Nabor Montoya of Truchas lost a cow to a mutilation. The cow was found in a pasture adjacent to the busy main street of Truchas, seemingly an unlikely location for a mutilation.

In 1977 and 1978, more than fifteen cattle were mutilated on New Mexico Indian Reservations. On December 21, 1978, a *Taos News* article by Phil Bateman speculated that a UFO sighting in Ranchitos earlier in July might be tied to the new epidemic of mysterious animal deaths.

In January of 1979, three expensive race horses near Malga were mutilated. According to the official OAM report,

INFORMATION OBTAINED FROM THE NEW MEXICO LIVESTOCK BOARD REVEALED… THE UPPER EYELID AS WELL AS THE UPPER TIPS OF THE EARS HAD BEEN EXCISED. IN ONE ANIMAL THE GENITAL AREA HAD BEEN REMOVED.

The official conclusion of the report: coyotes.

Two months later, in April, the town of Dulce experienced a wave of low-level sightings. On April 9, 1979, police officers observed a round silent craft hovering fifty feet above the ground, sending down a searchlight. Soon afterwards, several cattle mutilations were discovered nearby.

It was a result of these and other cases that then New Mexico senator Harrison Schmitt called for a multi-state mutilation conference in Albuquerque.

On April 20, 1979, Senator Schmitt and New Mexico U. S. Attorney R. E. Thompson co-sponsored a public hearing on the cattle mutilations at the Albuquerque Public Library. It was an informal hearing designed to bring together people who had experienced cattle mutilations. More than 200 people attended.

Senator Schmitt opened the hearing with a prepared statement saying that: the mutilations are taking place, that they are criminal acts, and that they are causing a great deal of damage, though the identity of the perpetrators remains a mystery. He closed his statement by saying that he hoped these hearings would define the scope of the problem and find a solution by obtaining assistance from official agencies, such as the FBI.

Eleven speakers (including researchers, law enforcement, and ranchers) presented speeches. During the proceedings, John Remming of the New

Mexico Criminal Justice Department revealed that his office had requested $50,000 from the LEAA for the purpose of investigating mutilation reports. Following the hearing, there was a press conference.

According to researcher Jim Marrs, authorities appeared to be hostile towards the ranchers, citizens, and mutilation researchers. As an example, Marrs pointed out that R. E. Thompson, the U.S. Attorney for New Mexico made a statement urging law enforcement officials "not to bring out any evidential material which might be used later at a trial."

The hearings were at least partially successful in that five days later, on April 25, it was announced on Albuquerque television that the state of New Mexico had granted $44,000 in an FBI project to investigate the mutilation reports. Chief FBI investigator Kenneth Rommel headed the project. Incredibly, and to the anger of many researchers and ranchers, Rommel concluded that the mutilations were the result of animal predators and bloating. Meanwhile, the mutilations continued.

In the summer of 1979, Carlos Miranda, a tribal police officer for the Bureau of Indian Affairs in Santa Fe, responded to a call about two dead heifers at Santa Clara Pueblo. One of the heifer's nipples was neatly cut off. The second heifer was missing its entire tongue and the anus was cored out. There were no tire tracks or footprints surrounding the bodies. Miranda reported the case to authorities. According to Miranda, officials from Los Alamos showed up and took the heifers for an investigation. They told him they would get back to him with a report. Miranda, however, says he was unable to get any report. He called them several times. Two months after the incident, he called them again and Los Alamos officials told him flat-out, "We don't know what you're talking about."

Miranda believes there is a cover-up. As he says, "I was told to hush for some reason. There was something going on. I was going around and around with the U.S. government. If they know something, they should let people know what's going on."

A few days after the mutilation, Miranda says he was chased by a red light that hovered forty feet above the ground in the same area of the mutilations. He was impressed by the way the light "moves fast and stops on a dime."

Meanwhile, the sightings of UFOs and unmarked helicopters over animal mutilation sites continued, and the FBI's field offices in New Mexico were deluged with reports and inquiries. Finally, in 1980, the FBI launched an investigation known as "Operational Animal Mutilation" (OAM).

The introduction to the OAM report reads as follows:

ACCORDING TO SOME ESTIMATES, BY 1979, 10,000 HEAD OF CATTLE HAD BEEN MYSTERIOUSLY MUTILATED. OF THE STATES THAT HAVE BEEN AFFECTED BY THIS PHENOMENON, NEW MEXICO HAS BEEN UNUSUALLY "HARD HIT." SINCE 1975, OVER 100 CASES HAVE BEEN REPORTED. THE NEW MEXICO REPORTS, LIKE THOSE FROM OTHER PARTS OF THE COUNTRY, DESCRIBE THE MUTILATIONS AS BEING CHARACTERIZED BY THE PRECISE SURGICAL REMOVAL OF CERTAIN PARTS OF THE ANIMAL, PARTICULARLY THE SEXUAL ORGANS AND RECTUM... MUTILATION ACCOUNTS ARE OFTEN ACCOMPANIED BY SIGHTINGS OF STRANGE HELICOPTERS OR UFOs.

The document continues:

THE LINK BETWEEN UFOs AND THE NEW MEXICO INCIDENTS IS FURTHER SUPPORTED BY THE ALLEGED DISCOVERIES OF CARCASSES WITH BROKEN LEGS AND VISIBLE CLAMP MARKS, INDICATING TO SOME INVESTIGATORS THAT THE ANIMALS ARE BEING AIRLIFTED TO ANOTHER PLACE WHERE THEY ARE MUTILATED, AND THEN RETURNED TO THE SPOT WHERE THEY ARE FOUND. THIS BELIEF IS FURTHER SUPPORTED BY TWO ADDITIONAL REPORTS – ONE OF A CASE IN WHICH THE COW'S HORN WAS STICKING IN THE GROUND AS IF THE ANIMAL HAD BEEN DROPPED THERE; THE OTHER OF A STEER FOUND IN A TREE FIVE FEET ABOVE THE GROUND.

THE MUTILATIONS CONTINUE

Despite the OAM report, mutilations continued. In early 1988, several cows belonging to longtime Pecos village Marshall, Andres Vigil, were found mutilated. Former cattleman and Pecos Mayor George Adela says that Vigil told him about the mutilations. No further details were revealed.

Several months later, in October 1988, David and Edie Cook found their neighbor's yearling colt lying dead in their side-yard, about 100 feet from their home. The colt's genitals and anus had been removed, and a portion of its hide was missing. The animal showed no sign of struggle. There were no footprints or tracks next to the body. Says Edie Cook,

THE HORSE WAS LYING IN SOME GRASS ABOUT THREE OR FOUR FEET HIGH, BUT NONE OF THE GRASS WAS CRUSHED. THE HIDE WAS CUT WITH LASER PRECISION.

However, Edie also noticed that there were no burn-marks, which a laser might leave. The Cooks also noticed three black dots in a perfect triangle above one eye, and that a pencil-wide hole of flesh had been cored out of the flesh next to the nostril.

Edie carefully examined the terrain around the horse and found two six-foot wide circular patches situated side-by-side. Inside the patches, the grass was flattened and swirled in a counter clockwise pattern. None of the grass next to the strange circles was disturbed.

A few days after the colt had been found mutilated, the Cooks found three mutilated chickens in the same field next to their home. Two of the chickens were decapitated. The third was missing its legs.

In 1989 and 1990, Tom Reed (the manager of a ranch north of Questa) lost eight cows and thirteen calves. While he admits that some of the deaths may have been attributable to natural causes, some definitely were not because as he says, "…predators don't make nice clean cuts."

Reed has found other strange evidence. On one occasion, he was running the young calves through the cattle chute when he discovered that their ears had been surgically cut. Says Reed,

> IT DID SEEM KIND OF STRANGE. ALL OF THEM HAD AT LEAST ONE EAR CROPPED; TWO OF THEM HAD BOTH — JUST AN INCH OFF THE TOP IN THAT SMOOTH CUT — BUT THEY WEREN'T DEAD.

Reed has found no pattern in the type of cattle being killed. In March 1996, he found a one-month-old calf dead, missing its tongue, right eye, and two front teeth. He said it appeared as if the teeth had been pulled.

He contacted state investigators who took away the calf, but never gave Reed any results. Says Reed,

> THEY ALWAYS SAY THEY HAVE NO INFORMATION, THEY CAN'T TELL YOU ANYTHING.

In March of 1993, a mutilated cow was found on a ranch located right in the center of Taos. Sandoval County rancher Ray Trujillo says that he has lost twenty cattle on his ranch in the Jemez Mountains since 1993. One of the animals, he said, had its spinal cord "excised" from its body. It was only one of seventeen cases that had occurred in this area that year.

Another 1993 case occurred in May on the 3,800-acre Tres Ritos Ranch north of Questa. According to manager Tom Reed, he found the mutilated steer in a field. An eyeball and the tongue were missing, and a hole had been cored out of the flesh adjacent to the anus.

Starting in March of 1994, another rash of mutilations occurred on ranches near Questa, Eagle Nest and Taos. One of the first was reported by Daniel Quintana of El Prado, who lost a heifer. He found the body lying in fresh snow, with no tracks around it. Says Quintana,

> I HAD TO BREAK TRACKS THROUGH THE SNOW TO GET TO IT. THERE WAS NO BLOOD AROUND IT. BUT I FOUND A LITTLE SPOT OF BLOOD TUNNELED INTO THE SNOW ABOUT 50 FEET AWAY OUTSIDE THE CORRAL. THEY DID A VERY NEAT JOB, PERFECT.

According to Quintana, the lower jaw, one horn, the tongue, and both eyes were missing, and the rear end was cored out. Say Quintana,

> THEY CUT A STRAIGHT LINE ACROSS THE FOREHEAD, PULLED OFF THE SKIN AND TOOK AN ALMOST SQUARE PATCH FROM THE SIDE. YOU COULD SEE THE RIBS.

Quintana immediately contacted authorities, who began an investigation. Says Quintana,

> INVESTIGATORS WERE EXCITED ABOUT IT. THEY WANTED TO COME AND CAMP ON MY LAND.

By May, five new mutilations had been reported, the last by Moreno Valley rancher Eli Hronich. On May 14, 1994, Hronich found two head of cattle with their right eyes, tongues, and sexual organs "surgically removed." He told the *Sangre de Cristo Chronicle* that there was no trace of blood, and that the flesh around the mysterious wounds looked "bleached."

In June of 1994, another mutilation case occurred on a ranch north of Taos. The case was investigated by state livestock inspector Jerry Valerio. He was deeply puzzled by what he found. As Valerio told reporters,

> I CUT INTO THAT HEIFER AND THERE WAS NO BLOOD. THE MEAT WAS REALLY FLAKY. IT LOOKED LIKE IT HAD BEEN PUT THROUGH A MICROWAVE OR PRESSURE-COOKED. THE ANIMAL HAD ONLY BEEN DEAD FIVE OR SIX HOURS.

Valerio said that after handling the body of the heifer, he and two other ranchers experienced tingling and burning sensations in their hands for several days afterwards.

On September 13, 1994, Larry Gardea was bear hunting near Luhan Canyon when he came upon a herd of cows, in the middle of which was a mutilated cow with her vagina and rectum missing. Ten feet away, another cow was on its knees, also dead. As he examined the first cow, he heard a strange sound like a welder's torch coming from the forest. All the cows in the herd moved away from the sound except one, which according to Gardea, *floated* in the air over the fence enclosing the herd, and towards the source of the sound. At the same moment, he observed another cow float down out of the sky and land in the pasture.

Confused and frightened, Gardea aimed his rifle and fired twice at the source of the noise. The sound immediately stopped. Says Gardea,

> THAT'S WHEN I FELT AFRAID FOR THE FIRST TIME. I FIGURED I HAD JUST ATTRACTED ATTENTION TO MYSELF AND IF THE SOUND COULD MOVE THAT COW, IT COULD MOVE ME. SO I TURNED AROUND AND RAN BACK TO THE RANCH HOUSE TO CALL THE SHERIFF.

Gardea returned to the site forty minutes later with the Mora County sheriff's deputy and several local residents. There were unable to locate the cow that Gardea had seen floating into the forest, nor could they find the cow that was dead on its knees. While Gardea never observed an actual UFO, the fact that the cows were levitated points to the likelihood that a craft may have been hidden nearby in the forest. (Baker, pp42-43)

One New Mexican rancher who has suffered badly from the epidemic is Eagle Nest resident Eli Hronich. In 1994, Hronich lost an eleventh head of cattle to the phenomenon. On this occasion, the cow's tongue, eye, and several vital organs were removed. The Hroniches say that they have had little help from state or federal investigators. Hronich says that he has suffered "a substantial financial loss" and that "this whole thing just doesn't make much sense." Hronich was forced to move his herd in the hopes of preventing further deaths. As he says, "I wish I knew why they were picking on me."

Gail Staehlin (a researcher from Albuquerque) has investigated many cases firsthand. She is certain that the mutilations are not the work of Satanic cults. Says Staehlin,

> FOR YOU TO WALK UP TO A COW THAT SIZE AND KILL IT, YOU'D HAVE TO SLIT ITS THROAT. THEY'D HAVE BLOOD ALL OVER THE PLACE. IF IT IS CONFIRMED THAT IT IS LASER CUTS, THE EQUIPMENT THEY'D HAVE TO USE IS FAIRLY GOOD-SIZED. THAT'S WHY I THINK THE COWS ARE REMOVED.

She says that although many ranchers do see unmarked helicopters, in many cases, it is after the mutilation and not before.

In most cases, officials blame the animal mutilations on predators, though not without some disagreement among them and the ranchers who are losing the cattle. In 1994, John Worthman, the executive director of the New Mexico Livestock Board said,

WE DON'T KNOW WHO'S DOING IT OR WHY, BUT WE KNOW FOR SURE IT'S NOT PREDATORS.

In late 1994, Santa Fe researcher David Perkins charted the locations of more than a dozen mutilation cases that had taken place in New Mexico in the prior sixteen months. The majority of these cases occurred in the Eagle Nest area, where – says Perkins – nuclear fallout from a May 1955 Nevada atomic test had landed. Perkins believes that the purpose of the mutilations might be to measure the effects of atomic pollution on the local animal population.

On July 8, 1996, rancher Jesse Gonzales found two mutilated cows on his ranch in Arroyo Hondo. Says Gonzales,

I'M A PROFESSIONAL HUNTER OF DEER AND ELK, AND I SLAUGHTER MY OWN ANIMALS FOR MEAT. SO I KNOW WHAT IT LOOKS LIKE WHEN YOU PULL THE GUTS OUT OF AN ANIMAL. THIS WAS NOT DONE BY ANYTHING HUMAN.

Gonzales described one of the mutilations in detail, saying that the bull had only been dead a few hours when he found it. The tongue and one eye were missing. A patch of skin around the lower jaw had been neatly removed. The hind end was cored out and the sexual organs removed. There were no tracks around the carcass, and the gate into the pasture was locked.

A few days following the incident, Gonzales reported seeing a UFO in the same area. Says Gonzales,

A COUPLE OF NIGHTS LATER I SAW THESE VERY WEIRD LIGHTS, BLUE AND RED, THREE OR FOUR OF THEM HOVERING OVER GALLINA CANYON.

Meanwhile, Gonzales' neighbor, Ben Valerio, said he lost a steer worth $1,500 on his ranch in lower Arroyo Hondo. The mutilation occurred around the same time as the Gonzales case. Says Valerio,

THE MALE ORGANS AND BACK PART OF IT HAD BEEN REMOVED. I HADN'T CHECKED MY CATTLE IN TWO OR THREE DAYS, BUT I DIDN'T SEE ANY TRACKS. THERE WAS NO BLOOD. IT WAS VERY NEAT.

A few weeks after the above incidents, a third cow was found in a pasture in El Prado. The heifer's anus and udders had been removed, and a round patch of skin had been cut out of the belly. Researcher Gail Staehlin examined the animal and said that the cuts were all smooth and symmetrical, and looked as if they had been burned. There was no trace of any blood.

There were other rare details that Staehlin discovered coincided with other cases. One was the fact that the mutilation occurred during violent weather, when most people were inside. Another was the bizarre fact that, as in other cases, dry cow patties were found flipped over.

Staehlin does believe there is a connection with the reported black helicopters. On one occasion, she was followed by an unmarked black helicopter. Another time, while investigating a mutilation site, a black helicopter hovered low overhead.

On September 30, 1996, a dead cow was found fifteen miles up Taos Canyon. The cow's rectum was cored-out and the udder and tongue had been cut away. There was no blood or tracks on the ground. A few days earlier, there was a report of a UFO sighting in the area.

In October 1996, rancher Robert Allen of Kanjilon came across his prized four-year-old bull, dead and mutilated in a field near his home. The genitals and anus had been neatly sliced away. There was no blood, no footprints, and no indication of what had killed the animals. They had heard a "strange helicopter" flying over their property the night before. When he told his family what happened, his wife became "completely terrified."

Allen believes that "visitors from outer space" is the explanation which best fits the evidence. Says Allen,

PEOPLE JUST CAN'T GRASP THIS UNLESS THEY HAVE ACTUALLY SEEN THE MUTILATED ANIMAL THEMSELVES.

The cuts are so precise that Allen believes that they are done by lasers. Also, there is the fact that the mutilated bodies remain untouched by local wildlife. As Allen says,

BUT NO PREDATOR WILL EAT OFF THE ANIMAL, AND COYOTES WILL EAT ANYTHING.

Dulce-based police officer Gabe Valdez was one of the pioneering investigators of cattle mutilations when the story broke in the 1970s. By 1996, he had investigated hundreds of cases, remaining one of the leading mutilation experts. In February of 1997, Valdez became a field investigator for the National Institute of Discovery Science, (NIDS), which has considerable funding to investigate the mystery. Shortly after joining, Valdez was called to investigate two new cases in the Dulce area. Valdez doesn't have any answers yet, but as he says,

I KNOW SOMEONE'S DOING IT. AND WHOEVER IS DOING IT IS PRETTY DAMN SMART... WHOEVER BREAKS THIS CASE, WELL, IT'S GOING TO BE ONE OF THE BIGGEST THINGS IN THE HISTORY OF MANKIND.

On April 12, 1997, rancher Tony Trujillo of northern New Mexico found that one of his cattle had been mutilated. Says Trujillo,

THE FUNNY THING IS THAT YOU DON'T SEE THE DOGS OR THE BIRDS. THEY DON'T GET NEAR IT.

In May 1997, rancher Floyd Archuleta lost a bull to mutilation on his Taos ranch. The bull's anus was removed, as were the tongue, right eye, and sex organs. There was also a pencil-thin hole in its neck. Later, during the autopsy, behind the pencil-thin hole, investigators found a bowling ball-sized cavity, where the bull's flesh had been cored out. In the ground next to the bull, investigators found strange V-shaped gouge marks eighteen to twenty-four inches in diameter and five to six inches deep. The investigators concluded,

IT APPEARED THAT SOME TYPE OF HEAVY MECHANICAL OBJECT HAD MADE INDENTATIONS 150 FEET SOUTH OF WHERE THE BULL WAS FOUND. THE ABSENCE OF OTHER TRACKS FURTHER AWAY LED TO THE HYPOTHESIS THAT THE OBJECT HAD BEEN AIRBORNE AND HAD LANDED NEAR THE ANIMAL.

In support of this hypothesis, at the time of the incident, numerous witnesses in the area reported seeing a strange green light flying around Arroyo Seco, where the bull was found. Taos District Attorney John Pasternoster says that although this was the first mutilation to be reported in 1996, he believes the phenomenon will continue. Says Pasternoster,

I DON'T THINK THESE CATTLE MUTILATIONS ARE GOING TO STOP SUDDENLY.

On November 24, 1997, rancher Jessie Gonzales was tending his cattle on his ranch in Arroyo Hondo when he found one of his prime bulls, dead and mysteriously mutilated. A sixteen-inch diameter hole had been neatly sliced out of the flank, and the penis and entire anus of the animal were missing. Says Gonzales,

> THERE WAS NO BLOOD. WHEN YOU GUT AN ELK, ESPECIALLY FROM THE REAR, YOU GET ABOUT TWO GALLONS OF BLOOD… WHEN YOU HAVE MYSTERIOUS DEATHS LIKE THESE, YOU HAVE QUESTIONS… I FEEL REALLY FRUSTRATED. IF I SEE ANYONE MESSING AROUND WITH MY COWS, I'M GOING TO SHOOT THEM.

Also in 1997, Blanko rancher Paul Velasquez lost two bulls. The animals' intestines were cut, the right ears were removed, the tongues sliced off, and the rectums cored out. The loss cost him $2,000.

Researcher John Paternoster has researched several cases and says that in 1997, although there were six deaths reported, he believes that many more went unreported. Says Paternoster,

> THE FARMERS AND RANCHERS HAVE BEEN RELUCTANT TO REPORT CATTLE MUTILATIONS, THEY DON'T WANT TO BE PAINTED…AS CRACKPOTS AND UFOLOGISTS.

In 1997, researcher Timothy Good interviewed Les Roberts, the manager of the 2,300-acre Double D ranch near Taos, and the location of a large number of mutilations. Roberts told Good that officials have not been able to help him or the other ranchers. As he says,

> ALL THE VETS CAN TELL YOU, THEY HAVE NO EARS. LAST YEAR I LOST A COW. I'VE NO IDEA WHAT HAPPENED. SHE WAS PREGNANT. (GOOD, 2000, 247)

On May 2, 1998, rancher John Mutz of Moreno Valley (10 miles southeast of Red River) found his four-year-old cow mutilated, missing its tongue, eye, and udders. There was no blood and no tracks at the scene.

On November 7, 1998, a cow belonging to rancher Leroy Graham was found mutilated on a 160-acre ranch near Black Lake, in the Angel Fire area. The cow's uterus had been neatly removed, the anus was cored out, and one eye was missing. Adjacent to the mutilation, investigators found a puzzling hole in the road about three feet in diameter.

While cattle seem to be the main target of the mutilations, various other animals have also been victims. In late November 1998, a rare case involving a mutilated piglet was discovered near the Talpa Reservoir. The piglet was found neatly laid out with a huge hole in its side and all the internal organs missing.

On May 4, 1999, ranch manager Tom Reed found a severely mutilated cow on the 3,200-acre Tres Ritos Ranch five miles north of Questa. Mutilation researchers Gabe Valdez and Gary Mora were called to the scene. The cow, they discovered, was missing its right ear and half the left ear. There was a large hole in the neck and one of the eyes was missing. There was no blood around the body.

Four days later, Reed found another mutilation in the same area. In this case, the victim was a calf less than two months old. Says Reed,

> ALL THE INNARDS WERE GONE — THE HEART, GUTS, LUNGS, STOMACH AND SEXUAL ORGANS.

Reed had already lost eight cows in the past decade. While investigators conducted an autopsy, they were unable to determine how the animal died, other than to say that the case followed the same pattern as observed in other classic mutilation cases.

Two weeks later, on May 23, Reed found a third mutilated cow on the Tres Ritos Ranch, only about fifty yards distant from the location of the mutilated calf. In this case, the cow's udder had been entirely removed, and the neck had a deep hole several inches in diameter. Valdez was again called to the case. He noted that several cow patties in large circumference around the body had been flipped over by some type of turbulence, however, there were no tracks surrounding the animal. An autopsy of the body revealed massive hemorrhaging of the muscle tissue. Says Valdez,

> IT WAS COOKED.

WHAT IS GOING ON?

The summer of 2000 brought a new rash of mutilations, including one involving a cow that was found mutilated and alive. On May 20, near Cuba, New Mexico, a rancher who insisted upon remaining anonymous found one of his cows still alive, but with its tongue and ears removed. He quickly rounded up his other cattle and discovered that other cows had been victims of vivisection. A two-year-old Charolais cow had both ears missing and severe lacerations on its lip. The condition of the first cow quickly worsened and the owner decided to shoot the animal.

On June 18, 2000, rancher Jerry Sanchez of Sunshine Valley north of Questa lost a four-year-old Black Angus cow. The cow was cut along it spine and leg, the udder was damaged, and the tongue had been removed from the back of the throat.

Shortly later, rancher Rumaldo Martinez, who lives two miles north of the Tres Ritos ranch, lost a cow to mutilation.

On November 28, 2003, a gentleman was walking his dog near his home in Cloudcroft (which borders the Lincoln National Forest) when he came upon the body of an elk lying in a shallow ravine, about 200 yards from the subdivision where he lived. Elk are common in the area, but it was unusual to find a body. The witness reports that the head had been removed, and the rectum had been "smoothly cored out" and the genital removed. The witness was a former Federal investigator.

On March 22, 2006, two sisters were driving near Socorro when they saw a dead cow about fifty yards from the road. They pulled over to examine it. Says one of the sisters,

ITS EYES WERE REMOVED, ITS RECTUM REMOVED AND ALSO ITS HEART REMOVED. NO BLOOD ON THE GROUND OR ON THE DEAD ANIMAL.

After a short examination and after taking several photographs, the sisters drove home to Tucson, Arizona. While neither claimed to know for certain if it was a genuine mutilation, they were inspired enough to send a photo and short explanation to MUFON. (See the photo section on page 304.)

The mutilations show no signs of ending. Rancher Joe Quintana owns a cattle ranch near New Mexico Highway 104, not far from Tucumcari. On July 29, 2007, he found one of his $1,600 Angus cows mutilated. Its udder was removed with what appeared to be a sharp instrument. There were no signs of struggle, trauma, or predators. New Mexico State Livestock Board inspector Matthew Romero investigated the case and released an official report on the case. Says Romero,

WE'RE NOT SURE WHAT HAPPENED. IT'S A POSSIBLE MUTILATION.

Rancher Joe Quintana is puzzled and angry. As he says,

> I'VE NEVER EXPERIENCED ANYTHING LIKE THIS. MY NEIGHBORS HAVEN'T EITHER…
> I CARRY MY RIFLE OUT HERE, AND I'LL APPREHEND [SUSPECTS] AND HOLD THEM FOR
> THE SHERIFF. I HOPE IT DOESN'T HAPPEN AGAIN.

As mentioned, some researchers have noted that unmarked helicopters have been seen in the vicinity of cattle mutilations and that human agencies may be responsible for at least some of the cases. Some researchers feel that both human and extraterrestrial agencies are involved.

Leading researcher John Pasternoster is convinced that the mutilations are not caused by Satanists, or by scavengers. The evidence, he says, demands a different explanation. Says Pasternoster,

> MAYBE IT HAS SOMETHING TO DO WITH BIOLOGICAL OR BIOCHEMICAL WEAPONS
> TESTING. OR MAYBE IT'S SOMETHING WE CAN'T EVEN COMPREHEND.

Researcher Gabe Valdez says,

> WHOEVER IT IS, THEY'RE COMING DOWN BY AIR. I DON'T KNOW WHO THEY ARE,
> BUT WHATEVER IS BEHIND IT, IT'S SOMETHING BIG.

Writes Richard Dolan,

> THE THEORY IS THAT THE MUTILATIONS ARE OCCURRING AS PART OF A COVERT,
> RANDOM SAMPLING OF CATTLE TO TEST FOR EXCESSIVE LEVELS OF RADIATION
> CONTAMINATION. THE AREA OF NORTHERN NEW MEXICO, WHICH WAS THE HOTSPOT
> OF MUTILATION ACTIVITY DURING THE 1990S, HAPPENS TO BE DOWNWIND FROM THE
> NUCLEAR TEST SITE IN NEVADA, POSSESSES SEVERAL ACTIVE URANIUM MINES, WAS THE
> SCENE OF MANY NUCLEAR DETONATIONS IN PAST DECADES, AND ALSO HAS TWO MAJOR
> NUCLEAR RESEARCH LABORATORIES. OVER THE YEARS, AN ESTIMATED 1,000 KILOTONS
> OF RADIOACTIVE DUST FELL ON NEW MEXICO, NEVADA, AND COLORADO.

Researcher David Perkins agrees. When mutilations first became popularized in the late 1970s, Perkins conducted a statistical study and found that many mutilations were occurring downwind of nuclear power plants, nuclear weapons laboratories, nuclear test sites, and military bases. In New Mexico, Perkins found that a great many cases were reported near uranium mining operations in Grant and Hidalgo counties, near the site of underground nuclear detonations in the 1960s. Perkins also discovered that mutilation events formed a tight ring around Los Alamos National

Laboratories, including Sandoval, Santa Fe, and Rio Arriba counties. Perkins doesn't believe the military is responsible. Says Perkins,

> MY THEORY IS THE GOVERNMENT DOESN'T KNOW ANY MORE THAN US.

While he stops short of saying that extraterrestrials are responsible, he does admit that he has seen apparent UFOs during his investigations into the mutilations. Says Perkins,

> RIGHT NOW I'M LEANING TOWARD THE MILITARY SECRET OPERATION THEORY. I SEE ALL KINDS OF LIGHTS ZOOMING AROUND HERE, BUT I DON'T KNOW WHAT THEY ARE.

Other explanations are that the UFOs are imitating helicopters. Or it could be that the government is monitoring the UFOs as they perform the mutilations. Yet another possibility is that the mutilations are being conducted by humans working together with extraterrestrials.

One of the strangest and most frightening stories regarding animal mutilations is the possible case of a human mutilation. The following case, if true, shows a darker aspect of the UFO phenomenon. In 1956, an Air Force major reported that he saw a landed disk-shaped object kidnap Sergeant Jonathan P. Louette.

Three days later, Louette's body was found in the New Mexico desert near the range. As with cattle, his genitals had been removed and his anus cored out with what appeared to be laser-type instruments. Officially, Louette's death was listed as "exposure." (Swartz, p25)

More possibilities and explanations exist, however, at this point all that is known for sure is that there is a connections between UFOs, mutilations, and unmarked black helicopters. Writes Fawcett and Greenwood,

> IT MAY TAKE SOME TIME BEFORE THE PIECES FALL TOGETHER, BUT ULTIMATELY, WE BELIEVE THAT THE GOVERNMENT WILL HAVE TO ADMIT TO DEEP INVOLVEMENT IN THIS ASPECT OF THE UFO MYSTERY.[173]

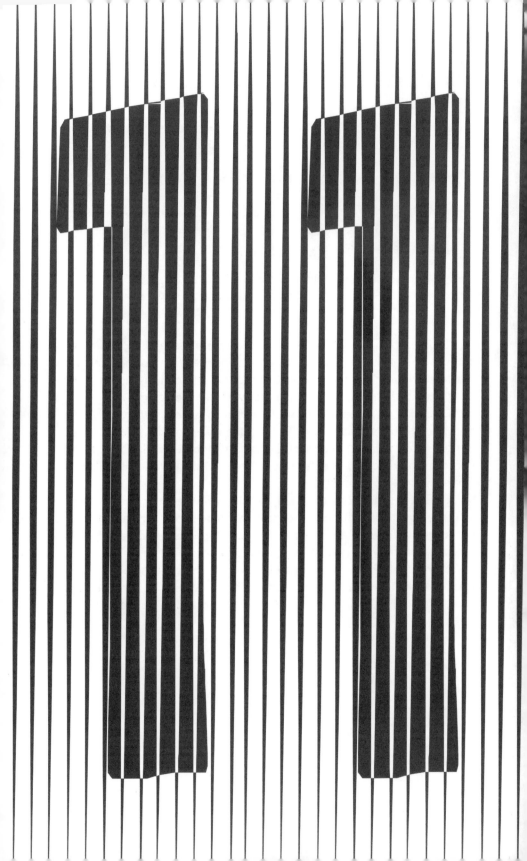

CHAPTER 11

THE Taos HUM

One of the newest and strangest mysteries to descend upon the Land of Enchantment comes in the form of a soft humming noise known as the Taos Hum. Starting in May 1991, a small group of *Taosenos* (Taos residents), began to complain of a low-pitched humming or buzzing noise that was keeping them awake at night and distracting them during the day. The mystery was, the source of the noise could not be found. As word of the hum spread, so did the number of people who claimed to hear it. While the hum was not only annoying, some people said that it was having a negative impact on their health.

Among the first "hearers" were Bob and Catanya Saltzman, who lived south of Taos. Bob Salztman described the noise as a combination of three sounds including "a low grinding, a staticky hiss, and a high ringing sound." Bothered by the constant noise, they finally hired an acoustical engineer who recorded a tone of 17 hertz with a harmonic rising to as high as 70 hertz.

Some of those who hear the tone say that it has led to severe health problems. Mrs. Whitted, who lives on Airport Road in Santa Fe says that she has suffered terribly from the hum. Says Whitted,

> IT'S HORRIBLE. IT'S KILLING ME. I WENT TO SEE MY DOCTOR ABOUT A YEAR AGO, AND I TOLD HIM I JUST COULDN'T MAKE IT ANY LONGER. I'M JUST IN SO MUCH PAIN.

Whitted's doctor prescribed her an antidepressant.

Some learned to live with it. Sara Allen, an engineer at KTAO radio in Taos, says she hears the hum which she describes as "a tractor running, off in the distance," but unable to do anything about it, she just ignores it. She theorizes that the hum is some sort of military communications signal. Thankfully, she says she hasn't suffered any physical symptoms, but she does believe that many people are suffering from the hum, even though they can't hear it.

Taos resident Steve Walters says that at first he didn't hear it, but then woke up one night and ever since then, the hum has not gone away. Says Walters,

> I WENT RUNNING AROUND THE HOUSE, CHECKING, BUT NOTHING WAS ON. I CUT OFF ALL THE CIRCUIT BREAKERS IN THE HOUSE, AND I COULD STILL HEAR IT. THEN IT OCCURRED TO ME, THIS WAS THE SOUND EVERYBODY WAS TALKING ABOUT.

Meanwhile, the Saltzman family was still hearing the noise and were continuing their campaign to solve the mystery. They organized a survey and learned that hundreds of Taos residents were hearing the noise. They wrote numerous letters to government officials, asking for an investigation. Finally, in May of 1993, scientists and engineers from the University of New Mexico conducted an investigation in the Saltzman's home and recorded a tone between 30 and 80 hertz. Unfortunately, they were unable to pinpoint a source. Their investigation cost more than $37,000.

Unable to get any relief, the sound eventually forced the Saltzmans out of their home. The University of New Mexico study found that two percent of the Taos County population was hearing the vibrations.

By this time, the Taos hum had become front-page news, not only across New Mexico, but across the world. People seemed fascinated by the unusual mystery. New Mexicans, however, wanted answers.

The hum continued to force additional residents out of their homes, including Paul Loumena and Alexandra Lorraine who sold *The Laughing Horse Inn* and moved away. Says Loumena,

> I DON'T NECESSARILY BELIEVE IT HAS TO BE A CONSPIRACY, BUT IF IT'S GENERATED BY THE INNER EAR, THEN WHY DO I FEEL THESE VIBRATIONS IN MY HEART? WHY DOES MY HEAD FEEL LIKE A TUNING FORK WHEN I WAKE UP IN THE MORNING?

Shatzie Hubbell used to live on Canyon Road in Santa Fe. The hum bothered her so much, she moved to a ranch near Fort Worth, Texas, where she no longer hears the tone.

Taos resident K. C. Grams describes it as "power lines throbbing with a whiny quality." She says that the noise is so pervasive and annoying, it sometimes drives her to tears. Writes Grams,

> CERTAINLY THE SOUND IS NOT INTERNAL. I HAVE TO USE A WAVE TAPE TO GET SLEEP HERE, BUT I WENT TO HOUSE-SIT FOR A FRIEND IN SANTA FE, AND I SLEPT THE WHOLE TIME.

When complaints continued to spread, officials were again forced to investigate. In 1993, New Mexico democratic Congressman Bill Richardson was quoted by reporters saying that the hum could be defense related, perhaps caused by three local weapons projects. Two months later, New Mexico's republican Senator Pete Domenici told reporters that he had queried Pentagon officials at the Defense Department and received a response in the form of a letter, which said in part,

> MY STAFF HAS REVIEWED OUR DEFENSE ACTIVITIES IN THIS AREA AND HAVE CONCLUDED THERE IS NO PROGRAM, CLASSIFIED OR NOT, WHICH WOULD CAUSE THE HUM.

Senator Dominici then said that underground aqueducts might be responsible, and that he was interested in seeing if the University of New Mexico or New Mexico's national laboratories can solve the mystery.

Meanwhile, a spokesperson for Congressman Bill Richardson backpedaled and said that Richardson's comments on the hum were not based on military intelligence, but rather on "rumors."

In 1993, a team of scientists from the University of New Mexico, the Sandia and Los Alamos National Laboratory, and the Phillips Laboratory of the U.S. Air Force collaborated together in an investigation to identify the sound. They worked for a month using electromagnetic, seismic, and acoustic sensors, each of which failed to register the hum.

Although the investigation ultimately failed to identify the hum, it did bring some needed attention. The investigation was headed by Joe Mullins, the chairman of the mechanical engineering department at the University of New Mexico. Mullins denied hearing the hum but said,

> THE PEOPLE WHO DO HEAR IT, THEY'RE CERTAINLY SENSING AND RESPONDING TO SOMETHING. I CAN'T SAY IT'S IMAGINARY AT ALL.

Says Senator Richardson,

> MY FEELING IS THAT IT'S SOME DEFENSE-RELATED PROJECT, NOT NECESSARILY BY THE DEPARTMENT OF DEFENSE. I DON'T THINK ANYBODY'S DOING A COVER-UP... IT MAY NOT BE AN URGENT PRIORITY, BUT BECAUSE MY CONSTITUENTS ARE BOTHERED, IT'S DEFINITELY SOMETHING TO LOOK INTO.

Meanwhile, engineering professor emeritus Joe Mullins of University of New Mexico led another study to locate the source of the hum. He interviewed 161 people, all of whom fell under normal demographic statistics. Unfortunately, he was unable to obtain any sizeable funding for his project and after several months of study, was unable to locate the source of the noise. He was convinced, however, of its existence. As he says,

> PEOPLE ARE REALLY SUFFERING.

In 1993, the University of Mexico mailed a questionnaire to 7,000 Taos homes. There were 1,440 responses. Eleven percent of the respondents reported hearing the hum.

Some of the "hearers" are not whom one might expect. For example, Horace Poteet, who lives in Albuquerque, is an electrical engineer who works at a Sandia National Laboratories. Poteet was also a member of Professor Mullins' team. Poteet reports that he has heard the hum for years, and still does, especially when he's in a quiet location.

In 1996, Taos resident K. C. Grams told reporters that she was still hearing the hum, and had been since it began years earlier. Says Grams,

I STILL NOTICE IT WHEN IT'S QUIET.

Sara Allen, also an early hearer says that the hum has not gone away. As she says,

MOST PEOPLE THINK THAT THE PHENOMENON HAS GONE AWAY, BUT I CAN ASSURE YOU IT HASN'T.

A more recent hearer is professional musician Jenny Bird, who has lived in Taos for eighteen years, but didn't start hearing the hum until 1994. Say Bird,

ONE DAY I WAS WAITING FOR THE SCHOOL BUS WITH MY KIDS. I THOUGHT THE BUS WAS PULLING UP BEHIND ME AND I TURNED AROUND AND NOTHING WAS THERE. I SAID, "MAYBE THAT'S WHAT THEY WERE TALKING ABOUT."

Although publicity has died down, the Taos hum remains. In 2003, Santa Fe resident P.J. Nelson wrote an editorial for the *Santa Fe New Mexican*, asking,

DOES ANYONE ELSE HEAR A CONSTANT HUMMING NOISE THAT SOUNDS LIKE DIESEL ENGINES RUNNING IN AND AROUND SANTA FE AND SURROUNDING COMMUNITIES AS FAR AS LAS VEGAS AND LOS ALAMOS? IT CAN BE HEARD OUTDOORS AS WELL AS INDOORS. SOME DAYS IT IS MUCH LOUDER THAN OTHER DAYS.

Nelson wrote that noise machines and ear-plugs have failed to mask the sound and did anybody have any suggestions? Anybody?[173]

CHAPTER 12

UFOsOver
NewMexicoTODAY

New Mexico's UFO history stretches back 130 years and continues strong today. The last decade from 2000 to 2010 has produced a whole new batch of dramatic sightings. Below are some of the most current prominent encounters. As can be seen, the UFOs are not going away.

FLOCK OF GEESE ABDUCTED?

On January 23, 2000, an anonymous witness sat in his car in a parking lot outside the building where he worked in Rio Rancho. He was enjoying his lunch break when he saw a flock of geese circling above the Rio Grande River. Says the witness,

THEY WERE IN THEIR USUAL "V" FORMATION BUT INSTEAD OF FLYING OFF INTO THE DISTANCE, THEY SEEMED TO BE CONFUSED AS TO WHAT DIRECTION TO GO. THEY SEEMED TO BE CONCERNED BECAUSE THEY WERE NOT MAKING THEIR USUAL HONKING... INSTEAD THE SOUNDS WERE DIFFERENT, MORE HIGH PITCHED AND STRESSFUL.

The geese continued circling and making sounds until they were directly above the witness. He looked away for fifteen seconds to continue eating his lunch, when suddenly the sounds stopped. He jumped out of his car and was stunned to see that the geese were gone.
Says the witness,

THIS WAS VERY STRANGE, AND I WAS IN DISBELIEF THAT THEY COULD HAVE VANISHED. AS I WAS STILL SEARCHING FOR THE GEESE I NOTICED A DARK ROUND OBJECT HANGING ABOVE THE RIVER SOUTH OF MY POSITION AND ABOUT A MILE AWAY.

He estimated that the object was at least 15 feet in diameter and at about 200 feet altitude. It bobbed up and down as if trying to maintain a stable position.

As his lunch break was over, he returned inside. When he came back outside two hours later, just before sunset, the object was still there. Later he reported his sighting to NUFORC.[174]

SILVERY ORB OVER ANGEL FIRE

On September 24, 2000, at 6:30 p.m., Marcia Wood was in the office of the *Sangre de Christo Chronicle* where she worked in the town of Angel Fire. Suddenly resident Richard Sutton rushed into the building, grabbed her arm and pulled her outside. Sutton, Wood and a group of others gathered in the Centro Plaza and viewed "a silver orb" that "glinted in the eastern sky....never moving, seemingly tethered in the air."

Residents Sue and Dave Huettner were driving home from Taos and also viewed the object. They used their cell-phone to call the *Sangre de Christo Chronicle* and alert them of the object.

Meanwhile, another Angel Fire couple was viewing the object through a telescope. Jack and Joan Graham saw the silvery orb and quickly aimed their powerful telescope at the mystery object. Jack Graham reports that through the telescope, the sphere appeared circular and had "things hanging on the side, almost like the balloons that cross the ocean."

After viewing the object, Joan Graham said it was "...amazing... It's the most beautiful sight we've ever seen."

The Grahams watched the object until the sky became dark at which point it became impossible to see. The next day it was gone. Says Marcia Wood of the *Sangre de Christo Chronicle*,

ALAS, IT REMAINS A BEAUTIFUL SILVERY MYSTERY.[175]

RING-SHAPED OBJECT OVER DEMING

On October 26, 2000 at around 8:10 p.m., Todd Hall was driving west through the mountains on Interstate Highway I-10 when he noticed an object hovering overhead. As he drove down the mountain, he approached the town of Deming and saw that the object was hovering in place at an altitude of about 1,000 to 2,000 feet. Realizing it was unusual, Hall kept his eye on the object, and was amazed when it began to change shape from a short, cylindrical object to a wedge shape. The object remained in place for at least thirty minutes. Says Hall,

AT ONE POINT, I EVEN PULLED TO THE SIDE OF THE ROAD TO PAY MORE ATTENTION TO THE THING.

Hall described the object as "dark in color with a slight metallic look." After about thirty minutes, the mysterious visitor changed to a flat shape, moved straight up for three seconds, and disappeared.[176]

DARTING LIGHT OVER ALAMOGORDO

As investigated by researcher Wayne Mattson, at around sunset on April 20, 2002, an anonymous Alamogordo resident was sitting on the porch of her home north of Indian Wells when she observed a light hovering over the Sacramento Mountains to the east. She watched the light for several minutes as it rose and fell in the sky, descending below the horizon in front of the mountains. The object then began to dart rapidly back and forth sometimes above the mountains, sometimes behind. The witness estimates the light moved about three-quarters of a mile in a matter of seconds. After several minutes of these incredible maneuvers, the object suddenly rose upwards and "blinked" out of sight.[177]

EXTRATERRESTRIAL CULTURE DAY

The politics of UFOs in New Mexico took a new twist on March 10, 2003, when Republican State Representative Daniel R. Foley of Roswell proposed some new legislation to help take advantage of New Mexico's reputation as a UFO hotspot. He put forth a bill that would make the second Tuesday of each February dedicated as "Extraterrestrial Culture Day." The proposal won approval in the house and reads as follows:

WHEREAS, NEW MEXICO HAS A UNIQUE AND DYNAMIC MOSAIC OF CULTURAL ANOMALIES; AND

WHEREAS, EXTRATERRESTRIALS HAVE CONTRIBUTED TO THE WORLDWIDE RECOGNITION OF NEW MEXICO THROUGH THEIR MANY AND ONGOING VISITATIONS, SIGHTINGS, UNEXPLAINED MYSTERIES, ATTRIBUTED TECHNOLOGICAL ADVANCES, EXPERIMENTATIONS, EXPEDITIONS, EXPLORATIONS, INTRIGUES, PROVISION OF STORY LINES FOR HOLLYWOOD EPICS AND ACCOMPLISHMENTS OF ALIEN BEINGS THROUGHOUT THE UNIVERSE;

NOW, THEREFORE, BE IT RESOLVED BY THE HOUSE OF REPRESENTATIVES OF THE HOUSE OF NEW MEXICO THAT THE SECOND TUESDAY OF FEBRUARY BE DESIGNATED "EXTRATERRESTRIAL CULTURE DAY" IN NEW MEXICO TO CELEBRATE AND HONOR ALL PAST, PRESENT AND FUTURE EXTRATERRESTRIAL VISITORS IN WAYS TO ENHANCE RELATIONSHIPS AMONG ALL CITIZENS OF THE COSMOS KNOWN AND UNKNOWN; AND

BE IT FUTHER RESOLVED THAT A COPY OF THIS MEMORIAL BE TRANSMITTED INTO SPACE WITH THE INTENT THAT IT BE RECEIVED AS A TOKEN OF PEACE AND FRIENDSHIP.[178]

UFO DISABLES CAMERA

There are easily hundreds of cases in the records of various UFO organizations in which people claim that their cameras strangely malfunctioned when they attempted to photograph a UFO. This following case is a typical example.

On April 5, 2003, just past midnight, the witness was standing on the balcony of his second-floor apartment smoking a cigarette when he observed "an extremely large craft" shaped like a giant wing, hover silently over a nearby shopping center. It was hard to see in the darkness, and was only visible because its metallic surface was reflecting the city lights.

The witness had a video camera with fresh batteries. He grabbed it and attempted to film the object, but as he says,

THE VIDEO CAMERA WOULD NOT TURN ON.

Says the witness,

I TRIED TO CALL A NEIGHBOR AT THE TIME, AND LOST ALL CELL PHONE SIGNAL.

After about fifteen minutes, the object moved southward and off into the darkness. Impressed, the witness reported his sighting to NUFORC.[179]

DISK OVER ALCALDE

Just before noon on April 3, 2003, a resident of Taos (a 37-year-old graphic designer) was returning to his home along Highway 68 returning from Santa Fe, and had just passed the town of Alcalde when he saw a "solid white shape" moving swiftly in his direction, paralleling the highway. When the object suddenly zoomed to a stop, he pulled his car over to observe it more closely. Says the witness,

DURING THE 55 MINUTES I OBSERVED IT, IT EXHIBITED THE FOLLOWING BEHAVIORS. FIRST IT BEHAVED LIKE A BEE HOVERING OVER FLOWERS, EXCEPT LESS ERRATIC AND A LITTLE BIT SLOWER. IT WOULD DIP DOWN ENOUGH TO MAKE THE HILLS BEHIND IT A BACKDROP AND THE WHITE ELLIPSOIDAL SHAPE POP OUT PRETTY CLEAR. IT MOVED SMOOTHLY, BUT NOT PERFECTLY SMOOTH. ACCELERATIONS TO THE LEFT, RIGHT, HIGHER AND LOWER, AND TO AND FRO, WERE NOT ALWAYS AT THE SAME RATE. AT ONE POINT IT WENT BELOW THE TREES, ALLOWING THE WITNESS TO ESTIMATE ITS DISTANCE AT ABOUT A QUARTER MILE. HE TRIED TO PHOTOGRAPH IT, BUT BY THE TIME HE GOT HIS CAMERA, THE OBJECT HAD DEPARTED.[180]

RECTANGULAR UFO PHOTOGRAPHED

While in some cases, cameras may malfunction during a UFO sighting, in other cases people photograph UFOs without ever having seen them. In early May 2005, a man and his friends were returning from a noonday climb in the Sandia Mountains near Albuquerque. The witness decided to stop and take a couple of panoramic views of the Sandia Mountains. He and his friends noticed nothing unusual at the time. However, when he returned home, the witness reviewed the photographs and was surprised to see that on one of them there was a weird aberration. Says the witness,

> ...THERE WAS SOME KIND OF BLUE-GREY RECTANGLE CENTERED IN THE UPPER PART OF THE PICTURE. MY FIRST REACTION WAS TO CONSIDER IT AS A SPECKLE... HOWEVER, WHEN MAGNIFYING THE PICTURE, IT SEEMED THAT THE RECTANGLE HAD SOME KIND OF THICKNESS.

The witness was aware that the Sandia Labs are located adjacent to the Sandia Mountains, and speculated if there might be a connection. He theorized that the rectangle might be the result of a government test, a temperature inversion, or perhaps a genuine UFO. Only one of the two photos he took showed the strange object. (See the photo section on page 300.)[181]

A FLUTTERY UFO OVER ALBUQUERQUE

At 12:50 p.m. on June 19, 2005, an anonymous witness in Albuquerque observed a bright white flashing light perform strange maneuvers, rising suddenly, hovering and diving at sharp angles. Says the witness,

I STOPPED AND WATCHED IT; THE FLASHING CONTINUED IN AN IRREGULAR, FLUTTERY FASHION, AND IT CONTINUED ITS SOUTHERLY MOTION AGAINST THE WIND. AFTER ABOUT TWO MINUTES OF OBSERVATION, THE OBJECT WAS DUE SOUTH OF ME. IT SUDDENLY ROSE VERY RAPIDLY TO A POSITION PROBABLY 70 DEGREES ABOVE THE HORIZON AND STOOD MOTIONLESS. IT CONTINUED TO FLASH, AND I COULD SEE A BLACK PHASE ALTERNATING BETWEEN THE BRIGHT ONES.

The witness was not able to discern the shape of the object behind the light, but he did get the impression that it was a solid object and not just a light. He later reported his sighting to NUFORC.[182]

UFOS VIDEOTAPED OVER LORDSBURG

After experiencing a wave of sightings in Lordsburg, Benjie Medina wrote to MUFON, saying that on February 22, 2006:

WE HAVE GREAT DEAL OF UFO ACTIVITY GOING ON DAY AND NIGHT THAT RAMON ORTIZ IS CAPTURING ON VIDEO. WE CAPTURED A CLOUD-LIKE OBJECT THAT WAS LIGHTER THAN THE SKY, WHEN SUDDENLY A STRANGE MANEUVERING LIGHT CAME OUT OF THE CLOUD. THE LIGHT HOVERED IN THE SKY, AND PERIODICALLY IT CHANGED SHAPE, BUT STAYED IN THE AREA FOR OVER FIVE MINUTES. TWO MANEUVERING OBJECTS WERE CAPTURED IN THIS VIDEO.[183]

ALBUQUERQUE DISKS AND TAOS TRIANGLES

Two days following the above case, at 1:12 p.m. on February 24, 2006, a pilot was driving his car along Yale Road in Albuquerque when he saw a "disc-shaped and light-colored, semi-reflective" object. It was at approximately 750 feet elevation and slightly larger than an F-15. It moved slowly and in a sideways motion. Suddenly, it darted away to the north "at an incredible speed" becoming a distant point before disappearing. The witness had a video camera with him and was able to capture nearly a minute of video of the object. The witness later reported his sighting to MUFON.

Four days later, at 8:57 p.m. on February 28, 2006, an anonymous witness observed a "dark triangular craft in the clouds with a red light on each of three corners." The witness was deeply impressed by the incredible fast speed of the craft. As he says,

THERE WAS NO NOISE, AND THE CRAFT WAS HUGE.

He later reported his sighting to NUFORC.[184]

LOW-LEVEL HOVERING LIGHTS

In early May 2006, 77-year-old Corrales Heights resident Charlotte Motter was inside her home late at night when she had a strange impulse to walk outside onto her front patio. Says Motter,

DON'T ASK ME WHY I WALKED OUT. I SAW ABOUT 6-8 WHITE LIGHTS AND IT WAS HOVERING. IT COULDN'T BE A HELICOPTER; A HELICOPTER CAN HOVER BUT IT'S NOT QUIET... I COULD NOT DETECT A SHAPE BECAUSE OF THE DARKNESS.

The lights, says Motter, were only twenty-five feet above the ground, and about an eighth-mile away. She watched them for just a few moments, when suddenly remembering what she'd heard and read about UFOs, she decided to retreat back inside. As she says,

I WISH I COULD HAVE REMAINED OUTSIDE LONGER BUT, KNOWING ABOUT ABDUCTIONS, I CAME INSIDE, FEELING VERY LUCKY HAVING WITNESSED THIS PHENOMENON... I WANT PEOPLE TO KNOW UFOS ARE IN RIO RANCHO. IT'S THE FIRST ONE I'VE SEEN IN RIO RANCHO.[185]

ANOTHER UFO PHOTOGRAPH

On May 13, 2006, a gentleman was driving east on Interstate 10 through New Mexico. He had just passed the town of Gage; he was surprised to see a strange object floating in the sky. It was gray in color, strangely-shaped, and stayed perfectly still in the sky. It made no audible noise. Surprised and bewildered, the witness pulled over and starting taking pictures. For the next forty minutes, he drove forward and parked again, trying to get closer to the object and get a different angle and more photographs. Says the witness,

IT DIDN'T MOVE. IT JUST HUNG THERE IN THE SKY, NO SOUND, NO MOVEMENT. I WAS AMAZED BECAUSE ALTHOUGH I CONSIDER MYSELF A LITTLE SKEPTICAL ABOUT THESE KINDS OF THINGS, THIS WAS SOMETHING I COULD NOT EXPLAIN AND I WAS LOOKING AT IT WITH MY OWN EYES.

At some point, the witness "got a little nervous feeling." He returned to his car and drove off, "trying to put as much distance between me and that thing as I could."

The witness sent the photos and a description of the sighting to MUFON, ending his report of the case with the request, "I would just like to know what it is." (See photo section page 300.)[186]

LIGHTS OVER RUIDOSO

On August 6, 2006, a resident of North Alto who prefers to remain anonymous says that she woke up at 2:15 a.m., and looking outside her window, observed a strange light "move erratically" across the sky. Going to the window she was shocked to see that it was moving towards a much larger rectangular-shaped object, which "seemed to be made up of web-shaped lights."

As she watched, yet another object approached the larger rectangular-shaped object. All three objects then moved slowly over the Ranches of Sonterra, passed over the Spencer Theater and moved out of sight.

She says that the next day, the area was swarming with fighter jets flying at low speed over Ruidoso.

Meanwhile, the *Ruidoso News* was receiving calls from residents reporting UFOs. One resident called to share his observation of a bright light hovering at horizon level near the Alto post office. Other residents of Gavilan Canyon and Hull Street also called to report their sightings of "strange lights."

The Ruidoso News contacted Tom Fuller, the public information officer for Holloman, who said,

NEITHER HOLLOMAN AIR FORCE BASE NOR WHITE SANDS MISSILE RANGE HAD ANYTHING FLYING OVER RUIDOSO AT 0200 ON 6 AUG.

When asked about the possibility of "otherworldly" sightings, Fuller replied,

WE'VE SPOKEN ON THIS AND HAVE NOTHING FURTHER TO SAY.[187]

METEOR OR UFO?

The need for careful investigation is illustrated by the following case. On October 1, 2006, the National UFO Reporting Center (NUFORC) received more than thirty calls from people across the mid-western United States reporting a bright orange fireball. Reports came from Arizona, Colorado, Wyoming, and New Mexico. Residents of Santa Fe, Silver City, Raton, Los Alamos, and Las Cruces were among the callers.

A Raton resident observed what appeared to be a large gold star split into three objects and then seven, which moved in straight lines and disappeared.

Menka Jain was driving through Los Alamos when she saw a fiery orange projectile which exploded into pieces.

Most reports are consistent with meteors or possibly space debris. Santa Fe resident Peggy Crumbacher, however, isn't so sure. She saw the object make a turn. Says Crumbacher,

IT WENT FROM WHITE TO BLUE, AND THEN I COULD SEE IT TURNED TOWARD THE NORTH, AND THEN IT ABSOLUTELY DISAPPEARED. THIS WAS NOT A METEOR. METEORS WOULD BE BRIGHT LIGHTS.

The lights were seen from 9:26 p.m. until about 11:20. FAA officials were contacted and replied that it was likely a meteor.[188]

UFO CAPTURED ON CELL-PHONE

The year of 2006 produced several interesting cases involving photographic evidence. Another addition to the collection includes image captured by Elizabeth Wall on her cell phone. On December 17, 2006, Wall, her husband, and a friend were driving along Interstate 40 when she noticed an interesting loop in one of the clouds. Says Wall,

AT THE TIME I DIDN'T NOTICE ANYTHING BUT THIS UNUSUAL CLOUD. IT WAS LIKE A RAINBOW-ARCH SHAPE, PRETTY COOL. SO I TOOK A PIC.

Actually, she took two pictures. She later uploaded them to her computer and was amazed to see that one of them showed a dark object resting at the bottom of the unusual loop in the clouds. She enlarged and enhanced the photo. Says Wall,

CLEARLY, IT'S AN OBJECT... IT IS SOMETHING, AND KIND OF STRANGELY OUT OF PLACE.... THIS WAS JUST A PICTURE OF A COOL CLOUD, AND I GOT A COOL SURPRISE WITH IT. IT MIGHT BE NOTHING, BUT IT SURE DOES LOOK WILD.

Wall showed the photo to several friends, and about one week after the incident, submitted her case and the photograph to MUFON. Interestingly, there are many other cases in which UFOs have punched holes in clouds or have been associated with strange clouds. (See photo section page 301.

HORSESHOE-SHAPED OBJECT OVER ROSWELL

On October 21, 2007 at around 5:20 a.m., sisters Patricia and Carole O'Rourke were out in their backyard in midtown Roswell watching a meteor shower when they saw a horseshoe-shaped object appear in the western sky moving towards the southeast. The object appeared to have a "smoky" texture, and brightened and dimmed in and out of visibility. The object was less than 500 feet away and was moving very slowly at treetop level. While they heard no sound coming from it, they could hear a succession of barking dogs that seemed to follow its path.

New Mexico MUFON field investigator Donald Burleson investigated the case. He writes,

> WE MAY NEVER KNOW EXACTLY WHAT THIS OBJECT WAS, BUT UNQUESTIONABLY THE WITNESSES ARE PERCEPTIVE, INTELLIGENT, DETAIL-CONSCIOUS, AND HIGHLY CREDIBLE OBSERVERS WHO HAVE PROVIDED THE SORT OF INFORMATION ANY UFO INVESTIGATOR SHOULD FIND OPTIMAL.[190]

TRUCKER ENCOUNTER

On March 18, 2008, a trucker was driving east on Interstate 40 outside of Tucumcari when he saw a light moving along the ridge to his left. Without warning, it veered and moved at super-high speeds, crossing the highway in front of his semi. All the electronics in his truck died as he observed a "huge dome of light about 300 feet across and 100 feet high" move over the road. Says the trucker,

> EVEN THOUGH THE OBJECT WAS BRIGHT, NO DETAILS WERE VISIBLE. IT DIDN'T LIGHT UP THE SURROUNDING DESERT LIKE IT SHOULD HAVE.

Within seconds, the object was gone. The witness never heard any noise from the object. Immediately after it disappeared, his electronics came back on and he continued on his way, puzzled enough to later report his sighting to MUFON[191]

A BOUNCING UFO

Not all UFOs are large saucer-shaped craft carrying ETs. Some appear to be much smaller probe-like devices, such as the following case, which occurred at 4 a.m. on March 20, 2008, to a young couple who was driving through Carlsbad. Says one of the witnesses,

> ME AND MY GIRLFRIEND WERE JUST DRIVING DOWN THE STREET WHEN THIS CIRCULAR OBJECT SHOT DOWN AND BOUNCED OFF THE GROUND MAYBE ONE FOOT IN FRONT OF THE CAR. IT APPEARED TO BE WHITE BUT CONSIDERING THE RATE OF SPEED, IT COULD HAVE BEEN SILVER... IT WAS MOVING FAST ENOUGH TO JUST CATCH A GLIMPSE OF IT AS IT CAME INTO VIEW OF THE FRONT WINDSHIELD. IT LOOKED LIKE IT CAME STRAIGHT DOWN AND SHOT BACK UP AT A SLIGHT ANGLE. IT WAS MOVING AT AN EXTREMELY HIGH RATE OF SPEED. THIS WAS THE MOST UNEXPLAINABLE THING THAT I HAVE EVER SEEN IN MY LIFE — AN OBJECT MAYBE FOUR-FEET IN DIAMETER, BOUNCING OFF THE STREET IN FRONT OF THE CAR AT AN UNEXPLAINABLE RATE OF SPEED, WITH NO NOISE.[192]

GALLUP UFOS

Two days later, on the evening of March 22, 2008, two brothers were hiking near their home in Gallup when they saw a "large round white object" hovering directly above them. They watched it for about a minute when the object suddenly doubled in size and turned bright red. It then began to rotate and change into different shapes. Says the witness,

> IT WOULD BECOME OVAL, ROUND, SQUARE, AND SOMETIMES APPEAR TO HAVE PROTRUSIONS THAT SEEMED TO COME OUT OF THE BODY OF THE OBJECT ITSELF.

At this point, several military jets appeared and began to vector in on the object which promptly disappeared. After a few moments, the object re-appeared briefly, then disappeared again. The next day, on March 23, 2008, the brothers and their wives and children witnessed a much more dramatic sighting.

They were driving along Highway 66 when they saw a bright white object. Moments later two additional objects appeared, followed by another. Suddenly there were six more. Says the witness,

THEY ZIPPED DOWN SO FAST THAT A FEW LOOKED ALMOST LIKE A METEOR COMING DOWN. THEY WERE ALL MOVING INDEPENDENT OF EACH OTHER, AND IT HAD GOTTEN TO A POINT WHERE I COULD COUNT UP TO TWELVE OF THEM.

Suddenly, military jets again appeared on the scene and attempted to chase the objects. Says the witness,

A FEW OF THE OBJECTS ACTUALLY APPEARED TO BE PLAYING WITH THE JETS. THEY FLEW IN VERY CLOSE PROXIMITY TO THE PLANES AND EVEN FLEW ALONGSIDE THEM FOR A MOMENT OR TWO. THE FORMATION ALMOST SEEMED LIKE A FLOCK OF GEESE OR A SCHOOL OF FISH IN THE OCEAN THE WAY THEY MOVED WITH EACH OTHER.

The objects darted around, finally disappearing into an approaching cloud.

Two months later, on March 31, a lady was driving her son and a friend near Truth or Consequences to go camping. The son noticed a bright light and pointed it out to her. She instructed him to grab the binoculars and examine it more closely. He shrieked that it was not a star, and that it appeared to be a cone-shaped object. Says the witness,

I IMMEDIATELY PULLED OVER AND BEGAN TAKING PICTURES WITH MY NIKON 200 MM.

Shortly later, the object began to move. Then it suddenly turned red and vanished. (See photo section page 302.[193]

MISS WITH A UFO!

Late in the evening of June 20, 2008, a gentleman was flying from Ontario, California to Atlanta, Georgia, and to his best guess, was over New Mexico at 34,000 feet when he saw a UFO pass below his plane, only a few hundred feet away. Says the witness,

I WAS SITTING ON A WINDOW SEAT ON THE RIGHT SIDE OF THE AIRPLANE IN THE VERY LAST ROW. THE MOVIE HAD JUST ENDED AND I RAISED MY WINDOW SHUTTER TO LOOK OUT. I WAS AMAZED TO SEE A SHINY ALUMINUM-APPEARING CYLINDER, APPROXIMATELY 60 FEET LONG AND TEN TO FIFTEEN FEET WIDE, PASS UNDER THE

PLANE FROM LEFT TO RIGHT AT A 45 DEGREE ANGLE TO THE AIRPLANE. IT APPEARED TO FLY UNDER THE PLANE AT APPROXIMATELY TWO TO THREE HUNDRED FEET. THE SKIN OF THE OBJECT HAD A SHINY, BRUSHED ALUMINUM APPEARANCE, ALMOST LIKE A NEW UN-PAINTED AIRPLANE, EXCEPT IT HAD NO WINGS OR PORTHOLES OF ANY KIND. IT ALSO HAD A ROUNDED NOSE AND BACK, AND THE BACK OF THE CRAFT WAS BLACK IN COLOR.

As he watched, the object darted to the left and then shot off to the north. The witness wrote to NUFORC and described his sighting in detail, adding,

I WAS SO STUNNED THAT I KEPT THINKING OVER AND OVER, "THEY ARE REAL!"[194]

AN ACCIDENTAL UFO PHOTOGRAPH

On October 7, 2008, a photographer was on a photo shoot in Moreno Valley. Using his Fuji S100 12 megapixels digital camera, he was near the end of shooting about 300 photographs of local autumn scenery when he decided to stop at a friend's house and get some panoramic views of the Moreno Valley. Writes the witness,

I NOTICED A FLOWER POT THAT LOOKED PRETTY, SO I SHOT FOUR PICTURES IN A ROW OF THEM, FROM ABOUT 20 FEET AWAY, USING A TELEPHOTO LENS. THE FIRST SHOT WAS A "SINGLE," THE NEXT THREE WERE A "BURST" TOWARDS THE NORTHWEST.

To the photographer's surprise, one of the photos contained a glowing orange object floating in the sky. Says the witness,

I MADE A COPY OF THE PHOTO AT FULL SIZE AND ENLARGED IT IN PHOTOSHOP. THE OBJECT APPEARED TO BE SOLID AND NOT THE RESULT OF CAMERA MALFUNCTIONS. I CHECKED AND RECHECKED THE OTHER THREE PHOTOS OF THE SAME SCENE AND FOUND NO TRACE OF THE OBJECT IN ANY OF THEM. THERE WAS ABOUT FIVE SECONDS BETWEEN SHOTS. (SEE PHOTO SECTION PAGE 303.)[195]

A PESKY UFO

One of the strange behaviors of UFOs is that they show up in the same location over a period of hours or days. The following case is a good example. On the evening of October 10, 2008, a gentleman was watching television with his family in their home in Rio Rancho when they looked out their window and saw a UFO right over their yard. Says the witness,

> SLOWLY MOVING OVER OUR YARD WAS A TORPEDO-SHAPED FIGURE WITH GLOWING LIGHTS: RED, YELLOW, AND GREEN. IT WAS TOO CLOSE TO THE GROUND TO BE A PLANE. THERE WAS NO NOISE AT ALL.

Two days later, around 10 a.m., the witness was walking with his cousin and looking up, saw another UFO.

> THERE WAS A METALLIC SAUCER MOVING SLOWLY THROUGH THE AIR. I QUICKLY TOLD MY COUSIN TO LOOK UP, AND SURE AS HECK, I WASN'T IMAGINING IT; HE SAW IT TOO.

The witness whipped out his cell-phone to take a picture. Right when he pressed the "TAKE" button, the object darted into a cloud bank. The witnesses returned home.

However, a few hours later the UFO was back. The witness was in his living room when he looked out and saw the same UFO he had just seen with his cousin. It floated slowly across the sky and moved off into the distance.[196]

A VERY BRIGHT OBJECT

On the evening of January 31, 2009, a family of four was driving along Highway 56 near Gladstone when the wife (who was driving) pulled over and said, "Look at this!"

Forty yards away and about fifty feet above the ground was a large object that was almost too bright to look at. Below it was a row of blue lights stretching an estimated thirty yards wide.

Several times the husband repeated "What is this?" Nobody in the car responded. The object made no sound and was sending bright beams of light up into the sky.

The husband said, "I'm going to grab my camera."

Instantly, as if in response, the object darted down the road behind them. The wife began to turn around the car, but their eighteen-year-old daughter cried out, "No, don't turn around! Do not turn around! Do not go after that thing!"

Says the husband, "I had never seen my daughter so scared."[197]

A VERY LARGE STEALTH-LIKE CRAFT

As reported to MUFON, an anonymous resident stepped out of his home in New Mexico to check the weather at 12:45 a.m., May 3, 2009, when he saw "...a very large stealth-like craft that made no sound." Says the witness,

THE OBJECT HAD DIM LIGHTS... WHEN IT WENT BY IT COVERED THE STARS. THE OBJECT MOVED FROM SOUTH TO NORTHWEST AT SMOOTH SPEED PASSING BY FOR ABOUT A MINUTE AND A HALF.

The witness mailed a sketch to investigators, and wrote,

I WAS SO EXCITED BY WHAT I SAW THAT I DIDN'T SLEEP AT ALL AFTER THE SIGHTING.

The sketch drawn by the witness portrays a manta ray-shaped object, with lights along the perimeter of the leading edges.[198]

LIGHTS OVER LAS CRUCES

On the western side of the mountains from the White Sands Missile Range lies a NASA facility in Las Cruces. At 7:45 p.m. on May 17, 2009, a resident of Las Cruces received a call from his friend, telling him to check out the "UFO" that was hovering in eastern sky. The witness went outside and was shocked to see three balloon-like white spheres hovering in a triangle formation. The objects became very bright as the sun went down. At this point, the witness received three other calls from various friends, each of who was observing the object from different locations.

Using the many reports, the resident was able to ascertain that the object was less than ten miles away, hovering over the NASA facility. He called out his neighbor and they both observed the object as it began to flash brightly. A small orb of light separated from the object and darted northwest toward Albuquerque. Over the course of about an hour, the object steadily dimmed and disappeared. The entire sighting lasted two hours. The witness reported his sighting to NUFORC a mere ten minutes after it occurred.[199]

OBJECT SPLITS IN TWO

Early in the evening of June 10, 2009, two vacationing friends from Los Angeles were traveling on Highway 230 toward Roswell. It was a dark moonless night and the highway had no cars on it. They decided to pull over and look at the stars. They had no sooner turned off the headlights when they saw a bright orange-red light moving about thirty degrees above the horizon. They instantly pointed it out to each other. At that moment, it disappeared and then reappeared further along its trajectory. Both were shocked by what happened next.

One witness writes,

> SUDDENLY THE OBJECT CLEAN SPLIT INTO TWO OBJECTS, EACH RETAIN ITS ORIGINAL ORANGISH-REDDISH COLOR. BOTH OBJECTS THEN TRAVELED PARALLEL TO THE OTHER, QUICKLY SEPARATING OR WIDENING APART IN A SORT OF AN ARC FASHION. THEN SUDDENLY BOTH OBJECTS DID SOMETHING BIZARRE: EACH DOVE RIGHT INTO EACH OTHER, REJOIN AND GIVING THE APPEARANCE AS IF BOTH LIGHTS HAD "MELTED" OR MORPHED BACK INTO ONE SINGLE OBJECT.

Seconds later, the object disappeared. Neither of the witnesses heard any noise associated with the object. One of the men had served in the Coast Guard and the Marine Corp and was familiar with most aircraft. He was impressed by the fact that the object made no sound and had no fuselage lights.[200]

FLOATING OBJECTS

On February 27, 2010, Alan X. of Albuquerque decided he wanted to take a picture of the Sandia Mountains to the west. He took his laptop and climbed onto the roof of his home. He snapped a picture.

He went back inside and examined the photo. To his amazement, there were "three cone-shaped objects in the distance towards the east that I didn't see when I took the picture... Their height off the ground and their solid appearance is truly baffling to me."

About five minutes after the first photograph, Alan returned to his roof and snapped more pictures. None showed any objects. Impressed by his photo, Alan reported his case to MUFON and submitted his photograph, which was published in the MUFON Journal.[201]

FARMINGTON TRIANGLE

On July 31, 2010, three men were standing and talking outside of a gas station in Farmington when all three observed a triangular-shaped UFO moving towards them at less than 500 feet altitude. The witnesses were "creeped out," and immediately reported the encounter to MUFON.[202]

SOCORRO SPHERES

The year of 2011 produced several new cases. On the evening of January 22, 2011, a professor who teaches an astronomy lab course at a university stepped outside his home in Socorro when he saw five red lights hovering at about seventy degrees of elevation in the southeast. Says the professor,

> "THESE OBJECTS WERE SILENT, SMALL AND VERY BRIGHT. THE CENTER OF THE LIGHT WAS A BRIGHT WHITE-RED AND SEEMED TO GLOW SOLID RED. I'VE NEVER SEEN ANYTHING LIKE IT."

The lights were moving toward the southwest, with four in a square formation and one trailing behind. Moments later, he noticed three additional objects following the others. He watched the entire fleet of glowing spheres cross the sky in about one minute.

Seeing nothing else, he returned inside. Baffled by his sighting, he returned outside about five minutes later and saw two more spheres. Intrigued, he climbed onto his roof to broaden his view and saw another glowing red object traveling an estimated five to ten miles away, moving south over the Rio Grande River.

The professor is convinced that he saw something very unusual and shortly following his encounter, reported his sighting to MUFON in the hopes that somebody else may have seen the objects or managed to film them. Says the professor,

"I AM FAMILIAR WITH CELESTIAL OBJECTS AND WHAT CONVENTIONAL AIRCRAFT LOOK LIKE AT NIGHT." (MUFON)

MOTORISTS BUZZED BY A UFO

Another case reported to MUFON occurred to three people who, on August 4, 2011, were traveling from Flagstaff, Arizona, to Silver City, New Mexico, through the Gila National Forest. They were listening to an audio book. Only Chris (pseudonym) in the rear seat on the left was looking out at the sky.

Suddenly he was puzzled to see a "very bright light" off in the distance. Almost immediately it began to get closer, becoming much brighter and larger. It was moving at an incredible speed. Says Chris,

"AT FIRST IT LOOKED TO ME LIKE IT WAS HEADING STRAIGHT FOR THE CAR. IT PASSED RELATIVELY LOW, MUCH LESS THAN THE HEIGHT OF AN AIRPLANE."

Chris knew instantly the object was not a plane. First, it was moving too fast. Second, it was way too low. Third was its shape, as Chris says,

"IT WAS SAUCER SHAPED. THE ENTIRE BOTTOM WAS LIT, BUT THE TOP WAS DARK."

Chris gasped loudly. By the time she could shout out, "UFO!" the object was gone. Says Chris,

"THE SIGHT OF IT TOOK MY BREATH AWAY... IT WAS FLYING SO FAST, YOU WOULD ONLY SEE IT IF YOU WERE LOOKING RIGHT AT IT AT THE TIME."

Chris told the other passengers and they scoured the skies for the rest of the trip, wondering if the UFO might return. Says Chris,

"I WAS PRAYING IN THE BACKSEAT THAT IT WOULD NOT. I WAS AFRAID. WE HAD NO CELL [PHONE] SERVICE AND WE WERE IN THE MIDDLE OF NOWHERE." (MUFON)

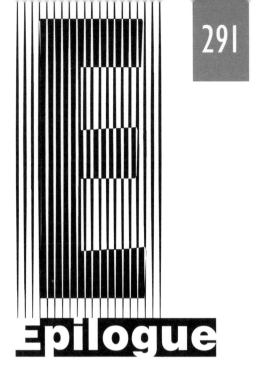

Epilogue

New Mexico's UFO history is among the most complicated of all states. The intensity of activity appears to be at least partly related to the existence of the many installations involved with the study and/or use of nuclear power. Certainly the number of reported UFO crashes is several magnitudes larger than any other state. The reason for this remains a mystery. The fact that extensive atomic research has been conducted in the area may hold the answer, and this theory has been raised by several researchers. It is also interesting to note that one-third of the state remains owned by the federal government.

Whatever the case, New Mexico has produced some of the most prominent UFO cases in history. The Roswell UFO crash, the landing of a UFO in Socorro, and the Farmington UFO display are only three of dozens of similar super high-profile cases that have shaped the way we perceive and feel about the UFO phenomenon.

Many other high profile cases could be mentioned. For example, the rash of car-stalling/UFO cases of November 1957 centered in New Mexico and Texas changed the way many people viewed UFOs, forcing the conclusion that the electromagnetic effects sometimes associated with UFOs were not always accidental, but – at least in some cases – intentional.

Many of the New Mexico cases show how badly the Air Force has bungled the UFO situation. Over and over again, military officials refuse to investigate UFO reports and conversely issue ludicrous and insulting conclusions in what is an obvious attempt to debunk the phenomenon. Roswell is, of course, the ultimate example, in which the military moved from insulting witnesses to physically threatening them with bodily harm, while at the same time denying the entire incident. The many other cases in which the Air Force postulated ridiculous and sometimes bizarre theories to explain away what now appear to genuine UFO cases illustrates not only that there is a UFO cover-up, but that the cover-up has been a dismal failure.

The cattle mutilations complicate New Mexico's UFO situation further, and again raise the question of the alien agenda, and the level of government knowledge and involvement with the phenomenon. Why are UFOs here? Why are they abducting people and mutilating animals? And what are we to make of the Taos hum? Is this a collective hallucination, evidence of underground activity or what?

While conclusive proof of UFOs is now in the public arena, these types of questions remain unanswered.

What will the future bring for UFOs over New Mexico? Clearly, there will be a continuing stream of sightings, landings, onboard experiences and – judging from the state's past history – probably more crashes, too. There appears to be a slow but steady escalation of activity. The UFOs show no signs of leaving. If trends continue as they have, we are leading towards open and official contact between humans and extraterrestrials, and an end to the official government cover-up of UFOs. The crumbling cover-up might be considered the most volatile area of UFO research, and one that holds great potential for change. Perhaps one day we will view the Roswell UFO craft in a museum for everyone to see.

Stranger things have happened.

Scores Report Seeing Saucers' Flight in Formation Over New Mexico

FARMINGTON, N.M., March 17 (U.P.)—A mass flight of flying saucers over this Northwestern New Mexico oil town of 5000 population was reported today by 50 persons, including businessmen and private pilots.

Detailed accounts of the flight varied, but the witnesses estimated the number of the objects, which appeared in groups commencing at 10:30 a.m., and lasting for one hour, from one to "hundreds."

The advertising manager of the Farmington Daily Times, Clayton Boddy, said he was with a group of five businessmen who saw a mass flight of the saucers. Boddy said they were all disk-shaped and fluttered through the air without descending to earth.

Among the saucers spotted by scores of persons on Farmington's streets was one low-flying, red-hued, saucer-shaped object which streaked across the sky.

Orville Ricketts, editor of the Times, said a cross check of witnesses revealed that the object cleared the horizon in its tremendous speed in about three seconds.

Ricketts said he did not see the objects, but that Boddy said that in the mass flight of the saucers he and five businessmen with whom he was standing believed they saw more than 100 of the strange objects.

The town's business was brought practically to a standstill while persons scanned the skies.

All of the objects were of a silvery color except for the one red "saucer," and all except the latter appeared to be at an extremely high altitude, Ricketts said.

Ricketts said that among the witnesses were airplane pilots.

On March 17, 1950 the small town of Farmington witnessed perhaps the single largest UFO wave in United States history during which several hundred objects were seen over a period of a few hours. This article appeared in the Los Angeles Times the day following the UFO wave. (Adventures Unlimited)

On May 11, 1967, two Mormon Sunday school teachers and their students were picnicking at Ponderosa Pines outside of Albuquerque when a metallic disk-shaped object approached. Dave Adams (one of the teachers) was able to snap a series of four photographs before the object departed. This photo shows the object moving at treetop level approaching the picnickers. (UFO Photo Archives)

New York Times.

NEW YORK, WEDNESDAY, JULY 9, 1947.

'Disk' Near Bomb Test Site Is Just a Weather Balloon

Warrant Officer Solves a Puzzle That Baffled His Superiors—'Flying Saucer' Tales Pour in From Round the World

By MURRAY SCHUMACH

Celestial crockery had the Army up in the air for several hours yesterday before an Army officer explained that what a colleague thought was "a flying disk" was nothing more than a battered Army weather balloon.

This denouement closed the New Mexico chapter in the "flying saucer" saga that already had contributions from forty-three other states in the Union as well as from Australia, England, South Africa, Mexico and Canada.

However, none of the previous or subsequent reports of strange heavenly bodies created as much confusion as the startling announcement from an Army lieutenant that "a flying disk" had been found on a ranch near Roswell, N. M., near the scene of atomic bomb tests. The officer, Lieut. Warren Haught, public information officer of the Roswell Army Air Field, made no bones about the discovery in his detailed report as carried by The Associated Press.

"The many rumors regarding the flying disk became a reality," his statement began. He told which Intelligence Office of what Bomb Group of the Eighth Air Force had passed "the flying disk" along "to higher headquarters."

Then phones began to buzz between Washington and New Mexico and the "disk" was well on the way to showing how the circle could be squared. One by one, as the rank of the investigating officer rose, the circle lost arcs and developed sides until it was roughly octagonal.

Within an hour after Lieutenant Haught had given new impetus to the "flying saucer" derby, his boss, Brig. Gen. Roger Ramey, had a somewhat different version of "the flying disk."

He said that while it was true it had been found on a ranch, no one had seen it in the air; it was "of flimsy construction," apparently

Continued on Page 10, Column 4

STIFF LEWIS TERMS ARE SIGNED BY 75% OF SOFT COAL MEN

UMW Get $13.05 for 8-Hour Day and Clauses to Free Union of Major Labor Act Rules

SOUTH'S PITS STAY IDLE

Its Operators See Union Head, to Decide Today—Mine Cost Rise Set at Half Billion

By LOUIS STARK
Special to The New York Times.

WASHINGTON, July 8—John L. Lewis signed up nearly 75 per cent of the bituminous coal industry today to unprecedented contract terms which apparently write the United Mine Workers of America out of major sections of the Taft-Hartley labor act.

Several hours after operators representing the "captive" mines and Northern, Midwestern and Western properties trooped wearily and disheartened from Mr. Lewis' office, spokesmen for the

This article appeared in the *New York Times* days after the Roswell UFO Crash and told the world that the explanation was a weather balloon. (Adventures Unlimited)

'Disk' Found on New Mexico Ranch Is Just an Army Weather Balloon

Continued From Page 1

made "of some sort of tin foil." Subsequently, it was reported being flown to a research laboratory at Wright Field, Ohio.

In Washington, Lieut. Gen. Hoyt Vandenberg, Deputy Chief of the Army Air Forces, hurried to his headquarters' press section. Atomic experts in the capital were certain that whatever had been found was not any of their doing, but no one seemed to know just how to dispose of the object.

Finally, a lowly warrant officer, Irving Newton, a forecaster at the Fort Worth, Tex., weather station, solved the mystery. He said it was just a part of a weather balloon, such as is used by eighty weather stations in the country to determine velocity and direction of winds at high altitudes.

Several hours before the New Mexico mystery had been solved, a Canadian meteorologist suggested the same answer in connection with rumors of "flying saucers" in Circleville, Ohio. This was soon after a couple in the Ohio town had jubilantly proclaimed their "capture" of a mysterious disk.

However, the midwest was spurred in its hunt by offers of $3,000 rewards for "proof" that America was not succumbing to an epidemic of hallucinations. One of the first to put in a claim for the prize was an Iowa salesman, who produced a steel disk, nearly seven inches in diameter. He said he found it in his yard in the morning after hearing it "crash through the trees." According to The United Press, reporters thought the disk was playing truant from an ash tray.

Then there was the Nebraska farmer who added a bucolic touch to the story. He said the heavenly bodies were "flaming straw hats," that careened through the night, sometimes pausing for a rest.

Michigan's contributor for the day was a toolmaker from Pontiac. According to The United Press, he turned over to newspapers a picture showing two circular objects against a black background. Examination showed holes in the disks.

Also in the act was Wisconsin, where it was reported that on Monday 250 pilots of that state's Civil Air Patrol would take off in search of "flying saucers."

Proof that "flying saucers" were not indigenous to the United States and Canada began coming in late in the afternoon. Two residents of Johannesburg, South Africa, said, according to Reuters, that they not only saw the objects, but that these "traveled at tremendous speed in V-formation and disappeared in a cloud of smoke."

In England, a clergyman's wife, who said she had kept her discovery secret for fear of derision, finally came forth yesterday with a story about seeing "a dark ring, with clear-cut edges," that sped across the sky on Monday.

The Australian variations of "the flying saucer," though reported by six persons in Sydney, were quite ordinary. Observers said they were a bit brighter than the moon, seemed to prefer an altitude of about 10,000 feet and moved along rather briskly.

It may have been the weather, but the only allusion to "flying saucers" in New York City were a few skeptical remarks by Admiral William H. P. Blandy, commander in chief of the Atlantic Fleet. Said the admiral, in response to questions:

"I remain to be convinced there is any such thing. I am convinced that they are nothing the Army and Navy is concerned with. I am curious, like everybody else, to see what's behind it."

In 1993, UFO researcher Chris Miller snapped this photograph of a UFO swooping down above the famous natural formation known as Shiprock. (MUFON CMS)

This image was one of several pictures taken in 1972 in Las Lunas, New Mexico when Villa observed and photographed a small UFO that dropped out of the sky and circled around his pick-up truck. He noticed a small round raised spot, on the object just above the rim. (UFO Photo Archives)

UFO Contact From
COMA BERENESIS
The Paul Villa Story

Peralta, New Mexico, 16 June 1963, 300' diameter craft from Coma Berenices.

By
Apolinar Villa – Wendelle Stevens

ISBN 0 934269-62-9

Apolinar Villa Jr., one of New Mexico's most famous UFO contactees, is perhaps known for taking hundreds of clear photographs of UFOs over New Mexico. This is the cover of an E-book detailing his case. (UFO Photo Archives)

On June 15, 1997, researcher Mike Hawkins had arrived early for the 50th anniversary festival of the Roswell UFO crash and was looking at real-estate in the area when he observed a helicopter chasing a metallic disk-shaped UFO. He snapped five photographs until the helicopter and disc departed. The above photo shows both the disk and the helicopter. (UFO Photo Archives)

At 1 p.m. on October 16, 1957, Miss Ella Louise Fortune observed a glowing object moving over Holloman Air Force Base. She snapped this now famous photograph. (Adventures Unlimited)

This photograph was taken by an anonymous man who was hiking with friends in the Sandia mountains near Albuquerque. They never saw a UFO when taking the photo. However, the photograph appears to show a rectangular shaped craft. (MUFON CMS)

Blimp or UFO? This photo was taken near the town of Gage. The witness took these two photos of the object, which he says remained perfectly still in the sky. The witness is convinced the object is "unexplained." (MUFON CMS)

On October 10, 2008, Alan X., a resident of Albuquerque took a digital picture of the Sandia Mountains. Examining the photo, he was shocked to see three silver objects hanging in the sky. He didn't notice anything unusual at the time the photo was taken. Subsequent attempts to duplicate the photo failed. (MUFON CMS)

Photo defect or UFO? On December 17, 2006, Elizabeth Wall observed a strange cloud formation while driving along Interstate 50. She whipped out her cell phone camera and snapped a photo. Later, upon examination, she noticed this strange object. The second image has been enhanced. (MUFON CMS)

On March 31, 2008, three witnesses (a mother and son and friend) observed this object near Truth or Consequences. They observed the object through binoculars before snapping these two photographs.(MUFON CMS)

On October 7, 2008, a nature photographer was taking pictures of the Moreno Valley. He shot four pictures of a flower pot. In one of the photos, a strange object appeared. (MUFON CMS)

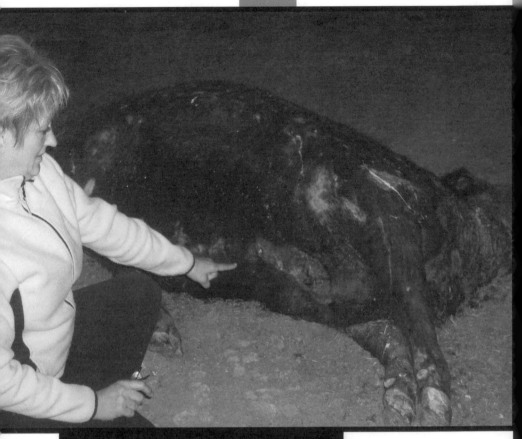

The phenomenon known as "Cattle Mutilations" seems to be centered in New Mexico. Thousands of cattle in the state have been targeted, at the cost of millions of dollars. In this 2006 case, two sisters came upon what appears to be a classic case outside of Socorro. (MUFON CMS)

Is this a "fairy ring" or an actual UFO landing spot? Taken in 2010 in the town of Angel Fire; the origins of this circle remain a mystery. (MUFON CMS)

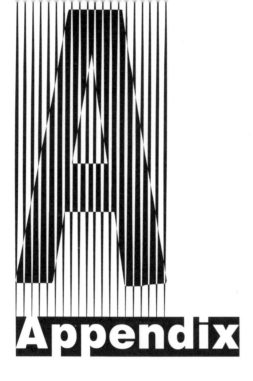

Appendix

Roswell UFO Museum
114 North Main Street, Roswell, NM

(HOURS: 9 A.M. TO 5 P.M.) THE MUSEUM WAS OPENED IN 1992 AND RECEIVES UPWARDS OF 700 VISITORS DAILY. IN JUNE 2001, THE MUSEUM RECEIVED ITS ONE MILLIONTH VISITOR. THE MUSEUM CONTAINS MORE THAN 3,300 BOOKS, 56,000 DOCUMENTS AND HUNDREDS OF VIDEOS.

Ah, the Blue Book Cases

Take a look at the following chart to get a quick view of the Blue Book's strange cases.

CHRONOLOGY OF UNEXPLAINED USAF BLUE BOOK CASES IN NEW MEXICO (1947-1969)

Case Number	Date	Location
Case #139	April 5, 1948	Holloman AFB
Case #358	April 24, 1949	Arrey
Case #642	February 24, 1950	Albuquerque
Case #645	February 25, 1950	Los Alamos
Case #955	August 25, 1951	Albuquerque
Case #1037	January 16, 1952	Artesia
Case #1151	May 24, 1952	Clovis
Case #1233	May 28, 1952	Albuquerque
Case #1256	June 5, 1952	Albuquerque
Case #1260	June 7, 1952	Albuquerque
Case #1263	June 8, 1952	Albuquerque
Case #1295	June 16, 1952	Walker AFB
Case #1538	July 22, 1952	Los Alamos
Case #1637	July 26, 1952	Kirtland AFB
Case #1755	July 30, 1952	Albuquerque
Case #1961	August 24, 1952	Hermanas
Case #1979	August 25, 1952	Holloman AFB
Case #2150	October 7, 1952	Alamogordo
Case #2171	October 17, 1952	Taos
Case #2173	October 17, 1952	Tierra Amarilla
Case #2219	November 12, 1952	Los Alamos
Case #2248	November 27, 1952	Albuquerque
Case #2524	March 27, 1953	Mount Taylor
Case #3382	January 1, 1955	Chochise
Case #3414	February 1, 1955	Chochise
Case #5227	November 6, 1957	Radium Springs
Case #8766	April 24, 1964	Socorro
Case #9971	September 25, 1965	Rodio

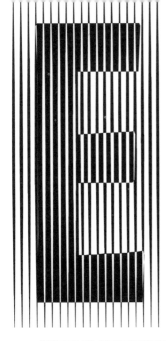

Endnotes

1. Greer MD, Steven, 1999, 26
2. Kerth, 9
3. Clark & Coleman, 131-132; Hall, 6; Vallee, 1993, 180
4. Dolan, p396; Hall, 1964, 19; MUFON CMS; NUFORC
5. NUFORC
6. Ibid
7. Berlitz & Moore, 18-21, 29; Blum & Blum, 39-40; Bourdais, 20; Burt, 44; Dolan, 19; Filer, Aug 2005, 15-16; Good, 2007, 56-57, 61, 65; Hall, 39-41, 64; Hall, 1964, 149; Last, 1; Lorenzen, 1962, 20-21; MUFON CMS
8. NUFORC
9. Dolan, 58; Gribble, Apr 1988, 19; Hall, 102
10. Bourdais, 20
11. Vallee, 1965, 59
12. Keyhoe, 1973, 5
13. Baker, 240; Dolan, 63-64, 67, 78, 162; Flammonde, 431; Gribble, 14; Hall, 114-115; Keyhoe, 1973, 169; Steiger, 1976, 278-279; Stringfield, 1957, 39-40, 58; Stringfield, 1977, 50; Wilkins, 1954, 265
14. Steiger, 1976, 280-281
15. Baker, 240; Dolan, 68-69, 76-77, 79, 398; Fawcett & Greenwood, 114-115; Good, 2007, 108; Hall, 115, 121-122; Hall, 1964, 2-3; Hall, 1988, 238-239; Hynek, 1972, 72-73, Hynek, 1977, 104-105; Johnson & Thomas, 46-47; Scully, 196; Wilkins, 1954, 110-112
16. Dolan, 146; Edwards, 1966, 45-46; Flammonde, 170-171; Hall, 128; Stringfield, 1977, 50-51
17. Johnson & Thomas, 54-55
18. Gribble, Mar 1990, 1; Hall, 130, Johnson & Thomas, 54, 240, 256; Mayeux, 2; McCool, 5; Scully, 212-213

19. Dolan, 82, 399; Good, 2007, 108; Hall, 115, 136; Lorenzen, 1962, 28-29; Maccabee, 1995, 5
20. Dolan, 400, Gribble, #280, 17; Hall, 1964, 56
21. Gribble #280, 17, Sutherly, 189, Vallee, 1965, 64-65
22. Lorenzen & Lorenzen, 1969, 40-41; Wilkins, 1954, 265-266
23. Dolan, 400; Hall 1964, 3, 131; Hall, 1999, 347; Hynek, 1972, 69-70; Vallee, 1966, 1-3
24. Kerth, 7; Vallee, 1965, 65; Wilkins, 1954, 265
25. Delgado, 5; Lorenzen, 1962, 37; Lorenzen & Lorenzen, 1969, 43
26. Hynek, 1972, 69, 265
27. Dolan, 113; Dolan 2009, 107-108, 403; Hynek, 1977, 61-63; Hall, 1964, 69-70; Nevada State Journal, Reno, NV: Aug 3, 1952
28. Dolan, 109; Flammonde, 433; Hall, 1964, 21
29. Good, 2007, 175; Gribble, #235, Nov 1987, 20
30. Barker, 40; Hall, 1964, 21
31. Swords, 20
32. Davenport, 85; Dolan, 407; Hall, 1999, 22, 150; Hall, 1964, 146
33. Cerny, 8; Gribble #256, Aug 1989; Keyhoe, 1973, 89
34. Campbell, Jan 15, 2008 (LA MUFON Meeting)
35. Dolan, 182
36. Last, 1
37. Roybal, 20
38. Haines, 70-71
39. MUFON CMS
40. Lorenzen & Lorenzen, 1969, 79
41. Hall, 1964, 101
42. Davenport, 68, 150; Dolan, 207, 410; Flammonde, 338, 435; Gribble, Nov 1987, #235, 20-21; Hall, 1964, 136, 153, 164; Lorenzen, 1962, 93-102, 152-153; Vallee, 1965, 148; Vallee, 1993, 263
43. Hynek, 1972, 87-90, 267
44. Blum & Blum, 102-103; Good, 207, 222; Gribble, July 1988, #243
45. Lorenzen & Lorenzen, 1969, 93-94
46. Lorenzen & Lorenzen, 1969, 226-227; Vallee, 1965, 174
47. Haines, 289-291; Hall, 1964, 12
48. NUFORC
49. Gribble, July 1987, #231, 17
50. Haines, 4; Kerth, 7; Vallee, 1993, 297-298
51. Beckley, 1992, 9-10; Steiger & Whritenhour, 1967, 23-24, 36-37
52. Dolan, 277; Lorenzen, 1962, 225-226; Lorenzen, 1967, 150-151
53. Lorenzen, 1962, 226-227; Steiger & Whritenhour, 1967, 15; Vallee, 1993, 299
54. Steiger & Steiger, 144-145
55. Edwards, 1967, 108, 116
56. Edwards, 1967, 56-57; Lorenzen, 1962, 238
57. NUFORC
58. Keyhoe, 1973, 181
59. MUFON CMS; NUFORC
60. Edwards, 1967, 105-106; Keyhoe, 1973, 100; Steiger & Whritenhour, 1967, 71

61. MUFON CMS; NUFORC
62. Lorenzen & Lorenzen, 1969, 274
63. Blum & Blum, 155; Hynek, 1972, 64, 265; Lorenzen & Lorenzen, 1969; 274; NUFORC; UFO Photo Archives
64. Andrus, Jan 1986, #213, 12-13; Gribble, Jun 1988, #242; Keyhoe, 1973, 10-11
65. Flammonde, 441; Kerth, 7
66. NUFORC
67. Good, 2007, 321-322
68. Dolan, 2009, 114-115; Editors Skylook, Feb 1979, #99, 14; Hartz, 349; NUFORC; Stanford, 8
69. Blann, 14; Kerth, 7; NUFORC
70. NUFORC
71. Kerth, 8
72. Walters & Maccabee, 122-123, 146-147
73. Kerth, 8
74. Bass, 92-94
75. Campbell, 139-141
76. Kerth, 8
77. NUFORC
78. Dennett, 1997, 71-77
79. NUFORC
80. Kerth, 9
81. Sauder, 69-70
82. MUFON CMS; NUFORC
83. Kaemper, 7; Kerth 8
84. Johnson, Bill, 9
85. Dennett, 2009, 82-84
86. MUFON CMS
87. NUFORC
88. Editors *Roswell Daily Record*, Sep 23, 1994; Linthicum, 2; Nelson, S, 9
89. Van Eyck, 7
90. Cordova, 4
91. UFO FILES, *Black Box UFOs,* 2006, History Channel
92. NUFORC
93. Bunch, 4-5
94. King, 8
95. Greenwood, *Taos News*, Aug 1, 1996 & Sep 5, 1996, 17
96. Delgado, 5
97. UFO Photo Archives
98. NUFORC
99. Sanner, 9
100. Terrell, 8
101. Friedburg, 18
102. Greenwood, *Taos News*, Jan 6, 2000
103. Brenner, Gallup Independent, Oct 19-20, 1999; Donovan, Gallup Independent, Oct 19-20, 1999; Maniaci, 4
104. Wiggins, 9

105. NUFORC
106. Gribble, July 1992, #291; Randle, 1997, 52-54
107. Vallee, 1993, 204; Wilkins, 1954, 216
108. MUFON; NUFORC
109. Wilkins, 1955, 44-45, 232
110. Vallee, 1993, 206
111. Blum & Blum, 102-103; Good, 2007, 219; Gribble, Sep 1991, #281, 10
112. Dolan, 205; Keyhoe, 1973, 19-21; Vallee, 1993, 262
113. NUFORC
114. Baker, 105
115. Baker, 227-228; Bowen, 130-142; DeGraw, 14-15; Dolan, 273-275; Druffel, 211-219; Edwards, 1966, 186-191; Hall, 268-29; Hynek, 223-229; Hynek, 1972, 165-166; Kimble, 1; Lorenzen & Lorenzen, 1969, 241-242; Moffett, 3; Steiger, 1976, 106-137; Vallee, 1993, 297
116. Dolan, 276; Vallee, 1993, 298
117. Dolan, 276; Lorenzen, 1962, 224-225; Randle, 1997, 44-45; Steiger & Steiger, 117-118; Steiger, 1966, 70-71
118. NUFORC
119. Brethwaite, 4
120. Dolan, 2009, 28-29
121. Kerth, 8
122. Dolan, 2009, 219; Fawcett & Greenwood, 224-225
123. MUFON
124. NUFORC
125. Leupold, 4
126. NUFORC
127. Ibid
128. Girand, 8; MUFON
129. NUFORC
130. Ibid
131. Logan, 1; MUFON
132. Steiger & Steiger, 144-145; Villa Jr. & Stevens, 1-88
133. Fry, 1-92; Reeve, 101-110
134. Clear, 38, 52-54, 191-194
135. MUFON
136. Cumber, 12-13
137. MUFON
138. NUFORC
139. Roney, 88-89
140. Stringfield, 1977, 177
141. Good, 2007, 323-325; Hall, 1988, 282-283
142. Stringfield, 1977, 177
143. Ring PhD, 81-83
144. Dongo, 57-59
145. Hawker, 1-223; Nott, 4
146. Baker, 47-48; Dolan, 2009, 212-213
147. NUFORC

148. Ibid
149. Boylan & Boylan, pp135-144
150. Dennett, 2001, 97-104
151. NUFORC
152. Editors, *New Mexican,* Santa Fe, NM-Jul 23, 2000
153. NUFORC
154. Burleson PhD, 12-14
155. MUFON
156. Good, 2007, 27-28; Wood, 52-57
157. Good, 2007, 57-58
158. Berlitz & Moore, 49, 94-95, 105-107; Burt, 87; Constable, 8-9; Corso 3-4, 32-33, 44-45; editor, MUFON Journal May 2003, p3; Friedman & Berliner, 1-220; McGivern, 11; McMahon, 10; Mendoza, 8; Randle & Schmitt, 1991, 1-320; Randle & Schmitt 1994, 1-220; Spencer, 1-150; Stein, 6; Stringfield, Status Report V, 1989, 12-14
159. Birnes, 29-30, 278-279; Friedman & Berliner, 86
160. Baker, 28; Berlitz & Moore, 118-119; Burt, 87; Good, 2007, 110; Mayeux, 2; Stringfield, 1977, 107; Stringfield, 1978, Status Report I, 2; Stringfield, 1991, 41-42
161. Wood, 99-102
162. Stringfield, 1978, 7-8
163. Hall, 1988, 78; Stringfield, 1982, Status Report III, p5-6; Wood, 110
164. Stringfield, 1982, Status Report III, p6-7; Wood, 118
165. Wood, 123
166. MUFON
167. Burt, p87, 260; Randle, 1995, 200; Stringfield, 1978, #1, pp15-16
168. Wood, 132-133
169. Burt, 1995, 205; Goode, 2007, 321-322; Randle, 1995, 205
170. Staff, p7, UFONs #226
171. Baker, 31, 34-35; Bird & Terrell, 11; Good, 2007, 110
172. Blann, 14-15; Chacon, 20; Dolan, 377-378; Dolan, 2009, 119, 201-203; Donovan, 18; Fawcett & Greenwood, 100-104, 110-111; Foster, 17; , Giuliani, 19; Greenwood, Aug 1, 1996, 17; Greenwood, Sep 5, 1996, Taos News, p17; Greenwood, Nov 26, 1997, Taos News, p18; Greenwood, Taos News, Nov 12, 1998, p18; Green, Taos News, May 7, 1998; Greenwood, *Taos News,* May 13, 1999, Greenwood, Taos News, May 27, 1999; Greenwood, *Taos News,* Jan 6, 2000, 1; Greenwood, *Taos News,* Dec 14, 2000; Taos News, Oct 10, 1996; Van Eyck, Sep 19, 1994; Kerch, 7; Miller-Goins, 20; NUFORC 11-28-03; Rolwing, p20; Romancito, p19; Stiny, p17; Stiny, New Mexican, May 22, 1997; Terrell, pp17-18
173. Dellios, 19; Nelson, 20; Pressley, 19; Sharpe, 19; Sharpe & Auslander, 17; www.taoshum.com
174. NUFORC
175. Wood, 6
176. Filer, Dec 2000, 15
177. Filer, Jun 2002, 12
178. Blum & Blum

179. NUFORC
180. Ibid
181. MUFON
182. Filer, Nov 2005, 15; NUFORC
183. Filer, Jun 2006, 18
184. Filer, May 2007, 16-17; NUFORC
185. Herron, 1
186. MUFON
187. Cheney, 4
188. Sharpe & Auslander, 7
189. MUFON
190. Burleson, May 2008, 15
191. MUFON
192. NUFORC
193. MUFON; NUFORC
194. NUFORC
195. MUFON
196. NUFORC
197. Ibid
198. Filer, May 2009, 17
199. NUFORC
200. Ibid
201. Filer, April 2010 #2010, 17; MUFON
202. MUFON

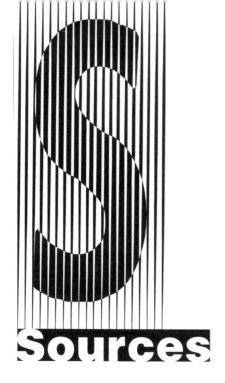

Sources

Books

Baker, Alan. *The Encyclopedia of Alien Encounters: A Complete Guide from Abductions to the Yeti.* New York: Checkmark Books, 2000.

Barker, Gray. *They Knew Too Much About Flying Saucers.* New York: University Books, 1956.

Beckley, Timothy Green. *Strange Encounters: Bizarre and Eerie Contacts with UFO Occupants.* New Brunswick, NJ: Inner Light Publications, 1992.

Berlitz, Charles and William L. Moore. *The Roswell Incident.* New York: Berkley Books, 1980.

Birnes, William J. (Editor) *The UFO Magazine Encyclopedia.* New York: Pocket Books, 2004.

Blum, Ralph and Judy Blum. *Beyond Earth: Man's Contact with UFOs.* New York: Bantam Books, 1974.

Bowen, Charles (Editor.) *The Humanoids: A Survey of Worldwide Reports of Landings of Unconventional Aerial Objects and Their Occupants.* Chicago, IL: Henry Regnery Company, 1969.

Boylan Ph.D., Richard J. and Lee K. Boylan. *Close Extraterrestrial Encounters: Positive Experiences With Mysterious Visitors.* Tigard, OR: Wild Flower Press, 1994.

Bryan, C. D. B. *Close Encounters of the Third Kind: Alien Abduction, UFOs, and the Conference at M. I. T.* New York, NY: Knopf, 1995

Burt, Harold E. *Flying Saucers 101: Everything You Ever Wanted to Know About Unidentified Flying Objects.* Sunland, CA: A UFO Book/ UFO Magazine, 2000.

Campbell, Arthur H. *UFO Crash at San Augustine.* Medford, OR: Art Campbell, 1998.

Clark, Jerome and Loren Coleman. *The Unidentified: Notes Towards Solving the UFO Mystery.* New York: Warner Books, Inc., 1975.

Clear MA, MSW, Constance. *Reaching For Reality: Seven Incredible True Stories of Alien Abduction.* San Antonio, TX: Consciousness Now, Inc., 1999.

Corso, Philip J. (Col., Ret.). *The Day After Roswell.* New York, NY: Pocket Books, 1997.

Davenport, Mark. *Visitors From Time: The Secret of the UFOs.* Tuscaloosa, AL: Greenleaf Publications, 1984.

Dennett, Preston. *Extraterrestrial Visitations: True Accounts of Contact.* St. Paul, MN: Llewellyn Publications, 2001.

----. *One In Forty – The UFO Epidemic: True Accounts of Close Encounters with UFOs.* Commack, NY: Nova Science Publishers, Inc., 1997.

Dolan, Richard M. *UFOs And The National Security State: Chronology of a Cover-up 1941-1973.* Charlottesville, VA: Hampton Roads Publishing Inc., 2000.

----. *UFOs And The National Security State: The Cover-up Exposed, 1973-1991*. Rochester, NY: Keyhole Publishing Company, 2009.

Dongo, Tom. *The Mysteries of Sedona: Book II*. Sedona, AZ: Hummingbird Publishing Company, 1990.

Druffel, Ann. *Firestorm: Dr. James E McDonald's Fight For UFO Science*. Columbus, NC: Wild Flower Press, 2003.

Edwards, Frank. *Flying Saucers – Here and Now!* New York: Bantam Books, 1967.

----. *Flying Saucers – Serious Business*. Secaucus, NJ: Citadel Press, 1966.

Fawcett, Lawrence and Barry Greenwood. *Clear Intent: The Government Coverup of the UFO Experience*. Englewood Cliffs, NJ: Prentice-Hall, Inc., 1984.

Flammonde, Paris. *UFO Exist!* New York: Ballantine Books, 1976.

Friedman, Stanton T. and Don Beliner. *Crash at Corona: the U.S. Military Retrieval and Cover-Up of a UFO*. New York, NY: Paragon House, 1992.

Fry, Dr. Daniel. *The White Sands Incident*. Louisville, KY: Best Books Inc., 1966.

Good, Timothy. *Need to Know: UFOs, the Military and Intelligence*. New York: Pegasus Books, 2007.

----. *Unearthly Disclosure*. London: Arrow Books, 2000.

Greer, MD, Steven M. *Extraterrestrial Contact: The Evidence and Implications*. Crozet, VA: Crossing Point, Inc., 1999.

Haines Ph.D., Richard F. *CE-5: Close Encounters of the Fifth Kind*. Naperville, IL: Sourcebooks, 1999.

Hall, Michael David. *UFOs: A Century of Sightings*. Lakeville, MN: Galde Press, Inc., 1999.

Hall, Richard H. (Editor). *The UFO Evidence: The National Investigations Committee on Aerial Phenomena (NICAP)* New York, Barnes & Noble Books, 1964, 1997.

Hall, Richard. *Uninvited Guests: A Documented History of UFO Sightings, Alien Encounters & Coverups*. Santa Fe, NM: Aurora Press, 1988.

Hartz, Marlena. "UFO Incident Resurfaces." *News Journal*. Clovis, NM – Jun 18, 2006. (See UFONS, Aug 2006, #445, p1)

Hynek, J. Allen. *The Hynek UFO Report*. New York: Dell Publishing, Co., Inc., 1977.

----. *The UFO Experience: A Scientific Inquiry*. New York: Ballantine Books, 1972.

Johnson, Dewayne B. & Kenn Thomas. *Flying Saucers Over Los Angeles: The UFO Craze of the 50's*. Kempton, IL: Adventures Unlimited Press, 1998.

Keyhoe, Major Donald E. (USMC Ret.). *Aliens From Space: The Real Story of Unidentified Flying Objects*. New York: The New American Library, Inc., 1973.

Lorenzen, Coral E. *Flying Saucers: The Startling Evidence of the Invasion From Outer Space*. New York: New American Library, 1962.

Lorenzen, Coral & Jim. *Flying Saucer Occupants*. New York: New American Library, 1967.

Randle, Kevin. *Faces of the Visitors: An Illustrated Reference to Alien Contact*. New York: Fireside, 1997.

Randle, Kevin. *A History of UFO Crashes*. New York: Avon Books, 1995.

Randle, Kevin D. (Capt USAFR) and Donald R. Schmitt. *The Truth About the UFO Crash at Roswell*. New York: M. Evans and Company, Inc., 1994.

----. *UFO Crash at Roswell*. New York: Avon Books, 1991.

Reeve, Bryant and Helen. *Flying Saucer Pilgrimage*. Amherst, WI: Amherst Press, 1957.

Ring Ph.D., Kenneth. *The Omega Project: Near-Death Experiences, UFO Encounters and Mind at Large*. New York: William Morrow and Company, Inc., 1992.

Scully, Frank. *Behind the Flying Saucers*. New York: Henry Holt and Company, 1950.

Spencer, Lawrence R. (Editor.) *Alien Interview: Based on Documents Provided by Matilda O'Donnell MacElroy*. Lawrence Spencer, 2008.

Steiger, Brad and Joan Whritenhour. *The Flying Saucers Are Hostile*. New York: Award Books, 1967.

Steiger, Brad. *Project Blue Book: The Top Secret UFO Findings Revealed*. New York: Ballantine Books, 1976.

Steiger, Brad and Sherry Hansen Steiger. *The Rainbow Conspiracy*. New York: Pinnacle Books, 1994.

Steiger, Brad. *Strangers From the Skies*. London: Tandem Publishing Ltd., 1966.

Stringfield, Leonard. *Inside Saucer Post...3-0 Blue*. Cincinnati, OH: CRIFO, 1957.

----. *Retrievals of the Third Kind: A Case Study of Alleged UFOs and Occupants in Military Custody – Status Report I*. Cincinnati, OH: Leonard H. Stringfield, 1978.

----. *Situation Red: The UFO Siege*. New York: Fawcett Crest Books, 1977

----. *UFO Crash Retrievals: Amassing the Evidence – Status Report III.* Cincinnati, OH: Leonard Stringfield, 1982.

----. *UFO Crash Retrievals: Is the Coverup Lid Lifting – Status Report V.* Cincinnati, OH: Leonard Stringfield, January 1989.

----. *UFO Crash/Retrievals: The Inner Sanctum – Status Report VI.* Cincinnati, OH: Leonard Stringfield, July1991.

Sutherly, Curt. *UFO Mysteries: A Reporter Seeks the Truth.* St. Paul, MN: Llewellyn, 2001.

Vallee, Jacques. *Challenge to Science: The UFO Enigma.* New York: Ballantine Books, 1966.

----. *Passport to Magonia: On UFOs, Folklore, and Parallel Worlds.* Chicago, IL: Contemporary Books, 1969, 1993.

Walters, Edward and Bruce Maccabee Ph.D. *UFOs Are Real: Here's the Proof.* New York: Avon Books, 1997.

Wilkins, Harold T. *Flying Saucers on the Attack.* New York: Ace Books Inc., 1954.

----. *Flying Saucers Uncensored.* New York: Pyramid Books, 1955.

Wood, Ryan S. *Majic: Eyes Only: Earth's Encounters with Extraterrestrial Technology.* Broomfield, CO: Wood Enterprises, 2005.

Magazines, Journals, Newspapers

Andrus, Walt. "Sighting Reports." *MUFON UFO Journal. MUFON UFO Journal.* 103 Oldtowne Rd, Seguin, TX 78155. Jan 1986, #213, pp12-13.

Bass, James. "UFO Forum: Green Orb." *Fate.* Lakeville, MN: Fate Magazine, Inc., June 2004.

Bird, Kay and Steve Terrell. "ETs Living in NM? Not Likely Investigators Say." *New Mexican.* Santa Fe, NM – Sep 11, 1988. (see UFONS, Oct 1988, #231, p11)

Blann, Tommy Roy. "UFO Connection in Dulce and Taos, New Mexico?" *MUFON UFO Journal.* Aug 1979, #138, pp14-15)

Bourdais, Gildas. "The Twining Letter: Part Two." *MUFON UFO Journal.* Feb 1998, #358, p19.

Brenner, Malcolm. "UFO Team Gets an Earful on Radio Show." *Independent.* Gallup, NM – Oct 20, 1999. (See UFONS, Dec 1999, #365, p7)

----. "Was UFO an AF Missile?" *Independent.* Gallup, NM – Oct 19, 1999. (See UFONS, Dec 1999, #365 p6)

Brethwaite, Chris. "Aliens Do Exist." *Journal.* Albuquerque, NM – Mar 15, 2005. (See UFONS, Apr 2005, #429)

Bunch, Jason. "Apparent UFO Reportedly Seen Over Midway." *Daily Record.* Roswell, NM – Feb 5, 1996. (see UFONS, Apr 1996, #321, p4)

----. "'UFO' Was Irrigation System, Some Witnesses & Farmer Say." *Daily Record.* Roswell, NM – Feb 11, 1996. (see UFONS, April 1996, #321, p5)

Burleson, Don. "Another Strange Object Over Roswell?" *MUFON UFO Journal.* Fort Collins, CO: Mutual UFO Network. May 2008, #481, pp14-15.

----. "Women Encounter Spiraling Light." *MUFON UFO Journal.* May 2004, #433.

Cerny, Paul C. "Air Force Warns Pilot." *MUFON UFO Journal.* Aug 1963, #186, p8.

Chacon, Daniel J. "Cow's Death Is Investigated as Possible Case of Mutilation." *New Mexican.* Santa Fe, NM – May 5, 1998.

Cheney, Deanna. "Objects in Sky Spark Inquiry." *Ruidoso News.* Ruidoso, NM – October 25, 2006.

Constable, Ann. "Something Happened." *New Mexican.* Santa Fe, NM – Mar 23-29, 1994. (see UFONS: Jun 1994, #299, pp8-9)

Cordova, Kathy. "The Truth is Out There." *The Taos News.* Taos, NM – March 16, 1995. (see UFONS: May 1995, #310, p4)

Cumber, Jim. "The Case of the Disappearing Air Force Jet Interceptor." *MUFON UFO Journal.* Dec 2000, #392, pp12-13.

Degraw, Ralph C. "Socorro Witness Interviews." *MUFON UFO Journal.* Oct 1978, #131.

Delgado, David. "Mysterious Lights Seen in Los Tanos Sky." *News.* Santa Rosa, NM – Oct 10, 1996. (see UFONS; Dec 1996, #329, p5)

Dellios, Hugh. "Taos Residents Making Noise Over Mystery Hum." *Tribune.* Chicago, IL – Dec 26, 1993. (see UFONS, Dec 1993, #?)

Deuley, Thomas P. "Mutilation Hearings Held in New Mexico." *The MUFON Journal.* Jul 1979, #137.

Donovan, Bill. "Mutilated Bull: No Blood, No Clue." *Independent.* Gallup, NM – May, 5, 2007 (See: UFONS, June 2007, #455, p18)

----. "Spotters of UFO Asked to Speak Up." *Independent*. Gallup, NM – Oct 18, 1999. (see UFONS, Dec 1999, #365, p6)

----. "The Truth Is Out There." *Independent*. Gallup, NM – May 5, 2007. (See UFONS, June 2007, #455, p18)

Editors. "Defense Department Denies Link To Taos Hum." *Journal*. Albuquerque, NM – April 7, 1993. (see UFO Newsclipping Service, [UFONS], Route 1, Box 220, Plumerville, ARK, 72127. May 1993, #286, p18)

Editors. "'Alien Baby' Woman Attempts Suicide." *New Mexican*. Santa Fe, NM – Jul 23, 2000. (see UFONS, 2000, #376, p5)

Editors. "Anonymous Tip Leads to Mutilated Cow." *News*. Taos, NM – Oct 10, 1996.

Editors. "Belief in UFOs Has Damaged Army Career, Sergeant Says." *Journal*. Albuquerque, NM – March 16, 1988. (see UFONS: May 1988, #226, p7)

Editors. "Clovis, NM Sightings." *Skylook: The UFO Monthly*. Quincy, IL: Dwight Connelly, Feb 1976, #99, p14.

Editors. "Flying Saucer Reports Mount Over Nation." *Nevada State Journal*. Reno, NV – Aug 3, 1952. (See UFOs, Nov 2010, #496, 12)

Editors. "Roswell Saga Continues." *MUFON UFO Journal*. Morrison, CO: Mutual UFO Network, Inc., May 2003, #421, p3

Editors. "Sightings on TV." *Daily Record*. Roswell, NM – Sep 23, 1994. (See UFONS, Nov 1994, #304)

Filer, George. "Filer's Files: New Mexico Disc at Rocket Launch." *MUFON UFO Journal*. Morrison, CO: Mutual UFO Network. Apr 2006, #456.

----. "Filer's Files: New Mexico Flashing Object." *MUFON UFO Journal*. Nov 2005, #451.

----. "Filer's Files: New Mexico Large Moving Object Blots Out Stars." *MUFON UFO Journal*. May 2009, #493.

----. "Filer's Files: New Mexico Triangle." & "New Mexico Video." *MUFON UFO Journal*. May 2006, #457.

----. "Filer's Files: New Mexico Video of UFO." *MUFON UFO Journal*. Jun 2006, #458, p17.

----. "Filer's Files: Objects Speeds and Stops in New Mexico. *MUFON UFO Journal*. Jun 2002, #412

----. "Filer's Files: Possible New Roswell Info." *MUFON UFO Journal*. Aug 2005, #448.

----. "Filer's Files: Ring Observed in New Mexico."

MUFON UFO Journal. Dec 2000, #392, p15.

Foster, Dick. "Four Mutilations Puzzle Ranchers." *Rocky Mountain News*. Denver, CO – Sep 23, 1994. (See UFONS, Apr 1995, #309, p17.)

Friedburg, Ruth. "Big Boom." *News Tribune*. Portales, NM – Oct 21, 1998. (See UFONS, Dec 1998, #353, p18)

Girand, Jan. "Midway Man Encounters Odd Circle in his Pasture." *Daily Record*. Roswell, NM – May 20, 2001. (See UFONS, Jul 2001, #384, p8)

Giulani, David. "Agency Labels Cattle Deaths as Possible Mutilation." *Las Vegas Optic*. Las Vegas, NM – Aug 29, 2007. (See UFONs, Oct 2007, #459, p19)

Greenwood, Phaedra. "Cattle Mutilation Mystery Continues; UFO Sightings Reported." *News*. Taos, NM – Aug 1, 1996. (See UFONS, Aug 1996, #325, p17)

----. "Cattle Mutilations: Questions Remain Despite Intensive Study." *News*. Taos, NM – Dec 14, 2000. (See UFONs, 2001, #378, p18)

----. "Local Resident Awed by UFO Sighting After Storm: Another Cattle Mutilation Discovered in El Prado Pasture." *News*. Taos, NM – Sep 5, 1996. (see UFONs, May 1997, #334, p17)

----. "Moreno Valley Rancher Reports Another Unusual Animal Death." *News*. Taos, NM – May 7, 1998. (see UFONS, July 1998, #348, p17)

----. "Rancher Frustrated By New Cattle Mutilation." *News*. Taos, NM – Nov 26, 1997. (see UFONS, Jan 1998, #342, p17)

----. "Recent Cattle Death Prompts Mutilation Investigation." *News*. Taos, NM – Nov 12, 1998. (See UFONS, Feb 1999, #355, p18)

----. "Something's Out There." *News*. Taos, NM – Jan 6, 2000. (See UFONS, Jan 6, 2000, #368, p1)

----. "Strange Cattle Deaths Renew Investigation." *News*. Taos, NM – May 13, 1999. (See UFONS, Jun 1999, #359, p17)

----. "A Third Cow Found Mutilated Near Questa." *News*. Taos, NM – May 27, 1999. (See UFONS, Jul 1999, #360, p17)

Gribble, Bob. "Looking Back Forty Years Ago: April 1948." *MUFON UFO Journal*. Apr 1988, #240, p19.

----. "Looking Back Forty Years Ago: December 1948." *MUFON UFO Journal*. Dec 1988, #248, p14.

----. "Looking Back Thirty Five Years Ago: November 1952. *MUFON UFO Journal*. Nov 1987, #235, p20.

----. "Looking Back Thirty Years Ago: November 1957." *MUFON UFO Journal*. Nov 1987, #235.

----. "Looking Back Twenty-Five Years Ago: July 1962." *MUFON UFO Journal*. Jul 1987, #231, p17.

----. "Looking Back: March 1950." *MUFON UFO Journal*. Mar 1990, #263, p21.

----. "Looking Back: August 1951." *MUFON UFO Journal*. Aug 1991, #280, p17.

----. "Looking Back: 1956." *MUFON UFO Journal*. Sep 1991, #281, p10.

----. "Looking Back: July 1972." *MUFON UFO Journal*. Seguin, TX: Mutual UFO Network, Inc., Jul 1992, #291, p17

----. "Looking Back Thirty Years Ago: July 1958." *MUFON UFO Journal*. Seguin, TX: Mutual UFO Network, Inc., Jul 1988, #243, p18.

----. "Looking Back Thirty Five Years Ago: August 1954." *MUFON UFO Journal*. Aug 1989, #256, p20.

----. "Looking Back Twenty Years Ago: June 1968." *MUFON UFO Journal*. Seguin, TX: Mutual UFO Network, Inc., Jun 1988 #242, p20.

Hartz, Marlena. "UFO Incident Resurfaces." *News Journal*. Clovis, NM – June 18, 2006. (see UFONS: Aug 2006, #445, p1.)

Herron, Gary. "Corrales Heights Woman Swears She Saw UFO Here." *Observer*. Rio Rancho, NM – June 1, 2006. (see UFONS, Jul 2006, #444)

Hunter, Mark H. "GAO to Investigate Mystery UFO Crash." *Valley Courier*. Alamosa, CO – Jan 22, 1994. (see UFONs, Mar 1994, #296, p2)

Johnson, Bill. "Strange Lights Fill Sky." *Sierra County Sentinel*. Truth or Consequences, NM – Dec 27, 1989. (see UFONS: Jan 1990, p246, p9)

Kaemper, Michael. "Callers Verify Sighting of Strange Lights." *Rio Grande Sun*. Espanola, NM – Dec 28, 1989. (see UFONS: Feb 1990, #247, p7)

Kerth, Linda. "Strange Things In the Sky: A Look at 40 Years of UFO Sightings Over Northern N.M." *Rio Grande Sun*. Espanola, NM – Jul 4, 1996)

Kimble, Valerie. "Socorro's UFO Incident Still Unexplained." *El Defensor Chieftain*. Socorro, NM – Jul 23, 2003. (see UFONS, Sep 2003, #410, p1)

King, Jack. "Several Local Residents Think They Spotted UFO Saturday." *Headlight*. Deming, NM – Aug 3, 1995. (see UFONS, Oct 1995, #315, p8)

Last, T. S. "As Roswell Goes Crazy, Belen Woman's Uncle Has Own Story." *News Bulletin*. Valencia, NM – July 5, 1997. (See UFONS, Sep 1997, #338, p1)

Leupold, Edwin H. "Deming Woman Recounts 50 Years of Real-life UFO 'Close Encounters.'" *Headlight*. Deming, NM: Jan 27, 1994. (See UFONS, Apr 1994, #297, p4.)

Linthicum, Leslie. "Saucer Slide Show." *Journal*. Albuquerque, NM – Mar 27, 1994. (see UFONs, Apr 1994, #297, pp2-3)

Logan, J. R. "UFO Site Found Near Angel Fire." *Sangre de Cristo Chronicle*. Angel Fire, NM: June 2, 2010. (See UFONS, Jun 2010, #491, p1)

Maccabee, Bruce. "The White Sands Films." *International UFO Reporter*. Chicago, IL: J. Allen Hynek Center for UFO Studies. Spring 1996, Vol 21, #1, pp22-25.

Maniaci, Jim. "UFO Eludes Navajo Cops." *Independent*. Gallup, NM – Oct 6, 1999. (See UFONS, Dec 1999, #365, p4)

Mayeux, Debra. "UFO Fever Growing." *Sun*. San Juan, NM – Mar 20, 2002. (see UFONS, May 2002, #394, p2)

McCool, Lewis. "Theories Abound at UFO Meeting." *Herald*. Durango, CO – Mar 25, 2002. (See UFONS, Apr 2002, #393, p5)

McGivern, Tim. "Alien Nation." *Nucity*. Albuquerque, NM – Feb 7-13, 1994. (see UFONS, Mar 1994, #296, p11)

McMahon, Nate. "Request Renews UFO Controversy." *Daily Record*. Roswell, NM – Jan 16, 1994. (see UFONS: Mar 1994, #296, p10)

Mendoza, Felipe. "Shirkey Writes Book On Roswell Incident." *Daily Record*. Roswell, NM – Jul 2, 1999. (See UFONS, Jul 1999, #360, p8)

Miller-Goins, Ellen. "Cattle Mutilations – No Joke for Eagle Nest Ranchers." *Sangre de Christo Chronicle*. Angel Fire, NM – Jul 28, 1994. (see UFONS, Nov 1994, #304, p20)

Moffett, Ben. "Exclusive: San Antonio Natives Tell 1945 UFO Tale." *Mountain Mail*. Socorro, NM – Oct 23, 2003. (See UFONS, Dec 2003, #413, p3)

Nelson, P. J. "Humm-mm-mm." *New Mexican*. Santa Fe, NM – Feb 1, 2003.

Nelson, Sylvie. "Midway Becoming Known For UFOs." *Daily Record*. Roswell, NM – June 24, 1994. (see UFOS: Aug 1994, #301, p9)

Nott, Robert. "An Abductee's Story." *The New Mexican.* Santa Fe, NM – July 4, 2003. (See UFONS, Aug 2003, #409, p4)

Pressley, Sue Anne. "'Taos Hum' Disturbs Artistic Colony's Good Vibrations." *Post.* Washington, DC – June 24, 1993. (See UFONS, Jul 1993, #288, p19)

Randall, Teri Thomas. "Extraterrestrial Culture Day." *The New Mexican.* Santa Fe, NM – July 4, 2003. (See UFONS, Aug 2003, #409, p5)

Rolwing, Rebecca. "Cattle Mutilations Puzzling Ranchers." *Chronicle.* Houston, TX – Mar 29, 1998. (See UFONS, Apr 1998, #345, p20)

Romancito, Rick. "Seminar Looks at Mutilations." *The Taos News.* Taos, NM – May 6 1994. (See UFONS: Jul 1994, #300, p5)

Roney, Steven T. "UFO/ET Readers Forum: A Roswell UFO." *Fate.* Lakeville, MN: Fate Magazine. Jan 2004, Vol 57, #1, Issue #645, pp88-89.

Roybal, David. "Dead Cows Are Fair Game For News Media." *New Mexican.* Santa Fe, NM – Sep 20, 1994. (see UFONS, Mar 1995, #308, p20)

Sanner, Tammy. "Strange Light Seen in Night Sky." *Daily Record.* Roswell, NM – June 18, 1998. (see UFONS, Aug 1998, #349, p9)

Sauder, Richard. "The Day the Spaceships Buzzed Albuquerque." *UFO Universe.* New York: Condor Books, Inc., Jan 1990, Vol 1, No 5, pp69-71.

Sharpe, Tom. "Pondering The Hum." *New Mexican.* Santa Fe, NM – Jul 24, 2001. (see UFONS, Aug 2001, #385, p17)

Sanner, Tammy. "Strange Light Seen in Night Sky." *Daily Record.* Roswell, NM – Jun 18, 1998. (See UFONS, Aug 1998, #349, p9)

Sharpe, Tom. "Mysterious Taos Noise Now Rouses a Ho-Hum." *Journal.* Albuquerque, NM – Aug 27, 1996. (See UFONS, Oct 1996, #327, p19)

Sharpe, Tom and Jason Auslander. "Strange, Bright Lights Surprise Stargazers." *New Mexican.* Santa Fe, NM – Oct 3, 2006. (See UFONS, Nov 2006, #448, p7)

Stanford, Ray. "Clovis, NM, 'UFO' Was Unfocused Saturn." *Skylook, The UFO Monthly.* May 1976, #102, pp8-9.

Stein, Steven. "Linguistics Expert Vouches For Paper." *Record.* Roswell, NM – April 17, 1988. (see UFONS: Jun 1988, #227, p6)

Stevens, Wendelle. "June 1993." *UFO Calendar 1993.* Tucson, AZ: UFO Photo Archives, 1993.

Stiny, Andrew. "Better Exams Sought in Mutilations." *Journal.* Albuquerque, NM – Oct. 4, 1994. (see UFONS, Feb 1995, #307, p17)

----. "Group Hopes Web Site Helps Solve Mutilation Mystery." *New Mexican.* Santa Fe, NM – May 22, 1997. (See UFONS, June 1997, #335, p18)

Swartz, Tim. "Cattle Mutilations Remain a Mystery." *Mysteries Magazine.* Walpole, NH: Phantom Press Publications, Winter/Spring 2007, #16.

Swords, Michael D. "Fun and Games in the Desert Near Las Cruces." *International UFO Reporter.* Chicago, IL: J. Allen Hynek Center For UFO Studies (CUFOS). May 2006, Vol 30, #3.

Terrell, Steve. "The Valdez Files." *New Mexican.* Santa Fe, NM – Dec 16, 1997. (see UFONS, Jan 1998, #342, pp17-18)

Van Eyck, Zack. "Horse's Death Never Forgotten." *New Mexican.* Santa Fe, NM – Sep 19, 1994. (see UFONS: Mar 1995, #308, p19)

----. "Hundreds Report Seeing UFOs." *New Mexican.* Santa Fe, NM – Nov 14, 1994. (See UFONS, Jan 1995, #306, p7)

Van Eyck, Zack. "Many Theories, Few Answers in Mutilation Mystery." *New Mexican.* Santa Fe, NM – Sep 19, 1994. (See UFONS, Apr 1995, #309, p17)

Wiggins, Jane. "Artesia Couple Observes UFOs Moving Through the Night Sky." *Daily Record.* Roswell, NM – Oct 5, 1999. (See UFONS, Dec 1999, #365, p9)

Wood, Marcia. "Silvery Mystery...Weather Balloon?" *Sangre de Christo Chronicle.* Angel Fire, NM – Sep 28, 2000. (see UFONS, Jan 2001, #378, p6)

Yozwiak, Steve. "'From the High Desert...'Art Bell Reigns as Radio's Kind of Weird Science." *Arizona Republic.* Phoenix, AZ – July 12, 1997. (See UFONS, Dec 1997, #341, p17)

Websites

www.mufon.com
www.nuforc.com
www.prestondennett.weebly.com

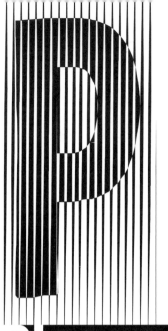

Places Index